THE SOURCE

RESOURCE GUIDE
FOR USING CREATIVE ARTS
IN CHURCH SERVICES

THE SOURCE

RESOURCE GUIDE
FOR USING CREATIVE ARTS
IN CHURCH SERVICES

compiled by
SCOTT DYER & *introduction by* NANCY BEACH

WILLOW CREEK RESOURCES™

ZondervanPublishingHouse
Grand Rapids, Michigan

A Division of HarperCollinsPublishers

The Source
Copyright © 1996 by Willow Creek Association

Requests for information should be addressed to:
ZondervanPublishingHouse
Grand Rapids, Michigan 49530

Library of Congress Cataloging-in-Publication Data

Dyer, Scott.
    The source: a resource guide for using creative arts in church services / Scott Dyer and Nancy Beach.
      p. cm.
    Includes index.
    ISBN: 0-310-50021-4 (pbk.)
    1. Church work—Audio-visual aids. I. Dyer, Scott. II. Title.
BV1535.B46   1996
246'.7—dc 00   96-10250
                                                           CIP

Printed in the United States of America

96 97 98 99 00 01 02 03 /❖ DH/ 10 9 8 7 6 5 4 3 2 1

Contents

Life Issues 121

Relationship with God 207

Relationships 257

Introduction

For as long as I can remember, I have believed in the power of the arts to touch a human soul. All of us can recall times when a song or a moment in theater or film deeply moved us and tapped into the heart of our humanity. I am thrilled that the arts were God's idea! He is the awesome Creator, the model for all that is beautiful and wonderful and true. When it comes to building a church that honors God, the arts must be embraced and supported as a vital part of both worship services and events designed for seekers. In many churches there has been an unfortunate attitude of mediocrity when it comes to planning services, and in some cases even a sense that the arts are too "worldly" and too risky to tamper with. How sad that what the heavenly Father gave us when he imagined the arts and then entrusted some of his children with artistic gifts has been neglected and even abandoned by some Christian communities. We are seeing a resurrection of the arts in recent years in many churches, and that surely delights the Master Artist, the Lord Almighty.

To harness the arts for the glory of God, therefore, may require a radical shift in our perspective as we plan corporate services and events in the local church. For those of us who are given the responsibility to prepare the "front-door" dimension of church life, we must begin with a sense that the time in those services is not dispensable; it is not a time that we dread filling. It is not entertainment before the "really important" thing happens (the sermon). The team at Willow Creek views the thirty minutes of "programming" in our seeker services and thirty to forty-five minutes in our worship services as a *treasure*. We think of every single minute as a potential treasure. What takes place in that half-hour can count for eternity. It can provide the turning point for a lost soul or healing for a wounded soldier. It does not compete with the message time; it need not devalue the role of solid biblical teaching. When the creative arts work together with well-crafted teaching—watch out! God can unleash his power in amazing ways.

Most of you are given a similar responsibility by God and your local church. It may entail twenty, thirty, or ninety minutes. You may design services primarily for believers. But like me and our team, you are entrusted with a treasure. So how can we be good stewards of thirty-minute treasures? I believe there are at least seven strategic choices we can make every week. These choices will in large part determine the effectiveness of the front-door dimension of our churches. I boldly challenge you to consciously make these seven choices as you plan your corporate gatherings. I believe you will honor God and bear lasting fruit as a result of these commitments.

Choose Planning Over Patchwork

The Old Testament contains several descriptions of major feasts, festivals, and times of worship for God's people. A favorite passage of mine is Nehemiah 12, where we learn about the dedication of the wall of Jerusalem. Spiritual leaders and musicians of all kinds were brought to Jerusalem to celebrate with songs of thanksgiving. Nehemiah assigned two large choirs to come from opposite directions on top of the wall. What careful planning was required for this massive day of celebration! Nehemiah 12:43 relates that "the sound of rejoicing in Jerusalem could be heard far away."

Many of us have attended church services where it was obvious that little if any planning was done. As we sat in the pew, we wondered how an element connects to any other element, whether anyone conferred with the preacher in advance, and why it was hard to keep our minds from wandering to other things. Worse yet, the perceptive person wondered whether anyone really cared about preparing something meaningful and may have felt that the time was wasted.

It is essential for those of us entrusted with the thirty-minute treasure to begin with a blank sheet of paper, ready to wrestle with difficult questions like these:

1. What exactly are we trying to accomplish through this service or event?
2. Who is our target audience, and in what specific ways do we hope that people might think or feel differently when they leave?
3. What would "success" look like as a result of this service? Will the audience know or understand something new? Will they be challenged or encouraged or convicted? If God empowers our efforts, what would we long to see?

Once we have wrestled with those questions, we take another blank sheet and begin to brainstorm and plan. We believe that our most effective services usually connect the arts with whatever will be taught by the speaker. This kind of planning requires that the teachers give basic information about the major theme of the message three or four weeks in advance.

Whenever my mother tries to reach me at our church offices, she is usually told that I am in a meeting. She teases me that my tombstone will say, "Gone to another meeting." I attend several meetings each week to plan and evaluate our services. Sometimes these meetings are enjoyable, fruitful, and invigorating. At other times they feel tedious, uninspired, and frustrating. But they are essential to everything we try to do with the thirty-minute treasures. We must pay the price of investing careful planning and attention to detail. Advertisers spend countless hours calculating what strategies to use to persuade us to purchase their product. Surely, as stewards of the eternal truths of salvation and hope, we can commit ourselves to a process of devoted planning.

Choose Excellence Over Mediocrity

Closely connected to a commitment to plan is the value of excellence. We have received a great deal of criticism over the years about our passion for excellence, and I believe in some cases we have been misunderstood. Let me define excellence in our ministry by clearly stating what it is not: Excellence is not perfectionism or bigness or prideful exclusion. Excellence is doing the best you can with what you have. It is refusing to drift to the lazy attitude that says, "It's only church; what's the big deal?" On the contrary, it is the bride of Christ we are nurturing, and nothing less than our best effort is acceptable.

It is tempting, when planning services, to take the easier road. Many times I have confessed to the sin of laziness in wanting to set the standards low and do just whatever we did last year. But then I visit Disney World or attend a great play or concert, and my passion is renewed to see the same measure for excellence brought to the most significant undertaking on earth—the building of the church.

In his book *Addicted to Mediocrity,* Franky Schaeffer wrote that "because of our mediocrity we Christians all too often provide the excuse the world is looking for to ignore the truth of Christianity." When we carefully brainstorm ideas, pay attention to detail and prepare like crazy, we can at least avoid giving seekers excuses to avoid God's truth based on what they perceive as shoddy effort. Much of our striving for excellence stems from a desire to minimize distractions.

The truth is that harnessing the arts and preparing effective services is hard work. There really are no shortcuts. I am inspired each week by the hundreds of volunteers at Willow Creek who place their gifts on the altar, refusing to bring a blemished lamb to the Lord. I see production teams hanging lights from a new angle every three days; I see vocalists memorizing the lyrics to yet another song so they can communicate with confidence; I see writers paying the price to craft a line word by word that rings true; I see men and women who have full-time jobs and families and all kinds of activities unwilling to give anything less than their very best when they serve God. These heroes of mine live out Colossians 3:23: "Whatever you do, work at it with all your might, as working for the Lord, not for men." If our pursuit of excellence shifts into unhealthy perfectionism, the Holy Spirit will convict us and lead us to reexamine our motives.

You may feel that your church lacks gifted artists or the necessary funds to pursue excellence. Remember that even the simplest things can be done with quality. Over the years we have attempted to learn from our mistakes and just get a little better each week. I believe your congregation will appreciate the extent to which you embrace this value. Eventually excellence will attract excellence, bringing more gifted artists your way. So let us simply commit to doing the best we can with what we have and trust that God will be glorified with our attitude.

Choose Teamwork Over Lone Rangers

Preparing the thirty-minute treasure is an awesome responsibility that I cannot imagine serving the church without a fierce devotion to *team.* That word *team* is used so much at Willow Creek, some folks wonder if a person ever does anything alone around this place. Certainly there are some masterful works of art created by a gifted artist with little assistance from a team. But we have discovered that in most situations, a gifted team can pool their resources to craft initial ideas and concepts and sometimes to engage in the actual writing or arranging. Regardless of how a "first draft" comes about, the team plays a vital role in making constructive suggestions for improvement. At Willow Creek we brainstorm as a team, usually create (at least partially) as a team, carry out the services as a team, and evaluate the results as a team. Proverbs 15:22 says, "Plans fail for lack of counsel, but with many advisers they succeed." We often say that we do together what none of us could ever do alone. While lone rangers may be considered heroes out on the range, in church work lone rangers are often insecure or prideful or perhaps just inexperienced in the wonders of community and teamwork.

Teamwork can get messy. The synergy we long for sometimes becomes unwieldy or fraught with conflict. Artists do not always agree, and it is difficult not to feel defensive when others are critical of one's ideas or treasured work. We have learned that creating a safe community environment for artists requires individual commitments to growing in godly character and to speaking the truth *in love*. As we seek to build an atmosphere of support and trust, it becomes a little easier to receive honest feedback. We have agreed that the Lord and his church are far better served when we work as a team.

You can begin to choose the practice of teamwork at any stage of church development. In the early years of Willow Creek, our planning team was quite small, composed of a few volunteers. In the same way, I would encourage you to pray and look for a few folks who

- Clearly understand and affirm your church's mission
- Are perceptive and intuitive about the arts and human nature
- Have a "can do" attitude and are positive, enthusiastic thinkers
- Are not overly defensive
- Are willing to speak the truth in love
- Are naturally "idea" people who have an appreciation for the arts and the vital role they can play in your services

The adventure of building a team and growing into a true community of Christian artists is one of the most fulfilling aspects of ministry. Please consider choosing the team approach over lone rangers—it will make an incredible difference.

Choose Variety Over Predictability

Several years ago, I was visiting a church and given a tour of the auditorium and stage. The young man who was my guide glowingly reported that all the lighting fixtures were set in permanent positions, as were also the staging and microphones for the choir and instrumentalists. He said with great pride, "This is a turnkey operation!"

How many parts of our weekly services have become "turnkey"? Do the attendees know what to expect moment to moment? When was the last time they were truly surprised in church? Whenever I read the biblical account of the Creation or walk through a botanical garden, I am struck by the incredible diversity of all that God made. Our Creator clearly loves variety.

This is not to say there is no room for tradition. But if our order of service, treatment of Scripture, style of music, and design of the stage do not reflect variety, most people will begin to tune out. I enjoy observing the reactions in our congregation when we prepare intriguing artwork for the side walls or begin a vocal selection from a new place in the auditorium or use dance or video in a fresh way. Human beings usually respond with greater attentiveness to new forms of communicating truth. Our production team changes the look of our stage setup, lighting plan, and backgrounds every single week. We agonize over designing an order of service that will feel fresh and different. The Young Life organization says, "It's a sin to bore a kid." I say it's also a sin to bore an adult! As you prepare your thirty-minute treasures, commit yourselves to variety and watch the enthusiasm of your church ignite.

Choose Moments Over Glitz

Few things have grieved me more in my twenty years of ministry than the criticism that our use of drama, contemporary music, dance, and other mediums has simply been a glitzy, showy display designed to impress or astonish people. I could not devote myself to such an unworthy, shallow goal. While we certainly have not always succeeded, our primary goal has been to use the arts to move the souls of people. We long to create *moments* that God can use to make people feel something deep down inside. Our Creator gave us music and all the other arts because he designed us to be emotive beings who respond to beauty and humor and celebration and tragedy. George Bernard Shaw once said that "you use a glass mirror to see your face; you use a work of art to see your soul." Often it is only a song or a dramatic scene that has the power to help a person feel understood, to get in touch with one's pain, or to be inspired to dance with joy.

One of our drama writers, Sharon Sherbondy, wrote a sketch years ago called "Great Expectations." This classic sketch portrays a couple on the day their adopted son had been due to arrive, but who are now dealing with the agony of being informed that the mother has changed her mind. After years of struggling with infertility, the wife explodes with anger and pain. She pounds her husband's chest and says, "I hate you! I hate God! I hate everybody." As she pours out her tears of anguish the scene leaves them just hoping that someday they will receive a child. I have never watched that sketch without feeling keenly the pain of that couple. Although I do not share the same struggle, I know what it is like to be angry toward God and to feel that, on the surface, life seems unfair. No preacher or book could move me on that subject quite the way that scene does.

When we carefully plan and pray over a thirty-minute treasure, there will be times when the Holy Spirit will use our efforts in amazing ways and the hearts of the attendees will be deeply moved. One of the greatest adventures of my ministry is being part of creating such moments for our congregation. As you prepare your services, commit yourself to that adventure as well. When artistic moments support great preaching, lives can be dramatically changed by God.

Choose Godliness Over Giftedness

Creating powerful moments requires a team of people who are both godly and gifted. We all try to find leaders, musicians, actors, and other artists who walk closely with the Lord and are growing to be more like him. We hope that those who participate in our ministries are authentic believers, willingly submitting to the Spirit's agenda in their daily lives. But when it comes to the arts, we also need people with gifts or God-given talents. There are many godly people in this world who unfortunately cannot sing on pitch or act believably or play an instrument skillfully.

As leaders of the thirty-minute treasure, we face the test when we find very gifted individuals who, for whatever reasons, are lacking in character. They may be prideful or greedy or immoral or bitter or angry. I am not talking about sinners—we are all in that camp—but about those who are not willing to walk in the light, confess their sins, and devote themselves to growth.

We have had a few painful experiences of asking some incredibly gifted artists to stop serving in our ministry until such problems are resolved. Some of you know how hard it is to face this test—especially if your talent pool is quite small. Everything in us wants to compromise because we think we desperately need a particular person's gifts. On the basis of experience, let me warn you that the price we pay for compromise is much too high. Proverbs 10:9 says, "The man of integrity walks securely, but he who takes crooked paths will be found out." The sinful attitudes and rebellion of just one person can seriously tarnish the thirty-minute treasure. If you are ever forced to make a choice, please select godliness over giftedness.

Choose Leadings Over Formulas

The majority of this book is a useful resource guide, a terrific jump-start of ideas. We all look for tools that might help us as we plan our services. But in that search we can never abdicate our God-given responsibility to *listen* to the Lord for his leadings in favor of simply seeking a quick-fix formula. Powerful church services result primarily from the voice of God giving ideas and inspiration to undeserving people like you and me. Isaiah 30:15 is a favorite verse: "In quietness and trust is your strength."

Inspiration is a mysterious thing to describe, isn't it? It can come in a Burger King or an airplane or in your favorite chair. God still speaks to those who listen. He is and always will be the Ultimate Creator—and I have learned that his storehouse will never grow empty of wonderful ideas. God knows exactly what each congregation needs in any given week. He even knows whether a vocalist will get sick, how weary we are, and when an unexpected blizzard will keep most of the people away. The Designer of the Universe invites us to come to him in quietness with our blank sheets of paper. Sometimes we will hear no leadings. At other times we will walk away amazed again by grace.

Please do not prepare your thirty-minute treasure without listening for leadings, both when alone and in your team meetings. The best ideas are usually not found in how-to manuals or other people's churches. Those tools can get us going, but they need to be filtered through the unique lens of one's own situation. I shudder to think of how many leadings I might have missed over the years because I am too busy or impatient to be still. Remember that God loves you and your church far more than you know. He longs for your people to experience powerful moments, and he wants you to be a conduit of creativity for his purposes.

When we choose

Planning over patchwork
Excellence over mediocrity
Teamwork over lone rangers
Variety over predictability
Moments over glitz
Godliness over giftedness, and
Leadings over formulas

we give God the best possible offering in the thirty-minute treasure. I wish I could say I have always been faithful to these seven choices—I have not. But to the extent any of us devote ourselves to these biblical values, God will be glorified and our congregations will be changed. Let us accept the responsibility for the treasures we are given with sober minds, willing hearts, and adventurous spirits. God bless you on your journey to serve him through the arts.

—Nancy Beach

How to Use This Book

The Purpose

The creative process can be one of the most rewarding and exciting features of ministry, but it can also be agonizing and frustrating. Sometimes great ideas flow like streams of inspiration. At other times the "right" ideas seem to be lost behind an impenetrable wall. The purpose of this book is to provide a source of ideas for people responsible for programming "relevant" church services. Our desire is that *The Source* would become a useful part of your creative arsenal—a place to start when you need one, a place to turn when you're stuck.

The word *relevant* can be interpreted many different ways, and because this is a Willow Creek Resource, you might be inclined to assume that "relevant" refers only to "seeker services." While many of these ideas came from Willow Creek's seeker services, *The Source* can be helpful to many different churches with many different styles. A song or a drama that works well in a seeker service might also have tremendous ministry impact in a service oriented more toward believers. The common denominator is that these elements seek to relate biblical truth and wisdom to specific aspects of life.

The Blanks

The Source is intended to be a supplement to your creative process, not a substitute for it. After each series of ideas you will find some blanks for you to fill in your own suggestions. At Willow Creek we are well aware of the fact that we are not the end-all when it comes to creative ideas. "A Source" would probably be a more accurate title for this book—it will only become "The Source" for you when you add your input. You and your creative team know your specific church audience better than anyone, and it is your ability to come up with fresh ideas and innovations that will ultimately make the biggest difference in your ministry.

The Content

The ideas listed in *The Source* represent the creative programming elements that have been used effectively at Willow Creek Community Church over the past five to seven years—in both the weekend seeker services and the believer-oriented New Community worship services—combined with a few of my own ideas. The ideas fall into four specific element categories: Message Titles, Dramas, Songs, and Movie Clips.

Message Titles

This is a listing of many of the titles that Willow Creek's teaching pastors have used over the years. We hope they will be useful to you, perhaps just to spur a thought for your pastor regarding his message title. The message titles are coded according to how they were used at Willow Creek. All actual message titles are listed in normal (roman) type. If a title is preceded by another title in *italics,* it means that the message was a part of a series (*the series title is in italics*). For example, a listing such as "*Seven Wonders of the Spiritual World:* God Can Be Trusted" means that the message "God Can Be Trusted" was one message in a series entitled *"Seven Wonders of the Spiritual World."* Titles in **boldface** indicate that all the following message titles were a part of the same series (**the series title is in boldface**). For example, the series **Faith Has Its Reasons** consisted of five messages, all of which are listed afterward. A message title not preceded by another title indicates a stand-alone message—one that was not part of a series.

Dramas

All the sketches listed are available through Willow Creek Resources at 1-800-876-SEEK. Next to each drama you will find three other pieces of information: Tone, Number of Characters, and Topics. The Tone refers to the general mood of the drama. Characters are listed by gender, although with some scripts one or more characters might work in either gender. The Topics will help you to determine whether a drama deals with the aspect of the subject you are exploring. For example, *Faith* can be a fairly broad topic. If you are dealing with the specific aspect of having reasoning behind your faith, the sketch "Reason Enough" would probably be a good one to consider, based on the Topics listing.

There is additional information about drama, including a brief synopsis of each sketch, in the **Drama Index** in the back of *The Source.*

Songs

There is probably no matter of greater diversity among churches than music. Consequently, you may have found recording artists or writers not listed in *The Source* whose songs work very well in your church setting. The blanks are for your suggestions. We have listed some recommended songs to consider for each topic, and we hope that the combination of our ideas and your ideas will give you a much larger pool of quality music from which to choose.

The song entries in *The Source* are coded according to some distinguishing factors. Songs in **bold type** have recently been used effectively at Willow Creek—providing a sort of "stamp of approval." That is, we have seen these songs work well in our services. Songs in *italics* are Willow Creek originals. The instrumental and vocal charts for these songs are available through the Willow Creek Association at (847) 765-0070. If a song is given in normal type, it doesn't necessarily mean that it is an inferior song—it simply means that we have not used it for a while or not used it at all.

Beside each song are four other categories: Artist, Style, Tempo, and Seeker-Sensitivity Rating. The first three are self-explanatory. The Seeker-Sensitivity Rating is very important. This is a scale from one to ten, with ten being the most seeker-oriented. The rating is not a quality rating, but rather a gauge for how relevant a song is to seekers and how understandable the language and concepts are to the heart and mind of someone who does not know Christ. Be cautious about using any song with a rating under 6 or 7 in a seeker-targeted or seeker-sensitive service. However, a high Seeker-Sensitivity Rating should not preclude your using a song in a believer-oriented service. A song with a 10 rating might be very effective in any type of service. With all the music, use your own judgment.

More information about each song, including the album, record label, and comments, is included in the **Song Index** in the back of this book. We recommend that you review the index information for any song you are seriously considering for a service.

Movie Clips

We do not use a lot of movie clips at Willow Creek, and many of the clips included in *The Source* have not been used at Willow Creek. When we do use movie clips, they are often—though not always—used during the message as an illustration of a particular point, rather than as a separate element in the service.

Several pieces of information are given for each clip: Movie Title, Specific Topic, Clip Description, Start Time, Start Cue, End Time, End Cue, and Comments (where applicable). The Start and End Times are measured from the point in each film when the movie studio's header fades to black (for example, when the Universal Globe fades to black) and the main titles begin. The Start and End Cues refer to suggested points in the dialogue or action to begin and end each clip.

Some clips have language that may or may not be acceptable in your church service. We have noted these instances in the Comments section, with the understanding that you will use discernment according to your church's standards. At Willow Creek we take a conservative approach to this issue. Also, some churches may have editing systems that allow you to "bleep" certain words.

Always make sure that you obtain copyright clearance before you use a movie clip.

Package Suggestions

One thing we have found particularly effective at Willow Creek is to use songs, dramas, and occasionally movie clips in a "package," in which one element immediately follows another. Many programs need bridging elements, such as a Scripture reading, to maintain creative and emotional flow; by contrast, when it fits, a drama/song package can be a powerful and moving tool for ministry. Where it is appropriate we have inserted packages for you to consider.

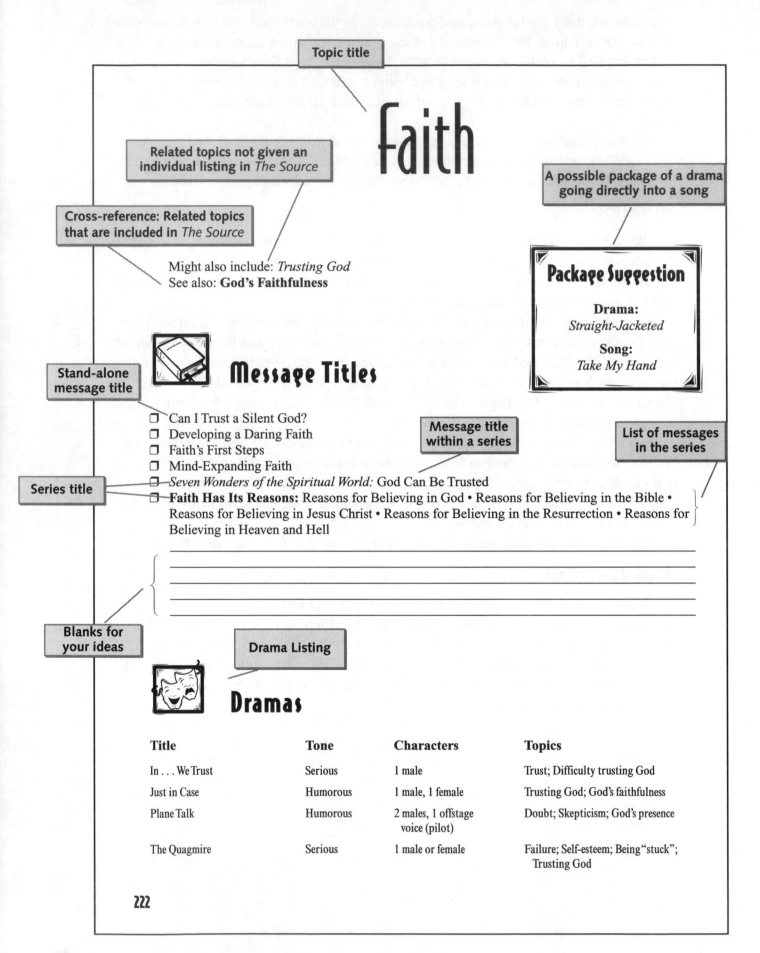

Topic title

Faith

Related topics not given an individual listing in *The Source*

A possible package of a drama going directly into a song

Cross-reference: Related topics that are included in *The Source*

Might also include: *Trusting God*
See also: **God's Faithfulness**

Package Suggestion

Drama:
Straight-Jacketed

Song:
Take My Hand

Stand-alone message title

Message Titles

Message title within a series

List of messages in the series

Series title

- ❑ Can I Trust a Silent God?
- ❑ Developing a Daring Faith
- ❑ Faith's First Steps
- ❑ Mind-Expanding Faith
- ❑ *Seven Wonders of the Spiritual World:* God Can Be Trusted
- ❑ **Faith Has Its Reasons:** Reasons for Believing in God • Reasons for Believing in the Bible • Reasons for Believing in Jesus Christ • Reasons for Believing in the Resurrection • Reasons for Believing in Heaven and Hell

Blanks for your ideas

Drama Listing

Dramas

Title	Tone	Characters	Topics
In . . . We Trust	Serious	1 male	Trust; Difficulty trusting God
Just in Case	Humorous	1 male, 1 female	Trusting God; God's faithfulness
Plane Talk	Humorous	2 males, 1 offstage voice (pilot)	Doubt; Skepticism; God's presence
The Quagmire	Serious	1 male or female	Failure; Self-esteem; Being "stuck"; Trusting God

222

Song Listing

Song that has worked well at Willow Creek (indicated by boldface)

WIllow Creek original (indicated by italics)

Blanks for your ideas

Songs

Title	Artist	Style	Tempo	Seeker-Sensitivity Rating
All That I Need	Steve Camp	Ballad	Slow	5
All the Faith You Need	*Willow Creek Music*	*Pop/rock*	*Up*	*10*
Build My World Around You	**Sandi Patty**	**Pop**	**Up**	**9**
Do I Trust You	Twila Paris	MOR	Mid	5
Every Step I Take	**Bob Carlisle**	**Bluesy pop**	**Mid**	**9**
Facts Are Facts	Steven Curtis Chapman	Rock/pop	Up	4
Faith, Hope and Love	**Point of Grace**	**Pop vocal group**	**Up**	**9**
From Here on Out	*Willow Creek Music*	*MOR pop*	*Mid*	*8*
The Future	First Call	Pop vocal group	Up	8
God Is in Control	**Twila Paris**	**Pop/rock**	**Up**	**1**
Hard Times	Wayne Watson	Ballad	Slow	4
He Won't Let Me Down	**Debbie McClendon**	**R & B/pop**	**Up**	**9**
Higher Ways	Steven Curtis Chapman	Acoustic guitar ballad	Mid/slow	8
I Choose to Follow	**Al Denson**	**Ballad**	**Slow**	**5**
I'll Be Believing	**Point of Grace**	**Pop vocal group**	**Up**	**9**
I'm Depending on You	Harv & Edythe	MOR	Mid	7
_____	_____	_____	_____	_____
_____	_____	_____	_____	_____
_____	_____	_____	_____	_____
_____	_____	_____	_____	_____

Movie Clip
Listing

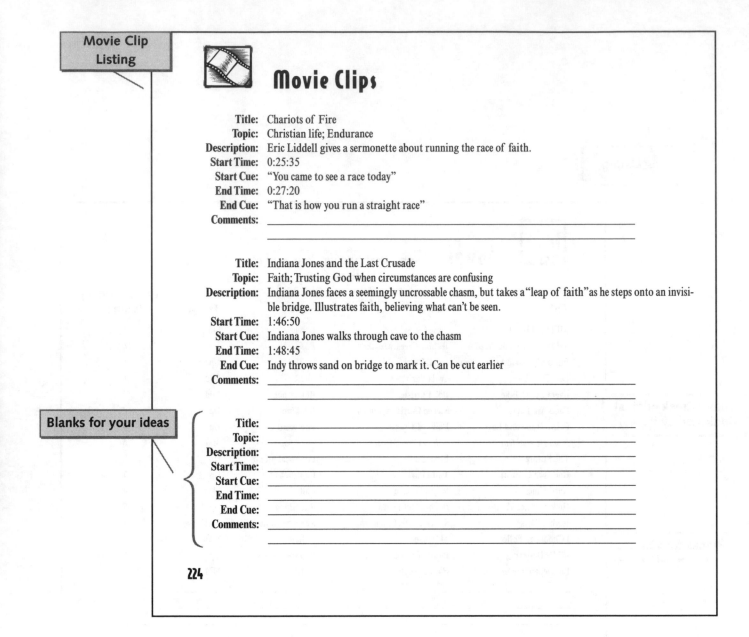

Movie Clips

Title: Chariots of Fire
Topic: Christian life; Endurance
Description: Eric Liddell gives a sermonette about running the race of faith.
Start Time: 0:25:35
Start Cue: "You came to see a race today"
End Time: 0:27:20
End Cue: "That is how you run a straight race"
Comments: _____

Title: Indiana Jones and the Last Crusade
Topic: Faith; Trusting God when circumstances are confusing
Description: Indiana Jones faces a seemingly uncrossable chasm, but takes a "leap of faith" as he steps onto an invisible bridge. Illustrates faith, believing what can't be seen.
Start Time: 1:46:50
Start Cue: Indiana Jones walks through cave to the chasm
End Time: 1:48:45
End Cue: Indy throws sand on bridge to mark it. Can be cut earlier
Comments: _____

Blanks for your ideas

Title: _____
Topic: _____
Description: _____
Start Time: _____
Start Cue: _____
End Time: _____
End Cue: _____
Comments: _____

224

The Future

One thing inherent in creative programming is change. A drama sketch that was great four years ago might not work as well now, for any number of reasons. Musical styles change, important issues change; trends in theater and movies and culture in general change. If we are to be truly "relevant," it is important to be aware of these things and make appropriate adjustments in the creative elements we choose.

With this in mind, our plan at this point is to update *The Source* from time to time to keep it current and fresh. We hope to continually expand and improve upon the material in this first edition.

May God inspire you and use the gifts he has given uniquely to you to bring honor and glory to him and to help bring a world that is lost back home to him.

—Scott Dyer

Acknowledgments

Whenever a book like this is put together, it is very easy to assume that the author is the primary contributor. This is not the case here. It is very important to me that you get a true picture of who really wrote this book. I have compiled and organized the information contained in these pages and have added some of my own ideas, but in reality there are many authors. I hope that by listing each person and the role he or she plays in the creative process, you will get a clear picture of how a team of creative people can function effectively—so much better than just one person trying to do it all.

Nancy Beach is the Programming Director at Willow Creek Community Church. For many years Nancy was the leader and a key innovator of the creative process in our programming ministry. While she still contributes to the creative teams and occasionally still leads that process, her primary role currently is to be a vision caster and manager of the programming department. She is a true champion of the use of the arts in the church and the high value of the artist in the body of Christ.

Corinne Ferguson is the Weekend Services Programming Director and Vocal Team Director at Willow Creek. She is the leader of the creative process for our seeker services. Corinne has a true gift of creative instinct—she can often tell when something is "missing," and she has a great sense of creative and emotional flow within a church service. She has been key to many of the new things we have done at Willow Creek over the past few years as she continues a legacy of creativity and innovation begun years ago by Dave Holmbo.

Steve Pederson is the Drama Director at Willow Creek. Steve is primarily responsible for overseeing the script creation process; he also directs many of the sketches on weekends and leads the drama team. He has a great sense of visual movement and flow on a stage and has the unique ability to create wonderful dramatic pictures. He has played a major role in creating many of the "moments" we have experienced from our stage.

Rory Noland is the Music Director. Rory has written many of the original songs that appear in *The Source,* and he contributes much to our ministry beyond his specific area of expertise. Rory always seems to be asking, "Are we hitting the target?" or "Are we accomplishing what we set out to do?" These questions help us refine and sharpen the end result. Rory is a man whose heart is vitally connected to Christ, which has a profound effect on his contribution to our team. He also does a great deal of music research, and his impact on this book is obviously significant.

Greg Ferguson is what we call a Creative Consultant. He brings a seemingly endless bag of ideas and insights with him every week. He is a "pure creator"—someone who takes a blank page and fills it with color and life. He is one of our primary songwriters and has composed many of the song medleys presented at Willow Creek.

Mark Demel is the Associate Drama Director. Mark is extremely visual. He is a cartoonist and artist and often draws our ideas on paper so we can get a visual concept. This tactic frequently serves as a logjam-breaker. Mark is also great at asking "what if . . ." questions: "What if we tried this?" or "What if we did this differently?" He often pushes the boundaries and that leads to innovation. Mark helped quite a bit with the drama sections of this book.

Others who have made very significant contributions recently to our weekend services and to this book include **John Carlson, Joe Horness, Tom Vitacco, Scott Pederson, Anne Rand,** and **Ted Thomas.**

My role on the team is as a Creative Consultant. I do much of our music research and serve as a resource of ideas and perspective.

There are many others who have contributed ideas presented in this book. Although most of the material in *The Source* is directed toward seeker services, the creative team for our New Community services (our midweek worship services for believers) has also provided many of the ideas. This team is led by **Pam Howell** and includes **Nancy Beach, Greg Ferguson, Todd Hiller, Joe Horness, Rory Noland, John Ortberg, Scott Pederson, Kim Anderson,** and **Dieter Zander.**

As you can see, the team approach to the creative process is absolutely critical to the effectiveness of the programming ministries at Willow Creek. Each person brings an essential piece to the puzzle that no one else can bring.

I hope this gives you a clear picture of who really wrote this book. As I was compiling this information, I was often ambushed by memories of moments when a drama or a song or a video penetrated my heart in a way that nothing else could have, giving me a clearer picture of the grace and amazing love of my Savior. I am amazed and privileged to work beside such gifted and passionately devoted servants of Christ.

—Scott Dyer

CHRISTIAN LIFE ISSUES

Authenticity

Refers to living out what you believe
Might also include: *Integrity*

 ## Message Titles

- [ ] Cosmetic Christianity
- [ ] *Becoming a Contagious Christian:* Authenticity
- [ ] *What Jesus Would Say to . . .* Billy Graham

_____

_____

_____

 ## Dramas

Title	Tone	Characters	Topics
A Day in the Life	Humorous	5 males	Christians in the marketplace; New Christian
Counting the Cost	Serious	2 males, 2 females	Commitment to Christ; Sacrifice; Spiritual maturity
Getting the Nod	Mixed	2 males, 1 either male or female	Honesty; Integrity; Business ethics; Handling failure
Impressions, Inc.	Humorous	2 males, 1 female	Skin-deep Christianity
Man of the Year	Serious	5 males, 1 female	Moralism; Our need for Christ
The Mystery of Robert Richardson	Mixed	3 males, 2 females, 1 narrator	Living the Christian life
One Step Up, One Step Down	Serious	4 males (1 can be female)	Ambition; Priorities
_____	_____	_____	_____
_____	_____	_____	_____
_____	_____	_____	_____

Songs

Title	Artist	Style	Tempo	Seeker-Sensitivity Rating
All I Ever Wanted	Margaret Becker	Pop/rock ballad	Slow/mid	4
Audience of One	*Willow Creek Music*	*Power ballad*	*Slow*	*8*
Casual Christian	**De Garmo & Key**	**Power ballad**	**Slow**	**6**
Changin'	**Acapella Vocal Band**	**Acapella vocal group**	**Up**	**8**
Chippin' Away	*Willow Creek Music*	*Folk pop*	*Mid/up*	*8*
The Dilemma	Sandi Patti	Pop	Up	6
For Who He Really Is	Steven Curtis Chapman	Folk/pop ballad	Mid/slow	1
Heart's Cry	**Steven Curtis Chapman**	**Acoustic ballad**	**Mid/slow**	**7**
If That's What It Takes	*Willow Creek Music*	*Pop/MOR*	*Mid/slow*	*5*
Look Me in the Eye	Margaret Becker	Pop ballad	Slow/mid	3
Love You With My Life	Steven Curtis Chapman	Pop	Up	5
Man of God	*Willow Creek Music*	*Pop/rock*	*Mid/up*	*7*
Most of the Time	Glad	Piano ballad	Slow	4
The Narrow Way	Wayne Watson	Pop	Mid	6
Show Yourselves to Be	Steven Curtis Chapman	Acoustic ballad	Slow/mid	4
There Is a Line	Susan Ashton	Folk pop	Mid	6
Whatever You Ask	**Steve Camp**	**Power ballad**	**Slow**	**5**
Who Makes the Rules	**Steven Curtis Chapman**	**Pop/folk rock**	**Up**	**7**
Would I Know You	Wayne Watson	Ballad	Slow	3
You've Got to Stand for Something	**Aaron Tippin**	**Country**	**Up**	**10**

Movie Clips

Title: Chariots of Fire
Topic: Integrity; Standing up for what you believe in; The Sabbath
Description: Eric Liddell refuses to run on the Sabbath. The English Olympic Committee tries to make him compromise, but he stands firm.
Start Time: 1:28:15

Start Cue: "We decided to invite you in for a little chat"
End Time: 1:30:00
End Cue: "But I can't make that sacrifice"
Comments: _____
_____

Title: _____
Topic: _____
Description: _____
Start Time: _____
Start Cue: _____
End Time: _____
End Cue: _____
Comments: _____
_____

Programming Tip

Vary the tone of your drama sketches
Presenting serious drama three or four weeks in a row
might wear out the congregation emotionally. Conversely,
doing humorous sketches several weeks in a row could
leave the people longing for something deeper. The first
priority is to choose a tone that fits the service, but it helps
to mix it up from week to week to keep things fresh.

Being Salt and Light

See also: **Evangelism**

Package Suggestion

Drama:
The Story of Rachel

Song:
Be the One

Message Titles

- ☐ Becoming a Contagious Christian
- ☐ Capturing the Heart of Christianity
- ☐ Salt and Light
- ☐ **Stronger Salt, Brighter Light:** Assessing Your Savor Factor • Increasing Your Candle Power

Dramas

Title	Tone	Characters	Topics
A Day in the Life	Humorous	5 males	Christians in the marketplace; New Christian
First-Day Jitters	Humorous	1 female	New Christian; Obeying God
On the Outside	Serious	1 female or male	Being salt and light; Negative church experiences
Parlor Talk	Mixed	3 males, 2 females	Making a difference with your life; Death; Workaholism
Reason Enough	Mixed, mostly serious	1 male, 1 female	Importance of faith grounded in reason
The Right Thing	Serious	1 male	Costly obedience; Christian character; Persecution
The Story of Rachel	Serious	3 females	Care for the poor; Compassion

Title	Tone	Characters	Topics

Songs

Title	Artist	Style	Tempo	Seeker-Sensitivity Rating
Be the One	**Al Denson**	**Power ballad**	**Slow**	7
Casual Christian	**De Garmo & Key**	**Power ballad**	**Slow**	6
The Door	Al Denson	Power ballad	Slow	1
For Who He Really Is	Steven Curtis Chapman	Folk/pop ballad	Mid/slow	1
Heart's Cry	**Steven Curtis Chapman**	**Acoustic ballad**	**Mid/slow**	7
Heaven in the Real World	**Steven Curtis Chapman**	**Pop/rock**	**Up**	7
Heroes	Paul Overstreet	Country	Mid/slow	8
Let's Stand Together	**The Kry**	**Rock**	**Mid/up**	1
Run to the Battle	Steve Camp	Pop/rock	Up/mid	1
Show Yourselves to Be	Steven Curtis Chapman	Acoustic ballad	Slow/mid	4
Who Makes the Rules	**Steven Curtis Chapman**	**Pop/folk rock**	**Up**	7

Movie Clips

Title: _____

Topic: _____

Description: _____

Start Time: _____

Start Cue: _____

End Time: _____

End Cue: _____

Comments: _____

The Bible

See also: **Apologetics, God's Wisdom**

Message Titles

- Objections to the Bible
- *Defining Family Values:* Origin of Values
- *Faith Has Its Reasons:* Reasons for Believing in the Bible

_____

_____

_____

_____

_____

Dramas

Title	Tone	Characters	Topics
Nice to Have Around	Mixed; Mime	2 males, 1 female	Attitudes toward the Bible
Pulpit Talk	Humorous	3 males, 2 females	Stereotypical church experiences; Sermons; Intro to Sermon on the Mount

Songs

Title	Artist	Style	Tempo	Seeker-Sensitivity Rating
Thy Word	Amy Grant	Ballad	Slow	4

Movie Clips

Title: _____

Topic: _____

Description: _____

Start Time: _____

Start Cue: _____

End Time: _____

End Cue: _____

Comments: _____

_____

Programming Tip

Build the "library" of your mind
Take time to feed your heart and mind with things that
stimulate you spiritually, emotionally, and artistically.
A regular diet of quality ideas will deepen the creative
well from which you can draw.

Christian Character
~ Compassion ~

Might also include: *Kindness*
See also: **Caring for the Poor, Comforting Others**

Package Suggestion

Drama:
The Story of Rachel

Song:
Not Too Far From Here

Message Titles

- ❏ Random Acts of Senseless Kindness
- ❏ *Becoming a Contagious Christian:* Compassion
- ❏ *What Jesus Would Say to . . .* Mother Teresa

Dramas

Title	Tone	Characters	Topics
The Boy Who Never Got Dirty	Humorous	1 male, 1 female, 1 narrator	Service; Risk taking
Family Snapshots—Take IV	Serious	2 males, 3 females, 1 jr. high boy	Family; Self-sacrifice
Just As I Am	Serious	1 male	Homosexuality
The Killing Spree	Humorous	1 male, 3 females	Sixth Commandment; Murder; Gossip
A Nice Guy	Serious	2 males	Regret; Admitting failures; Effects of sin; Confession

Title	Tone	Characters	Topics
On the Outside	Serious	1 female or male	Being salt and light; Negative church experiences
The Right Thing	Serious	1 male	Costly obedience; Christian character; Persecution
The Story of Rachel	Serious	3 females	Care for the poor; Compassion
___	___	___	___
___	___	___	___
___	___	___	___

Songs

Title	Artist	Style	Tempo	Seeker-Sensitivity Rating
Heaven in the Real World	**Steven Curtis Chapman**	**Pop/rock**	**Up**	7
Helping Hand	Amy Grant	Pop	Mid/up	10
Holding Out Hope to You	Michael English	Power ballad	Slow	9
In Heaven's Eyes	**Sandi Patti**	**Inspirational ballad**	**Slow**	**9**
Love Can Open the Door	Sandi Patti	Pop	Up	10
Not Too Far From Here	**Kim Boyce**	**Pop ballad**	**Slow**	7
We Are the People	Bob Carlisle	Power ballad	Slow	5
___	___	___	___	___
___	___	___	___	___
___	___	___	___	___

Movie Clips

Title: _____

Topic: _____

Description: _____

Start Time: _____

Start Cue: _____

End Time: _____

End Cue: _____

Comments: _____

~ Contentment ~

See also: **Fulfillment, Materialism/Greed**

Message Titles

- ☐ It All Goes Back Into the Box
- ☐ Our Need for Contentment
- ☐ What Can Fill an Empty Frame
- ☐ *Rare and Remarkable Virtues:* Contentment

_____

_____

_____

_____

Dramas

Title	Tone	Characters	Topics
Catalog-itis	Humorous	1 male, 1 female, 2 jr. high age girls	Self-control; Contentment
Confessions of an Ad-aholic	Humorous	1 male, 1 female	Materialism; Power of the media; The American dream
Early One Morning Just After the Dawn of History As We Know It	Humorous	3 males	Materialism; "Keeping up with the Joneses"
In Pursuit of Happiness	Mixed	1 male, 1 female	Contentment; Possessions
Lifestyles of the Obscured and Indebted	Humorous	4 males, 3 females	Materialism; Coveting
The Mirror Thought of It	Mixed	1 male, 1 female, 1 offstage voice	Materialism; Workaholism; Striving for more
Oh, What a Feeling!	Humorous	2 males, 1 female	Decision making; Self-control; Money management
What's the Ticket?	Mixed	2 females, 4 either male or female	Need for Christ; Contentment; Needs and wants

Title	Tone	Characters	Topics
_____	_____	_____	_____
_____	_____	_____	_____
_____	_____	_____	_____

 # Songs

Title	Artist	Style	Tempo	Seeker-Sensitivity Rating
Audience of One	*Willow Creek Music*	*Power ballad*	*Slow*	8
How Could I Ask for More	Cindy Morgan	Piano ballad	Slow	9
Reaching	Carolyn Arends	Ballad	Slow	6
Strength in You	*Willow Creek Music*	*MOR pop*	*Slow/mid*	10
_____	_____	_____	_____	___
_____	_____	_____	_____	___
_____	_____	_____	_____	___

 # Movie Clips

Title: Cool Runnings
Topic: Success; Ambition
Description: A bobsledder asks his coach why he cheated 20 years ago in the Olympics. The answer has a lot to say about the trap of success and its ultimate lack of fulfillment.
Start Time: 1:25:15
Start Cue: Coach enters hotel room
End Time: 1:27:15
End Cue: "When you cross that finish line, you'll know"
Comments: _____

Title: _____
Topic: _____
Description: _____
Start Time: _____
Start Cue: _____
End Time: _____
End Cue: _____
Comments: _____

- Courage -

Might also include: *Confidence*
See also: **Heroes, Risk Taking**

Message Titles

- ❏ Our Need for Confidence
- ❏ Turning Zeroes Into Heroes
- ❏ *Endangered Character Qualities:* Courage

_____

_____

_____

_____

Dramas

Title	Tone	Characters	Topics
The Comfort Zone	Humorous	1 male, 2 females (1 TV announcer on tape)	Risk taking
Counting the Cost	Serious	2 males, 2 females	Commitment to Christ; Sacrifice; Spiritual maturity
The Eggshell Family	Humorous	2 males, 1 female, 1 male or female	Decision making
The Quitter	Serious	2 males, 1 female	Quitting; Failure
The Speculators	Humorous	2 males, 1 female	Risk taking; Missed opportunities

Songs

Title	Artist	Style	Tempo	Seeker-Sensitivity Rating
Be the One	**Al Denson**	**Power ballad**	**Slow**	7
For the Sake of the Call	Steven Curtis Chapman	Anthemic pop	Up	3
Heroes	Paul Overstreet	Country	Mid/slow	8
Man of God	*Willow Creek Music*	*Pop/rock*	*Mid/up*	7
Seize the Day	Carolyn Arends	Folk pop, in 3	Mid	8
Whatever You Ask	**Steve Camp**	**Power ballad**	**Slow**	5
When You Are a Soldier	**Steven Curtis Chapman**	**Keyboard ballad**	**Slow/mid**	4

Movie Clips

Title: Chariots of Fire
Topic: Perseverence; Determination; Courage
Description: Runner Eric Liddell gets knocked down in a race and comes back to win.
Start Time: 0:34:25
Start Cue: "Gentlemen, get to your marks"
End Time: 0:35:45
End Cue: Liddell falls down in exhaustion at the finish
Comments: _____

_____

Title: Forrest Gump
Topic: Friendship; Laying your life down for a friend
Description: Forrest goes into the jungle of Vietnam to find his fallen friend, Bubba, and runs him out of the battle zone.
Start Time: 0:53:30
Start Cue: "I gotta find Bubba!"
End Time: 0:55:00
End Cue: Forrest runs out of frame, with jungle exploding behind him. Can also end at "That's all I have to say about that"
Comments: _____

_____

Title: Indiana Jones and the Last Crusade

Topic: Faith; Trusting God when circumstances are confusing

Description: Indiana Jones faces a seemingly uncrossable chasm, but takes a "leap of faith" as he steps onto an invisible bridge. Illustrates faith, believing what can't be seen.

Start Time: 1:46:50

Start Cue: Indiana Jones walks through cave to the chasm

End Time: 1:48:45

End Cue: Indy throws sand on bridge to mark it—can be cut earlier

Comments: _____

_____

Title: Rudy

Topic: Quitting; Perseverence

Description: Rudy decides to quit the football team. Fortune, his friend and former boss, challenges him because he used to play for Notre Dame, but quit.

Start Time: 1:29:10

Start Cue: Just before "What're you doing here"

End Time: 1:31:20

End Cue: "Do you hear me clear enough?"

Comments: Contains 2 potentially objectionable words.

_____

Title: _____

Topic: _____

Description: _____

Start Time: _____

Start Cue: _____

End Time: _____

End Cue: _____

Comments: _____

_____

- Honesty -

Message Titles

- ❑ Honest to God?
- ❑ Simple Truth Telling
- ❑ Telling the Truth
- ❑ Truth or Consequences
- ❑ *Ninth Commandment:* Refuse to Lie

_____

_____

_____

_____

_____

Dramas

Title	Tone	Characters	Topics
All Gummed Up	Serious	1 male, 1 female, 1 offstage voice	Adultery; Dealing with past hurts; The pain of lies
Mr. P. Nocchio	Humorous	2 males, or 1 female and 1 male	Honesty
The Okra Windy Show	Humorous	3 males, 3 females	Honesty in relationships; Communication

Songs

*No songs specifically on Honesty. Try looking at **Authenticity** or **Truth Telling**.*

Title	Artist	Style	Tempo	Seeker-Sensitivity Rating
_____	_____	_____	_____	_____
_____	_____	_____	_____	_____
_____	_____	_____	_____	_____

Movie Clips

Title: _____

Topic: _____

Description: _____

Start Time: _____

Start Cue: _____

End Time: _____

End Cue: _____

Comments: _____

- Purity -

See also: **Sex, Temptation**

Message Titles

❏ Christians in a Sex-Crazed Culture
❏ Defining Our Code of Conduct
❏ How to "Affair Proof" Your Marriage
❏ Looking, Lusting or Loving?

- ❏ The Payoff for Sexual Purity
- ❏ The Pornography Problem
- ❏ What Causes Affairs?

_____

_____

_____

_____

_____

 # Dramas

Title	Tone	Characters	Topics
The Big Sell	Humorous	3 males, 2 females	Obsession with sex in society; Effect of the media
It's Only a Movie	Humorous	2 males, 2 females, 1 offstage voice	The power of media; The effects of what we see; Male/female differences
Just Looking	Mixed; Light	1 male, 1 female	Eye causing you to stumble; Purity of thoughts

 # Songs

Title	Artist	Style	Tempo	Seeker-Sensitivity Rating
The Dilemma	Sandi Patti	Pop	Up	6
I Stand, I Fall	*Willow Creek Music*	*Piano ballad*	*Slow*	7
Keep My Mind	**Margaret Becker**	**Pop**	**Mid/up**	**7**
Man of God	*Willow Creek Music*	*Pop/rock*	*Mid/up*	7
Miracle of Mercy	**Steven Curtis Chapman**	**Acoustic ballad**	**Slow**	**4**
Run Away	Steven Curtis Chapman	Pop	Up	7
Stranger to Holiness	Steve Camp	Ballad	Slow/mid	2
There Is a Line	Susan Ashton	Folk pop	Mid	6
Walk on By	**Susan Ashton**	**Folk pop**	**Mid/up**	**8**

Title	Artist	Style	Tempo	Seeker-Sensitivity Rating

Movie Clips

Title: _____
Topic: _____
Description: _____
Start Time: _____
Start Cue: _____
End Time: _____
End Cue: _____
Comments: _____
_____

- Self-Control -

Refers to being able to control your actions and words—can deal with finances, gossip, physical health, and sexuality

Message Titles

☐ *Rare and Remarkable Virtues:* Self-Control
☐ **The Secret of Self-Control:** Your Body • Your Money • Your Passion

_____
_____
_____
_____
_____

Dramas

Title	Tone	Characters	Topics
Catalog-itis	Humorous	1 male, 1 female, 2 jr. high age girls	Self-control; Contentment
Check Mates	Humorous	1 male, 1 female	Personal finances; Debt
Confessions of an Ad-aholic	Humorous	1 male, 1 female	Materialism; Power of the media; The American dream
Donuts & Deadbeats	Humorous	1 male, 1 female	Self-control; Physical health
The Killing Spree	Humorous	1 male, 3 females	Sixth Commandment; Murder; Gossip
Oh, What a Feeling!	Humorous	2 males, 1 female	Decision making; Self-control; Money management
____	____	____	____
____	____	____	____
____	____	____	____
____	____	____	____
____	____	____	____

Songs

Title	Artist	Style	Tempo	Seeker-Sensitivity Rating
Behind Every Fantasy	*Willow Creek Music*	*Country pop*	*Up*	*10*
The Dilemma	Sandi Patti	Pop	Up	6
There Is a Line	Susan Ashton	Folk pop	Mid	6
Walk on By	**Susan Ashton**	**Folk pop**	**Mid/up**	**8**
Whatever You Ask	**Steve Camp**	**Power ballad**	**Slow**	**5**
____	____	____	____	____
____	____	____	____	____
____	____	____	____	____
____	____	____	____	____
____	____	____	____	____

Movie Clips

Title: _____

Topic: _____

Description: _____

Start Time: _____

Start Cue: _____

End Time: _____

End Cue: _____

Comments: _____

_____

Programming Tip

Risk taking

Do not be afraid to take calculated risks. The stakes
are high, so we need to use discernment—some risks are
unwarranted—but there are times when the potential
for something wonderful happening outweighs the risks.
Innovation is a process, and failure is sometimes a
part of that process.

Christian Life, General

Message Titles

- **Becoming a Contagious Christian:** Authenticity • Compassion • Sacrifice
- **Building Bigger Hearts:** Energy Management • Relationship Management • Soul Management
- **Capturing the Heart of Christianity:** How to Become a Christian • How a Christian Relates to God • Discovering Community • A Day in the Life of a Christian • A Night in the Life of a Christian
- **Endangered Character Qualities:** Courage • Discipline • Vision • Endurance
- **Life's Defining Moments:** Defining Our Beliefs • Defining Our Code of Conduct • Defining Our Personal Aspirations
- **Rare and Remarkable Virtues:** Self-Control • Confidence • Patience • Contentment

_____
_____
_____
_____

Dramas

Title	Tone	Characters	Topics
A Day in the Life	Humorous	5 males	Christians in the marketplace; New Christian
First-Day Jitters	Humorous	1 female	New Christian; Obeying God
Horsefeathers and Nosefly	Humorous	2 male or female "helpers"	Christian living; Obedience
Impressions, Inc.	Humorous	2 males, 1 female	Skin-deep Christianity
"It"	Humorous	2 males, 1 female	Becoming a Christian doesn't mean having no problems; Vulnerability of new believers

Title	Tone	Characters	Topics
The Mystery of Robert Richardson	Mixed	3 males, 2 females, 1 narrator	Living the Christian life
No Fun	Humorous	3 males, 1 female	Christian lifestyle; Misconceptions about Christianity
A Problem of Perception	Humorous	3 males, 1 female	Misconceptions about Christianity; Christian life
Seeing Is Believing	Humorous	1 male, 1 female, 1 narrator	A Savior you can trust; Easy faith
Welcome to the Family	Humorous	2 males, 1 female	New Christian; Growing in Christ
_____	_____	_____	_____
_____	_____	_____	_____
_____	_____	_____	_____
_____	_____	_____	_____

 **Songs**

Title	Artist	Style	Tempo	Seeker-Sensitivity Rating
All I Ever Wanted	Margaret Becker	Pop/rock ballad	Slow/mid	4
Audience of One	*Willow Creek Music*	*Power ballad*	*Slow*	*8*
Casual Christian	**De Garmo & Key**	**Power ballad**	**Slow**	**6**
Changin'	**Acapella Vocal Band**	**Acapella vocal group**	**Up**	**8**
Chippin' Away	*Willow Creek Music*	*Folk pop*	*Mid/up*	*8*
Ever Devoted	*Willow Creek Music*	*Ballad*	*Slow*	*6*
For Who He Really Is	Steven Curtis Chapman	Folk/pop ballad	Mid/slow	1
Heart's Cry	**Steven Curtis Chapman**	**Acoustic ballad**	**Mid/slow**	**7**
If That's What It Takes	*Willow Creek Music*	*Pop/MOR*	*Mid/slow*	*5*
Isn't It Good	*Willow Creek Music*	*Ballad*	*Mid/slow*	*4*
Look Me in the Eye	Margaret Becker	Pop ballad	Slow/mid	3
Love You With My Life	Steven Curtis Chapman	Pop	Up	5
Man of God	*Willow Creek Music*	*Pop/rock*	*Mid/up*	*7*
Most of the Time	Glad	Piano ballad	Slow	4
The Narrow Way	Wayne Watson	Pop	Mid	6
No Better Place	Steven Curtis Chapman	Pop/folk rock	Up	7
Show Yourselves to Be	Steven Curtis Chapman	Acoustic ballad	Slow/mid	4
There Is a Line	Susan Ashton	Folk pop	Mid	6
Whatever You Ask	**Steve Camp**	**Power ballad**	**Slow**	**5**

Title	Artist	Style	Tempo	Seeker-Sensitivity Rating
When You Are a Soldier	Steven Curtis Chapman	Keyboard ballad	Slow/mid	4
Who Makes the Rules	Steven Curtis Chapman	Pop/folk rock	Up	7
Would I Know You	Wayne Watson	Ballad	Slow	3
_____	_____	_____	_____	_____
_____	_____	_____	_____	_____
_____	_____	_____	_____	_____
_____	_____	_____	_____	_____

 # Movie Clips

Title: Chariots of Fire
Topic: Christian life; Endurance
Description: Eric Liddell gives a sermonette about running the race of faith.
Start Time: 0:25:35
Start Cue: "You came to see a race today"
End Time: 0:27:20
End Cue: "That is how you run a straight race"
Comments: _____
_____

Title: _____
Topic: _____
Description: _____
Start Time: _____
Start Cue: _____
End Time: _____
End Cue: _____
Comments: _____
_____

The Church

Can refer to the biblical model for the church as well as issues within the church or between churches

Might also include: *Denominational Differences*

See also: **Community**

Message Titles

- ❏ What Catholics Can Learn From Protestants
- ❏ What Protestants Can Learn From Catholics
- ❏ *Changing Times:* The Changing American Church
- ❏ **The Story of Seven Churches (Rev. 2–3:22):** The Heartless Church • The Tested Church • The Compromising Churches • The Church of the Open Door • The Lukewarm Church

_____

_____

_____

_____

Dramas

Title	Tone	Characters	Topics
Differences	Humorous	2 males, 1 female	Catholicism vs. Protestantism
On the Outside	Serious	1 female or male	Being salt and light; Negative church experiences
Pastor General	Humorous	2 males, 2 females	Abusive leadership; The church; Authoritarianism
Pulpit Talk	Humorous	3 males, 2 females	Stereotypical church experiences; Sermons; Intro to Sermon on the Mount
_____	_____	_____	_____
_____	_____	_____	_____
_____	_____	_____	_____

Songs

Title	Artist	Style	Tempo	Seeker-Sensitivity Rating
Bridge Between Two Hearts	**Bob Carlisle**	**Pop**	**Up**	**9**
I Commit My Love to You	Twila Paris	Ballad	Slow	5
Isn't It Good	*Willow Creek Music*	*Ballad*	*Mid/slow*	*4*
Let's Build a Bridge	Michael English	Pop	Up	8
Let's Stand Together	**The Kry**	**Rock**	**Mid/up**	**1**
Undivided	**First Call**	**Ballad—trio**	**Slow**	**5**
We Are an Army	Trace Balin	Power ballad	Slow/mid	1
We Need Each Other	**Trace Balin**	**Power ballad**	**Slow/mid**	**7**
_____	_____	_____	_____	_____
_____	_____	_____	_____	_____
_____	_____	_____	_____	_____
_____	_____	_____	_____	_____

 # Movie Clips

Title: Sister Act
Topic: The church; Reasons people don't go to church
Description: Humorous clip of a boring preacher and a horrible choir, illustrating a couple of reasons why people don't go to church.
Start Time: 0:30:25
Start Cue: "We are a small congregation this morning"
End Time: 32:25
End Cue: Whoopi Goldberg winces
Comments: _____
_____

Title: _____
Topic: _____
Description: _____
Start Time: _____
Start Cue: _____
End Time: _____
End Cue: _____
Comments: _____
_____

Evangelism

Primarily intended for a Christian audience, on the importance of evangelism
For evangelistic ideas, see: **Baptism, Grace, Salvation**

 ## Message Titles

☐ Becoming a Contagious Christian
☐ People Matter to God
☐ **Adventures in Personal Evangelism:** The Motivations for Evangelism • The Mindset of an Evangelist • The Message of an Evangelist • The Style of an Evangelist
☐ **Stronger Salt, Brighter Light:** Assessing Your Savor Factor • Increasing Your Candle Power • Impacting the Irreligious • Discovering Your Evangelism Style • Communicating the Message of Hope • Enfolding New Believers • Coping With Questions

_____
_____
_____
_____

 ## Dramas

Title	Tone	Characters	Topics
The Lane of Life	Serious; Mime	5 either male or female, 1 offstage narrator	Salvation; Our value to God; Self-esteem
Life Cycle	Humorous	2 females	Evangelism
Reason Enough	Mixed, mostly serious	1 male, 1 female	Importance of faith grounded in reason
Trying Time	Serious	1 male, 2 females	Marriage; Spiritual mismatch
Wait 'Til Halftime	Mixed	1 male, 1 female	Eternity; Heaven and hell; Evangelism

_____	_____	_____	_____
_____	_____	_____	_____
_____	_____	_____	_____

Songs

Title	Artist	Style	Tempo	Seeker-Sensitivity Rating
Be the One	**Al Denson**	**Power ballad**	**Slow**	**7**
The Door	Al Denson	Power ballad	Slow	1
For Who He Really Is	Steven Curtis Chapman	Folk/pop ballad	Mid/slow	1
People Need the Lord	Steve Green	Inspirational ballad	Slow	1
Run to the Battle	Steve Camp	Pop/rock	Up/mid	1

 Movie Clips

*There are several good video clips, illustrating various evangelistic styles, in the *Becoming a Contagious Christian* evangelism training course, available through Willow Creek Resources.

Title: _____

Topic: _____

Description: _____

Start Time: _____

Start Cue: _____

End Time: _____

End Cue: _____

Comments: _____

_____

Gossip/Slander

See also: **Relational Conflict, Self-Control, Sin**

Package Suggestion

Drama:
The Killing Spree

Song:
Words

Message Titles

- ❏ *Sixth Commandment:* Respect Human Life
- ❏ *What Jesus Would Say to . . .* Rush Limbaugh

_____

_____

_____

_____

_____

Dramas

Title	Tone	Characters	Topics
The Killing Spree	Humorous	1 male, 3 females	Sixth Commandment; Murder; Gossip

Songs

Title	Artist	Style	Tempo	Seeker-Sensitivity Rating
Words	Kim Hill	Pop/rock	Up	10

Movie Clips

Title: _____

Topic: _____

Description: _____

Start Time: _____

Start Cue: _____

End Time: _____

End Cue: _____

Comments: _____

_____

Hypocrisy

See also: **Authenticity**

Message Titles

Package Suggestion

Drama:
On the Outside

Song:
For Who He Really Is

☐ Watch Out for Wolves
☐ *Private Conversations:* Jesus Talks to a Religious Person
☐ **Religion Run Amok:** How Good Groups Go Bad • How Good Christians Go Bad • How [name of your church] Could Go Bad

_____

_____

_____

_____

Dramas

Title	Tone	Characters	Topics
Impressions, Inc.	Humorous	2 males, 1 female	Skin-deep Christianity
On the Outside	Serious	1 female or male	Being salt and light; Negative church experiences
Reason Enough	Mixed, mostly serious	1 male, 1 female	Importance of faith grounded in reason
Sweet Hour of Prayer	Humorous	2 males, 1 female	Prayer; Hypocrisy; Faith
A Visitor	Serious	2 males, 1 female	Wolves in sheep's clothing; Discernment; Spiritual manipulation

Songs

Title	Artist	Style	Tempo	Seeker-Sensitivity Rating
Casual Christian	De Garmo & Key	Power ballad	Slow	6
For Who He Really Is	Steven Curtis Chapman	Folk/pop ballad	Mid/slow	1
Who Makes the Rules	Steven Curtis Chapman	Pop/folk rock	Up	7
Would I Know You	Wayne Watson	Ballad	Slow	3

 # Movie Clips

Title: _____

Topic: _____

Description: _____

Start Time: _____

Start Cue: _____

End Time: _____

End Cue: _____

Comments: _____

Programming Tip

Avoid "slot-filling"

Do not choose a song or drama just because you need something for that particular "slot." Have a well-thought-out purpose for every element that you program.

Joy of the Christian Life

Addresses the misconception of many seekers that Christianity is boring or stifling

Package Suggestion

Drama:
D-Day

Song:
What a Ride

 ## Message Titles

- ❐ The Adventure of Christianity
- ❐ The Benefits of Knowing God
- ❐ *Christianity's Toughest Competition:* Adventurism
- ❐ *A Taste of Christianity:* A Better Kind of Freedom
- ❐ *Three Things God Loves (That Most People Think He Doesn't):* Laughter
- ❐ *Yeah God:* For Being Joyful

_____

_____

_____

_____

 ## Dramas

Title	Tone	Characters	Topics
D-Day	Humorous	2 males, 1 female	Misconceptions about Christianity
Fully Devoted Sailors	Humorous	1 male, 1 female, 7 either male or female	Joy of Christian life; Misconceptions about Christianity
Monday Night Meeting	Humorous	4 males	New Christian; Joy of Christian life; Discipleship
No Fun	Humorous	3 males, 1 female	Christian lifestyle; Misconceptions about Christianity

_____	_____	_____	_____
_____	_____	_____	_____
_____	_____	_____	_____

Songs

Title	Artist	Style	Tempo	Seeker-Sensitivity Rating
Change in My Life	**John Pagano**	**Gospel**	**Mid/up**	**9**
Ever Devoted	*Willow Creek Music*	*Ballad*	*Slow*	*6*
The Great Adventure	Steven Curtis Chapman	Pop/rock	Up	5
How Could I Ask for More	Cindy Morgan	Piano ballad	Slow	9
I Could Live Without You	Wayne Watson	Ballad	Slow	6
Isn't It Good	*Willow Creek Music*	*Ballad*	*Mid/slow*	*4*
No Better Place	**Steven Curtis Chapman**	**Pop/folk rock**	**Up**	**7**
This Is the Life	**Phillips, Craig and Dean**	**Pop/rock**	**Up**	**6**
Treasure	**Gary Chapman**	**Acoustic ballad**	**Slow**	**9**
Want the World to Know	*Willow Creek Music*	*Pop*	*Up*	*9*
We've Got a Reason to Celebrate	Billy and Sarah Gaines	R & B pop	Up	3
What a Ride	*Willow Creek Music*	*Pop/rock*	*Up*	*9*
_____	_____	_____	_____	_____
_____	_____	_____	_____	_____
_____	_____	_____	_____	_____
_____	_____	_____	_____	_____

 # Movie Clips

Title: _____

Topic: _____

Description: _____

Start Time: _____

Start Cue: _____

End Time: _____

End Cue: _____

Comments: _____

_____

Servanthood

Refers to serving others and having the attitude and heart of a servant
Might also include: *Self-Sacrifice*
See also: **Compassion, Selfishness/Pride**

 Message Titles

- ❏ *Becoming a Contagious Christian:* Sacrifice
- ❏ *Giving and Receiving Love:* Sacrificial Love
- ❏ **Serving Lessons:** Exposing the "Me First" Mindset • Breaking the Back of Self-Centeredness •
  Imagine Everyone Serving • Gifted to Serve • The Servant's Survival Kit • Inspiring Others to
  Serve • Serving Through Sharing • The Rewards of Servanthood • My Life, a Living Sacrifice

_____

_____

_____

_____

_____

 Dramas

Title	Tone	Characters	Topics
Am I Missing Something?	Serious	3 males, 2 females	Attitudes in serving; Giving; Self-deception; Rationalizing
The Boy Who Never Got Dirty	Humorous	1 male, 1 female, 1 narrator	Service; Risk taking
Full-Service Stations and Other Myths	Humorous	1 male, 1 female	Servanthood
Good Friday 1991, Scene 1	Serious	Jesus character, 12 disciples, 2 females	Good Friday; Serving others
Mr. Hibbs' Day Off	Mixed; mime	3 males, 1 female, 1 child	Serving others; Self-denial; Being used by God

Title	Tone	Characters	Topics
Parlor Talk	Mixed	3 males, 2 females	Making a difference with your life; Death; Workaholism
The Story of Rachel	Serious	3 females	Care for the poor; Compassion
Suit and Volly	Humorous	2 males, 2 females	Motives in serving others
___	___	___	___
___	___	___	___
___	___	___	___

Songs

Title	Artist	Style	Tempo	Seeker-Sensitivity Rating
Be the One	**Al Denson**	**Power Ballad**	**Slow**	7
The Extra Mile	Al Denson	Power Ballad	Slow	9
Helping Hand	**Amy Grant**	**Pop**	**Mid/up**	**10**
Love Can Open the Door	Sandi Patti	Pop	Up	10
Love You With My Life	Steven Curtis Chapman	Pop	Up	5
___	___	___	___	___
___	___	___	___	___
___	___	___	___	___
___	___	___	___	___
___	___	___	___	___

Movie Clips

Title: _____

Topic: _____

Description: _____

Start Time: _____

Start Cue: _____

End Time: _____

End Cue: _____

Comments: _____

Serving God

Refers to what you do with your gifts to serve God, most likely in the church
Might also include: *Spiritual Gifts*
See also: **Commitment to Christ, Discipleship**

Package Suggestion

Drama:
Suit and Volly

Song:
Audience of One

Message Titles

- ☐ Redefining Commitment
- ☐ *Discovering the Way God Wired You Up:* Spiritually
- ☐ *Seven Wonders of the Spiritual World:* God Uses Me
- ☐ **Values Vital to Our Future:** The Gift of Leadership • The Gift of Evangelism • The Gift of Giving • The Gift of Helps • The Gifts of Exhortation and Mercy • The Gifts of Shepherding and Hospitality

_____
_____
_____
_____

Dramas

Title	Tone	Characters	Topics
Call of the Wild	Mixed	1 male, 1 female	Serving God; Serving in a place consistent with your gifts and temperament
Somebody's Got to Do It	Humorous	1 male, 1 female	Spiritual gifts; Serving God
Suit and Volly	Humorous	2 males, 2 females	Motives in serving others
Tired When Needed	Humorous	1 male, 1 female	Burnout; Boundaries; Saying "no"
_____	_____	_____	_____
_____	_____	_____	_____
_____	_____	_____	_____
_____	_____	_____	_____

Songs

Title	Artist	Style	Tempo	Seeker-Sensitivity Rating
Audience of One	*Willow Creek Music*	*Power ballad*	*Slow*	8
Be the One	**Al Denson**	**Power ballad**	**Slow**	7
My Soul Desire	Deniece Williams	R & B ballad	Slow	5
Power of God	Imperials	Pop/rock	Up	5
Run to the Battle	Steve Camp	Pop/rock	Up/mid	1
Surrender Medley	*Willow Creek Music*	*Ballad medley—duet*	*Slow*	6
Whatever You Ask	**Steve Camp**	**Power ballad**	**Slow**	5
With All My Heart	Babbie Mason	Ballad	Slow	6
___	___	___	___	___
___	___	___	___	___
___	___	___	___	___

Movie Clips

Title: Chariots of Fire
Topic: Being true to whom God made you; Honoring God with your gifts
Description: Eric Liddell talks to his sister, who wants him to forsake running to be a missionary. Eric talks about the fact that God made him fast, and when he runs, he can feel God's pleasure.
Start Time: 0:58:20
Start Cue: First line is "I've decided . . . I'm going back to China"
End Time: 0:59:15
End Cue: "To win is to honor him"
Comments: _____

Title: Sister Act
Topic: Spiritual gifts; Celebrating uniqueness
Description: Sister Mary Robert confides in Sister Mary Clarence that she wants to give something that's "only me, and nobody else."
Start Time: 0:38:40
Start Cue: After "Have a seat"; Mary Robert sits down
End Time: 0:40:05
End Cue: "Good night, Mary Robert"
Comments: _____

Tithing

See also: **Money Management**

Message Titles

- ☐ *Financial Freedom:* Giving Money
- ☐ *Your Money Matters:* Discovering the Rewards of Giving

_____
_____
_____
_____
_____

Dramas

Title	Tone	Characters	Topics
Am I Missing Something?	Serious	3 males, 2 females	Attitudes in serving; Giving; Self-deception; Rationalizing
The Offering	Humorous	3 males, 1 female	Tithing
_____	_____	_____	_____
_____	_____	_____	_____
_____	_____	_____	_____
_____	_____	_____	_____

Songs

No songs specifically on Tithing. *Try looking at* Commitment to Christ, Discipleship, Materialism, Thanksgiving.

Title	Artist	Style	Tempo	Seeker-Sensitivity Rating

Movie Clips

Title: _____

Topic: _____

Description: _____

Start Time: _____

Start Cue: _____

End Time: _____

End Cue: _____

Comments: _____
_____

Programming Tip

Variety, variety, variety!
Do not allow your service order or the elements themselves to become predictable and stale. If the congregation can tell exactly what will happen in the service from week to week, you are in a rut. Variety can bring life and excitement to a church service.

HOLIDAYS/SPECIAL SERVICES

Baptism

See also: **Changed Life, New Christians, Salvation**

 ## Dramas

Title	Tone	Characters	Topics
The Book of Life	"Energetic mime"; mixed	3 males, 3 females	Baptism; Faith; Basic Christianity; Eternal life
A Clean Slate	Serious	1 male, 2 or 3 males or females	Forgiveness; Redemption; Guilt
Going Public	Humorous	2 males, 2 females, 1 offstage narrator	Baptism; Living openly for Christ
The Lane of Life	Mixed; mime	5 either male or female, 1 offstage narrator	Salvation; Our value to God; Self-esteem
Measuring Up	Mixed; mime	2 males, 1 female, 1 other male or female	God's acceptance of us; Self-esteem
Sitters, Strivers, Standers, and Saints	Mixed	4 either male or female, 1 narrator	God changing lives; God completing us
The Stickholders	Serious	3 males, 1 female, 1 narrator	Relationship with God; Freedom from rules
"X" Marks the Spot	Serious; mime	1 female, 1 male, and 3 either female or male	Sin; Redemption; Forgiveness; Guilt
___	___	___	___
___	___	___	___
___	___	___	___
___	___	___	___

Songs

Title	Artist	Style	Tempo	Seeker-Sensitivity Rating
Change in My Life	John Pagano	Gospel	Mid/up	9
Cross Medley	*Willow Creek Music*	*Ballad medley— hymns*	*Slow*	7
From This Moment On	Newsong	**Ballad**	Slow	**8**
I'm Amazed	*Willow Creek Music*	*Ballad*	*Slow*	7
_____	_____	_____	_____	_____
_____	_____	_____	_____	_____
_____	_____	_____	_____	_____

Movie Clips

Title: _____

Topic: _____

Description: _____

Start Time: _____

Start Cue: _____

End Time: _____

End Cue: _____

Comments: _____

_____

Programming Tip

Servanthood

No matter how gifted a person may be, he or she should not be allowed to minister if there are serious ego problems, patterns of sin, or an inability to receive the truth with humility.

Christmas

Message Titles

- ☐ The Aftermath of Christmas
- ☐ Christmas Is More Than Jesus' Birth
- ☐ The Christmas Story
- ☐ On the Outside Looking In
- ☐ Out of the Ordinary
- ☐ A Promise for Peace
- ☐ Who Is Lying in the Manger?

_____

_____

_____

_____

Dramas

Title	Tone	Characters	Topics
Family Snapshots—Take V (Christmas Eve)	Mixed— touching end	2 males, 2 females, 1 jr. high boy	Christmas
Little What's His Face	Mixed	3 males, 3 females	Christmas; Parenting
Merry Christmas With Love	Mixed	1 female, 3 male or female carolers	Christmas
Mistaken Identity	Mixed	3 males, 2 females, 1 young girl	Christmas; Doubting
Stolen Jesus	Mixed; touching	2 females	Christmas
Unaverage Joe	Mixed	2 males, 1 female	Christmas; Obeying God's call
_____	_____	_____	_____
_____	_____	_____	_____
_____	_____	_____	_____

Songs

Title	Artist	Style	Tempo	Seeker-Sensitivity Rating
Away in a Manger	Steven Curtis Chapman	Folk pop	Mid	10
Heirlooms	Amy Grant	Ballad	Slow	8
Love Has Come	Amy Grant	MOR	Mid	8
The Music of Christmas	Steven Curtis Chapman	Folk pop	Mid	10
Our God Is With Us	Steven Curtis Chapman	Folk pop	Mid	9
This Baby	Steven Curtis Chapman	Pop	Up	9

We also use our own arrangements of standards, such as "O Holy Night."

_____	_____	_____	____	____
_____	_____	_____	____	____
_____	_____	_____	____	____

Movie Clips

Title:	A Christmas Story
Topic:	Christmas memories
Description:	A funny clip showing memories of visiting Santa at the department store.
Start Time:	1:09:35
Start Cue:	Elf says, "Quit dragging your feet"
End Time:	1:11:40
End Cue:	Ralphie goes down the slide after being pushed by Santa
Comments:	It's hard to understand Ralphie's request to Santa. It may need to be explained to the congregation

Title:	A Christmas Story
Topic:	Christmas memories
Description:	Christmas is over, and Ralphie hasn't gotten the BB gun he wanted. His dad points out one present he hasn't opened yet—it's the BB gun.
Start Time:	1:20:30
Start Cue:	Mom says, "Did you have a nice Christmas?"
End Time:	1:22:43
End Cue:	"I had one when I was eight years old"
Comments:	_____

Communion

See also: **Salvation, God's Forgiveness of Us, Grace**

 ## Dramas

Title	Tone	Characters	Topics
The Wall	Serious	3 males, 2 females, 1 child	Importance of remembering

We celebrate Communion during the midweek services, where we rarely use drama.

_____ _____ _____ _____

_____ _____ _____ _____

_____ _____ _____ _____

_____ _____ _____ _____

 ## Songs

Title	Artist	Style	Tempo	Seeker-Sensitivity Rating
Cross Medley	*Willow Creek Music*	*Ballad medley—hymns*	*Slow*	7
Forgive Me	Tim Miner	Ballad	Slow	4
Just Come In	Margaret Becker	Pop ballad	Slow	5
Miracle of Mercy	**Steven Curtis Chapman**	**Acoustic ballad**	**Slow**	**4**
Remember Your Chains	Steven Curtis Chapman	Acoustic MOR	Mid	2
Who Am I	Margaret Becker	Power ballad	Slow	7
Why Me	*Willow Creek Music*	*Ballad*	*Slow*	9

_____ _____ _____ _____ _____

_____ _____ _____ _____ _____

_____ _____ _____ _____ _____

_____ _____ _____ _____ _____

Movie Clips

Title: _____

Topic: _____

Description: _____

Start Time: _____

Start Cue: _____

End Time: _____

End Cue: _____

Comments: _____

Programming Tip

The process is as important as the product

If in the process of producing a great service we abuse or overuse our volunteers or staff members, we have not honored God. Do the things in the process of planning and executing a program that will build and protect a sense of community.

Easter

See also: **Jesus, Salvation**

Message Titles

- ❑ Easter Celebration
- ❑ God's Wake-up Calls
- ❑ People Matter to God
- ❑ The Relevance of the Resurrection

_____

_____

_____

_____

Package Suggestions

Drama:
Happy Easter

Song:
Love That Will Not Let Me Go

. . .

Drama:
These Parts

Song:
They Could Not

Dramas

Title	Tone	Characters	Topics
Happy Easter	Humorous	3 males, 5 females, 1 ten-year-old girl	Easter
Lonely at the Top	Serious	1 male	The perils of power, authority; Easter
The Prisoner	Serious	3 males, 1 female	Easter; Freedom from sin; New Christian
The Stickholders	Serious	3 males, 1 female, 1 narrator	Relationship with God; Freedom from rules
These Parts	Mixed	3 adults in any combination of male and female 1 child, 1 narrator	The Resurrection; Our need for Christ; Easter

 Songs

Title	Artist	Style	Tempo	Seeker-Sensitivity Rating
I've Been Released	*Willow Creek Music*	*Pop/rock—Chicago sound*	*Up*	9
They Could Not	Sandi Patti	Inspirational ballad	Slow	5
Up From the Dead	Dana Key	Pop	Mid	8
Via Dolorosa	Sandi Patti	Inspirational ballad	Slow	7
Want the World to Know	*Willow Creek Music*	*Pop*	*Up*	9

 Movie Clips

Title: _____

Topic: _____

Description: _____

Start Time: _____

Start Cue: _____

End Time: _____

End Cue: _____

Comments: _____

_____

Father's Day

Message Titles

- ❏ Dads . . . Whatever You Do
- ❏ Fathers: An Endangered Species
- ❏ Fathers: Heavenly and Otherwise
- ❏ Gracious Fathers
- ❏ Leaving a Living Legacy
- ❏ Phantom Fathers
- ❏ Rediscovering Discipline
- ❏ The Soft Side of Fathering
- ❏ Understanding Dad's Dilemma
- ❏ Unforgettable Fathers

_____

_____

_____

_____

Dramas

Title	Tone	Characters	Topics
Definitely Safe	Serious— heartwarming	2 males, 1 female	Father's Day; Prodigal son; Unconditional love
Fishin'	Mixed; touching	2 males	Expressing positive emotions; Father/son relationships
Lucky Day at the Ballpark	Mixed	2 males, 1 boy	Father's Day; Proper priorities
Misjudged Love	Serious	2 males, 1 female	Homosexuality; AIDS; Father/son relationship
One Day at the Zoo	Humorous	1 narrator, 3 males, 2 females, and some offstage voices	Fatherhood

Title	Tone	Characters	Topics
Out of Control	Humorous	2 males, 1 female	Fatherhood; Parenting
Quality Time	Serious	1 male, 1 female, 2 teenage girls	Fatherhood; Workaholism

Songs

Title	Artist	Style	Tempo	Seeker-Sensitivity Rating
If I Had Only Known	Reba McEntire	Ballad	Slow	10
I Want to Be Just Like You	Phillips, Craig and Dean	MOR	Mid/slow	9
The Last Song	Elton John	Ballad	Slow	10
The Living Years	Mike & the Mechanics	Pop	Mid/up	10
Man of God	*Willow Creek Music*	*Pop/rock*	*Mid/up*	*7*

Movie Clips

Title:	8 Seconds
Topic:	Regret; Communicating love
Description:	A father, whose son has recently died, breaks down in remorse over not telling his son that he loved him.
Start Time:	1:27:10
Start Cue:	Pallbearers carry casket out of church
End Time:	1:28:33
End Cue:	"I loved him"
Comments:	_____

Title: Dad

Topic: Father/son relationships

Description: Ted Danson and Jack Lemmon play a father and son. Lemmon is dying in a hospital bed, and the two have a poignant exchange, ending with Danson crawling into bed with his dad.

Start Time: 1:46:20

Start Cue: "How you feeling?"

End Time: 1:50:35

End Cue: "I must have done something right." End after wide shot

Comments: _____

_____

Title: Father of the Bride

Topic: Parenthood; Father/daughter relationship

Description: Steve Martin plays basketball with his daughter as "My Girl" plays in the background. Shows the warmth and fun of their relationship.

Start Time: 0:14:55

Start Cue: "Suppose you're not in the mood for a little one-on-one?"

End Time: 0:17:00

End Cue: Steve Martin and his daughter walk off together

Comments: _____

_____

Title: Indiana Jones and the Last Crusade

Topic: Father/son relationships

Description: Indiana Jones mildly confronts his father about the lack of a relationship between them.

Start Time: 1:13:45

Start Cue: "Remember the last time we had a quiet drink?"

End Time: 1:15:05

End Cue: "I can't think of anything"

Comments: Conversation is over a drink. May be offensive to some churches

_____

Title: Parenthood

Topic: Parental neglect; Dealing with past hurts

Description: Funny, bittersweet scene where young Gil (Steve Martin plays the adult Gil) is taken to a baseball game by his father and then left with an usher. We find out it's actually a combination of memories of his strained childhood.

Start Time: 0:00:05

Start Cue: Start at fade-up. This is the opening scene.

End Time: 0:02:28

End Cue: "Strong, happy, confident kids"

Comments: Profanity immediately follows cutoff point

_____

Title: Searching for Bobby Fischer

Topic: Fatherhood; Failure; Destructive parenting

Description: Eight-year-old Josh loses chess match, and his dad angrily confronts him about losing. Illustrates a dad who has too much invested in son's success.

Start Time: 1:06:30
Start Cue: Shot of clock tower. "Seven moves" is first line
End Time: 1:08:20
End Cue: "Sorry"
Comments: _____
_____

Title: _____
Topic: _____
Description: _____
Start Time: _____
Start Cue: _____
End Time: _____
End Cue: _____
Comments: _____
_____

Programming Tip

Details matter

Think through every moment of a service several days before it is to take place. Anticipate what transitions are needed, what cues need to be given to the technical team, what music you might play beforehand and afterward, and so on. Leave nothing to chance.

Good Friday

Dramas

Title	Tone	Characters	Topics
Adulterous Woman/Soldier at the Cross	Serious	1 female, 1 male	Good Friday
Good Friday 1990	Serious	2 males, 1 female	Good Friday
Good Friday 1991, Scene 1	Serious	Jesus character, 12 disciples, 2 females	Good Friday; Serving others
Good Friday 1991, Scene 2	Serious	Jesus character, 12 disciples, 2 females	Good Friday
Lonely at the Top	Serious	1 male	The perils of power, authority; Easter
_____	_____	_____	_____
_____	_____	_____	_____
_____	_____	_____	_____

Songs

Title	Artist	Style	Tempo	Seeker-Sensitivity Rating
Via Dolorosa	Sandi Patti	Inspirational ballad	Slow	7
What I Wouldn't Give	_Willow Creek Music_	_Acoustic ballad_	_Slow_	10
Where Would I Be Now	_Willow Creek Music_	_Ballad/Broadway feel_	_Slow_	6
Why Me	_Willow Creek Music_	_Ballad_	_Slow_	9
_____	_____	_____	_____	_____
_____	_____	_____	_____	_____
_____	_____	_____	_____	_____
_____	_____	_____	_____	_____

Movie Clips

Title: _____

Topic: _____

Description: _____

Start Time: _____

Start Cue: _____

End Time: _____

End Cue: _____

Comments: _____

_____

Programming Tip

Discover what fuels your creativity
For some, creativity may be stimulated by a walk in a forest preserve; for others it may come through watching a movie or reading a great book. Find out what spurs you to creative thoughts and make time for those activities.

Mother's Day

See also: **Parent—Child Relationships**

Message Titles

- ❑ How Much Should Mothers Work?
- ❑ The Nobility of Motherhood
- ❑ A Tribute to Mothers

_____

_____

_____

_____

_____

Dramas

Title	Tone	Characters	Topics
Let Me Go	Mixed	2 females	Parenting; Letting go of adult children
The Luncheon	Serious	3 females	Mother/daughter conflict; Honesty in relationships
A Mother's Day	Mixed	1 male, 2 females	Mother's Day
Reflections	Mixed	1 male, 2 females, 2 children	Motherhood
Worth Keeping	Mixed; touching	1 male, 2 females	The nobility of motherhood; Single parenting

Songs

Title	Artist	Style	Tempo	Seeker-Sensitivity Rating
Hats	Amy Grant	Pop	Up	10
Midnight Oil	**Phillips, Craig and Dean**	**Acoustic ballad**	**Slow**	**7**
Thanks for So Much Love	Harry Newman	Ballad	Slow	10

Movie Clips

Title: _____

Topic: _____

Description: _____

Start Time: _____

Start Cue: _____

End Time: _____

End Cue: _____

Comments: _____

_____

Thanksgiving

See also: **God's Goodness**

 ## Dramas

*We don't usually use drama in Thanksgiving services.

Title	Tone	Characters	Topics
_____	_____	_____	_____
_____	_____	_____	_____
_____	_____	_____	_____
_____	_____	_____	_____
_____	_____	_____	_____

 ## Songs

Title	Artist	Style	Tempo	Seeker-Sensitivity Rating
He's Been Faithful	**Brooklyn Tabernacle Choir**	**Ballad with choir**	**Slow**	**6**
How Could I Ask for More	Cindy Morgan	Piano ballad	Slow	9
I'm Amazed	*Willow Creek Music*	*Ballad*	*Slow*	7
Listen to Our Hearts	**Geoff Moore & the Distance (with Steven Curtis Chapman)**	**Acoustic ballad— duet**	**Slow/mid**	**2**
Love That Will Not Let Me Go	**Steve Camp**	**Ballad**	**Slow**	**10**
My Redeemer Is Faithful and True	**Steven Curtis Chapman**	**Ballad**	**Slow**	**9**
My Turn Now	Steven Curtis Chapman	Country bop	Up	6
Remember Your Chains	Steven Curtis Chapman	Acoustic MOR	Mid	2

Title	Artist	Style	Tempo	Seeker-Sensitivity Rating
Thankful	*Willow Creek Music*	*Pop*	*Up*	7
Who Am I	Margaret Becker	Power ballad	Slow	7
Why Me	*Willow Creek Music*	*Ballad*	*Slow*	9

Movie Clips

Title: _____

Topic: _____

Description: _____

Start Time: _____

Start Cue: _____

End Time: _____

End Cue: _____

Comments: _____

_____

Programming Tip

Develop a "safe place" for creativity
It is important for each member of a creative team to know that he or she can share ideas with freedom and confidence, without fear of ridicule or disapproval. In the initial free-flowing phase of the creative process, "no idea is a bad idea."

IDENTITY OF GOD

God as a Refuge

Might also include: *God's Protection*

Message Titles

☐ *Yeah God:* For Being a Refuge

_____
_____
_____
_____
_____
_____

Dramas

Title	Tone	Characters	Topics
The Stickholders	Serious	3 males, 1 female, 1 narrator	Relationship with God; Freedom from rules

Songs

Title	Artist	Style	Tempo	Seeker-Sensitivity Rating
Almighty God	**Jim Murray**	**Traditional ballad**	Slow	7
A Place to Call Home	*Willow Creek Music*	*Gospel ballad*	*Slow, in 3*	*10*
Gentle Hands	Truth	Traditional ballad	Slow	8
He Covers Me	Steve Camp	Power ballad	Slow/mid	4
Here in My Heart	Susan Ashton	Folk rock	Up	8
He's All You Need	**Steve Camp**	**Ballad**	Slow	8
He Won't Let Me Down	**Debbie McClendon**	**R & B/pop**	Up	9
Hiding Place	Steven Curtis Chapman	Pop ballad	Mid/slow	9
His Love Is Strong	**Clay Crosse**	**Pop**	Up	10
His Strength Is Perfect	**Steven Curtis Chapman**	**Ballad**	Slow	9
I Go to the Rock	**Dottie Rambo**	**Swing/big band**	Mid	7
I'll Find You There	The Kry	Folk rock ballad	Slow	9
I'm Depending on You	Harv & Edythe	MOR	Mid	7
In His Sanctuary	Morris Chapman & Friends	Ballad	Slow	6
Jesus Will Still Be There	**Point of Grace**	**Ballad**	Slow	9
Let the Lord Love You	*Willow Creek Music*	*Acoustic guitar ballad*	*Slow*	*9*
Love That Will Not Let Me Go	**Steve Camp**	**Ballad**	Slow	10
Never Be Another	Paul Smith	Power ballad	Slow	8
No One Knows My Heart	Susan Ashton	Folk/pop ballad	Slow/mid	9
Peace Be Still	**Al Denson**	**Ballad**	Slow	10
Rock of Ages	James Ward	Ballad	Slow	1
Safe	Steve Archer	Ballad—duet	Slow/mid	8
Say It to Him	Teri Gibbs	Funky pop	Up	9
Say the Name	Margaret Becker	Ballad	Slow/mid	4
Strength in You	*Willow Creek Music*	*MOR pop*	*Slow/mid*	*10*
When You Are a Soldier	**Steven Curtis Chapman**	**Keyboard ballad**	Slow/mid	4
Wings of Love	Imperials	Pop	Up	8
Your Love Stays With Me	**Gary Chapman**	**Piano ballad**	Slow	10
_____	_____	_____	_____	_____
_____	_____	_____	_____	_____
_____	_____	_____	_____	_____
_____	_____	_____	_____	_____
_____	_____	_____	_____	_____

Movie Clips

Title: _____

Topic: _____

Description: _____

Start Time: _____

Start Cue: _____

End Time: _____

End Cue: _____

Comments: _____

_____

Title: _____

Topic: _____

Description: _____

Start Time: _____

Start Cue: _____

End Time: _____

End Cue: _____

Comments: _____

_____

Programming Tip

Celebrate!
When God does something powerful in a service,
take time to celebrate it with your team and to
affirm those whom he used.

God as Creator/Creation

Might also include: *God's Majesty*

Message Titles

- ❏ The Case for Creation
- ❏ *Faith Has Its Reasons:* Reasons for Believing in God
- ❏ *Yeah God:* For Being Expressive

_____
_____
_____
_____
_____

Dramas

Title	Tone	Characters	Topics
Is "Nothing" Sacred?	Humorous	3 males, and at least 4 others in group	Evolution vs. Creation; Modern science
The Nature of Life	Mixed	2 males, 2 females	Wonder of Creation; Family

Songs

Title	Artist	Style	Tempo	Seeker-Sensitivity Rating
Lord of All	First Call	Ballad—trio	Slow	6
Mighty Lord	Kathy Troccoli	Funky pop	Up	8
_____	_____	_____	_____	_____
_____	_____	_____	_____	_____
_____	_____	_____	_____	_____
_____	_____	_____	_____	_____

 Movie Clips

Title: _____

Topic: _____

Description: _____

Start Time: _____

Start Cue: _____

End Time: _____

End Cue: _____

Comments: _____

_____

Programming Tip

Bring something to the table

Spend time alone thinking creatively about the service before you get together as a team. The more thought each person has put into the topic in advance, the better equipped you will be as a team for brainstorming.

God as Father

Message Titles

- ❏ Father Knows Best
- ❏ *Our 3-D God:* God as Father

_____

_____

_____

_____

_____

_____

Dramas

Title	Tone	Characters	Topics
Definitely Safe	Serious— heartwarming	2 males, 1 female	Father's Day; Prodigal son; Unconditional love
The Intruder	Serious	1 male, 1 female	Self-image; Destructive parenting; God's love in spite of failure

Songs

Title	Artist	Style	Tempo	Seeker-Sensitivity Rating
A Place to Call Home	*Willow Creek Music*	*Gospel ballad*	*Slow, in 3*	*10*
He Won't Let Me Down	Debbie McClendon	R & B/pop	Up	9
In My Father's Hands	Susan Ashton	Folk/pop	Mid	9
_____	_____	_____	_____	_____
_____	_____	_____	_____	_____
_____	_____	_____	_____	_____
_____	_____	_____	_____	_____

Movie Clips

Title: _____

Topic: _____

Description: _____

Start Time: _____

Start Cue: _____

End Time: _____

End Cue: _____

Comments: _____

_____

Programming Tip

Excellence

"Because of our mediocrity, we Christians all too often provide the excuse the world is looking for to ignore the truth of Christianity"—Franky Schaeffer.

When we serve God, he deserves our best, our "unblemished lamb" (Malachi 1). Excellence is not the same as perfectionism; it is doing the best we can with what we have.

God's Character, General

Refers to God's attributes—understanding who God is, to the extent that we can. Attributes that are similar in nature have been combined, so the individual categories are rather broad.

 Message Titles

- ❐ **Illustrating the Identity of God:** Our Loving God • Our Forgiving God • Our Attentive God • Our Providing God • Our Gracious God • Our Giving God • Our Just God
- ❐ **Seven Wonders of the Spiritual World:** God Loves Me • God Can Be Trusted • God Forgives My Failures • God Transforms Me • God Guides Me • God Uses Me • God Satisfies Me
- ❐ **God Has Feelings, Too:** What Delights God • What Frustrates God • What Makes God Jealous
- ❐ **Surprised By God:** A Surprising God • Surprised by God's Love • Surprised by God's Truth • Surprised by God's Holiness • Surprised by God's Power • Surprised by God's Satisfaction
- ❐ **Three Things God Loves (That Most People Think He Doesn't):** Leisure • Laughter • Love Making
- ❐ **Our 3-D God:** God as Father • God as Forgiver • God as Friend
- ❐ **Yeah God:** For Being Relational • For Being Expressive • For Being Wise • For Being Joyful • For Being an Equal Opportunity Employer • For Being Patient • For Being a Refuge • For Being Righteous • For Being Gracious • For Being Committed to Me • For Being Generous • For Being a Guide • For Being Powerful • For Being a Servant

_____

_____

_____

 Dramas

Title	Tone	Characters	Topics
I Don't Want to Fight You Anymore	Serious	1 female	Relationship with God; Giving up control; Our value to God
Just in Case	Humorous	1 male, 1 female	Trusting God; God's faithfulness
Will the Real God Please Stand Up?	Humorous	3 males, 1 female	Second Commandment; What is God like?
_____	_____	_____	_____
_____	_____	_____	_____

Songs

Title	Artist	Style	Tempo	Seeker-Sensitivity Rating
Almighty God	**Jim Murray**	**Traditional ballad**	Slow	7
Awesome God	Rich Mullins	Pop anthem	Mid/up	1
God Is Great	**Babbie Mason**	**R & B/pop**	Up	5
His Eyes	**Steven Curtis Chapman**	**Acoustic guitar ballad**	**Mid/slow**	9
If I Could Look Through Your Eyes	*Willow Creek Music*	*Piano ballad*	*Slow*	10
I'm Amazed	*Willow Creek Music*	*Ballad*	*Slow*	7
Lion and the Lamb	Maranatha! Singers	Ballad—trio	Slow	4
Lord of All	**First Call**	**Ballad—trio**	**Slow**	6
Love That Will Not Let Me Go	**Steve Camp**	**Ballad**	**Slow**	10
Mighty Lord	**Kathy Troccoli**	**Funky pop**	**Up**	8
More Than Words	Steven Curtis Chapman	Acoustic guitar ballad	Mid/slow	4
My Redeemer Is Faithful and True	**Steven Curtis Chapman**	**Ballad**	**Slow**	9
Never Be Another	Paul Smith	Power ballad	Slow	8
_____	_____	_____	_____	_____
_____	_____	_____	_____	_____
_____	_____	_____	_____	_____
_____	_____	_____	_____	_____

Movie Clips

Title: _____

Topic: _____

Description: _____

Start Time: _____

Start Cue: _____

End Time: _____

End Cue: _____

Comments: _____

_____

God's Faithfulness

Might also include: *God's Trustworthiness*

Message Titles

- ☐ *Seven Wonders of the Spiritual World:* God Can Be Trusted
- ☐ *Yeah God:* For Being Committed to Me

_____

_____

_____

_____

_____

Package Suggestion

Drama:
In . . . We Trust

Song:
Love That Will Not Let Me Go

Dramas

Title	Tone	Characters	Topics
In . . . We Trust	Serious, not heavy	1 male	Trust; Difficulty trusting God
Just in Case	Humorous	1 male, 1 female	Trusting God; God's faithfulness
Seeing Is Believing	Humorous	1 male, 1 female, 1 narrator	A Savior you can trust; Easy faith

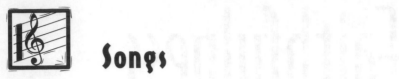

Songs

Title	Artist	Style	Tempo	Seeker-Sensitivity Rating
A Beautiful Place	Wayne Watson	MOR ballad	Mid/slow	9
Build My World Around You	Sandi Patty	Pop	Up	9
Do I Trust You	Twila Paris	MOR	Mid	5
Every Step I Take	Bob Carlisle	Bluesy pop	Mid	9
Facts Are Facts	Steven Curtis Chapman	Rock/pop	Up	4
Foundations	Geoff Moore & the Distance	Folk/pop ballad	Slow/mid	8
From Here on Out	*Willow Creek Music*	*MOR pop*	*Mid*	*8*
From This Moment On	Newsong	Ballad	Slow	8
The Future	First Call	Pop vocal group	Up	8
He'll Find a Way	Billy and Sarah Gaines	MOR ballad—duet	Slow/mid	8
Here in My Heart	Susan Ashton	Folk rock	Up	8
He's All You Need	Steve Camp	Ballad	Slow	8
He's Been Faithful	Brooklyn Tabernacle Choir	Ballad with choir	Sow	6
He Won't Let Me Down	Debbie McClendon	R & B/pop	Up	9
He Won't Let You Go	The Kry	Piano ballad	Slow	10
His Eyes	Steven Curtis Chapman	Acoustic guitar ballad	Mid/slow	9
His Love Is Strong	Clay Crosse	Pop	Up	10
His Strength Is Perfect	Steven Curtis Chapman	Ballad	Slow	9
I Go to the Rock	Dottie Rambo	Swing/big band	Mid	7
I Need to Stop	*Willow Creek Music*	*Pop*	*Up*	*3*
I'll Find You There	The Kry	Folk rock ballad	Slow	9
I'm Amazed	*Willow Creek Music*	*Ballad*	*Slow*	*7*
I'm Depending on You	Harv & Edythe	MOR	Mid	7
In My Father's Hands	Susan Ashton	Folk/pop	Mid	9
Jesus Will Still Be There	Point of Grace	Ballad	Slow	9
Lord of All	First Call	Ballad—trio	Slow	6
Love Is Always There	Carolyn Arends	Folk/pop	Up	9
The Love of God	Phillip Bailey	Ballad	Slow	8
The Love of God	Willow Creek Music	Acapella vocal group	Slow	6
Love That Will Not Let Me Go	Steve Camp	Ballad	Slow	10
My Life Is in Your Hands	Kathy Troccoli	Ballad	Slow	9
My Redeemer Is Faithful and True	Steven Curtis Chapman	Ballad	Slow	9
Rock Steady	Wayne Watson	Pop/rock	Up	7
Solid as the Rock	Michael English	Pop	Up	8

Title	Artist	Style	Tempo	Seeker-Sensivity Rating
Still Listening	Steven Curtis Chapman	Acoustic ballad	Slow/mid	7
Strength in You	*Willow Creek Music*	*MOR pop*	*Slow/mid*	*10*
Take My Hand	The Kry	Acoustic ballad	Mid/slow	9
Thankful	*Willow Creek Music*	*Pop*	*Up*	*7*
There Is a Love	Michael English	Pop	Up	9
When You Are a Soldier	Steven Curtis Chapman	Keyboard ballad	Slow/mid	4
You're the One He Loves	Truth	Pop	Up	10
Your Love Stays With Me	Gary Chapman	Piano ballad	Slow	10
Your Steadfast Love	Alleluia Music	MOR	Mid/slow	3
___	___	___	___	___
___	___	___	___	___
___	___	___	___	___
___	___	___	___	___

 # Movie Clips

Title:	Indiana Jones and the Last Crusade
Topic:	Faith; Trusting God when circumstances are confusing
Description:	Indiana Jones faces a seemingly uncrossable chasm, but takes a "leap of faith" as he steps onto an invisible bridge. Illustrates faith, believing what can't be seen.
Start Time:	1:46:50
Start Cue:	Indiana Jones walks through cave to the chasm
End Time:	1:48:45
End Cue:	Indy throws sand on bridge to mark it. Can be cut earlier
Comments:	_____
	_____

Title:	_____
Topic:	_____
Description:	_____
Start Time:	_____
Start Cue:	_____
End Time:	_____
End Cue:	_____
Comments:	_____

God's Forgiveness of Us

See also: **Grace, Salvation**

Message Titles

□ *Illustrating the Identity of God:* Our Forgiving God
□ *Our 3-D God:* God as Forgiver
□ *Seven Wonders of the Spiritual World:* God Forgives My Failures
□ *What Jesus Would Say to . . .* O. J. Simpson
□ *Yeah God:* For Being Gracious

Package Suggestion

Drama:
A Clean Slate

Song:
Face of Forgiveness

Dramas

Title	Tone	Characters	Topics
The Brow Beater	Mixed, mostly serious	1 male, 1 female	Self-esteem; Failures; Forgiveness
A Clean Slate	Serious	1 male, 2 or 3 males or females	Forgiveness; Redemption; Guilt
A Failure Tale	Mixed	5 males, 1 narrator	Failing; Obeying rules
Forgive Again?	Serious	1 male, 1 female	Forgiving others
Only Child	Serious	1 male, 2 females	Grace; Outrageous forgiveness; Doctrine of adoption
The Prisoner	Serious	3 males, 1 female	Easter; Freedom from sin; New Christian
"X" Marks the Spot	Serious; Mime	1 female, 1 male, and 3 either female or male	Sin; Redemption; Forgiveness; Guilt

Songs

Title	Artist	Style	Tempo	Seeker-Sensitivity Rating
Ball and Chain	**Susan Ashton**	**Folk/pop**	**Mid**	**9**
Cross Medley	*Willow Creek Music*	*Ballad medley— hymns*	*Slow*	*7*
Face of Forgiveness	*Willow Creek Music*	*Ballad*	*Slow*	*10*
Forgive Me	Tim Miner	Ballad	Slow	4
The Great Divide	Point of Grace	Power ballad	Slow	9
He Covers Me	Steve Camp	Power ballad	Slow/mid	4
He's All You Need	**Steve Camp**	**Ballad**	**Slow**	**8**
His Grace Is Greater	Larnelle Harris	Inspirational ballad	Slow	8
I Found Myself in You	**Clay Crosse**	**Gospel ballad**	**Mid/slow**	**10**
If I Could Look Through Your Eyes	*Willow Creek Music*	*Piano ballad*	*Slow*	*10*
I Stand, I Fall	*Willow Creek Music*	*Piano ballad*	*Slow*	*7*
I've Been Released	*Willow Creek Music*	*Pop/rock— Chicago sound*	*Up*	*9*
Just Come In	Margaret Becker	Pop ballad	Slow	5
Love That Will Not Let Me Go	**Steve Camp**	**Ballad**	**Slow**	**10**
Mercy for the Memories	**Geoff Moore & the Distance**	**Folk/pop ballad**	**Slow**	**9**
Never Be an Angel	Margaret Becker	Pop	Mid	4
The Prodigal (I'll Be Waiting)	Amy Grant	Ballad	Slow	7
Why Me	*Willow Creek Music*	*Ballad*	*Slow*	*9*
___	___	___	___	___
___	___	___	___	___
___	___	___	___	___
___	___	___	___	___

Movie Clips

Title: Hoosiers
Topic: Unconditional love; Forgiveness
Description: Dennis Hopper's character, a recovering alcoholic, is in the hospital drying out. His son visits him and tells him he loves him.

Start Time: 1:30:15
Start Cue: "No school this small . . ."
End Time: 1:32:30
End Cue: "Anyway, no school this small has ever been in the state championship!"
Comments: Needs some setup for those who haven't seen the movie

_____

Title: _____
Topic: _____
Description: _____
Start Time: _____
Start Cue: _____
End Time: _____
End Cue: _____
Comments: _____
_____
_____

Programming Tip

Choose quality over topicality
When programming a service, it is better to use an
element that doesn't perfectly fit the message but is a
proven "winner" than an element that is thematically
on target but is of questionable quality.

God's Goodness

Might also include: *God's Providence, God's Generosity*
See also: **Thanksgiving**

 ## Message Titles

☐ *Yeah God:* For Being Generous
☐ *Illustrating the Identity of God:* Our Giving God

_____
_____
_____
_____
_____
_____

 ## Dramas

Title	Tone	Characters	Topics
Conversations in a Field	Humorous	2 males, 2 females	Anxiety; Worry; God's providence
I Know What You Want	Serious	2 males, 2 females	God's love; Dysfunctional families

Songs

Title	Artist	Style	Tempo	Seeker-Sensitivity Rating
Facts Are Facts	Steven Curtis Chapman	Rock/pop	Up	4
God Is Great	**Babbie Mason**	**R & B/pop**	**Up**	**5**
He Won't Let Me Down	**Debbie McClendon**	**R & B/pop**	**Up**	**9**
I'm Amazed	*Willow Creek Music*	*Ballad*	*Slow*	*7*
Lord of All	**First Call**	**Ballad—trio**	**Slow**	**6**
My Redeemer Is Faithful and True	**Steven Curtis Chapman**	**Ballad**	**Slow**	**9**
My Turn Now	Steven Curtis Chapman	Country bop	Up	6
Never Be Another	Paul Smith	Power ballad	Slow	8
Thankful	*Willow Creek Music*	*Pop*	*Up*	*7*
Who Am I	Margaret Becker	Power ballad	Slow	7
Your Steadfast Love	Alleluia Music	MOR	Mid/slow	3
_____	_____	_____	____	____
_____	_____	_____	____	____
_____	_____	_____	____	____
_____	_____	_____	____	____

Movie Clips

Title: _____

Topic: _____

Description: _____

Start Time: _____

Start Cue: _____

End Time: _____

End Cue: _____

Comments: _____

_____

God's Holiness

Might also include: *God's Justice, God's Righteousness*
See also: **Praise and Worship**

 ## Message Titles

- ❏ *Yeah God:* For Being Righteous
- ❏ *Surprised by God:* Surprised by God's Holiness
- ❏ *Illustrating the Identity of God:* Our Just God

_____
_____
_____
_____
_____
_____

 ## Dramas

Title	Tone	Characters	Topics
Everything's Relative	Humorous	3 males, 1 female	God's holiness; Benefits of God's laws

Songs

Title	Artist	Style	Tempo	Seeker-Sensitivity Rating
The Beauty of Holiness	Steve Camp	Ballad	Slow	1
Lord of All	**First Call**	**Ballad—trio**	**Slow**	**6**
Stranger to Holiness	Steve Camp	Ballad	Slow/mid	2
_____	_____	_____	_____	_____
_____	_____	_____	_____	_____
_____	_____	_____	_____	_____
_____	_____	_____	_____	_____

Movie Clips

Title:	_____
Topic:	_____
Description:	_____
Start Time:	_____
Start Cue:	_____
End Time:	_____
End Cue:	_____
Comments:	_____

Programming Tip

Contextualize without compromise

When programming for seekers, the goal is to contextualize the message of the gospel without watering it down or distorting it. Seek creative and relevant ways to communicate the undiluted, challenging message of the gospel so that it can be understood by people outside of the Christian culture.

God's Love

Might also include: *Unconditional Love*

 ## Message Titles

- ☐ Coming Home (The Prodigal Son's Father)
- ☐ *Illustrating the Identity of God:* Our Loving God
- ☐ *Seven Wonders of the Spiritual World:* God Loves Me
- ☐ *Surprised by God:* Surprised by God's Love

_____

_____

_____

_____

 ## Dramas

Title	Tone	Characters	Topics
Another Day at the Bus Stop	Mixed	1 male, 1 female	Our relationship with God; Self-esteem
The Black Hole	Serious, but light	2 males, 1 female, 1 narrator	Filling the void; Contentment; God's love
I Know What You Want	Serious	2 males, 2 females	God's love; Dysfunctional families
The Intruder	Serious	1 male, 1 female	Self-image; Destructive parenting; God's love in spite of failure
Keeping Tabs	Humorous	1 male, 1 female	Gifts of grace; Undeserved love
The Lane of Life	Mixed; mime	5 either male or female, 1 offstage narrator	Salvation; Our value to God; Self-esteem
Measuring Up	Mixed; mime	2 males, 1 female, 1 other male or female	God's acceptance of us; Self-esteem
Only Child	Serious	1 male, 2 females	Grace; Outrageous forgiveness; Doctrine of adoption

Title	Tone	Characters	Topics
The Quagmire	Serious	1 male or female	Failure; Self-esteem; Being "stuck"; Trusting God
The Stickholders	Serious	3 males, 1 female, 1 narrator	Relationship with God; Freedom from rules
Take Heart	Mixed; mime	2 males, 2 females	God heals the brokenhearted; Disappointment
These Parts	Mixed	2 males, 1 female, 3 either male or female, 1 child, 1 narrator	The Resurrection; Our need for Christ; Easter
Tom, Dick, and Mary	Serious	3 males, 1 female, 1 narrator	Hearing God's voice; Crowding God out of your life
"X" Marks the Spot	Serious; mime	1 female, 1 male, and 3 either female or male	Sin; Redemption; Forgiveness; Guilt
___	___	___	___
___	___	___	___
___	___	___	___

 # Songs

Title	Artist	Style	Tempo	Seeker-Sensitivity Rating
Almighty God	**Jim Murray**	**Traditional ballad**	**Slow**	**7**
A Place to Call Home	*Willow Creek Music*	*Gospel ballad*	*Slow, in 3*	*10*
At Jesus' Feet	**Billy & Sarah Gaines**	**Ballad**	**Slow**	**6**
Bridge Between Two Hearts	**Bob Carlisle**	**Pop**	**Up**	**9**
Cross Medley	*Willow Creek Music*	*Ballad medley— hymns*	*Slow*	*7*
Face of Forgiveness	*Willow Creek Music*	*Ballad*	*Slow*	*10*
Faith, Hope and Love	**Point of Grace**	**Pop vocal group**	**Up**	**9**
Friend of a Wounded Heart	Wayne Watson	Power ballad	Slow	8
Gentle Hands	Truth	Traditional ballad	Slow	8
He Won't Let Me Down	**Debbie McClendon**	**R & B/pop**	**Up**	**9**
He Won't Let You Go	**The Kry**	**Piano ballad**	**Slow**	**10**
Here in My Heart	Susan Ashton	Folk rock	Up	8
He's All You Need	**Steve Camp**	**Ballad**	**Slow**	**8**
His Eyes	**Steven Curtis Chapman**	**Acoustic guitar ballad**	**Mid/slow**	**9**
His Grace Is Greater	Larnelle Harris	Inspirational ballad	Slow	8

Title	Artist	Style	Tempo	Seeker-Sensitivity Rating
His Love Is Strong	**Clay Crosse**	**Pop**	**Up**	**10**
I Don't Deserve Your Love	Trace Balin	Ballad	Slow	9
If I Could Look Through Your Eyes	*Willow Creek Music*	*Piano ballad*	*Slow*	*10*
I'll Find You There	The Kry	Folk rock ballad	Slow	9
I'm Amazed	*Willow Creek Music*	*Ballad*	*Slow*	*7*
In Heaven's Eyes	**Sandi Patti**	**Inspirational ballad**	**Slow**	**9**
Jesus Loves Me	**Whitney Houston**	**R & B/pop**	**Slow/mid**	**8**
Just Come In	Margaret Becker	Pop ballad	Slow	5
Let the Lord Love You	*Willow Creek Music*	*Acoustic guitar ballad*	*Slow*	*9*
Lion and the Lamb	Maranatha! Singers	Ballad—trio	Slow	4
Lord of All	**First Call**	**Ballad—trio**	**Slow**	**6**
Love Conquers All	**Pam Thum**	**Pop**	**Up**	**10**
Love Is Always There	Carolyn Arends	Folk/pop	Up	9
The Love of God	Phillip Bailey	Ballad	Slow	8
The Love of God	*Willow Creek Music*	*Acapella vocal group*	*Slow*	*6*
Love That Will Not Let Me Go	**Steve Camp**	**Ballad**	**Slow**	**10**
Mercy for the Memories	**Geoff Moore & the Distance**	**Folk pop ballad**	**Slow**	**9**
Miracle of Mercy	**Steven Curtis Chapman**	**Acoustic ballad**	**Slow**	**4**
Never Be Another	Paul Smith	Power ballad	Slow	8
No One Knows My Heart	**Susan Ashton**	**Folk/pop ballad**	**Slow/mid**	**9**
Original Love	Imperials	Pop	Up	9
Peace Be Still	**Al Denson**	**Ballad**	**Slow**	**10**
The Prodigal (I'll Be Waiting)	Amy Grant	Ballad	Slow	7
Safe	Steve Archer	Ballad—duet	Slow/mid	8
Thankful	Willow Creek Music	Pop	Up	7
There Is a Love	**Michael English**	**Pop**	**Up**	**9**
Treasure of You	Steven Curtis Chapman	Driving rock	Up	10
True Devotion	Margaret Becker	R & B/pop	Up	6
What I Wouldn't Give	*Willow Creek Music*	*Acoustic ballad*	*Slow*	*10*
When It Hurts the Most	Brent Lamb	Ballad	Slow	9
Who Am I	Margaret Becker	Power ballad	Slow	7
Why Me	*Willow Creek Music*	*Ballad*	*Slow*	*9*
Wings of Love	Imperials	Pop	Up	8
You're the One He Loves	**Truth**	**Pop**	**Up**	**10**
Your Love	Alleluia Music	MOR—duet	Mid	4
Your Love Stays With Me	**Gary Chapman**	**Piano ballad**	**Slow**	**10**
Your Steadfast Love	Alleluia Music	MOR	Mid/slow	3
_____	_____	_____	_____	_____
_____	_____	_____	_____	_____

Movie Clips

Title: Forrest Gump

Topic: Friendship; Laying your life down for a friend

Description: Forrest goes back into the jungle of Vietnam to find his fallen friend, Bubba, and runs him out of the battle zone.

Start Time: 0:53:30

Start Cue: "I gotta find Bubba!"

End Time: 0:55:00

End Cue: Forrest runs out of frame, with jungle exploding behind him. Can also end at "That's all I have to say about that"

Comments: _____

_____

Title: Forrest Gump

Topic: Love; Friendship

Description: Forrest, driving a shrimp boat, sees his friend Lt. Dan and jumps off the boat to greet him.

Start Time: 1:31:10

Start Cue: Shot of Forrest's hands steering the boat

End Time: 1:32:50

End Cue: "That's my boat." Can end earlier

Comments: _____

_____

Title: Hoosiers

Topic: Unconditional love; Forgiveness

Description: Dennis Hopper's character, a recovering alcoholic, is in the hospital drying out. His son visits him and tells him he loves him.

Start Time: 1:30:15

Start Cue: "No school this small . . ."

End Time: 1:32:30

End Cue: "Anyway, no school this small has ever been in the state championship!"

Comments: Needs some setup for those who haven't seen the movie

_____

Title: _____

Topic: _____

Description: _____

Start Time: _____

Start Cue: _____

End Time: _____

End Cue: _____

Comments: _____

_____

God's Majesty

Dramas

Title	Tone	Characters	Topics
The Nature of Life	Mixed	2 males, 2 females	Wonder of Creation; Family

Songs

Title	Artist	Style	Tempo	Seeker-Sensitivity Rating
Almighty	Wayne Watson	Praise & worship/pop	Up	2
Awesome God	Rich Mullins	Pop anthem	Mid/up	1
Lord of All	First Call	Ballad—trio	Slow	6
Mighty Lord	Kathy Troccoli	Funky pop	Up	8
We've Got a Reason to Celebrate	Billy and Sarah Gaines	R & B pop	Up	3

Movie Clips

Title: _____

Topic: _____

Description: _____

Start Time: _____

Start Cue: _____

End Time: _____

End Cue: _____

Comments: _____

_____

Programming Tip

Evaluate

If possible, videotape the services and evaluate them with the creative team. Be truthful but appropriately sensitive in your critique. If handled with a gracious spirit, honest evaluations can significantly raise the quality of your programs. Ask questions such as these: Did we accomplish our purpose for the service? Did it flow well thematically? How effectively did the actors and vocalists communicate? Were there any technical problems? What worked particularly well? What could we have done better? Was there a powerful "moment"?

God's Mercy

Might also include: *God's Patience*

 Message Titles

☐ *Yeah God:* For Being Patient

_____

_____

_____

_____

_____

_____

 Dramas

Title	Tone	Characters	Topics
Another Day at the Bus Stop	Mixed	1 male, 1 female	Our relationship with God; Self-esteem
Measuring Up	Mixed; mime	2 males, 1 female, 1 other male or female	God's acceptance of us; Self-esteem
Take Heart	Mixed; mime	2 males, 2 females	God heals the brokenhearted; Disappointment
"X" Marks the Spot	Serious; mime	1 female, 1 male, and 3 either female or male	Sin; Redemption; Forgiveness; Guilt
_____	_____	_____	_____
_____	_____	_____	_____
_____	_____	_____	_____
_____	_____	_____	_____

Songs

Title	Artist	Style	Tempo	Seeker-Sensitivity Rating
At Jesus' Feet	Billy & Sarah Gaines	Ballad	Slow	6
Build My World Around You	Sandi Patty	Pop	Up	9
I Don't Deserve Your Love	Trace Balin	Ballad	Slow	9
In Heaven's Eyes	Sandi Patti	Inspirational ballad	Slow	9
Let the Lord Love You	*Willow Creek Music*	*Acoustic guitar ballad*	*Slow*	9
Lord of All	First Call	Ballad—trio	Slow	6
Love Is Always There	Carolyn Arends	Folk/pop	Up	9
Mercy for the Memories	Geoff Moore & the Distance	Folk/pop ballad	Slow	9
Miracle of Mercy	Steven Curtis Chapman	Acoustic ballad	Slow	4
My Redeemer Is Faithful and True	Steven Curtis Chapman	Ballad	Slow	9
Remember Your Chains	Steven Curtis Chapman	Acoustic MOR	Mid	2
Who Am I	Margaret Becker	Power ballad	Slow	7
Why Me	*Willow Creek Music*	*Ballad*	*Slow*	9
_____	_____	_____	_____	_____
_____	_____	_____	_____	_____
_____	_____	_____	_____	_____
_____	_____	_____	_____	_____
_____	_____	_____	_____	_____

Movie Clips

Title: _____

Topic: _____

Description: _____

Start Time: _____

Start Cue: _____

End Time: _____

End Cue: _____

Comments: _____

_____

God's Power

Might also include: *God's Strength*

Message Titles

- ❏ Connect With the Source of Strength
- ❏ *God's Outrageous Claims:* Unlocking Our Power
- ❏ *Surprised by God:* Surprised by God's Power

_____

_____

_____

_____

Dramas

Title	Tone	Characters	Topics
The Quagmire	Serious	1 male or female	Failure; Self-esteem; Being "stuck"; Trusting God
The Safe	Mixed	1 male, 1 female, 3 either male or female	Inner strength; Needing God's strength
These Parts	Mixed	2 males, 1 female, 3 either male or female, 1 child, 1 narrator	The Resurrection; Our need for Christ; Easter

Songs

Title	Artist	Style	Tempo	Seeker-Sensitivity Rating
Almighty	Wayne Watson	Praise & worship/pop	Up	2
Awesome God	Rich Mullins	Pop anthem	Mid/up	1
Every Step I Take	**Bob Carlisle**	**Bluesy pop**	**Mid**	**9**
God Is Great	**Babbie Mason**	**R & B/pop**	**Up**	**5**
God Is in Control	**Twila Paris**	**Pop/rock**	**Up**	**1**
His Love Is Strong	**Clay Crosse**	**Pop**	**Up**	**10**
His Strength Is Perfect	**Steven Curtis Chapman**	**Ballad**	**Slow**	**9**
I Go to the Rock	**Dottie Rambo**	**Swing/big band**	**Mid**	**7**
Lion and the Lamb	Maranatha! Singers	Ballad—trio	Slow	4
Lord of All	**First Call**	**Ballad—trio**	**Slow**	**6**
Mighty Lord	**Kathy Troccoli**	**Funky pop**	**Up**	**8**
Power of God	Imperials	Pop/rock	Up	5
Rock of Ages	James Ward	Ballad	Slow	1
Strength in You	*Willow Creek Music*	*MOR pop*	*Slow/mid*	*10*
Take My Hand	**The Kry**	**Acoustic ballad**	**Mid/slow**	**9**
We Are an Army	Trace Balin	Power ballad	Slow/mid	1
When You Are a Soldier	**Steven Curtis Chapman**	**Keyboard ballad**	**Slow/mid**	**4**
_____	_____	_____	_____	_____
_____	_____	_____	_____	_____
_____	_____	_____	_____	_____
_____	_____	_____	_____	_____

Movie Clips

Title: _____

Topic: _____

Description: _____

Start Time: _____

Start Cue: _____

End Time: _____

End Cue: _____

Comments: _____

_____

God's Presence

Message Titles

☐ **Discovering the Presence of God:** Discovering the Presence of God • Practicing the Presence of God • The Power of the Presence of God

_____
_____
_____
_____
_____
_____

Dramas

Title	Tone	Characters	Topics
Chameleon	Mixed	3 males	Controlling our emotions; God's presence in our lives
Go Away God	Humorous	2 males, 1 female	Conscience; Guilt; Hearing God's voice

Songs

Title	Artist	Style	Tempo	Seeker-Sensitivity Rating
His Eyes	**Steven Curtis Chapman**	**Acoustic guitar ballad**	**Mid/slow**	**9**
In His Presence	Sandi Patti	Traditional ballad	Slow	6
Lord of All	**First Call**	**Ballad—trio**	**Slow**	**6**
When It Hurts the Most	Brent Lamb	Ballad	Slow	9
Your Love Stays With Me	**Gary Chapman**	**Piano ballad**	**Slow**	**10**
_____	_____	_____	_____	_____
_____	_____	_____	_____	_____
_____	_____	_____	_____	_____
_____	_____	_____	_____	_____
_____	_____	_____	_____	_____

Movie Clips

Title: _____

Topic: _____

Description: _____

Start Time: _____

Start Cue: _____

End Time: _____

End Cue: _____

Comments: _____

_____

God's Tenderness

Might also include: *God's Gentleness*

Message Titles

☐ *Yeah God:* For Being Expressive

_____

_____

_____

_____

_____

Dramas

Title	Tone	Characters	Topics
Another Day at the Bus Stop	Mixed	1 male, 1 female	Our relationship with God; Self-esteem
The Stickholders	Serious	3 males, 1 female, 1 narrator	Relationship with God; Freedom from rules
Take Heart	Mixed; mime	2 males, 2 females	God heals the brokenhearted; Disappointment

Songs

Title	Artist	Style	Tempo	Seeker-Sensitivity Rating
A Place to Call Home	*Willow Creek Music*	*Gospel ballad*	*Slow, in 3*	*10*
At Jesus' Feet	**Billy & Sarah Gaines**	**Ballad**	**Slow**	**6**
Gentle Hands	Truth	Traditional ballad	Slow	8
He Won't Let You Go	**The Kry**	**Piano ballad**	**Slow**	**10**
His Eyes	**Steven Curtis Chapman**	**Acoustic guitar ballad**	**Mid/slow**	**9**
If I Could Look Through Your Eyes	*Willow Creek Music*	*Piano ballad*	*Slow*	*10*
In Heaven's Eyes	**Sandi Patti**	**Inspirational ballad**	**Slow**	**9**
Jesus Loves Me	**Whitney Houston**	**R & B/pop**	**Slow/mid**	**8**
Jesus Will Still Be There	**Point of Grace**	**Ballad**	**Slow**	**9**
Let the Lord Love You	*Willow Creek Music*	*Acoustic guitar ballad*	*Slow*	*9*
Lion and the Lamb	Maranatha! Singers	Ballad—trio	Slow	4
The Love of God	Phillip Bailey	Ballad	Slow	8
The Love of God	*Willow Creek Music*	*Acapella vocal group*	*Slow*	*6*
Never Be Another	Paul Smith	Power ballad	Slow	8
No One Knows My Heart	**Susan Ashton**	**Folk/pop ballad**	**Slow/mid**	**9**
Peace Be Still	**Al Denson**	**Ballad**	**Slow**	**10**
Treasure of You	Steven Curtis Chapman	Driving rock	Up	10
When It Hurts the Most	Brent Lamb	Ballad	Slow	9
_____	_____	_____	_____	_____
_____	_____	_____	_____	_____
_____	_____	_____	_____	_____

 # Movie Clips

Title: _____

Topic: _____

Description: _____

Start Time: _____

Start Cue: _____

End Time: _____

End Cue: _____

Comments: _____

_____

God's Wisdom

Might also include: *God's Guidance*
See also: **Decision Making**

 Message Titles

- ❐ God's Wisdom Works
- ❐ *The Art of Decision Making:* How to Acquire Wisdom
- ❐ *The Art of Decision Making:* Father Knows Best
- ❐ *Seven Wonders of the Spiritual World:* God Guides Me
- ❐ *Yeah God:* For Being a Guide
- ❐ *Yeah God:* For Being Wise

_____
_____
_____
_____
_____

 Dramas

Title	Tone	Characters	Topics
Permanent Solution	Humorous	4 females	Decision making; Who to listen to?
A Second Chance	Serious	3 males, 1 female	Decision making; Father/son relationships

Songs

Title	Artist	Style	Tempo	Seeker-Sensitivity Rating
A Beautiful Place	**Wayne Watson**	**MOR ballad**	**Mid/slow**	**9**
Every Step I Take	**Bob Carlisle**	**Bluesy pop**	**Mid**	**9**
Higher Ways	Steven Curtis Chapman	Acoustic guitar ballad	Slow/mid	6
In My Father's Hands	**Susan Ashton**	**Folk/pop**	**Mid**	**9**
Lord of All	**First Call**	**Ballad—trio**	**Slow**	**6**
My Life Is in Your Hands	**Kathy Troccoli**	**Ballad**	**Slow**	**9**
Thy Word	Amy Grant	Ballad	Slow	4
Walk in the Dark	Wayne Watson	Pop	Up	2
Who to Listen To	Amy Grant	Pop	Mid	8
____	____	____	____	____
____	____	____	____	____
____	____	____	____	____
____	____	____	____	____
____	____	____	____	____

Movie Clips

Title: _____

Topic: _____

Description: _____

Start Time: _____

Start Cue: _____

End Time: _____

End Cue: _____

Comments: _____

_____

Jesus

See also: **Christmas, Easter, Salvation**

 ## Message Titles

- ❏ The Relevance of Jesus Christ
- ❏ Sinner • Jesus Talks to the Father
- ❏ *Our 3-D God:* God as Friend
- ❏ *Surprised by God:* A Surprising God
- ❏ *What Jesus Would Say to . . .* (various people)
- ❏ *Yeah God:* For Being a Servant
- ❏ **Private Conversations:** Jesus Talks to a Religious Person

_____

_____

_____

_____

 ## Dramas

Title	Tone	Characters	Topics
Another Day at the Bus Stop	Mixed	1 male, 1 female	Our relationship with God; Self-esteem
Lonely at the Top	Serious	1 male	The perils of power, authority; Easter
These Parts	Mixed	2 males, 1 female, 3 either male or female, 1 child, 1 narrator	The Resurrection; Our need for Christ; Easter
"X" Marks the Spot	Serious; mime	1 female, 1 male, and 3 either female or male	Sin; Redemption; Forgiveness; Guilt
_____	_____	_____	_____
_____	_____	_____	_____
_____	_____	_____	_____
_____	_____	_____	_____

Songs

Title	Artist	Style	Tempo	Seeker-Sensitivity Rating
Cross Medley	*Willow Creek Music*	*Ballad medley— hymns*	*Slow*	*7*
He Won't Let Me Down	**Debbie McClendon**	**R & B/pop**	**Up**	**9**
His Eyes	**Steven Curtis Chapman**	**Acoustic guitar ballad**	**Mid/slow**	**9**
If That's What It Takes	*Willow Creek Music*	*Pop/MOR*	*Mid/slow*	*5*
Jesus Loves Me	**Whitney Houston**	**R & B/pop**	**Slow/mid**	**8**
Lion and the Lamb	Maranatha! Singers	Ballad—trio	Slow	4
One of Us	Geoff Moore & the Distance	Ballad	Slow	8
Say the Name	Margaret Becker	Ballad	Slow/mid	4
Where Would I Be Now	*Willow Creek Music*	*Ballad— Broadway feel*	*Slow*	*6*
Why Me	*Willow Creek Music*	*Ballad*	*Slow*	*9*

Movie Clips

Title: _____

Topic: _____

Description: _____

Start Time: _____

Start Cue: _____

End Time: _____

End Cue: _____

Comments: _____

LIFE ISSUES

Death

Can refer to the issue of our own death or the death of people close to us
See also: **Grief**

Message Titles

- ❐ A Better Kind of Grieving
- ❐ The Fear of Death ("What's going to happen to you the first 15 minutes after you die?")
- ❐ **Living With Dying:** Facing Death • Grief • Grieving Process • Heaven and Hell: How to Be Saved • View for True Believers

_____
_____
_____
_____

Dramas

Title	Tone	Characters	Topics
In the Dark	Serious	1 male, 1 female	Death of a child; Grief
Mr. Peepers Goes to Sleep	Mixed	1 male, 2 females, 1 child	Death; Facing the truth
The Old Man and the Laundromat	Mixed, mostly serious	1 male, 1 female, 1 child	Grieving; Dealing with death of a loved one; Letting go
Parlor Talk	Mixed	3 males, 2 females	Making a difference with your life; Death; Workaholism
What Now?	Serious	2 males, 4 females	Coping with a crisis; Dealing with death

Songs

Title	Artist	Style	Tempo	Seeker-Sensitivity Rating
Healing River	*Willow Creek Music*	*Ballad*	*Slow/mid*	9
He Won't Let You Go	**The Kry**	**Piano ballad**	**Slow**	**10**
Home Free	Wayne Watson	Ballad	Slow/mid	6
If I Had Only Known	**Reba McEntire**	**Ballad**	**Slow**	**10**
If You Could See Me Now	Truth	Ballad	Slow	5
Only Here for a Little While	**Billy Dean**	**Country**	**Mid/up**	**10**
Treasure	**Gary Chapman**	**Acoustic ballad**	**Slow**	**9**
___	___	___	___	___
___	___	___	___	___
___	___	___	___	___
___	___	___	___	___

Movie Clips

Title: 8 Seconds
Topic: Regret; Communicating love
Description: A father, whose son has recently died, breaks down in remorse over not telling his son that he loved him.
Start Time: 1:27:10
Start Cue: Pallbearers carry casket out of church
End Time: 1:28:33
End Cue: "I loved him"
Comments: _____
_____

Title: Shadowlands
Topic: Grief; Death; Need for a mother
Description: C. S. Lewis tells Joy Gresham about when his mother died.
Start Time: 0:28:15
Start Cue: "I have been really hurt, you know"
End Time: 0:29:25
End Cue: "Yes, I'd like that"
Comments: _____
_____

Title: Shadowlands

Topic: Death; Sharing the dying process

Description: Jack and Joy talk about her imminent death. She makes a couple of profound statements about sharing the dying process.

Start Time: 1:45:30

Start Cue: "I don't want to be somewhere else anymore"

End Time: 1:47:55

End Cue: Jack and Joy kiss

Comments: _____

_____

Title: Shadowlands

Topic: Grief

Description: C. S. Lewis talks to his stepson Douglass about his mother dying. Very moving.

Start Time: 2:00:55

Start Cue: Jack walks up behind Douglass and says "hi"

End Time: 2:04:00

End Cue: Shot, from behind them, of Jack and Douglass embracing

Comments: _____

_____

Title: _____

Topic: _____

Description: _____

Start Time: _____

Start Cue: _____

End Time: _____

End Cue: _____

Comments: _____

_____

Programming Tip

Song selection: You get only one shot
The congregation will usually hear a particular song only once in the service, so choose songs that will be clear and compelling the first time they are heard. Many songs require repeated listening to be fully understood.

Decision Making

See also: **God's Wisdom**

 ## Message Titles

- ❐ **The Art of Decision Making:** Decisions, Decisions, Decisions • How to Acquire Wisdom • Father Knows Best
- ❐ **Negotiating the Maze of Life:** Thinkers, Feelers and Procrastinators • God's Role in Decision Making • Developing a Personal Board of Directors

_____

_____

_____

 ## Dramas

Title	Tone	Characters	Topics
The Crowd, The Conscience, and Curt	Serious	2 males, 4 males or females	Broad vs. narrow way; Conscience; Peer pressure
The Eggshell Family	Humorous	2 males, 1 female, 1 male or female	Decision making
The Eggshells Break Out	Humorous	3 males, 1 female	Risk taking; Facing challenges
The Game of Life	Humorous	1 male, 1 female, 1 narrator	Decision making; Search for meaning
Oh, What a Feeling!	Humorous	2 males, 1 female	Decision making; Self-control; Money management
Permanent Solution	Humorous	4 females	Decision making; Who to listen to?
A Second Chance	Serious	3 males, 1 female	Decision making; Father/son relationships
The Speculators	Humorous	2 males, 1 female	Risk taking; Missed opportunities

_____	_____	_____	_____
_____	_____	_____	_____

Songs

Title	Artist	Style	Tempo	Seeker-Sensitivity Rating
Seize the Day	Carolyn Arends	Folk pop, in 3	Mid	8
Who Makes the Rules	**Steven Curtis Chapman**	**Pop/folk rock**	**Up**	**7**
Who to Listen To	Amy Grant	Pop	Mid	8
_____	_____	_____	_____	_____
_____	_____	_____	_____	_____
_____	_____	_____	_____	_____
_____	_____	_____	_____	_____

Movie Clips

Title: Indiana Jones and the Last Crusade

Topic: Decision making

Description: Walter Donovan, an evil antiquities collector, has to choose the true holy grail from a roomful of false grails. Because he doesn't know the humble character of Christ, he chooses "poorly."

Start Time: 1:50:35

Start Cue: Elsa and Donovan enter the "grail room"

End Time: 1:53:55

End Cue: "You have chosen wisely"; could also end at "He chose poorly"

Comments: Very gruesome scene when Donovan chooses wrong. Has been shown on network TV, but might scare kids and may be judged inappropriate by some churches

Title: _____

Topic: _____

Description: _____

Start Time: _____

Start Cue: _____

End Time: _____

End Cue: _____

Comments: _____

_____

Emotional Issues
~ Anger ~

See also: **Anger Toward God, Bondage to the Past, Relational Conflict**

 ## Message Titles

☐ **The Age of Rage:** The Roots of Rage • Expressing Anger Appropriately • Responding to the Anger of Others

_____

_____

_____

_____

 ## Dramas

Title	Tone	Characters	Topics
The Angry Woman	Serious	2 males, 3 females, 1 narrator	The roots of anger
Because I Love You	Serious	1 male, 1 female	Adultery; The consequences of sin
Chameleon	Mixed	3 males	Controlling our emotions; God's presence in our lives
Great Expectations	Mixed—ends very serious	1 male, 2 females	Unanswered prayer
A Problem of Perspective	Humorous	1 male, 1 female, 1 either male or female	Marriage; Marital conflict
Remembrances	Serious	1 male, 1 female	Parent/child relationships; Forgiveness

Title	Tone	Characters	Topics
Richard: 1992	Serious	2 males, 1 female	Anger; Rebellion; Decay of the family
Straight-Jacketed	Serious	1 male	Bondage to past and to sin; Anger toward God
Tired of Trying	Serious	1 male, 2 females	Dealing with the anger of others; Confronting injustice
Watching From the Window	Serious	1 female, 1 child	Stress of life; Challenge of motherhood; Draining relationships
_____	_____	_____	_____
_____	_____	_____	_____
_____	_____	_____	_____
_____	_____	_____	_____

 # Songs

No songs were found specifically about anger. Take a look at Relational Conflict *and* Anger Toward God

Title	Artist	Style	Tempo	Seeker-Sensitivity Rating
_____	_____	_____	_____	_____
_____	_____	_____	_____	_____
_____	_____	_____	_____	_____
_____	_____	_____	_____	_____
_____	_____	_____	_____	_____

 # Movie Clips

Title: City Slickers
Topic: Dysfunctional families; Friendship
Description: Three friends share the best and worst days of their lives.
Start Time: 1:12:45
Start Cue: "All right, I got one"
End Time: 1:14:50
End Cue: "Same day"
Comments: Could start earlier, but Billy Crystal swears briefly during his worst-day description

Title: Forrest Gump
Topic: Child abuse; Bondage to the past
Description: Jenny and Forrest walk by the house where Jenny was abused as a child. She throws rocks at it.
Start Time: 1:45:30
Start Cue: After "Jenny, most of the times, was real quiet"
End Time: 1:46:50
End Cue: "Sometimes there just aren't enough rocks"
Comments: _____
_____

Title: _____
Topic: _____
Description: _____
Start Time: _____
Start Cue: _____
End Time: _____
End Cue: _____
Comments: _____
_____

~ Bondage to the Past ~

Refers to how events in our past still affect us and often keep us from becoming whole
See also: **Healing, Regret**

 Message Titles

- ❏ From Stuck to Starting Over
- ❏ Life Without Regret
- ❏ Resolving Regrets
- ❏ Hostility in the Home
- ❏ Why Did This Happen to Me?
- ❏ *The Age of Rage:* The Roots of Rage
- ❏ *Measuring How Much You Matter to God:* What Scars Self-Esteem

_____
_____
_____
_____

Dramas

Title	Tone	Characters	Topics
All Gummed Up	Serious	1 male, 1 female, 1 offstage voice	Adultery; Dealing with past hurts; The pain of lies
Conversations	Serious	2 males, 1 female, 1 offstage female voice	Self-esteem; Self-criticism; Failure
Funny Girl	Mixed	1 male, 2 females (multiple roles for 1 man and 1 woman)	Self-esteem; Need for acceptance
Honestly Speaking	Mixed	3 males, 3 females	Positive self-talk; Self-esteem
I Don't Want to Fight You Anymore	Serious	1 female	Relationship with God; Giving up control; Our value to God
The Intruder	Serious	1 male, 1 female	Self-image; Destructive parenting; God's love in spite of failure
The Lane of Life	Serious; mime	5 males or females, 1 offstage narrator	Salvation; Our value to God; Self-esteem
The Quagmire	Serious	1 male or female	Failure; Self-esteem; Being "stuck"; Trusting God
Straight-Jacketed	Serious	1 male	Bondage to past and to sin; Anger toward God
_____	_____	_____	_____
_____	_____	_____	_____
_____	_____	_____	_____
_____	_____	_____	_____

 # Songs

Title	Artist	Style	Tempo	Seeker-Sensitivity Rating
Ask Me	Amy Grant	Pop	Mid	9
Ball and Chain	**Susan Ashton**	**Folk/pop**	**Mid**	**9**
Desperado	Eagles	Ballad	Slow	10
He's All You Need	**Steve Camp**	**Ballad**	**Slow**	**8**
I've Been Released	_Willow Creek Music_	_Pop/rock— Chicago sound_	_Up_	9

Title	Artist	Style	Tempo	Seeker-Sensitivity Rating
I Will Be Free	Cindy Morgan	Ballad	Slow	7
Just Come In	Margaret Becker	Pop ballad	Slow	5
Let the Lord Love You	*Willow Creek Music*	*Acoustic guitar ballad*	*Slow*	*9*
Mercy for the Memories	**Geoff Moore & the Distance**	**Folk/pop ballad**	**Slow**	**9**
Take My Hand	**The Kry**	**Acoustic ballad**	**Mid/slow**	**9**

Movie Clips

Title: Forrest Gump

Topic: Child abuse; Bondage to the past

Description: Jenny and Forrest walk by the house where Jenny was abused as a child. She throws rocks at it.

Start Time: 1:45:30

Start Cue: After "Jenny, most of the times, was real quiet"

End Time: 1:46:50

End Cue: "Sometimes there just aren't enough rocks"

Comments: _____

_____

Title: Parenthood

Topic:

Description: Funny, bittersweet scene where young Gil (Steve Martin plays the adult Gil) is taken to a baseball game by his father and then left with an usher. We find out it's actually a combination of memories from his strained childhood.

Start Time: 0:00:05

Start Cue: Start at fade-up. This is the opening scene

End Time: 0:02:28

End Cue: "Strong, happy, confident kids"

Comments: Profanity immediately follows cutoff point

_____

Title: Shadowlands

Topic: Grief; Death; Need for a mother

Description: C. S. Lewis tells Joy Gresham about when his mother died.

Start Time: 0:28:15

Start Cue: "I have been really hurt, you know"
End Time: 0:29:25
End Cue: "Yes, I'd like that"
Comments: _____
_____

Title: _____
Topic: _____
Description: _____
Start Time: _____
Start Cue: _____
End Time: _____
End Cue: _____
Comments: _____
_____

- Disappointment -

Message Titles

- ❏ Dealing With Disappointment
- ❏ **Disappointment With God:** What Causes Disappointment? • Where Is God When You Need Him? • When God Seems Silent

_____
_____
_____

Dramas

Title	Tone	Characters	Topics
Great Expectations	Serious	1 male, 2 females	Unanswered prayer
"It"	Humorous	2 males, 1 female	Becoming a Christian doesn't mean having no problems; Vulnerability of new believers

Title	Tone	Characters	Topics
The Surprise Party	Mixed	2 males, 1 female	Disappointments are a part of life
Take Heart	Mixed; mime	2 males, 2 females	God heals the brokenhearted; Disappointment

Songs

Title	Artist	Style	Tempo	Seeker-Sensitivity Rating
A Beautiful Place	**Wayne Watson**	**MOR ballad**	**Mid/slow**	**9**
A Place to Call Home	*Willow Creek Music*	*Gospel ballad*	*Slow, in 3*	*10*
Hard Times	Wayne Watson	Ballad	Slow	4
His Strength Is Perfect	**Steven Curtis Chapman**	**Ballad**	**Slow**	**9**
Jesus Will Still Be There	**Point of Grace**	**Ballad**	**Slow**	**9**
Peace Be Still	**Al Denson**	**Ballad**	**Slow**	**10**
There Is a Love	**Michael English**	**Pop**	**Up**	**9**

Movie Clips

Title: _____

Topic: _____

Description: _____

Start Time: _____

Start Cue: _____

End Time: _____

End Cue: _____

Comments: _____

~ Disillusionment ~

Might also include: *Apathy, Discouragement, Hopelessness*

 ## Message Titles

- ❏ From Stuck to Starting Over
- ❏ From Stuck to Making a Difference
- ❏ *Understanding the Times:* The '70s

_____
_____
_____
_____
_____
_____

 ## Dramas

Title	Tone	Characters	Topics
Grand Canyon	Serious	1 male, 1 female	Marital breakdown
Great Expectations	Mixed—ends very serious	1 male, 2 females	Unanswered prayer
The Quagmire	Serious	1 male or female	Failure; Self-esteem; Being "stuck"; Trusting God
The Quitter	Serious	2 males, 1 female	Quitting; Failure
Richard: 1974	Serious	5 males, 1 female	Disillusionment; Crumbling dreams
Richard: 1992	Serious	2 males, 1 female	Anger; Rebellion; Decay of the family

Songs

Title	Artist	Style	Tempo	Seeker-Sensitivity Rating
A Place Called Hope	Michael English	Pop gospel	Mid/up	8
A Place to Call Home	*Willow Creek Music*	*Gospel ballad*	*Slow, in 3*	*10*
Ball and Chain	Susan Ashton	Folk/pop	Mid	9
Desperado	Eagles	Ballad	Slow	10
Down on My Knees	Susan Ashton	Folk rock	Mid/up	6
Eleanor Rigby	**Beatles**	**Acoustic ballad**	**Slow/mid**	**10**
Heaven in the Real World	**Steven Curtis Chapman**	**Pop/rock**	**Up**	**7**
His Strength Is Perfect	**Steven Curtis Chapman**	**Ballad**	**Slow**	**9**
Jesus Will Still Be There	**Point of Grace**	**Ballad**	**Slow**	**9**
More to This Life	Steven Curtis Chapman	MOR Pop	Mid/up	9
Somebody Make Me Laugh	**Patti Austin**	**Ballad**	**Slow**	**10**
Treasure of You	Steven Curtis Chapman	Driving rock	Up	10
_____	_____	_____	_____	_____
_____	_____	_____	_____	_____
_____	_____	_____	_____	_____
_____	_____	_____	_____	_____

Movie Clips

Title: City Slickers
Topic: Disillusionment; Life fulfillment
Description: Billy Crystal speaks at his son's school. Disillusioned with life in general, he gives a very funny, very depressing discourse on the stages of life.
Start Time: 0:44:38
Start Cue: "As Danny said"
End Time: 0:45:30
End Cue: "Any questions"
Comments: _____

_____

Title: Forrest Gump
Topic: Despair; Disillusionment
Description: Forrest's friend Jenny, in a moment of despair, gets onto the ledge of a tall building, then decides not to jump, collapsing in tears.

Start Time: 1:29:35
Start Cue: Start after Jenny's boyfriend's hand disappears
End Time: 1:30:55
End Cue: Shot of full moon
Comments: _____
_____

Title: _____
Topic: _____
Description: _____
Start Time: _____
Start Cue: _____
End Time: _____
End Cue: _____
Comments: _____
_____

- Failure -

See also: **God's Forgiveness of Us**

 # Message Titles

- ❏ From Stuck to Starting Over
- ❏ From Stuck to Making a Difference
- ❏ Victim or Victor?
- ❏ When I'm Mad at Myself
- ❏ *Facing Up to Fear:* The Fear of Failure
- ❏ *The God of the Second Chance:* Getting a Second Chance
- ❏ *Learning Through Life's Crises:* Learning Through Failing
- ❏ *Seven Wonders of the Spiritual World:* God Forgives My Failures

_____
_____
_____
_____

 **Dramas**

Title	Tone	Characters	Topics
The Brow Beater	Mixed, mostly serious	1 male, 1 female	Self-esteem; Failures; Forgiveness
A Clean Slate	Serious	1 male, 2 or 3 males or females	Forgiveness; Redemption; Guilt
Conversations	Serious	2 males, 1 female, 1 offstage female voice	Self-esteem; Self-criticism; Failure
A Failure Tale	Mixed	5 males, 1 narrator	Failing; Obeying rules
Getting the Nod	Mixed	2 males, 1 either male or female	Honesty; Integrity; Business ethics; Handling failure
Honestly Speaking	Mixed	3 males, 3 females	Positive self-talk; Self-esteem
The Intruder	Serious	1 male, 1 female	Self-image; Destructive parenting; God's love in spite of failure
Measuring Up	Mixed; mime	2 males, 1 female, 1 other male or female	God's acceptance of us; Self-esteem
A Nice Guy	Serious	2 males	Regret; Admitting failures; Effects of sin; Confession
The Quagmire	Serious	1 male or female	Failure; Self-esteem; Being "stuck"; Trusting God
The Quitter	Serious	2 males, 1 female	Quitting; Failure
"X" Marks the Spot	Serious; mime	1 female, 1 male, and 3 either female or male	Sin; Redemption; Forgiveness; Guilt
_____	_____	_____	_____
_____	_____	_____	_____
_____	_____	_____	_____
_____	_____	_____	_____

Songs

Title	Artist	Style	Tempo	Seeker-Sensitivity Rating
A Beautiful Place	**Wayne Watson**	**MOR ballad**	**Mid/slow**	**9**
A Place to Call Home	*Willow Creek Music*	*Gospel ballad*	*Slow, in 3*	*10*
Bound to Come Some Trouble	**Rich Mullins**	**Ballad**	**Slow**	**10**
Face of Forgiveness	*Willow Creek Music*	*Ballad*	*Slow*	*10*
Forgive Me	Tim Miner	Ballad	Slow	4
Friend of a Wounded Heart	Wayne Watson	Power ballad	Slow	8
He Covers Me	Steve Camp	Power ballad	Slow/mid	4
He's All You Need	**Steve Camp**	**Ballad**	**Slow**	**8**
His Grace Is Greater	Larnelle Harris	Inspirational ballad	Slow	8
His Strength Is Perfect	**Steven Curtis Chapman**	**Ballad**	**Slow**	**9**
If I Could Look Through Your Eyes	*Willow Creek Music*	*Piano ballad*	*Slow*	*10*
I'm Amazed	*Willow Creek Music*	*Ballad*	*Slow*	*7*
In Heaven's Eyes	**Sandi Patti**	**Inspirational ballad**	**Slow**	**9**
I Stand, I Fall	*Willow Creek Music*	*Piano ballad*	*Slow*	*7*
Jesus Will Still Be There	**Point of Grace**	**Ballad**	**Slow**	**9**
Let the Lord Love You	*Willow Creek Music*	*Acoustic guitar ballad*	*Slow*	*9*
Love That Will Not Let Me Go	**Steve Camp**	**Ballad**	**Slow**	**10**
Mercy for the Memories	**Geoff Moore & the Distance**	**Folk/pop ballad**	**Slow**	**9**
Most of the Time	Glad	Piano ballad	Slow	4
Peace Be Still	**Al Denson**	**Ballad**	**Slow**	**10**
The Prodigal (I'll Be Waiting)	Amy Grant	Ballad	Slow	7
Stranger to Holiness	Steve Camp	Ballad	Slow/mid	2
Take My Hand	**The Kry**	**Acoustic ballad**	**Mid/slow**	**9**
When It Hurts the Most	Brent Lamb	Ballad	Slow	9
_____	_____	_____	_____	_____
_____	_____	_____	_____	_____
_____	_____	_____	_____	_____
_____	_____	_____	_____	_____
_____	_____	_____	_____	_____

Movie Clips

Title: Chariots of Fire

Topic: Failure

Description: Harold Abrahams loses a race, his first loss ever, then plays it over in his mind. He grieves over his failure to his girlfriend.

Start Time: 0:47:50

Start Cue: Begin after the starter walks across the track

End Time: 0:50:05

End Cue: "If you don't run, you can't win," or "Try growing up"

Comments: _____

_____

Title: Searching for Bobby Fischer

Topic: Success; Fear of failure

Description: Josh Waitzkin, a chess prodigy, has a late-night talk with his dad about the possibility of losing. Shows the pressure of staying on top.

Start Time: 1:01:30

Start Cue: Josh's dad is reading him a story

End Time: 1:03:40

End Cue: "Maybe it's better not to be the best. Then you can lose and it's okay"

Comments: _____

_____

Title: Searching for Bobby Fischer

Topic: Fatherhood; Failure; Destructive parenting

Description: Eight-year-old Josh loses a chess match, and his dad angrily confronts him about losing. Illustrates a man who has too much invested in his son's success.

Start Time: 1:06:30

Start Cue: Shot of clock tower. "Seven moves" is first line

End Time: 1:08:20

End Cue: "Sorry"

Comments: _____

_____

Title: _____

Topic: _____

Description: _____

Start Time: _____

Start Cue: _____

End Time: _____

End Cue: _____

Comments: _____

_____

~ Fear ~

See also: **Courage, God as a Refuge, Risk Taking**

Message Titles

☐ **Facing Up to Fear:** The Fear of Failure • The Fear of Living Alone • The Fear of Death

_____

_____

_____

_____

Dramas

Title	Tone	Characters	Topics
The Boy Who Never Got Dirty	Humorous	1 male, 1 female, 1 narrator	Service; Risk taking
The Eggshell Family	Humorous	2 males, 1 female, 1 either male or female	Decision making
The Eggshells Break Out	Humorous	3 males, 1 female	Risk taking; Facing challenges
Mr. Peepers Goes to Sleep	Mixed	1 male, 2 females, 1 child	Death; Facing the truth
The Quagmire	Serious	1 male or female	Failure; Self-esteem; Being "stuck"; Trusting God
Straight-Jacketed	Serious	1 male	Bondage to past and to sin; Anger toward God
What If . . .	Humorous	3 males, 1 female	Worry; Anxiety
_____	_____	_____	_____
_____	_____	_____	_____
_____	_____	_____	_____
_____	_____	_____	_____

Songs

Title	Artist	Style	Tempo	Seeker-Sensitivity Rating
All That I Need	Steve Camp	Ballad	Slow	5
Ball and Chain	**Susan Ashton**	**Folk/pop**	**Mid**	**9**
Bound to Come Some Trouble	**Rich Mullins**	**Ballad**	**Slow**	**10**
Every Step I Take	**Bob Carlisle**	**Bluesy pop**	**Mid**	**9**
The Future	First Call	Pop vocal group	Up	8
Gentle Hands	Truth	Traditional ballad	Slow	8
He Won't Let Me Down	**Debbie McClendon**	**R & B/pop**	**Up**	**9**
He Won't Let You Go	**The Kry**	**Piano ballad**	**Slow**	**10**
Here in My Heart	Susan Ashton	Folk rock	Up	8
His Grace Is Greater	Larnelle Harris	Inspirational ballad	Slow	8
His Love Is Strong	**Clay Crosse**	**Pop**	**Up**	**10**
I'll Find You There	The Kry	Folk rock ballad	Slow	9
I'm Depending on You	Harv & Edythe	MOR	Mid	7
In My Father's Hands	**Susan Ashton**	**Folk/pop**	**Mid**	**9**
Love Is Always There	Carolyn Arends	Folk/pop	Up	9
One Step at a Time	First Call	Pop vocal group	Up	8
Peace Be Still	**Al Denson**	**Ballad**	**Slow**	**10**
Seize the Day	Carolyn Arends	Folk pop, in 3	Mid	8
Take My Hand	**The Kry**	**Acoustic ballad**	**Mid/slow**	**9**
Walk in the Dark	Wayne Watson	Pop	Up	2
When You Are a Soldier	**Steven Curtis Chapman**	**Keyboard ballad**	**Slow/mid**	**4**
Wings of Love	Imperials	Pop	Up	8
Your Love Stays With Me	**Gary Chapman**	**Piano ballad**	**Slow**	**10**
_____	_____	_____	_____	_____
_____	_____	_____	_____	_____
_____	_____	_____	_____	_____
_____	_____	_____	_____	_____

Movie Clips

Title: _____
Topic: _____
Description: _____
Start Time: _____
Start Cue: _____
End Time: _____
End Cue: _____
Comments: _____
_____

- Grief -

See also: **Death**

Package Suggestion

Drama:
In the Dark

Song:
Healing River

Message Titles

❏ A Better Kind of Grieving
❏ *Disappointment With God:* Where is God When You Need Him?
❏ *Learning Through Life's Crises:* Learning Through Losing
❏ *Living With Dying:* Grief
❏ *Living With Dying:* Grieving Process

_____
_____
_____
_____
_____

Dramas

Title	Tone	Characters	Topics
Attack of the Well-Meaners	Mixed, mostly humorous	1 male, 2 females	Dealing with crisis; Friendship
In the Dark	Serious	1 male, 1 female	Death of a child; Grief
The Old Man and the Laundromat	Mixed, mostly serious	1 male, 1 female, 1 child	Grieving; Dealing with death of a loved one; Letting go
What Now?	Serious	2 males, 4 females	Coping with a crisis; Dealing with death

 # Songs

Title	Artist	Style	Tempo	Seeker-Sensitivity Rating
Bound to Come Some Trouble	**Rich Mullins**	**Ballad**	**Slow**	**10**
Gentle Hands	Truth	Traditional ballad	Slow	8
Healing River	*Willow Creek Music*	*Ballad*	*Slow/mid*	*9*
Home Free	Wayne Watson	Ballad	Slow/mid	6
Honesty	Margaret Becker	Power ballad	Slow	9
If I Had Only Known	**Reba McEntire**	**Ballad**	**Slow**	**10**
Peace Be Still	**Al Denson**	**Ballad**	**Slow**	**10**
When It Hurts the Most	Brent Lamb	Ballad	Slow	9
Your Love Stays With Me	**Gary Chapman**	**Piano ballad**	**Slow**	**10**

Movie Clips

Title: Shadowlands
Topic: Suffering; Pain; Why does God allow bad things to happen?
Description: C. S. Lewis delivers a speech about why God allows suffering.
Start Time: 0:10:00
Start Cue: "Yesterday I received a letter"
End Time: 0:11:40
End Cue: "Thank you very much"
Comments: The last line is a bit hard to understand

Title: Shadowlands
Topic: Grief; Death; Need for a mother
Description: C. S. Lewis tells Joy Gresham about when his mother died.
Start Time: 0:28:15
Start Cue: "I have been really hurt, you know"
End Time: 0:29:25
End Cue: "Yes, I'd like that"
Comments: _____

Title: Shadowlands
Topic: Grief
Description: C. S. Lewis talks to his stepson Douglass about his mother dying. Very moving.
Start Time: 2:00:55
Start Cue: Jack walks up behind Douglass and says "hi"
End Time: 2:04:00
End Cue: Shot, from behind, of Jack and Douglass embracing
Comments: _____

Title: _____
Topic: _____
Description: _____
Start Time: _____
Start Cue: _____
End Time: _____
End Cue: _____
Comments: _____

~ Guilt ~

See also: **Confession, God's Forgiveness of Us, Grace, Sin**

 Message Titles

- ☐ *Amazing Grace:* The God of Grace
- ☐ *Seven Wonders of the Spiritual World:* God Forgives My Failures

_____

_____

_____

_____

_____

 Dramas

Title	Tone	Characters	Topics
A Clean Slate	Serious	1 male, 2 or 3 males or females	Forgiveness; Redemption; Guilt
Go Away God	Humorous	2 males, 1 female	Conscience; Guilt; Hearing God's voice
A Nice Guy	Serious	2 males	Regret; Admitting failures; Effects of sin; Confession
On Vacation	Humorous	2 males, 1 female, 1 either male or female	Leisure time; Guilt; Slowing down
The Prisoner	Serious	3 males, 1 female	Easter; Freedom from sin; New Christian
"X" Marks the Spot	Serious; Mime	1 female, 1 male, and 3 females or males	Sin; Redemption; Forgiveness; Guilt

Songs

Title	Artist	Style	Tempo	Seeker-Sensitivity Rating
Ball and Chain	**Susan Ashton**	**Folk/pop**	**Mid**	**9**
Face of Forgiveness	*Willow Creek Music*	*Ballad*	*Slow*	*10*
He's All You Need	**Steve Camp**	**Ballad**	**Slow**	**8**
His Grace Is Greater	Larnelle Harris	Inspirational ballad	Slow	8
I Don't Deserve Your Love	Trace Balin	Ballad	Slow	9
If I Could Look Through Your Eyes	*Willow Creek Music*	*Piano ballad*	*Slow*	*10*
I'm Amazed	*Willow Creek Music*	*Ballad*	*Slow*	*7*
I Stand, I Fall	*Willow Creek Music*	*Piano ballad*	*Slow*	*7*
I've Been Released	*Willow Creek Music*	*Pop/rock— Chicago sound*	*Up*	*9*
Just Come In	Margaret Becker	Pop ballad	Slow	5
Mercy for the Memories	**Geoff Moore & the Distance**	**Folk/pop ballad**	**Slow**	**9**
Never Be an Angel	Margaret Becker	Pop	Mid	4
Why Me	*Willow Creek Music*	*Ballad*	*Slow*	*9*
_____	_____	_____	_____	_____
_____	_____	_____	_____	_____
_____	_____	_____	_____	_____
_____	_____	_____	_____	_____

Movie Clips

Title: _____

Topic: _____

Description: _____

Start Time: _____

Start Cue: _____

End Time: _____

End Cue: _____

Comments: _____

_____

- Hardship -

See also: **Endurance, Healing**

 ## Message Titles

❐ How to Be Strong When It Counts
❐ Victim or Victor?
❐ **Learning Through Life's Crises:** Learning Through Losing • Learning Through Failing • Learning Through Falling • Learning Through Physical Affliction
❐ **Strength for the Storms of Life:** Why Storms Strike • Staying Steady in the Storm • The Strength That Storms Produce

_____
_____
_____
_____

 ## Dramas

Title	Tone	Characters	Topics
The Breakfast Club	Mixed, mostly serious	4 males, 1 female	Friendship; Small groups; Friends in crisis
Final Judgment	Mixed, mostly humorous	4 males, 2 females, 1 child	Suffering
Great Expectations	Serious	1 male, 2 females	Unanswered prayer
In the Dark	Serious	1 male, 1 female	Death of a child; Grief
"It"	Humorous	2 males, 1 female	Becoming a Christian doesn't mean having no problems; Vulnerability of new believers
The Safe	Mixed	1 male, 1 female, 3 either male or female	Inner strength; Needing God's strength
Shop Talk	Serious	2 males, 2 females	Failure; Adversity; Small groups

Title	Tone	Characters	Topics
Take Heart	Mixed; mime	2 males, 2 females	God heals the brokenhearted; Disappointment
What Now?	Serious	2 males, 4 females	Coping with a crisis; Dealing with death

 # Songs

Title	Artist	Style	Tempo	Seeker-Sensitivity Rating
A Beautiful Place	**Wayne Watson**	**MOR ballad**	**Mid/slow**	**9**
All That I Need	Steve Camp	Ballad	Slow	5
A Place Called Hope	Michael English	Pop gospel	Mid/up	8
A Place to Call Home	*Willow Creek Music*	*Gospel ballad*	*Slow, in 3*	*10*
Ball and Chain	**Susan Ashton**	**Folk/pop**	**Mid**	**9**
Bound to Come Some Trouble	**Rich Mullins**	**Ballad**	**Slow**	**10**
Desperado	Eagles	Ballad	Slow	10
Down the Road	**Triloje**	**Acapella vocal group**	**Slow**	**6**
The Extra Mile	Al Denson	Power Ballad	Slow	9
Faith, Hope and Love	**Point of Grace**	**Pop vocal group**	**Up**	**9**
Friend of a Wounded Heart	Wayne Watson	Power ballad	Slow	8
Gentle Hands	Truth	Traditional ballad	Slow	8
Hard Times	Wayne Watson	Ballad	Slow	4
Healing River	*Willow Creek Music*	*Ballad*	*Slow/mid*	*9*
He'll Find a Way	**Billy and Sarah Gaines**	**MOR ballad—duet**	**Slow/mid**	**8**
Here in My Heart	Susan Ashton	Folk rock	Up	8
He's All You Need	**Steve Camp**	**Ballad**	**Slow**	**8**
He Won't Let Me Down	**Debbie McClendon**	**R & B/pop**	**Up**	**9**
Hiding Place	Steven Curtis Chapman	Pop ballad	Mid/slow	9
Higher Ways	Steven Curtis Chapman	Acoustic guitar ballad	Mid/slow	8
His Love Is Strong	**Clay Crosse**	**Pop**	**Up**	**10**
His Strength Is Perfect	**Steven Curtis Chapman**	**Ballad**	**Slow**	**9**
Holding Out Hope to You	Michael English	Power ballad	Slow	9

Title	Artist	Style	Tempo	Seeker-Sensitivity Rating
Honesty	Margaret Becker	Power ballad	Slow	9
I'll Be Believing	**Point of Grace**	**Pop vocal group**	**Up**	**9**
I'm Depending on You	Harv & Edythe	MOR	Mid	7
In His Sanctuary	Morris Chapman & Friends	Ballad	Slow	6
Jesus Will Still Be There	**Point of Grace**	**Ballad**	**Slow**	**9**
Love Can Open the Door	Sandi Patti	Pop	Up	10
Love That Will Not Let Me Go	**Steve Camp**	**Ballad**	**Slow**	**10**
My Life Is in Your Hands	**Kathy Troccoli**	**Ballad**	**Slow**	**9**
Peace Be Still	**Al Denson**	**Ballad**	**Slow**	**10**
Safe	Steve Archer	Ballad—duet	Slow/mid	8
Strength in You	*Willow Creek Music*	*MOR pop*	*Slow/mid*	*10*
Suffer in Silence	Susan Ashton	Folk/pop	Mid	10
There Is a Love	**Michael English**	**Pop**	**Up**	**9**
Walk in the Dark	Wayne Watson	Pop	Up	2
When It Hurts the Most	Brent Lamb	Ballad	Slow	9
When You Are a Soldier	**Steven Curtis Chapman**	**Keyboard ballad**	**Slow/mid**	**4**
Wings of Love	Imperials	Pop	Up	8
Your Love Stays With Me	**Gary Chapman**	**Piano ballad**	**Slow**	**10**
_____	_____	_____	_____	_____
_____	_____	_____	_____	_____
_____	_____	_____	_____	_____
_____	_____	_____	_____	_____

Movie Clips

Title: Chariots of Fire

Topic: Christian life; Endurance

Description: Eric Liddell gives a sermonette about running the race of faith.

Start Time: 0:25:35

Start Cue: "You came to see a race today"

End Time: 0:27:20

End Cue: "That is how you run a straight race"

Comments: _____

_____

Title: Shadowlands
Topic: Suffering; Pain; Why does God allow bad things to happen?
Description: C. S. Lewis delivers a speech about why God allows suffering.
Start Time: 0:10:00
Start Cue: "Yesterday I received a letter"
End Time: 0:11:40
End Cue: "Thank you very much"
Comments: The last line is a bit hard to understand

Title: Shadowlands
Topic: Grief; Death; Need for a mother
Description: C. S. Lewis tells Joy Gresham about when his mother died.
Start Time: 0:28:15
Start Cue: "I have been really hurt, you know"
End Time: 0:29:25
End Cue: "Yes, I'd like that"
Comments: _____

Title: Shadowlands
Topic: Death; Sharing the dying process
Description: Jack and Joy talk about her imminent death. She makes a couple of profound statements about sharing the dying process.
Start Time: 1:45:30
Start Cue: "I don't want to be somewhere else anymore"
End Time: 1:47:55
End Cue: Jack and Joy kiss
Comments: _____

Title: _____
Topic: _____
Description: _____
Start Time: _____
Start Cue: _____
End Time: _____
End Cue: _____
Comments: _____

~ Healing ~

See also: **Comforting Others, God's Love, God's Tenderness**

Message Titles

- ❏ Connect With the Source of Strength
- ❏ A Hunger for Healing
- ❏ *Measuring How Much You Matter to God:* Rebuilding Self-Esteem
- ❏ *Strength for the Storms of Life:* The Strength That Storms Produce

_____

_____

_____

Dramas

Title	Tone	Characters	Topics
The Angry Woman	Serious	2 males, 3 females, 1 narrator	The roots of anger
Another Day at the Bus Stop	Mixed	1 male, 1 female	Our relationship with God; Self-esteem
Because I Love You	Serious	1 male, 1 female	Adultery; The consequences of sin
The Old Man and the Laundromat	Mixed, mostly serious	1 male, 1 female, 1 child	Grieving; Dealing with death of a loved one; Letting go
Take Heart	Mixed; mime	2 males, 2 females	God heals the brokenhearted; Disappointment
Taking Step Four	Humorous	1 female	Self-examination; Self-delusion; Confession of sin
These Parts	Mixed	2 males, 1 female, 3 either male or female, 1 child, 1 narrator	The Resurrection; Our need for Christ; Easter
_____	_____	_____	_____
_____	_____	_____	_____
_____	_____	_____	_____

Songs

Title	Artist	Style	Tempo	Seeker-Sensitivity Rating
A Beautiful Place	**Wayne Watson**	**MOR ballad**	**Mid/slow**	**9**
A Place to Call Home	*Willow Creek Music*	*Gospel ballad*	*Slow, in 3*	*10*
Ball and Chain	**Susan Ashton**	**Folk/pop**	**Mid**	**9**
Bound to Come Some Trouble	**Rich Mullins**	**Ballad**	**Slow**	**10**
Down on My Knees	Susan Ashton	Folk rock	Mid/up	6
Down the Road	**Triloje**	**Acapella vocal group**	**Slow**	**6**
Faith, Hope and Love	**Point of Grace**	**Pop vocal group**	**Up**	**9**
Friend of a Wounded Heart	Wayne Watson	Power ballad	Slow	8
Gentle Hands	Truth	Traditional ballad	Slow	8
Hard Times	Wayne Watson	Ballad	Slow	4
He's All You Need	**Steve Camp**	**Ballad**	**Slow**	**8**
Healing River	*Willow Creek Music*	*Ballad*	*Slow/mid*	*9*
Hiding Place	Steven Curtis Chapman	Pop ballad	Mid/slow	9
His Love Is Strong	**Clay Crosse**	**Pop**	**Up**	**10**
Honesty	Margaret Becker	Power ballad	Slow	9
If You Could See Me Now	Truth	Ballad	Slow	5
I'll Find You There	**The Kry**	**Folk rock ballad**	**Slow**	**9**
I Will Be Free	Cindy Morgan	Ballad	Slow	7
Jesus Will Still Be There	**Point of Grace**	**Ballad**	**Slow**	**9**
Love Can Open the Door	Sandi Patti	Pop	Up	10
Mercy for the Memories	**Geoff Moore & the Distance**	**Folk/pop ballad**	**Slow**	**9**
Peace Be Still	**Al Denson**	**Ballad**	**Slow**	**10**
Safe	Steve Archer	Ballad—duet	Slow/mid	8
Suffer in Silence	Susan Ashton	Folk/pop	Mid	10
When It Hurts the Most	Brent Lamb	Ballad	Slow	9
Your Love Stays With Me	**Gary Chapman**	**Piano ballad**	**Slow**	**10**
_____	_____	_____	_____	_____
_____	_____	_____	_____	_____
_____	_____	_____	_____	_____
_____	_____	_____	_____	_____
_____	_____	_____	_____	_____

Movie Clips

Title: _____

Topic: _____

Description: _____

Start Time: _____

Start Cue: _____

End Time: _____

End Cue: _____

Comments: _____

~ Loneliness ~

Message Titles

- ❏ God Knows Your Name
- ❏ *Facing Up to Fear:* The Fear of Living (Being) Alone
- ❏ *What Jesus Would Say to . . .* Madonna

_____

_____

_____

Dramas

Title	Tone	Characters	Topics
Funny Girl	Mixed	1 male, 2 females (multiple roles for 1 man and 1 woman)	Self-esteem; Need for acceptance
The Old Man and the Laundromat	Mixed, mostly serious	1 male, 1 female, 1 child	Grieving; Dealing with death of a loved one; Letting go

Title	Tone	Characters	Topics
The Quagmire	Serious	1 male or female	Failure; Self-esteem; Being "stuck"; Trusting God
Single?	Mixed	1 male, 1 female	Singleness; Loneliness; Fear of living alone
_____	_____	_____	_____
_____	_____	_____	_____
_____	_____	_____	_____
_____	_____	_____	_____

 # Songs

Title	Artist	Style	Tempo	Seeker-Sensitivity Rating
A Place to Call Home	*Willow Creek Music*	*Gospel ballad*	*Slow, in 3*	*10*
Change in My Life	**John Pagano**	**Gospel**	**Mid/up**	**9**
Desperado	Eagles	Ballad	Slow	10
Eleanor Rigby	**Beatles**	**Acoustic ballad**	**Slow/mid**	**10**
Friend of a Wounded Heart	Wayne Watson	Power ballad	Slow	8
Gentle Hands	Truth	Traditional ballad	Slow	8
He Won't Let You Go	**The Kry**	**Piano ballad**	**Slow**	**10**
Hiding Place	Steven Curtis Chapman	Pop ballad	Mid/slow	9
In Heaven's Eyes	**Sandi Patti**	**Inspirational ballad**	**Slow**	**9**
Jesus Will Still Be There	**Point of Grace**	**Ballad**	**Slow**	**9**
Peace Be Still	**Al Denson**	**Ballad**	**Slow**	**10**
Somebody Make Me Laugh	**Patti Austin**	**Ballad**	**Slow**	**10**
Treasure of You	Steven Curtis Chapman	Driving rock	Up	10
You're the One He Loves	**Truth**	**Pop**	**Up**	**10**
Your Love Stays With Me	**Gary Chapman**	**Piano ballad**	**Slow**	**10**
_____	_____	_____	_____	_____
_____	_____	_____	_____	_____
_____	_____	_____	_____	_____
_____	_____	_____	_____	_____
_____	_____	_____	_____	_____

Movie Clips

Title: _____

Topic: _____

Description: _____

Start Time: _____

Start Cue: _____

End Time: _____

End Cue: _____

Comments: _____

- Self-Esteem -

See also: **Our Value to God**

Message Titles

❏ The Curse of Comparison
❏ Truly Significant
❏ *What Jesus Would Say to . . .* David Letterman
❏ *What Jesus Would Say to . . .* Madonna
❏ **Measuring How Much You Matter to God:** The Source of Your Self-Esteem • What Scars Self-Esteem • Rebuilding Self-Esteem • Building Self-Esteem Into Others

_____
_____
_____
_____
_____

Package Suggestion

Drama:
The Intruder

Song:
Let the Lord Love You

Dramas

Title	Tone	Characters	Topics
The Angry Woman	Serious	2 males, 3 females, 1 narrator	The roots of anger
Another Day at the Bus Stop	Mixed	1 male, 1 female	Our relationship with God; Self-esteem
The Brow Beater	Mixed, mostly serious	1 male, 1 female	Self-esteem; Failures; Forgiveness
Call Waiting	Mixed—ends serious	2 males	Marketplace pressures; Search for significance; Mid-life crisis
Conversations	Serious	2 males, 1 female, 1 offstage female voice	Self-esteem; Self-criticism; Failure
Funny Girl	Mixed	1 male, 2 females (multiple roles for 1 man and 1 woman)	Self-esteem; Need for acceptance
Honestly Speaking	Mixed	3 males, 3 females	Positive self-talk; Self-esteem
The Intruder	Serious	1 male, 1 female	Self-image; Destructive parenting; God's love in spite of failure
The Lane of Life	Mixed; mime	5 either male or female, 1 offstage narrator	Salvation; Our value to God; Self-esteem
Masterpiece	Mixed; touching	1 male, 1 female, 2 teenage females	Self-esteem; Parenting
Measuring Up	Mixed; mime	2 males, 1 female, 1 other male or female	God's acceptance of us; Self-esteem
The Quagmire	Serious	1 male or female	Failure; Self-esteem; Being "stuck"; Trusting God
Wonderfully Made	Serious	2 females, 2 males, 1 narrator	Affirming a child's uniqueness
_____	_____	_____	_____
_____	_____	_____	_____
_____	_____	_____	_____
_____	_____	_____	_____

Songs

Title	Artist	Style	Tempo	Seeker-Sensitivity Rating
A Place to Call Home	*Willow Creek Music*	*Gospel ballad*	*Slow, in 3*	*10*
A Rose Is a Rose	Susan Ashton	Piano ballad	Slow	9
Almighty God	**Jim Murray**	**Traditional ballad**	**Slow**	**7**
I Believe in You	Steve Camp	Pop	Up	10
If I Could Look Through Your Eyes	*Willow Creek Music*	*Piano ballad*	*Slow*	*10*
If You Could See What I See	Geoff Moore & the Distance	Folk ballad	Slow	10
I'll Find You There	**The Kry**	**Folk rock ballad**	**Slow**	**9**
I'm Amazed	*Willow Creek Music*	*Ballad*	*Slow*	*7*
In Heaven's Eyes	**Sandi Patti**	**Inspirational ballad**	**Slow**	**9**
Jesus Loves Me	**Whitney Houston**	**R & B/pop**	**Slow/mid**	**8**
Let the Lord Love You	*Willow Creek Music*	*Acoustic guitar ballad*	*Slow*	*9*
Peace Be Still	**Al Denson**	**Ballad**	**Slow**	**10**
Place in This World	Michael W. Smith	Power ballad	Slow	9
Somebody Love Me	Michael W. Smith	Power ballad	Slow	9
Treasure of You	Steven Curtis Chapman	Driving rock	Up	10
You're the One He Loves	**Truth**	**Pop**	**Up**	**10**
_____	_____	_____	_____	_____
_____	_____	_____	_____	_____
_____	_____	_____	_____	_____
_____	_____	_____	_____	_____

Movie Clips

Title: _____

Topic: _____

Description: _____

Start Time: _____

Start Cue: _____

End Time: _____

End Cue: _____

Comments: _____

_____

~ Worry ~

Might also include: *Anxiety*
See also: **Faith, God's Faithfulness**

Package Suggestion

Drama:
What If . . .

Song:
My Life Is in Your Hands

Message Titles

- ☐ *If You Only Knew the Father:* Why Worry?
- ☐ *Illustrating the Identity of God:* Our Providing God

_____

_____

_____

_____

Dramas

Title	Tone	Characters	Topics
Conversations in a Field	Humorous	2 males, 2 females	Anxiety; Worry; God's providence
The Eggshell Family	Humorous	2 males, 1 female, 1 either male or female	Decision making
The Eggshells Break Out	Humorous	3 males, 1 female	Risk taking; Facing challenges
What If . . .	Humorous	3 males, 1 female	Worry; Anxiety

Songs

Title	Artist	Style	Tempo	Seeker-Sensitivity Rating
All That I Need	Steve Camp	Ballad	Slow	5
Bound to Come Some Trouble	**Rich Mullins**	**Ballad**	**Slow**	**10**
From Here on Out	*Willow Creek Music*	*MOR pop*	*Mid*	*8*
The Future	First Call	Pop vocal group	Up	8
Gentle Hands	Truth	Traditional ballad	Slow	8
He'll Find a Way	**Billy and Sarah Gaines**	**MOR ballad—duet**	**Slow/mid**	**8**
He Won't Let Me Down	**Debbie McClendon**	**R & B/pop**	**Up**	**9**
Hiding Place	Steven Curtis Chapman	Pop ballad	Mid/slow	9
His Love Is Strong	**Clay Crosse**	**Pop**	**Up**	**10**
I'll Find You There	The Kry	Folk rock ballad	Slow	9
I'm Depending on You	Harv & Edythe	MOR	Mid	7
In My Father's Hands	**Susan Ashton**	**Folk/pop**	**Mid**	**9**
Jesus Will Still Be There	**Point of Grace**	**Ballad**	**Slow**	**9**
Let the Lord Love You	*Willow Creek Music*	*Acoustic guitar ballad*	*Slow*	*9*
My Life Is in Your Hands	**Kathy Troccoli**	**Ballad**	**Slow**	**9**
Take My Hand	**The Kry**	**Acoustic ballad**	**Mid/slow**	**9**
Your Love Stays With Me	**Gary Chapman**	**Piano ballad**	**Slow**	**10**
_____	_____	_____	_____	_____
_____	_____	_____	_____	_____
_____	_____	_____	_____	_____

Movie Clips

Title: _____

Topic: _____

Description: _____

Start Time: _____

Start Cue: _____

End Time: _____

End Cue: _____

Comments: _____

_____

Endurance

Might also include: *Quitting* and *Perseverance*
See also: **God's Power**, **God's Faithfulness**

Message Titles

- ☐ Anyone Can Quit
- ☐ Secrets of Survivng
- ☐ Staying Steady in the Storm
- ☐ Surviving a Slump
- ☐ Quitting Points
- ☐ *Endangered Character Qualities*: Endurance
- ☐ *Signs of the Times*: No U-Turn
- ☐ **Staying Power:** The Power of Perseverance • Power Beyond Yourself

_____
_____
_____
_____
_____

Package Suggestion

Drama:
What Now

Song:
When It Hurts the Most

Dramas

Title	Tone	Characters	Topics
The Quagmire	Serious	1 male or female	Failure; Self-esteem; Being "stuck"; Trusting God

Songs

Title	Artist	Style	Tempo	Seeker-Sensitivity Rating
A Beautiful Place	Wayne Watson	MOR ballad	Mid/slow	9
Faith, Hope and Love	Point of Grace	Pop vocal group	Up	9
His Strength Is Perfect	Steven Curtis Chapman	Ballad	Slow	9
Keep the Flame Burning	Debby Boone	MOR	Mid	5
Love That Will Not Let Me Go	Steve Camp	Ballad	Slow	10
A Rose Is a Rose	Susan Ashton	Piano ballad	Slow	9
When You Are a Soldier	Steven Curtis Chapman	Keyboard ballad	Slow/mid	4

Movie Clips

Title: Chariots of Fire
Topic: Christian life; Endurance
Description: Eric Liddell gives a sermonette about running the race of faith.
Start Time: 0:25:35
Start Cue: "You came to see a race today"
End Time: 0:27:20
End Cue: "That is how you run a straight race"
Comments: _____

_____

Title: Chariots of Fire
Topic: Perseverence; Determination; Courage
Description: Runner Eric Liddell gets knocked down in a race and comes back to win.
Start Time: 0:34:25
Start Cue: "Gentlemen, get to your marks"
End Time: 0:35:45
End Cue: Liddell falls down in exhaustion at the finish
Comments: _____

_____

Title: Rudy

Topic: Quitting; Perseverence

Description: Rudy decides to quit the football team. Fortune, his friend and former boss, challenges him because he used to play for Notre Dame but quit.

Start Time: 1:29:10

Start Cue: Just before "What're you doing here"

End Time: 1:31:20

End Cue: "Do you hear me clear enough?"

Comments: Contains two possibly objectionable words

Title: _____

Topic: _____

Description: _____

Start Time: _____

Start Cue: _____

End Time: _____

End Cue: _____

Comments: _____

Heroes

At a time when heroes seemingly fall every day, it's rare to see a truly worthy role model. This topic can be used to inspire people to be difference makers.

 ## Message Titles

- ☐ Difference Makers
- ☐ *What Jesus Would Say to . . .* Billy Graham
- ☐ *What Jesus Would Say to . . .* Michael Jordan
- ☐ *What Jesus Would Say to . . .* Mother Teresa
- ☐ **Everyday Heroes:** Hallmarks of a Hero • Heroes of the Heart • Heroes of the Home

Package Suggestion

Drama:
Parlor Talk

Song:
Treasure

_____

_____

_____

 ## Dramas

Title	Tone	Characters	Topics
Be Like Mike	Humorous	4 males, 2 females (actors play multiple roles)	Fame; Pressures of success
Parlor Talk	Mixed	3 males, 2 females	Making a difference with your life; Death; Workaholism
A Real Hero	Humorous	6 males	Manhood; Hero; Christian men
The Right Thing	Serious	1 male	Costly obedience; Christian character; Persecution
The Story of Rachel	Serious	3 females	Care for the poor; Compassion

Songs

Title	Artist	Style	Tempo	Seeker-Sensitivity Rating
Audience of One	*Willow Creek Music*	*Power ballad*	*Slow*	8
Be the One	**Al Denson**	**Power ballad**	**Slow**	7
Heroes	Paul Overstreet	Country	Mid/slow	8
Man of God	*Willow Creek Music*	*Pop/rock*	*Mid/up*	7

 Movie Clips

Title:	Chariots of Fire
Topic:	Integrity; Standing up for what you believe in; The Sabbath
Description:	Eric Liddell refuses to run on the Sabbath. The English Olympic Committee tries to make him compromise, but he stands firm.
Start Time:	1:28:15
Start Cue:	"We decided to invite you in for a little chat"
End Time:	1:30:00
End Cue:	"But I can't make that sacrifice"
Comments:	_____

Title:	Chariots of Fire
Topic:	Perseverence; Determination; Courage
Description:	Runner Eric Liddell gets knocked down in a race and comes back to win.
Start Time:	0:34:25
Start Cue:	"Gentlemen, get to your marks"
End Time:	0:35:45
End Cue:	Liddell falls down in exhaustion at the finish
Comments:	_____

Leadership

Message Titles

☐ *What Jesus Would Say to . . .* Bill Clinton
☐ **Bringing Out the Best in People:** Becoming a People Builder • The How-Tos • Bringing Out the Best in Yourself

_____
_____
_____
_____
_____

Dramas

Title	Tone	Characters	Topics
Lonely at the Top	Serious	1 male	The perils of power, authority; Easter
Pastor General	Humorous	2 males, 2 females	Abusive leadership; The church; Authoritarianism
Wonderfully Made	Serious	2 females, 2 males, 1 narrator	Affirming a child's uniqueness

Songs

Title	Artist	Style	Tempo	Seeker-Sensitivity Rating
Audience of One	*Willow Creek Music*	*Power ballad*	*Slow*	8
Be the One	**Al Denson**	**Power ballad**	**Slow**	7
Seize the Day	Carolyn Arends	Folk pop, in 3	Mid	8
Strength in You	*Willow Creek Music*	*MOR pop*	*Slow/mid*	10
You've Got to Stand for Something	**Aaron Tippin**	**Country**	**Up**	**10**

Movie Clips

Title: Hoosiers
Topic: Leadership
Description: A small-town basketball team enters a huge fieldhouse to play the state championship. The players are in awe. The coach has the players measure the basket to show them that it's the same as their gym at home.
Start Time: 1:33:20
Start Cue: Team enters Butler Fieldhouse
End Time: 1:35:20
End Cue: "It *is* big"
Comments: _____

_____

Title: Rudy
Topic: Quitting; Perseverence
Description: Rudy decides to quit the football team. Fortune, his friend and former boss, challenges him because he used to play for Notre Dame but quit.
Start Time: 1:29:10
Start Cue: Just before "What're you doing here"
End Time: 1:31:20
End Cue: "Do you hear me clear enough?"
Comments: Contains two possibly objectionable words

Materialism/Greed

Might also include: *Greed*
See also: **Contentment, Fulfillment**

Message Titles

- ❏ It All Goes Back Into the Box
- ❏ Money, Sex, and Power: Money
- ❏ The Power of Money
- ❏ The Profit of Financial Integrity
- ❏ Tenth Commandment: Restrain Material Desires
- ❏ The Truth About Earthly Treasures
- ❏ What Jesus Would Say to . . . Bill Gates
- ❏ You Can't Serve Two Masters
- ❏ *Changing Times:* The Changing American Dream
- ❏ *Understanding the Times:* The '80s

Package Suggestions

Drama:
Confessions of an Ad-aholic

Song:
Lay It on Down

. . .

Drama:
The Lures of Life

Song:
Unimportant Things

Dramas

Title	Tone	Characters	Topics
All I Want for Christmas	Mixed	3 males, 2 females, 1 female child	Greed; Desire to acquire possesions
Catalog-itis	Humorous	1 male, 1 female, 2 jr. high age girls	Self-control; Contentment
Check Mates	Humorous	1 male, 1 female	Personal finances; Debt

Title	Tone	Characters	Topics
Confessions of an Ad-aholic	Humorous	1 male, 1 female	Materialism; Power of the media; The American dream
Early One Morning Just After the Dawn of History as We Know It	Humorous	3 males	Materialism; "Keeping up with the Joneses"
For the Love of Money	Humorous	3 males, 3 females	Money
In Pursuit of Happiness	Mixed	1 male, 1 female	Contentment; Possessions
Lifestyles of the Obscured and Indebted	Humorous	4 males, 3 females	Materialism; Coveting
Lizzy and Leroy	Humorous	1 male, 1 female, piano player (optional)	Life fulfillment; Material things don't satisfy
The Lures of Life	Mixed mime; light	5 males, 1 female	Adventurism; Life fulfillment
The Mirror Thought of It	Mixed	1 male, 1 female, 1 offstage voice	Materialism; Workaholism; Striving for more
Oh, What a Feeling!	Humorous	2 males, 1 female	Decision making; Self-control; Money management
One Step Up, One Step Down	Serious	4 males (1 can be female)	Ambition; Priorities
Parlor Talk	Mixed	3 males, 2 females	Making a difference with your life; Death; Workaholism
Richard: 1985	Serious	2 males	Workaholism; Materialism vs. idealism
A Serf's Tale	Humorous	1 male, 1 female	Serving two masters; Materialism
What's the Ticket?	Mixed	2 females, 4 either male or female	Need for Christ; Contentment; Needs and wants
_____	_____	_____	_____
_____	_____	_____	_____
_____	_____	_____	_____
_____	_____	_____	_____

 # Songs

Title	Artist	Style	Tempo	Seeker-Sensitivity Rating
Build My World Around You	**Sandi Patty**	Pop	**Up**	9
Busy Man	**Steven Curtis Chapman**	Pop	**Mid/up**	10
Ever Devoted	_Willow Creek Music_	_Ballad_	_Slow_	6

Title	Artist	Style	Tempo	Seeker-Sensitivity Rating
Lay It on Down	**Bruce Carroll**	**Country**	**Mid/up**	8
Money Is a Powerful Thing	*Willow Creek Music*	*Motown/pop*	*Up*	*10*
Only Here for a Little While	**Billy Dean**	**Country**	**Mid/up**	10
Only You	*Willow Creek Music*	*Ballad*	*Slow*	*9*
Something to Hold on To	Truth	R & B/pop	Mid	10
Strength in You	*Willow Creek Music*	*MOR pop*	*Slow/mid*	*10*
Treasure	**Gary Chapman**	**Acoustic ballad**	**Slow**	9
Unimportant Things	**Paul Smith**	**Ballad**	**Slow**	8
Walk on By	Susan Ashton	Folk pop	Mid/up	8
Who Makes the Rules	**Steven Curtis Chapman**	**Pop/folk rock**	**Up**	7

Movie Clips

Title: Indiana Jones and the Last Crusade
Topic: Greed
Description: Elsa, Indy's girlfriend, chooses to reach for the grail in a chasm and falls to her death. Indy also reaches for it, but his father persuades him to let it go. Some good imagery.
Start Time: 1:55:50
Start Cue: Elsa grabs the grail
End Time: 1:57:40
End Cue: Indy's dad pulls him up
Comments: Elsa's deathfall may scare kids

_____

Title: She's Having a Baby
Topic: Life in suburbia; Emptiness of suburban life/American dream
Description: Funny parody of suburban life shows men in bad clothes dancing with lawnmowers, and their wives dancing around them with refreshments.
Start Time: 0:53:00
Start Cue: Start after the bicyclist leaves
End Time: 0:54:30
End Cue: End when music stops
Comments: _____

_____

> ## Package Suggestion
>
> **Movie Clip:**
> *Wall Street*
>
> **Song:**
> *Money Is a Powerful Thing*

Title: Wall Street
Topic: Greed/materialism; Money
Description: Corporate raider Gordon Gecko addresses a stockholders' meeting by extolling the virtues of greed.
Start Time: 1:17:00
Start Cue: "The new law of evolution in corporate America"
End Time: 1:18:15
End Cue: ". . . that other malfunctioning corporation called the U.S.A."
Comments: _____
_____

Title: _____
Topic: _____
Description: _____
Start Time: _____
Start Cue: _____
End Time: _____
End Cue: _____
Comments: _____
_____

Programming Tip

Song selection: Authenticity

Some Christian songs seem to present Christianity as a life without hardship: "If you trust in Jesus, you will be happy all the time." Or a song might present a difficult issue and then give a trite or overspiritualized response. Be careful to choose songs that portray the Christian life accurately and authentically.

Men's Issues

Message Titles

- *Changing Times:* The Changing American Male
- *Marriage Werks:* When a Man Loves a Woman
- *The "Amazing American" Stereotype:* The Amazing American Husband
- *The "Amazing American" Stereotype:* The Amazing American Male
- **The Benefits of Brotherhood:** Overcoming Independence • Superficial or Significant • The Cost of Commitment • The Rewards of Relationships

_____

_____

Dramas

Title	Tone	Characters	Topics
Any Time?	Mixed, mostly serious	1 male	Making Time for God
Call Waiting	Mixed—ends serious	2 males	Marketplace pressures; Search for significance; Mid-life crisis
Just an Acquaintance	Mixed	2 males, 2 females	Relationships between men; Superficial relationships
Mr. X, Mr. Y, and Mr. Z	Humorous	4 males, 1 female, and a narrator	Friendship; Intimacy
A Real Hero	Humorous	6 males	Manhood; Hero; Christian men
A Real Man	Humorous	4 males, 1 female	The American male; Finding the right man
Regarding Rodney	Humorous	4 males, 1 female	Workaholism; Marriage; Roles of men

Songs

Title	Artist	Style	Tempo	Seeker-Sensitivity Rating
Chippin' Away	*Willow Creek Music*	*Folk pop*	*Mid/up*	*8*
In Christ Alone	**Michael English**	**Power ballad**	**Slow**	**8**
Man of God	*Willow Creek Music*	*Pop/rock*	*Mid/up*	*7*
That's What a Brother Is For	**Michael James**	**Ballad—male duet**	**Slow**	**5**
_____	_____	_____	____	____
_____	_____	_____	____	____
_____	_____	_____	____	____
_____	_____	_____	____	____

 # Movie Clips

Title: _____

Topic: _____

Description: _____

Start Time: _____

Start Cue: _____

End Time: _____

End Cue: _____

Comments: _____

_____

Money Management

Different from **Materialism/Greed** in that it refers more to the way we spend and govern our financial resources

Might also include: *Stewardship*

 ## Message Titles

- [ ] **Your Money Matters:** Determining a Standard of Living • Developing a Financial Plan • Discovering the Rewards of Giving
- [ ] **Financial Freedom:** Earning Money • Managing Money • Giving Money

_____

_____

_____

_____

 ## Dramas

Title	Tone	Characters	Topics
Catalog-itis	Humorous	1 male, 1 female, 2 jr. high age girls	Self-control; Contentment
Check Mates	Humorous	1 male, 1 female	Personal finances; Debt
Confessions of an Ad-aholic	Humorous	1 male, 1 female	Materialism; Power of the media; The American dream
For the Love of Money	Humorous	3 males, 3 females	Money
Lifestyles of the Obscured and Indebted	Humorous	4 males, 3 females	Materialism; Coveting
The Offering	Humorous	3 males, 1 female	Tithing
Oh, What a Feeling!	Humorous	2 males, 1 female	Decision making; Self-control; Money management
_____	_____	_____	_____
_____	_____	_____	_____
_____	_____	_____	_____

Songs

For other songs, look at Commitment to Christ, Discipleship, *and* Obeying God.

Title	Artist	Style	Tempo	Seeker-Sensitivity Rating
Money Is a Powerful Thing	Willow Creek Music	Motown/pop	Up	10

Movie Clips

Title: _____

Topic: _____

Description: _____

Start Time: _____

Start Cue: _____

End Time: _____

End Cue: _____

Comments: _____

_____

Programming Tip

Be sensitive to "moments"

When something moving or inspiring happens on stage, whoever follows it must be sensitive to the "moment." For instance, a speaker who follows a moving song by barreling right into a message, without acknowledging and identifying with what the congregation is feeling, might jolt someone out of a tender moment with God.

Moral Issues

See also: **Sin, Values**

Message Titles

❏ The High Cost of a Cheap Thrill
❏ *Life's Defining Moments:* Defining Our Code of Conduct
❏ *Games We Play:* Scruples
❏ **Returns on Moral Investments:** The Payoff for Sexual Purity • The Reward of Relational Authenticity • The Benefits of Being a Seeker • The Profit of Financial Integrity
❏ **Modern-Day Madness:** The Agony of Escapism • The Pornography Problem • Hope for the Homosexual • Unwanted Pregnancies

_____
_____
_____
_____

> ## Package Suggestion
>
> **Drama:**
> *The Crowd, the Conscience, and Curt*
>
> **Song:**
> *I Could Live Without You*

Dramas

Title	Tone	Characters	Topics
Because I Love You	Serious	1 male, 1 female	Adultery; The consequences of sin
The Big Sell	Humorous	3 males, 2 females	Obsession with sex in society; Effect of the media
The Crowd, the Conscience, and Curt	Serious	2 males, 4 males or females	Broad vs. narrow way; Conscience; Peer pressure
Family Snapshots—Take II	Humorous	2 males, 2 females, 1 jr. high boy	Families; Values; Priorities
Finding Evidence	Serious	2 males, 1 female	Trust; Jumping to conclusions
Horsefeathers and Nosefly	Humorous	2 male or female "helpers"	Christian living; Obedience

Title	Tone	Characters	Topics
It's Only a Movie	Humorous	2 males, 2 females, 1 offstage voice	The power of media; The effects of what we see; Male/female differences
Just Looking	Mixed; light	1 male, 1 female	Eye causing you to stumble; Purity of thoughts
Man of the Year	Serious	5 males, 1 female	Moralism; Our need for Christ
Mere Technicality	Serious	1 male, 1 female	Living together; The cost of taking a stand for Christ
One Step Up, One Step Down	Serious	4 males (1 can be female)	Ambition; Priorities
The Resolve Dissolve	Humorous	2 males, 1 female	Sexuality; Dating
Richard: 1992	Serious	2 males, 1 female	Anger; Rebellion; Decay of the family
_____	_____	_____	_____
_____	_____	_____	_____
_____	_____	_____	_____
_____	_____	_____	_____

 **Songs**

Title	Artist	Style	Tempo	Seeker-Sensitivity Rating
Behind Every Fantasy	_Willow Creek Music_	_Country pop_	_Up_	_10_
Man of God	_Willow Creek Music_	_Pop/rock_	_Mid/up_	_7_
The Narrow Way	Wayne Watson	Pop	Mid	6
There Is a Line	Susan Ashton	Folk pop	Mid	6
Time to Return	_Willow Creek Music_	_Ballad_	_Slow_	_7_
Walk on By	**Susan Ashton**	**Folk pop**	**Mid/up**	**8**
Who Makes the Rules	**Steven Curtis Chapman**	**Pop/folk rock**	**Up**	**7**
Who to Listen To	Amy Grant	Pop	Mid	8
You've Got to Stand for Something	**Aaron Tippin**	**Country**	**Up**	**10**
_____	_____	_____	_____	_____
_____	_____	_____	_____	_____
_____	_____	_____	_____	_____
_____	_____	_____	_____	_____

Movie Clips

Title: City Slickers
Topic: Adultery; Temptation
Description: Billy Crystal's friend asks him if he would cheat on his wife if no one would ever know. His answer shows integrity.
Start Time: 0:44:38
Start Cue: "What if you could have great sex"
End Time: 0:45:30
End Cue: "I wouldn't like myself . . . that's all"
Comments: May be too straightforward for some. Profanity precedes the clip

Title: _____
Topic: _____
Description: _____
Start Time: _____
Start Cue: _____
End Time: _____
End Cue: _____
Comments: _____
_____

Programming Tip

Stepping stones

"Stepping stones are . . . provocative ideas that stimulate us to think about other ideas"—Roger von Oech, _A Whack on the Side of the Head._
Encourage the free flow of ideas, even if some seem impractical. Perhaps an idea will not get used in its original form, but someone may use it as a springboard to try something else that works. Some of our best ideas would not have come without "stepping stones."

Pace of Life/Balance

Might also include: *Hurry* and *Living a Balanced Life*
See also: **Workaholism**

Message Titles

❐ Balance in Your Life
❐ Called or Driven?
❐ The Fourth Commandment: Remember the Sabbath Day
❐ What Drives the Workaholic?
❐ *Ordering Your Private World:* Ordering Your Recreational World
❐ *Signs of the Times:* Reduce Speed
❐ *Three Things That God Loves (That Most People Think He Doesn't):* Leisure

_____

_____

_____

_____

Package Suggestion

Drama:
The Plate Spinner

Song:
I'm in a Hurry

Dramas

Title	Tone	Characters	Topics
Any Time?	Mixed, mostly serious	1 male	Making Time for God
The Brotherhood	Humorous	2 males, 4 either male or female	Workaholism; Balancing your life
Driven	Serious	1 male, 1 female	Workaholism; Marriage
Hank's Handles	Humorous	5 males, 3 females	Pace of life; Time management
An Hour on Wednesday	Mixed— ends serious	1 male, 1 female	Marriage; Damaging effects of a fast-paced life
It's No Picnic	Humorous	3 males, 3 females	Work stress; Surface relationships
Lifetime Deal	Serious	2 males	Workaholism

Title	Tone	Characters	Topics
On Vacation	Humorous	2 males, 1 female, 1 either male or female	Leisure time; Guilt; Slowing down
One Step Up, One Step Down	Serious	4 males (1 can be female)	Ambition; Priorities
One Sunday in the Parking Lot	Humorous	4 males or females	Pace of life; Making changes
The Plate Spinner	Humorous	5 males, 4 female, 1 narrator	Pace of life; Being in control
Quality Time	Serious	1 male, 1 female, 2 teenage girls	Fatherhood; Workaholism
Regarding Rodney	Humorous	4 males, 1 female	Workaholism; Marriage; Roles of men
Richard: 1985	Serious	2 males	Workaholism; Materialism vs. idealism
Tired When Needed	Humorous	1 male, 1 female	Burnout; Boundaries; Saying "no"
Up on the Roof	Mixed	1 male, 1 female	Emotional refueling; Building compassion
Vince Bueller's Day Off	Humorous	1 male, 1 female, 1 boy	Workaholism; Importance of rest/leisure
Winning Strategy	Mixed	2 males, 4 males or females	Good vs. evil; Busyness
_____	_____	_____	_____
_____	_____	_____	_____
_____	_____	_____	_____

Songs

Title	Artist	Style	Tempo	Seeker-Sensitivity Rating
Busy Man	**Steven Curtis Chapman**	**Pop**	**Mid/up**	**10**
Cat's in the Cradle	Harry Chapin; Ugly Kid Joe	Folk	Mid	10
Crisis Mode	*Willow Creek Music*	*Piano ballad*	*Slow*	*9*
I'm in a Hurry (and Don't Know Why)	**Alabama**	**Country pop**	**Up**	**10**
I Need to Stop	*Willow Creek Music*	*Pop*	*Up*	*3*
King of the Jungle	Steven Curtis Chapman	Pop shuffle with African touches	Mid/up	9
Lay It on Down	**Bruce Carroll**	**Country**	**Mid/up**	**8**
On My Knees	*Willow Creek Music*	*Acoustic guitar ballad*	*Slow*	*5*

Title	Artist	Style	Tempo	Seeker-Sensitivity Rating
Only Here for a Little While	Billy Dean	Country	Mid/up	10
Time Out	Clark Sisters	R & B	Up	9
_____	_____	_____	_____	_____
_____	_____	_____	_____	_____
_____	_____	_____	_____	_____
_____	_____	_____	_____	_____

Movie Clips

Title: _____

Topic: _____

Description: _____

Start Time: _____

Start Cue: _____

End Time: _____

End Cue: _____

Comments: _____

_____

Programming Tip

Song selection: Look for a "hook"
In songwriting terms, a "hook" is a melody line or lyric in a song that draws the listeners in and causes them to remember the song. If someone leaves a service humming the hook from a song you played and internalizes the lyric, you have planted your message.

Power

Refers to the desire for power, control
See also: **Control Issues**

 ## Message Titles

- ❏ *Money, Sex and Power:* Power
- ❏ *What Jesus Would Say to . . .* Bill Clinton

_____
_____
_____
_____
_____
_____

 ## Dramas

Title	Tone	Characters	Topics
The Gardeners	Humorous	1 male, 1 female	New Age movement
Lonely at the Top	Serious	1 male	The perils of power, authority; Easter
Wheel of Power	Serious	4 males, 1 female, 1 child	Power

Songs

Title	Artist	Style	Tempo	Seeker-Sensitivity Rating
Audience of One	*Willow Creek Music*	*Power ballad*	*Slow*	*8*
Power of God	Imperials	Pop/rock	Up	5
Strength in You	*Willow Creek Music*	*MOR pop*	*Slow/mid*	*10*
Treasure	**Gary Chapman**	**Acoustic ballad**	**Slow**	**9**
_____	_____	_____	_____	_____
_____	_____	_____	_____	_____
_____	_____	_____	_____	_____
_____	_____	_____	_____	_____

 # Movie Clips

Title: _____

Topic: _____

Description: _____

Start Time: _____

Start Cue: _____

End Time: _____

End Cue: _____

Comments: _____

_____

Regret

See also: **Guilt**

Message Titles

- ❐ Life Without Regret
- ❐ Resolving Regrets
- ❐ *Telling the Truth:* Expressing Positive Emotions

_____
_____
_____
_____
_____

Dramas

Title	Tone	Characters	Topics
The Angry Woman	Serious	2 males, 3 females, 1 narrator	The roots of anger
The Boy Who Never Got Dirty	Humorous	1 male, 1 female, 1 narrator	Service; Risk taking
The Brow Beater	Mixed, mostly serious	1 male, 1 female	Self-esteem; Failures; Forgiveness
A Nice Guy	Serious	2 males	Regret; Admitting failures; Effects of sin; Confession
The Painful Process	Serious	1 female	Abortion
_____	_____	_____	_____
_____	_____	_____	_____
_____	_____	_____	_____
_____	_____	_____	_____

Songs

Title	Artist	Style	Tempo	Seeker-Sensitivity Rating
Cat's in the Cradle	Harry Chapin; Ugly Kid Joe	Folk	Mid	10
If I Had Only Known	**Reba McEntire**	**Ballad**	**Slow**	**10**
The Living Years	Mike & the Mechanics	Pop	Mid/up	10
Mercy for the Memories	**Geoff Moore & the Distance**	**Folk/pop ballad**	**Slow**	**9**
Only Here for a Little While	**Billy Dean**	**Country**	**Mid/up**	**10**
Seize the Day	Carolyn Arends	Folk pop, in 3	Mid	8
_____	_____	_____	_____	_____
_____	_____	_____	_____	_____
_____	_____	_____	_____	_____
_____	_____	_____	_____	_____

 # Movie Clips

Title: 8 Seconds

Topic: Regret; Communicating love

Description: A father, whose son has recently died, breaks down in remorse over not telling his son that he loved him.

Start Time: 1:27:10

Start Cue: Pallbearers carry casket out of church

End Time: 1:28:33

End Cue: "I loved him"

Comments: _____

_____

Title: Dad

Topic: Father/son relationships; Regret for lost time

Description: Ted Danson and Jack Lemmon play a father and son. Lemmon is dying in a hospital bed, and they have a very poignant exchange, ending with Danson crawling into bed with his dad.

Start Time: 1:46:20

Start Cue: "How you feeling?"

End Time: 1:50:35

End Cue: "I must have done something right." End after wide shot

Comments: _____

_____

Title: Rudy

Topic: Quitting; Perseverence

Description: Rudy decides to quit the football team. Fortune, his friend and former boss, challenges him because he used to play for Notre Dame but quit.

Start Time: 1:29:10

Start Cue: Just before "What're you doing here"

End Time: 1:31:20

End Cue: "Do you hear me clear enough?"

Comments: Two potentially objectionable words are used

Title: The Shawshank Redemption

Topic: Regret; Consequences of sin

Description: Red, a 40-year inmate, stands before the parole board and talks about his regret over his lost years.

Start Time: 2:05:30

Start Cue: Bars slide open, door opens to parole board room

End Time: 2:07:32

End Cue: Stop immediately after "I gotta live with that"

Comments: _____

Title: _____

Topic: _____

Description: _____

Start Time: _____

Start Cue: _____

End Time: _____

End Cue: _____

Comments: _____

Risk Taking

Might also include: *Apathy*
See also: **Fear**

Message Titles

- ❏ Opportunity Knocks
- ❏ Seizing Spiritual Opportunities
- ❏ The Rewards of Spiritual Risk Taking
- ❏ *Games We Play:* Risk

_____
_____
_____
_____

Package Suggestion

Drama:
The Comfort Zone

Song:
Seize the Day

Dramas

Title	Tone	Characters	Topics
The Boy Who Never Got Dirty	Humorous	1 male, 1 female, 1 narrator	Service; Risk taking
The Comfort Zone	Humorous	1 male, 2 females (1 TV announcer on tape)	Risk taking
Conversations	Serious	2 male, 1 female, 1 offstage female voice	Self-esteem; Self-criticism; Failure
The Eggshell Family	Humorous	2 males, 1 female, 1 either male or female	Decision making

Title	Tone	Characters	Topics
The Eggshells Break Out	Humorous	3 males, 1 female	Risk taking; Facing challenges
Mr. X, Mr. Y, and Mr. Z	Humorous	4 males, 1 female, a narrator	Friendship; Intimacy
The Speculators	Humorous	2 males, 1 female	Risk taking; Missed opportunities
Straight-Jacketed	Serious	1 male	Bondage to past and to sin; Anger toward God
Ya, But . . .	Humorous	3 males, 2 females	Doubt; Physical fitness; Fear of change
_____	_____	_____	_____
_____	_____	_____	_____
_____	_____	_____	_____
_____	_____	_____	_____
_____	_____	_____	_____

 # Songs

Title	Artist	Style	Tempo	Seeker-Sensitivity Rating
Be the One	**Al Denson**	**Power ballad**	**Slow**	7
Desperado	Eagles	Ballad	Slow	10
Every Step I Take	**Bob Carlisle**	**Bluesy pop**	**Mid**	**9**
For the Sake of the Call	Steven Curtis Chapman	Anthemic pop	Up	3
One Step at a Time	First Call	Pop vocal group	Up	8
Seize the Day	Carolyn Arends	Folk pop, in 3	Mid	8
Take My Hand	**The Kry**	**Acoustic ballad**	**Mid/slow**	**9**
_____	_____	_____	_____	_____
_____	_____	_____	_____	_____
_____	_____	_____	_____	_____
_____	_____	_____	_____	_____
_____	_____	_____	_____	_____

Movie Clips

Title: Dead Poet's Society
Topic: Risk taking
Description: Robin Williams plays a teacher who encourages his students to "seize the day."
Start Time: 0:13:42
Start Cue: Student reads "Gather ye rosebuds while ye may"
End Time: 0:16:25
End Cue: "Make your lives extraordinary"
Comments: _____
_____

Title: _____
Topic: _____
Description: _____
Start Time: _____
Start Cue: _____
End Time: _____
End Cue: _____
Comments: _____
_____

Programming Tip

Song selection: Is it compelling?
Look for songs that have a clear focus, that accomplish their purpose in a way that moves the congregation and compels it to respond. Some songs don't seem to know what they are trying to say—they meander, or they try to say too much in three or four minutes. Ask yourself these questions: Can I grasp the main point of the song? Does it bring something important to my life? Would I crawl out of bed on a Sunday morning just to hear this song?

Selfishness/Pride

Selfishness and pride are somewhat different, but arise from the same issue—being centered on ourselves.

Might also include: *Humility*

See also: **Lordship of Christ, Obeying God**

 Message Titles

❐ The Altar of Ego
❐ An Audience of One
❐ The Blessedness of Brokenness
❐ A Check-up From the Neck Up
❐ *Christianity's Toughest Competition:* Individualism
❐ *Understanding the Times:* The '80s

_____
_____
_____
_____
_____

 Dramas

Title	Tone	Characters	Topics
Am I Missing Something?	Serious	3 males, 2 females	Attitudes in serving; Giving; Self-deception; Rationalizing
Any Time?	Mixed, mostly serious	1 male	Making Time for God
Credit Due	Mixed	2 males, 2 females, 2 children's voices offstage	When others use you

Title	Tone	Characters	Topics
You Cramp My Style	Serious	1 male, 1 female, 1 either male or female	Reasons people don't believe; Society's view of God

_____

_____

_____

Songs

Title	Artist	Style	Tempo	Seeker-Sensitivity Rating
Altar of Ego	Carolyn Arends	Folk/pop	Mid/up	6
Audience of One	*Willow Creek Music*	*Power ballad*	*Slow*	*8*
Call of the Wild	Susan Ashton	Country	Mid	10
Chippin' Away	*Willow Creek Music*	*Folk pop*	*Mid/up*	*8*
Down on My Knees	Susan Ashton	Folk rock	Mid/up	6
Ever Devoted	*Willow Creek Music*	*Ballad*	*Slow*	*6*
If That's What It Takes	*Willow Creek Music*	*Pop/MOR*	*Mid/slow*	*5*
In Christ Alone	**Michael English**	**Power ballad**	**Slow**	**8**
Miracle of Mercy	**Steven Curtis Chapman**	**Acoustic ballad**	**Slow**	**4**
Strength in You	*Willow Creek Music*	*MOR pop*	*Slow/mid*	*10*

_____

_____

_____

Movie Clips

Title: _____

Topic: _____

Description: _____

Start Time: _____

Start Cue: _____

End Time: _____

End Cue: _____

Comments: _____

_____

Values

Refers specifically to what we believe and what is important to us—what we value
See also: **Moral Issues**

Message Titles

- ☐ The Upside-Down Priorities
- ☐ *Life's Defining Moments:* Defining Our Beliefs
- ☐ **Defining Family Values:** Origin of Values • Transmitting Values • Endangered Values

Package Suggestion

Drama:
Richard: 1992

Song:
Time to Return

_____

Dramas

Title	Tone	Characters	Topics
The Big Sell	Humorous	3 males, 2 females	Obsession with sex in society; Effect of the media
Driven	Serious	1 male, 1 female	Workaholism; Marriage
Family Snapshots–Take II	Humorous	2 males, 2 females, 1 jr. high boy	Families; Values; Priorities
Getting the Nod	Mixed	2 males, 1 either male or female	Honesty; Integrity; Business ethics; Handling failure
Guidance Counselors	Humorous	2 males, 1 female	The power of TV; Sources for values
It's Only a Movie	Humorous	2 males, 2 females, 1 offstage voice	The power of media; The effects of what we see; Male/female differences
Just Looking	Mixed; light	1 male, 1 female	Eye causing you to stumble; Purity of thoughts
The Lamaze Class	Humorous	3 males, 4 females	Sources for values; Parenting

Title	Tone	Characters	Topics
Mere Technicality	Serious	1 male, 1 female	Living together; The cost of taking a stand for Christ
Richard: 1968	Mixed	2 males, 2 females	Youthful idealism; Changing societal values; Generation gap; The '60s
Richard: 1992	Serious	2 males, 1 female	Anger; Rebellion; Decay of the family
The Right Thing	Serious	1 male	Costly obedience; Christian character; Persecution
___	___	___	___
___	___	___	___
___	___	___	___

Songs

Title	Artist	Style	Tempo	Seeker-Sensitivity Rating
Man of God	*Willow Creek Music*	*Pop/rock*	*Mid/up*	7
There Is a Line	Susan Ashton	Folk pop	Mid	6
Time to Return	*Willow Creek Music*	*Ballad*	*Slow*	7
Who Makes the Rules	**Steven Curtis Chapman**	**Pop/folk rock**	**Up**	**7**
Who to Listen To	Amy Grant	Pop	Mid	8
You've Got to Stand for Something	**Aaron Tippin**	**Country**	**Up**	**10**
___	___	___	___	___
___	___	___	___	___
___	___	___	___	___

Movie Clips

Title: _____

Topic: _____

Description: _____

Start Time: _____

Start Cue: _____

End Time: _____

End Cue: _____

Comments: _____

_____

Women's Issues

See also: **Mother's Day**

 ## Message Titles

- ☐ *The Amazing American Stereotype:* The Amazing American Female
- ☐ *The Amazing American Stereotype:* The Amazing American Wife
- ☐ *Changing Times:* The Changing American Female
- ☐ *Fanning the Flames of Marriage:* Wisdom for Wives
- ☐ *Marriagewerks:* Loving a Man Without Losing Yourself
- ☐ *Taking Care of Business:* How Much Should Mothers Work?

_____

_____

_____

_____

_____

 ## Dramas

Title	Tone	Characters	Topics
Watching From the Window	Serious	1 female, 1 child	Stress of life; Challenge of motherhood; Draining relationships

Songs

Title	Artist	Style	Tempo	Seeker-Sensitivity Rating
Charm Is Deceitful	Kim Hill	Ballad	Slow	5
_____	_____	_____	_____	_____
_____	_____	_____	_____	_____
_____	_____	_____	_____	_____
_____	_____	_____	_____	_____

Movie Clips

Title: _____

Topic: _____

Description: _____

Start Time: _____

Start Cue: _____

End Time: _____

End Cue: _____

Comments: _____

_____

Work Issues
~ Marketplace Pressures ~

Might also include: *Christians in the Marketplace*

Message Titles

- ❏ Christians in the Marketplace
- ❏ A Day in the Life of a Christian
- ❏ Keeping Your Head Up When Your Job Gets You Down

_____

_____

_____

_____

Dramas

Title	Tone	Characters	Topics
A Day in the Life	Humorous	5 males	Christians in the marketplace; New Christian
An Hour on Wednesday	Mixed— ends serious	1 male, 1 female	Marriage; Damaging effects of a fast-paced life
Call Waiting	Mixed— ends serious	2 males	Marketplace pressures; Search for significance; Mid-life crisis
Driven	Serious	1 male, 1 female	Workaholism; Marriage
First-Day Jitters	Humorous	1 female	New Christian; Christians in the marketplace
It's No Picnic	Humorous	3 males, 3 females	Work stress; Surface relationships

Title	Tone	Characters	Topics
The Plate Spinner	Humorous	5 males, 4 females, 1 narrator	Pace of life; Being in control
Tired When Needed	Humorous	1 male, 1 female	Burnout; Boundaries; Saying "no"
Up on the Roof	Mixed	1 male, 1 female	Emotional refueling; Building compassion
___	___	___	___
___	___	___	___
___	___	___	___

 # Songs

Title	Artist	Style	Tempo	Seeker-Sensitivity Rating
I'm in a Hurry (and Don't Know Why)	**Alabama**	**Country pop**	**Up**	**10**
King of the Jungle	Steven Curtis Chapman	Pop shuffle with African touches	Mid/up	9
On My Knees	*Willow Creek Music*	*Acoustic guitar ballad*	*Slow*	5
___	___	___	___	___
___	___	___	___	___
___	___	___	___	___
___	___	___	___	___

 # Movie Clips

Title: _____

Topic: _____

Description: _____

Start Time: _____

Start Cue: _____

End Time: _____

End Cue: _____

Comments: _____

~ Success ~

Might also include: *Ambition, Fame*
See also: **Fulfillment**

 ## Message Titles

- ❏ Achievement's Shadow
- ❏ Essential Ingredients for Successful Living
- ❏ *Life's Defining Moments:* Defining Our Personal Aspirations
- ❏ *Taking Care of Business:* Called or Driven?
- ❏ *Understanding the Times:* The '80s
- ❏ *What Jesus Would Say to . . .* Bill Gates
- ❏ *What Jesus Would Say to . . .* Michael Jordan

_____

_____

_____

_____

_____

 ## Dramas

Title	Tone	Characters	Topics
Be Like Mike	Humorous	4 males, 2 females (actors play multiple roles)	Fame; Pressures of success
Driven	Serious	1 male, 1 female	Workaholism; Marriage
Lifetime Deal	Serious	2 males	Workaholism
Lizzie and Leroy	Humorous	1 male, 1 female, piano player (optional)	Life fulfillment; Material things don't satisfy
The Mirror Thought of It	Mixed	1 male, 1 female, 1 offstage voice	Materialism; Workaholism; Striving for more

Title	Tone	Characters	Topics
One Step Up, One Step Down	Serious	4 males (1 can be female)	Ambition; Priorities

Songs

Title	Artist	Style	Tempo	Seeker-Sensitivity Rating
Audience of One	*Willow Creek Music*	*Power ballad*	*Slow*	*8*
Busy Man	**Steven Curtis Chapman**	**Pop**	**Mid/up**	**10**
Ever Devoted	*Willow Creek Music*	*Ballad*	*Slow*	*6*
In Christ Alone	**Michael English**	**Power ballad**	**Slow**	**8**
More to This Life	Steven Curtis Chapman	MOR pop	Mid/up	9
Something to Hold on To	Truth	R & B/pop	Mid	10
Strength in You	*Willow Creek Music*	*MOR pop*	*Slow/mid*	*10*
Treasure	**Gary Chapman**	**Acoustic ballad**	**Slow**	**9**
Who Makes the Rules	**Steven Curtis Chapman**	**Pop/folk rock**	**Up**	**7**

Movie Clips

Title:	Cool Runnings
Topic:	Success; Ambition
Description:	A bobsledder asks his coach why he cheated 20 years ago in the Olympics. The answer speaks about the trap of success and its ultimate lack of fulfillment.
Start Time:	1:25:15
Start Cue:	Coach enters hotel room
End Time:	1:27:15
End Cue:	"When you cross that finish line, you'll know"
Comments:	

Title:	Searching for Bobby Fischer
Topic:	Success; Fear of failure
Description:	Josh Waitzkin, a chess prodigy, has a late-night talk with his dad about the possibility of losing. Shows the pressure of staying on top.
Start Time:	1:01:30
Start Cue:	Josh's dad is reading him a story
End Time:	1:03:
End Cue:	"Maybe it's better not to be the best. Then you can lose and it's okay"
Comments:	_____
	_____

Title:	Searching for Bobby Fischer
Topic:	Fatherhood; Failure; Destructive parenting
Description:	Eight-year-old Josh loses a chess match, and his dad angrily confronts him about losing. Illustrates a man who has invested too much in his son's success.
Start Time:	1:06:30
Start Cue:	Shot of clock tower. "Seven moves" is first line
End Time:	1:08:20
End Cue:	"Sorry"
Comments:	_____
	_____

Title:	She's Having a Baby
Topic:	Life in suburbia; Emptiness of suburban life/American dream
Description:	Funny parody of suburban life shows men in bad clothes dancing with lawnmowers, and their wives dancing around them with refreshments.
Start Time:	0:53:00
Start Cue:	Start after the bicyclist leaves
End Time:	0:54:30
End Cue:	End when music stops
Comments:	_____
	_____

Title:	_____
Topic:	_____
Description:	_____
Start Time:	_____
Start Cue:	_____
End Time:	_____
End Cue:	_____
Comments:	_____
	_____

~ Work/Marketplace Issues ~

A general category. For more specific topics, see: **Leadership, Marketplace Pressures, Success, Workaholism**

Might also include: *Labor Day*

 Message Titles

- ❏ Achievement's Shadow
- ❏ Four Advantages Christians Have at Work
- ❏ Keeping Your Head Up When Your Job Gets You Down
- ❏ Your Work Matters to God
- ❏ **Christians in the Workplace:** The Value of Human Labor • The Secret of Job Satisfaction • Missionaries in the Marketplace • Women in the Workplace • Profits or People • Please Pass the Paycheck
- ❏ **Taking Care of Business:** The Rewards of Human Labor • Keys to Job Satisfaction • How Much Should Mothers Work? • What Drives the Workaholic? • The Character Crisis • Called or Driven?

_____

_____

_____

_____

 Dramas

Title	Tone	Characters	Topics
The Brotherhood	Humorous	2 males, 4 either male or female	Workaholism; Balancing your life
Call Waiting	Mixed— ends serious	2 males	Marketplace pressures; Search for significance; Mid-life crisis
Credit Due	Mixed	2 males, 2 females, two children's voices offstage	When others use you
A Day in the Life	Humorous	5 males	Christians in the marketplace; New Christian

Title	Tone	Characters	Topics
Don't Mention It	Mixed, mostly humorous	2 males, 2 females	Unemployment; Being open about problems
Driven	Serious	1 male, 1 female	Workaholism; Marriage
Getting the Nod	Mixed	2 males, 1 either male or female	Honesty; Integrity; Business ethics; Handling failure
An Hour on Wednesday	Mixed— ends serious	1 male, 1 female	Marriage; Damaging effects of a fast-paced life
It's No Picnic	Humorous	3 males, 3 females	Work stress; Surface relationships
Lifetime Deal	Serious	2 males	Workaholism
One Step Up, One Step Down	Serious	4 males (1 can be female)	Ambition; Priorities
One Sunday in the Parking Lot	Humorous	4 males or females	Pace of life; Making changes
Parlor Talk	Mixed	3 males, 2 females	Making a difference with your life; Death; Workaholism
Quality Time	Serious	1 male, 1 female, 2 teenage girls	Fatherhood; Workaholism
Regarding Rodney	Humorous	4 males, 1 female	Workaholism; Marriage; Roles of men
Richard: 1985	Serious	2 males	Workaholism; Materialism vs. idealism
The Right Niche	Humorous	2 males, 1 female	Job satisfaction; Finding your niche
Shop Talk	Serious	2 males, 2 females	Failure; Adversity; Small groups
Tired When Needed	Humorous	1 male, 1 female	Burnout; Boundaries; Saying "no"
Up on the Roof	Mixed	1 male, 1 female	Emotional refueling; Building compassion
Wasted	Mixed	2 males	Job satisfaction; Christians and work
_____	_____	_____	_____
_____	_____	_____	_____
_____	_____	_____	_____

 **Songs**

Title	Artist	Style	Tempo	Seeker-Sensitivity Rating
Audience of One	*Willow Creek Music*	*Power ballad*	*Slow*	*8*
Build My World Around You	**Sandi Patty**	**Pop**	**Up**	9
Busy Man	**Steven Curtis Chapman**	**Pop**	**Mid/up**	10

Title	Artist	Style	Tempo	Seeker-Sensitivity Rating
Cat's in the Cradle	Harry Chapin; Ugly Kid Joe	Folk	Mid	10
I'm in a Hurry (and Don't Know Why)	**Alabama**	**Country pop**	**Up**	**10**
King of the Jungle	Steven Curtis Chapman	Pop shuffle with African touches	Mid/up	9
Lay It on Down	**Bruce Carroll**	**Country**	**Mid/up**	**8**
Only Here for a Little While	**Billy Dean**	**Country**	**Mid/up**	**10**
Only You	*Willow Creek Music*	*Ballad*	*Slow*	*9*
Something to Hold on To	Truth	R & B/pop	Mid	10
Strength in You	*Willow Creek Music*	*MOR pop*	*Slow/mid*	*10*
Time Out	Clark Sisters	R & B	Up	9
Treasure	**Gary Chapman**	**Acoustic ballad**	**Slow**	**9**
_____	_____	_____	_____	_____
_____	_____	_____	_____	_____
_____	_____	_____	_____	_____
_____	_____	_____	_____	_____

Movie Clips

Title: Chariots of Fire
Topic: Being true to whom God made you; Honoring God with your gifts
Description: Eric Liddell talks to his sister, who wants him to forsake running to be a missionary. Eric responds that God made him fast, and when he runs, he can feel God's pleasure.
Start Time: 0:58:20
Start Cue: First line is "I've decided . . . I'm going back to China"
End Time: 0:59:15
End Cue: "To win is to honor him"
Comments: _____

Title: Cool Runnings
Topic: Success; Ambition
Description: A bobsledder asks his coach why he cheated 20 years ago in the Olympics. The answer speaks about the trap of success and its ultimate lack of fulfillment.
Start Time: 1:25:15
Start Cue: Coach enters hotel room
End Time: 1:27:15
End Cue: "When you cross that finish line, you'll know"
Comments: _____

Title: _____

Topic: _____

Description: _____

Start Time: _____

Start Cue: _____

End Time: _____

End Cue: _____

Comments: _____

_____

~ Workaholism ~

Different from **Pace of Life** in that it deals specifically with work

 Message Titles

- ❐ Balance in Your Life
- ❐ It All Goes Back Into the Box
- ❐ Profession or Obsession
- ❐ *Signs of the Times:* Reduce Speed
- ❐ *Taking Care of Business:* What Drives the Workaholic?
- ❐ *What Jesus Would Say to . . .* Bill Gates

_____

_____

_____

 Dramas

Title	Tone	Characters	Topics
An Hour on Wednesday	Mixed— ends serious	1 male, 1 female	Marriage; Damaging effects of a fast-paced life
The Brotherhood	Humorous	2 males, 4 either male or female	Workaholism; Balancing your life

Title	Tone	Characters	Topics
Driven	Serious	1 male, 1 female	Workaholism; Marriage
It's No Picnic	Humorous	3 males, 3 females	Work stress; Surface relationships
Lifetime Deal	Serious	2 males	Workaholism
The Mirror Thought of It	Mixed	1 male, 1 female, 1 offstage voice	Materialism; Workaholism; Striving for more
One Step Up, One Step Down	Serious	4 males (1 can be female)	Ambition; Priorities
One Sunday in the Parking Lot	Humorous	4 males or females	Pace of life; Making changes
Parlor Talk	Mixed	3 males, 2 females	Making a difference with your life; Death; Workaholism
Quality Time	Serious	1 male, 1 female, 2 teenage girls	Fatherhood; Workaholism
Regarding Rodney	Humorous	4 males, 1 female	Workaholism; Marriage; Roles of men
Richard: 1985	Serious	2 males	Workaholism; Materialism vs. idealism
Vince Bueller's Day Off	Humorous	1 male, 1 female, 1 boy	Workaholism; Importance of rest/leisure
_____	_____	_____	_____
_____	_____	_____	_____
_____	_____	_____	_____
_____	_____	_____	_____

 # Songs

Title	Artist	Style	Tempo	Seeker-Sensitivity Rating
Busy Man	**Steven Curtis Chapman**	**Pop**	**Mid/up**	**10**
Cat's in the Cradle	Harry Chapin; Ugly Kid Joe	Folk	Mid	10
Crisis Mode	*Willow Creek Music*	*Piano ballad*	*Slow*	9
I'm in a Hurry (and Don't Know Why)	**Alabama**	**Country pop**	**Up**	**10**
King of the Jungle	Steven Curtis Chapman	Pop shuffle with African touches	Mid/up	9
Lay It on Down	**Bruce Carroll**	**Country**	**Mid/up**	**8**
Only Here for a Little While	**Billy Dean**	**Country**	**Mid/up**	**10**
Something to Hold on To	Truth	R & B/pop	Mid	10

Title	Artist	Style	Tempo	Seeker-Sensitivity Rating
Strength in You	*Willow Creek Music*	*MOR pop*	*Slow/mid*	*10*
Time Out	Clark Sisters	R & B	Up	9
_____	_____	_____	_____	_____
_____	_____	_____	_____	_____
_____	_____	_____	_____	_____
_____	_____	_____	_____	_____

 # Movie Clips

Title: _____

Topic: _____

Description: _____

Start Time: _____

Start Cue: _____

End Time: _____

End Cue: _____

Comments: _____

_____

Programming Tip

Song selection: Songs only a musician could love
Beware of choosing songs that require a musician's ear and mind-set to appreciate. Remember that the audience is composed primarily of non-musicians. This does not mean that you have to play bland, uninteresting songs, but put the listeners first and the performers second when choosing the music.

RELATIONSHIP WITH GOD

Anger Toward God

Message Titles

- ☐ Why Did This Happen to Me?
- ☐ When I'm Mad at God
- ☐ *The Power of Prayer:* The Mystery of Unanswered Prayer
- ☐ **Disappointment With God:** What Causes Disappointment? • Where Is God When You Need Him? • When God Seems Silent

_____

_____

_____

_____

Dramas

Title	Tone	Characters	Topics
Another Day at the Bus Stop	Mixed	1 male, 1 female	Our relationship with God; Self-esteem
Great Expectations	Mixed—ends very serious	1 male, 2 females	Unanswered prayer
Straight-Jacketed	Serious	1 male	Bondage to past and to sin; Anger toward God
___	___	___	___
___	___	___	___
___	___	___	___
___	___	___	___

Songs

See also God's Love, God's Wisdom

Title	Artist	Style	Tempo	Seeker-Sensitivity Rating
Honesty	Margaret Becker	Power ballad	Slow	9

Movie Clips

Title:	Shadowlands
Topic:	Suffering; Pain; Why does God allow bad things to happen?
Description:	C. S. Lewis delivers a speech about why God allows suffering.
Start Time:	0:10:00
Start Cue:	"Yesterday I received a letter"
End Time:	0:11:40
End Cue:	"Thank you very much"
Comments:	Last line is a bit hard to understand

Title: _____

Topic: _____

Description: _____

Start Time: _____

Start Cue: _____

End Time: _____

End Cue: _____

Comments: _____

Changed Life

Message Titles

- ❏ *Faith Has Its Reasons:* Reasons for Believing in Jesus Christ
- ❏ *God's Outrageous Claims:* Unleashing Our Potential
- ❏ *Seven Wonders of the Spiritual World:* God Transforms Me

_____

_____

_____

_____

Dramas

Title	Tone	Characters	Topics
Counting the Cost	Serious	2 males, 2 females	Commitment to Christ; Sacrifice; Spiritual maturity
First-Day Jitters	Humorous	1 female	New Christian; Obeying God
It's a New Year . . . Again	Humorous	2 males, 1 female	New Year's; Growth/change is difficult
The Lane of Life	Serious; mime	5 either male or female, 1 offstage narrator	Salvation; Our value to God; Self-esteem
Measuring Up	Mixed; mime	2 males, 1 female, 1 other male or female	God's acceptance of us; Self-esteem
Sitters, Strivers, Standers, and Saints	Mixed	4 either male or female, 1 narrator	God changing lives; God completing us
Take Heart	Mixed; mime	2 males, 2 females	God heals the brokenhearted; Disappointment
"X" Marks the Spot	Serious; mime	1 female, 1 male, 3 other females or males	Sin; Redemption; Forgiveness; Guilt

_____ _____ _____ _____

_____ _____ _____ _____

_____ _____ _____ _____

Songs

Title	Artist	Style	Tempo	Seeker-Sensitivity Rating
Change in My Life	**John Pagano**	**Gospel**	**Mid/up**	**9**
Changin'	Acapella Vocal Band	Acapella vocal group	Up	8
Chippin' Away	*Willow Creek Music*	*Folk pop*	*Mid/up*	8
Come Into My Life	Imperials	Power ballad	Slow	10
Cross Medley	*Willow Creek Music*	*Ballad medley— hymns*	*Slow*	7
I Found Myself in You	**Clay Crosse**	**Gospel ballad**	**Mid/slow**	**10**
I'm Amazed	*Willow Creek Music*	*Ballad*	*Slow*	7
I've Been Released	*Willow Creek Music*	*Pop/rock— Chicago sound*	*Up*	9
Love That Will Not Let Me Go	**Steve Camp**	**Ballad**	**Slow**	**10**
Mind, Body, Heart and Soul	**Bob Carlisle**	**Pop/rock**	**Up**	**9**
Only by Grace	*Willow Creek Music*	*Pop/rock*	*Mid*	10
Original Love	Imperials	Pop	Up	9
Remember Your Chains	Steven Curtis Chapman	Acoustic MOR	Mid	2
There Is a Love	**Michael English**	**Pop**	**Up**	**9**
This Is the Life	**Phillips, Craig and Dean**	**Pop/rock**	**Up**	**6**
Want the World to Know	*Willow Creek Music*	*Pop*	*Up*	9
What a Ride	*Willow Creek Music*	*Pop/rock*	*Up*	9
Why Me	*Willow Creek Music*	*Ballad*	*Slow*	9
_____	_____	_____	_____	_____
_____	_____	_____	_____	_____
_____	_____	_____	_____	_____

Movie Clips

Title: _____

Topic: _____

Description: _____

Start Time: _____

Start Cue: _____

End Time: _____

End Cue: _____

Comments: _____

_____

Commitment to Christ

Refers not to the point of salvation, but to a believer's covenant to serve and walk with Christ
See also: **Being Salt and Light**

 ## Message Titles

- ☐ Be There!
- ☐ Cosmetic Christianity
- ☐ Redefining Commitment
- ☐ Unmasking Your Master
- ☐ *Seasons of the Spiritual Life:* Spiritual Adulthood

_____

_____

_____

_____

 ## Dramas

Title	Tone	Characters	Topics
Counting the Cost	Serious	2 males, 2 females	Commitment to Christ; Sacrifice; Spiritual maturity
Impressions, Inc.	Humorous	2 males, 1 female	Skin-deep Christianity
Mere Technicality	Serious	1 male, 1 female	Living together; The cost of taking a stand for Christ
The Right Thing	Serious	1 male	Costly obedience; Christian character; Persecution
Unaverage Joe	Mixed	2 males, 1 female	Christmas; Obeying God's call

Songs

Many of these songs work well in response to topics such as Hypocrisy and Sin.

Title	Artist	Style	Tempo	Seeker-Sensitivity Rating
All I Ever Wanted	Margaret Becker	Pop/rock ballad	Slow/mid	4
Be the One	**Al Denson**	**Power ballad**	**Slow**	7
Build My World Around You	**Sandi Patty**	**Pop**	**Up**	9
Casual Christian	**De Garmo & Key**	**Power ballad**	**Slow**	6
Ever Devoted	*Willow Creek Music*	*Ballad*	*Slow*	6
Facts Are Facts	Steven Curtis Chapman	Rock/pop	Up	4
For the Sake of the Call	Steven Curtis Chapman	Anthemic pop	Up	3
From Here on Out	*Willow Creek Music*	*MOR pop*	*Mid*	8
Heart's Cry	**Steven Curtis Chapman**	**Acoustic ballad**	**Mid/slow**	7
I Am Determined	Tim Shepherd	Inspirational ballad	Slow	2
I Choose to Follow	**Al Denson**	**Ballad**	**Slow**	5
If That's What It Takes	*Willow Creek Music*	*Pop/MOR*	*Mid/slow*	5
I'll Be Believing	**Point of Grace**	**Pop vocal group**	**Up**	9
In Christ Alone	**Michael English**	**Power ballad**	**Slow**	8
Keep the Flame Burning	Debby Boone	MOR	Mid	5
Let's Stand Together	**The Kry**	**Rock**	**Mid/up**	1
Look Me in the Eye	Margaret Becker	Pop ballad	Slow/mid	3
Lord, I Want to Be Like Jesus	**Fernando Ortega**	**Ballad**	**Slow**	3
Love You With My Life	Steven Curtis Chapman	Pop	Up	5
Man of God	*Willow Creek Music*	*Pop/rock*	*Mid/up*	7
Mind, Body, Heart and Soul	**Bob Carlisle**	**Pop/rock**	**Up**	9
My Life Is In Your Hands	**Kathy Troccoli**	**Ballad**	**Slow**	9
My Soul Desire	Deniece Williams	R & B ballad	Slow	5
My Turn Now	Steven Curtis Chapman	Country bop	Up	6
The Narrow Way	Wayne Watson	Pop	Mid	6
No Better Place	Steven Curtis Chapman	Pop/folk rock	Up	7
Only You	*Willow Creek Music*	*Ballad*	*Slow*	9
Show Yourselves to Be	Steven Curtis Chapman	Acoustic ballad	Slow/mid	4
Solid as the Rock	**Michael English**	**Pop**	**Up**	8
There Is a Line	Susan Ashton	Folk pop	Mid	6
This Is the Life	**Phillips, Craig and Dean**	**Pop/rock**	**Up**	6
Treasure	**Gary Chapman**	**Acoustic ballad**	**Slow**	9
True Devotion	Margaret Becker	R & B/pop	Up	6
Want the World to Know	*Willow Creek Music*	*Pop*	*Up*	9

Title	Artist	Style	Tempo	Seeker-Sensitivity Rating
Whatever You Ask	Steve Camp	Power ballad	Slow	5
With All my Heart	Babbie Mason	Ballad	Slow	6

 # Movie Clips

Title: Chariots of Fire
Topic: Integrity; Standing up for what you believe in; The Sabbath
Description: Eric Liddell refuses to run on the Sabbath. The English Olympic Committee tries to make him compromise, but he stands firm.
Start Time: 1:28:15
Start Cue: "We decided to invite you in for a little chat"
End Time: 1:30:00
End Cue: "But I can't make that sacrifice"
Comments: _____
_____

Title: _____
Topic: _____
Description: _____
Start Time: _____
Start Cue: _____
End Time: _____
End Cue: _____
Comments: _____
_____

Confession

Might also include: *Conviction of Sin*
See also: **Communion, Sin**

 ## Message Titles

- ❑ *Do You Have What It Takes to Grow?:* Tell Somebody
- ❑ *Games We Play:* Sorry
- ❑ *The "S" Word:* Sin in a No-Fault Society

_____
_____
_____
_____
_____

 ## Dramas

Title	Tone	Characters	Topics
Go Away God	Humorous	2 males, 1 female	Conscience; Guilt; Hearing God's voice
A Nice Guy	Serious	2 males	Regret; Admitting failures; Effects of sin; Confession

Songs

Title	Artist	Style	Tempo	Seeker-Sensitivity Rating
At Jesus' Feet	**Billy & Sarah Gaines**	**Ballad**	Slow	6
The Dilemma	Sandi Patti	Pop	Up	6
Forgive Me	Tim Miner	Ballad	Slow	4
I Stand, I Fall	*Willow Creek Music*	*Piano ballad*	*Slow*	7
Just Come In	Margaret Becker	Pop ballad	Slow	5
Miracle of Mercy	**Steven Curtis Chapman**	**Acoustic ballad**	**Slow**	4
Most of the Time	Glad	Piano ballad	Slow	4
_____	_____	_____	_____	_____
_____	_____	_____	_____	_____
_____	_____	_____	_____	_____
_____	_____	_____	_____	_____

 Movie Clips

Title: _____

Topic: _____

Description: _____

Start Time: _____

Start Cue: _____

End Time: _____

End Cue: _____

Comments: _____

_____

Discipleship

Refers to a person committed to *following* Christ
See also: **Obeying God**

Package Suggestion

Drama:
Counting the Cost

Song:
I Choose to Follow

Message Titles

- ☐ Difference Makers
- ☐ How Do You Recognize a Disciple?
- ☐ How to Be Strong When It Counts
- ☐ The Marks of a Mature Christian
- ☐ Ordinary Folks Make Great Disciples
- ☐ *Developing a Daring Faith:* Following God
- ☐ *Seasons of a Spiritual Life:* Spiritual Adulthood

_____

_____

_____

Dramas

Title	Tone	Characters	Topics
Counting the Cost	Serious	2 males, 2 females	Commitment to Christ; Sacrifice; Spiritual maturity
First-Day Jitters	Humorous	1 female	New Christian; Obeying God
I Don't Want to Fight You Anymore	Serious	1 female	Relationship with God; Giving up control; Our value to God
Monday Night Meeting	Humorous	4 males	New Christian; Joy of Christian life; Discipleship
The Mystery of Robert Richardson	Mixed	3 males, 2 females, 1 narrator	Living the Christian life

Title	Tone	Characters	Topics
One Sunday in the Parking Lot	Humorous	4 males or females	Pace of life; Making changes
Quiet Time?	Humorous	1 female	Prayer
A Real Hero	Humorous	6 males	Manhood; Hero; Christian men
The Right Thing	Serious	1 male	Costly obedience; Christian character; Persecution
Seeing Is Believing	Humorous	1 male, 1 female, 1 narrator	A Savior you can trust; Easy faith
Sweet Hour of Prayer	Humorous	2 males, 1 female	Prayer; Hypocrisy; Faith
Unaverage Joe	Mixed	2 males, 1 female	Christmas; Obeying God's call
_____	_____	_____	_____
_____	_____	_____	_____
_____	_____	_____	_____
_____	_____	_____	_____

 # Songs

Title	Artist	Style	Tempo	Seeker-Sensitivity Rating
All I Ever Wanted	Margaret Becker	Pop/rock ballad	Slow/mid	4
Build My World Around You	**Sandi Patty**	**Pop**	**Up**	**9**
Casual Christian	**De Garmo & Key**	**Power ballad**	**Slow**	**6**
Changin'	Acapella Vocal Band	Acapella vocal group	Up	8
Fill Me, Lord	DeGarmo & Key	Ballad	Slow	2
For the Sake of the Call	Steven Curtis Chapman	Anthemic pop	Up	3
The Great Adventure	Steven Curtis Chapman	Pop/rock	Up	5
Hunger and Thirst	Susan Ashton	Folk pop	Mid/up	6
I Am Determined	Tim Shepherd	Inspirational ballad	Slow	2
I Choose to Follow	**Al Denson**	**Ballad**	**Slow**	**5**
I Stand, I Fall	*Willow Creek Music*	*Piano ballad*	*Slow*	7
I Want to Change	Russ Taff	MOR	Mid	7
If That's What It Takes	*Willow Creek Music*	*Pop/MOR*	*Mid/slow*	5
Keep the Flame Burning	Debby Boone	MOR	Mid	5
Look Me in the Eye	Margaret Becker	Pop ballad	Slow/mid	3
Love You With My Life	Steven Curtis Chapman	Pop	Up	5
Man of God	*Willow Creek Music*	*Pop/rock*	*Mid/up*	7
Mind, Body, Heart and Soul	**Bob Carlisle**	**Pop/rock**	**Up**	**9**
My Turn Now	Steven Curtis Chapman	Country bop	Up	6

Title	Artist	Style	Tempo	Seeker-Sensitivity Rating
The Narrow Way	Wayne Watson	Pop	Mid	6
On My Knees	**Willow Creek Music**	**Acoustic guitar ballad**	**Slow**	**5**
Show Yourselves to Be	Steven Curtis Chapman	Acoustic ballad	Slow/mid	4
Surrender Medley	*Willow Creek Music*	*Ballad medley—duet*	*Slow*	6
Take My Hand	**The Kry**	**Acoustic ballad**	**Mid/slow**	**9**
This Is the Life	**Phillips, Craig and Dean**	**Pop/rock**	**Up**	**6**
Treasure	**Gary Chapman**	**Acoustic ballad**	**Slow**	**9**
Walk in the Dark	Wayne Watson	Pop	Up	2
Want the World to Know	*Willow Creek Music*	*Pop*	*Up*	9
Whatever You Ask	**Steve Camp**	**Power ballad**	**Slow**	**5**
With All My Heart	Babbie Mason	Ballad	Slow	6

Movie Clips

Title: Chariots of Fire
Topic: Christian life; Endurance
Description: Eric Liddell gives a sermonette about running the race of faith.
Start Time: 0:25:35
Start Cue: "You came to see a race today"
End Time: 0:27:20
End Cue: "That is how you run a straight race"
Comments: _____
_____

Title: Chariots of Fire
Topic: Integrity; Standing up for what you believe in; The Sabbath
Description: Eric Liddell refuses to run on the Sabbath. The English Olympic Committee tries to make him compromise, but he stands firm.
Start Time: 1:28:15
Start Cue: "We decided to invite you in for a little chat"
End Time: 1:30:00
End Cue: "But I can't make that sacrifice"
Comments: _____
_____

Doubting

See also: **Apologetics, Faith**

Message Titles

- ❐ Can I Trust a Silent God?
- ❐ Doubters Welcome
- ❐ I Have My Doubts
- ❐ *The Power of Prayer:* The Mystery of Unanswered Prayer

_____

_____

_____

_____

Dramas

Title	Tone	Characters	Topics
Great Expectations	Mixed—ends very serious	1 male, 2 females	Unanswered prayer
Mistaken Identity	Mixed	3 males, 2 females, 1 young girl	Christmas; Doubting
On the Outside	Serious	1 female or male	Being salt and light; Negative church experiences
Plane Talk	Humorous	2 males, 1 offstage voice (pilot)	Doubt; Skepticism; God's presence
Reason Enough	Mixed, mostly serious	1 male, 1 female	Importance of faith grounded in reason

Songs

Title	Artist	Style	Tempo	Seeker-Sensitivity Rating
Honesty	Margaret Becker	Power ballad	Slow	9
Show Me the Way	Styx	**Power ballad**	**Slow/mid**	**10**

 # Movie Clips

Title: _____

Topic: _____

Description: _____

Start Time: _____

Start Cue: _____

End Time: _____

End Cue: _____

Comments: _____

_____

Programming Tip

Identify the target audience

Who exactly are you trying to reach in your services? What age group? What kind of jobs do they typically have? Is your audience made up primarily of single people or families? What is the ethnic makeup? Are you targeting Christians, or seekers, or both? The answers to these questions will be determined in large part by the community in which the church resides. Not knowing whom you are trying to reach is like shooting blindfolded at a moving target—your chances of hitting the mark will not be very good.

faith

Might also include: *Trusting God*
See also: **God's Faithfulness**

Package Suggestion

Drama:
Straight-Jacketed

Song:
Take My Hand

 ## Message Titles

- ☐ Can I Trust a Silent God?
- ☐ Developing a Daring Faith
- ☐ Faith's First Steps
- ☐ Mind-Expanding Faith
- ☐ *Seven Wonders of the Spiritual World:* God Can Be Trusted
- ☐ **Faith Has Its Reasons:** Reasons for Believing in God • Reasons for Believing in the Bible • Reasons for Believing in Jesus Christ • Reasons for Believing in the Resurrection • Reasons for Believing in Heaven and Hell

_____

_____

_____

_____

_____

 # Dramas

Title	Tone	Characters	Topics
In . . . We Trust	Serious	1 male	Trust; Difficulty trusting God
Just in Case	Humorous	1 male, 1 female	Trusting God; God's faithfulness
Plane Talk	Humorous	2 males, 1 offstage voice (pilot)	Doubt; Skepticism; God's presence
The Quagmire	Serious	1 male or female	Failure; Self-esteem; Being "stuck"; Trusting God

Title	Tone	Characters	Topics
Reason Enough	Mixed, mostly serious	1 male, 1 female	Importance of faith grounded in reason
Seeing Is Believing	Humorous	1 male, 1 female, 1 narrator	A Savior you can trust; Easy faith
Straight-Jacketed	Serious	1 male	Bondage to past and to sin; Anger toward God
Sweet Hour of Prayer	Humorous	2 males, 1 female	Prayer; Hypocrisy; Faith
_____	_____	_____	_____
_____	_____	_____	_____
_____	_____	_____	_____
_____	_____	_____	_____

 # Songs

Title	Artist	Style	Tempo	Seeker-Sensitivity Rating
All That I Need	Steve Camp	Ballad	Slow	5
All the Faith You Need	*Willow Creek Music*	*Pop/rock*	*Up*	*10*
Build My World Around You	**Sandi Patty**	**Pop**	**Up**	**9**
Do I Trust You	Twila Paris	MOR	Mid	5
Every Step I Take	**Bob Carlisle**	**Bluesy pop**	**Mid**	**9**
Facts Are Facts	**Steven Curtis Chapman**	**Rock/pop**	**Up**	**4**
Faith, Hope and Love	**Point of Grace**	**Pop vocal group**	**Up**	**9**
From Here on Out	*Willow Creek Music*	*MOR pop*	*Mid*	*8*
The Future	First Call	Pop vocal group	Up	8
God Is in Control	**Twila Paris**	**Pop/rock**	**Up**	**1**
Hard Times	Wayne Watson	Ballad	Slow	4
He Won't Let Me Down	**Debbie McClendon**	**R & B/pop**	**Up**	**9**
Higher Ways	Steven Curtis Chapman	Acoustic guitar ballad	Mid/slow	8
I Choose to Follow	**Al Denson**	**Ballad**	**Slow**	**5**
I'll Be Believing	**Point of Grace**	**Pop vocal group**	**Up**	**9**
I'm Depending on You	Harv & Edythe	MOR	Mid	7
In My Father's Hands	**Susan Ashton**	**Folk/pop**	**Mid**	**9**
My Life Is in Your Hands	**Kathy Troccoli**	**Ballad**	**Slow**	**9**
One Step at a Time	First Call	Pop vocal group	Up	8
Seize the Day	Carolyn Arends	Folk pop, in 3	Mid	8
Shepherd of My Heart	Sandi Patti	Ballad	Slow	4
Solid as the Rock	**Michael English**	**Pop**	**Up**	**8**

Title	Artist	Style	Tempo	Seeker-Sensitivity Rating
Take My Hand	**The Kry**	**Acoustic ballad**	**Mid/slow**	**9**
There Is a Love	**Michael English**	**Pop**	**Up**	**9**
Walk in the Dark	Wayne Watson	Pop	Up	2
_____	_____	_____	_____	_____
_____	_____	_____	_____	_____
_____	_____	_____	_____	_____

Movie Clips

Title:	Chariots of Fire
Topic:	Christian life; Endurance
Description:	Eric Liddell gives a sermonette about running the race of faith.
Start Time:	0:25:35
Start Cue:	"You came to see a race today"
End Time:	0:27:20
End Cue:	"That is how you run a straight race"
Comments:	_____
	_____

Title:	Indiana Jones and the Last Crusade
Topic:	Faith; Trusting God when circumstances are confusing
Description:	Indiana Jones faces a seemingly uncrossable chasm, but takes a "leap of faith" as he steps onto an invisible bridge. Illustrates faith, believing what can't be seen.
Start Time:	1:46:50
Start Cue:	Indiana Jones walks through cave to the chasm
End Time:	1:48:45
End Cue:	Indy throws sand on bridge to mark it. Can be cut earlier
Comments:	_____
	_____

Title:	_____
Topic:	_____
Description:	_____
Start Time:	_____
Start Cue:	_____
End Time:	_____
End Cue:	_____
Comments:	_____
	_____

Freedom in Christ

Might also include: *Freedom From Sin*
See also: **Grace vs. Works/Legalism, Joy of the Christian Life**

 ## Message Titles

❑   A Better Kind of Freedom

_____
_____
_____
_____
_____

 ## Dramas

Title	Tone	Characters	Topics
D-Day	Humorous	2 males, 1 female	Misconceptions about Christianity
Measuring Up	Mixed; mime	2 males, 1 female, 1 other male or female	God's acceptance of us; Self-esteem
No Fun	Humorous	3 males, 1 female	Christian lifestyle; Misconceptions about Christianity
The Prisoner	Serious	3 males, 1 female	Easter; Freedom from sin; New Christian
The Stickholders	Serious	3 males, 1 female, 1 narrator	Relationship with God; Freedom from rules

Songs

Title	Artist	Style	Tempo	Seeker-Sensitivity Rating
Ball and Chain	Susan Ashton	Folk/pop	Mid	9
Change in My Life	**John Pagano**	**Gospel**	**Mid/up**	**9**
I've Been Released	*Willow Creek Music*	*Pop/rock— Chicago sound*	*Up*	9
Remember Your Chains	Steven Curtis Chapman	Acoustic MOR	Mid	2
This Is the Life	**Phillips, Craig and Dean**	**Pop/rock**	**Up**	**6**
_____	_____	_____	_____	_____
_____	_____	_____	_____	_____
_____	_____	_____	_____	_____
_____	_____	_____	_____	_____

Movie Clips

Title: _____

Topic: _____

Description: _____

Start Time: _____

Start Cue: _____

End Time: _____

End Cue: _____

Comments: _____

_____

Glorifying God

Refers to honoring God in our words and deeds
See also: **Praise and Worship**

Message Titles

☐ **Secret Christianity:** An Audience of One • Secret Giving •
Secret Praying • Secret Fasting

Package Suggestion

Drama:
The Mystery of Robert Richardson

Song:
In Christ Alone

_____
_____
_____
_____

Dramas

Title	Tone	Characters	Topics
Counting the Cost	Serious	2 males, 2 females	Commitment to Christ; Sacrifice; Spiritual maturity
Mr. Hibbs' Day Off	Mixed; mime	3 males, 1 female, 1 child	Serving others; Self-denial; Being used by God
The Mystery of Robert Richardson	Mixed	3 males, 2 females, 1 narrator	Living the Christian life
Parlor Talk	Mixed	3 males, 2 females	Making a difference with your life; Death; Workaholism
10	Humorous	3 males, 2 females	Ten Commandments: First Commandment

Songs

Title	Artist	Style	Tempo	Seeker-Sensitivity Rating
All I Ever Wanted	Margaret Becker	Pop/rock ballad	Slow/mid	4
Always Before Me	**Steven Curtis Chapman**	**Worship ballad, in 3**	**Slow/mid**	**1**
Audience of One	*Willow Creek Music*	*Power ballad*	*Slow*	*8*
Casual Christian	**De Garmo & Key**	**Power ballad**	**Slow**	**6**
Heart's Cry	**Steven Curtis Chapman**	**Acoustic ballad**	**Mid/slow**	**7**
I Am Determined	Tim Shepherd	Inspirational ballad	Slow	2
In Christ Alone	**Michael English**	**Power ballad**	**Slow**	**8**
Look Me in the Eye	Margaret Becker	Pop ballad	Slow/mid	3
Love You With My Life	Steven Curtis Chapman	Pop	Up	5
My Turn Now	Steven Curtis Chapman	Country bop	Up	6
With All My Heart	Babbie Mason	Ballad	Slow	6
_____	_____	_____	_____	_____
_____	_____	_____	_____	_____
_____	_____	_____	_____	_____

Movie Clips

Title:	Chariots of Fire
Topic:	Being true to whom God made you; Honoring God with your gifts
Description:	Eric Liddell talks to his sister, who wants him to forsake running to be a missionary. Eric responds that God made him fast and when he runs, he can feel God's pleasure.
Start Time:	0:58:20
Start Cue:	First line is "I've decided . . . I'm going back to China"
End Time:	0:59:15
End Cue:	"To win is to honor him"
Comments:	_____
	_____

Title:	_____
Topic:	_____
Description:	_____
Start Time:	_____
Start Cue:	_____
End Time:	_____
End Cue:	_____
Comments:	_____

God's Acceptance of Us

Addresses the belief of many seekers that they are beyond salvation
See also: **Grace**

 ## Message Titles

- ❏ Come As You Are
- ❏ *Private Conversations:* Jesus Talks to a Sinner
- ❏ *What Jesus Would Say to . . .* O. J. Simpson

_____
_____
_____
_____
_____

 ## Dramas

Title	Tone	Characters	Topics
Another Day at the Bus Stop	Mixed	1 male, 1 female	Our relationship with God; Self-esteem
I Know What You Want	Serious	2 males, 2 females	God's love; Dysfunctional families
Measuring Up	Mixed; mime	2 males, 1 female, 1 other male or female	God's acceptance of us; Self-esteem

Songs

Title	Artist	Style	Tempo	Seeker-Sensitivity Rating
Change in My Life	**John Pagano**	**Gospel**	**Mid/up**	**9**
The Door	Al Denson	Power ballad	Slow	1
If I Could Look Through Your Eyes	**Willow Creek Music**	**Piano ballad**	**Slow**	**10**
In Heaven's Eyes	**Sandi Patti**	**Inspirational ballad**	Slow	9
Jesus Loves Me	**Whitney Houston**	**R & B/pop**	**Slow/mid**	**8**
Love Is Always There	Carolyn Arends	Folk/pop	Up	9
There Is a Love	**Michael English**	**Pop**	**Up**	**9**
Who Am I	Margaret Becker	Power ballad	Slow	7
_____	_____	_____	_____	_____
_____	_____	_____	_____	_____
_____	_____	_____	_____	_____
_____	_____	_____	_____	_____

Movie Clips

Title: _____

Topic: _____

Description: _____

Start Time: _____

Start Cue: _____

End Time: _____

End Cue: _____

Comments: _____

_____

God's Laws

The Ten Commandments work well as a series. For ideas on individual listings on commandments, look up a related topic—for example, Tenth Commandment (**Contentment, Materialism/Greed**).
See also: **God's Wisdom, Obeying God**

 ## Message Titles

- ❏ The Benefits of God's Laws
- ❏ Laws That Liberate
- ❏ **The Ten Commandments:** Honor God as God • Refuse to Reduce God • Revere the Name of God • Remember the Sabbath Day • Honor Your Parents • Respect Human Life • Restrain Sexual Desires • Respect the Property of Others • Refuse to Lie • Restrain Material Desires

_____
_____
_____
_____
_____

 ## Dramas

Title	Tone	Characters	Topics
Everything's Relative	Humorous	3 males, 1 female	God's holiness; Benefits of God's laws
Idol Minds	Humorous	3 males, 2 females	False gods; Priorities
10	Humorous	3 males, 2 females	First Commandment
A Thief's Carol	Mixed	3 males, 2 females	Stealing; Eighth Commandment

Songs

Title	Artist	Style	Tempo	Seeker-Sensitivity Rating
Only by Grace	*Willow Creek Music*	*Pop/rock*	*Mid*	*10*
There Is a Line	Susan Ashton	Folk pop	Mid	6
_____	_____	_____	_____	_____
_____	_____	_____	_____	_____
_____	_____	_____	_____	_____
_____	_____	_____	_____	_____

Movie Clips

Title: Chariots of Fire

Topic: Integrity; Standing up for what you believe in; The Sabbath

Description: Eric Liddell refuses to run on the Sabbath. The English Olympic Committee tries to make him compromise, but he stands firm.

Start Time: 1:28:15

Start Cue: "We decided to invite you in for a little chat"

End Time: 1:30:00

End Cue: "But I can't make that sacrifice"

Comments: _____

_____

Title: _____

Topic: _____

Description: _____

Start Time: _____

Start Cue: _____

End Time: _____

End Cue: _____

Comments: _____

Heaven

See also: **Death, Salvation**

Message Titles

- ☐ Hang On for Heaven
- ☐ Reasons for Believing in Heaven and Hell
- ☐ *Facing Up to Fear:* The Fear of Death

_____

_____

_____

Dramas

Title	Tone	Characters	Topics
Security Check	Mixed	1 male, 1 female, 1 offstage voice	Salvation; Works vs. grace
_____	_____	_____	_____
_____	_____	_____	_____
_____	_____	_____	_____

Songs

Title	Artist	Style	Tempo	Seeker-Sensitivity Rating
Another Time, Another Place	Sandi Patti (with Wayne Watson)	Power ballad	Slow	8
Down the Road	Triloje	Acapella vocal group	Slow	6
Healing River	*Willow Creek Music*	*Ballad*	*Slow/mid*	9

Title	Artist	Style	Tempo	Seeker-Sensitivity Rating
He Won't Let You Go	**The Kry**	**Piano ballad**	**Slow**	**10**
Home Free	Wayne Watson	Ballad	Slow/mid	6
If You Could See Me Now	Truth	Ballad	Slow	5
I Will Be Free	Cindy Morgan	Ballad	Slow	7
No More Night	Morris Chapman	Inspirational	Slow	6
Reaching	Carolyn Arends	Ballad	Slow	6
_____	_____	_____	_____	_____
_____	_____	_____	_____	_____
_____	_____	_____	_____	_____
_____	_____	_____	_____	_____

 # Movie Clips

Title: _____

Topic: _____

Description: _____

Start Time: _____

Start Cue: _____

End Time: _____

End Cue: _____

Comments: _____

_____

Lordship of Christ

Refers to the rightful place of Christ as Lord in the life of a believer; also encompasses the commandment "You shall have no other gods before me"

Message Titles

- ☐ Unmasking Your Master
- ☐ *First Commandment:* Honor God as God
- ☐ *God Has Feelings Too:* What Makes God Jealous
- ☐ *What Jesus Would Say to* . . . Oprah Winfrey

_____

_____

_____

_____

_____

Dramas

Title	Tone	Characters	Topics
Counting the Cost	Serious	2 males, 2 females	Commitment to Christ; Sacrifice; Spiritual maturity
I Don't Want to Fight You Anymore	Serious	1 female	Relationship with God; Giving up control; Our value to God
A Serf's Tale	Humorous	1 male, 1 female	Serving two masters; Materialism
10	Humorous	3 males, 2 females	First Commandment

Songs

Title	Artist	Style	Tempo	Seeker-Sensitivity Rating
All I Ever Wanted	Margaret Becker	Pop/rock ballad	Slow/mid	4
Build My World Around You	**Sandi Patty**	**Pop**	**Up**	**9**
Ever Devoted	*Willow Creek Music*	*Ballad*	*Slow*	6
Foundations	Geoff Moore & the Distance	Folk/pop ballad	Slow/mid	8
The Future	First Call	Pop vocal group	Up	8
God Is in Control	**Twila Paris**	**Pop/rock**	**Up**	**1**
I Am Determined	Tim Shepherd	Inspirational ballad	Slow	2
I Choose to Follow	**Al Denson**	**Ballad**	**Slow**	**5**
I Found Myself in You	**Clay Crosse**	**Gospel ballad**	**Mid/slow**	**10**
If That's What It Takes	*Willow Creek Music*	*Pop/MOR*	*Mid/slow*	5
I Go to the Rock	Dottie Rambo	Swing/big band	Mid	7
In Christ Alone	**Michael English**	**Power ballad**	**Slow**	**8**
In My Father's Hands	**Susan Ashton**	**Folk/pop**	**Mid**	**9**
King of the Jungle	Steven Curtis Chapman	Pop shuffle with African touches	Mid/up	9
Most of the Time	Glad	Piano ballad	Slow	4
My Soul Desire	Deniece Williams	R & B ballad	Slow	5
My Turn Now	Steven Curtis Chapman	Country bop	Up	6
Strength in You	*Willow Creek Music*	*MOR pop*	*Slow/mid*	10
Want the World to Know	*Willow Creek Music*	*Pop*	*Up*	9
We Believe in God	Amy Grant	Acoustic ballad	Slow	3
We Belong to Him	Wayne Watson	MOR ballad	Slow/mid	2
We've Got a Reason to Celebrate	Billy and Sarah Gaines	R & B pop	Up	3
Whatever You Ask	**Steve Camp**	**Power ballad**	**Slow**	5
Where Else Could I Go	*Willow Creek Music*	*Inspirational ballad*	*Slow*	8
Who Makes the Rules	**Steven Curtis Chapman**	**Pop/folk rock**	**Up**	7
_____	_____	_____	_____	_____
_____	_____	_____	_____	_____
_____	_____	_____	_____	_____
_____	_____	_____	_____	_____
_____	_____	_____	_____	_____

Movie Clips

Title: _____

Topic: _____

Description: _____

Start Time: _____

Start Cue: _____

End Time: _____

End Cue: _____

Comments: _____

_____

Programming Tip

Bridging elements

Often we will use programming elements that fit the topic but don't necessarily connect smoothly. In those cases, a "bridge" is needed—something to help the congregation follow the thematic flow of the service. Bridges can take various forms—a Scripture reading, for example, or preceding or following a song or drama with a personal story.

Obeying God

See also: **Commitment to Christ**

Message Titles

- ❏ Life in the Comfort Zone
- ❏ Living by Dying
- ❏ Unmasking Your Master
- ❏ *Developing a Daring Faith:* Obeying God
- ❏ *Leadings From God:* Obeying God's Leadings
- ❏ *Seasons of a Spiritual Life:* Spiritual Adulthood

_____

_____

_____

_____

Dramas

Title	Tone	Characters	Topics
Counting the Cost	Serious	2 males, 2 females	Commitment to Christ; Sacrifice; Spiritual maturity
A Failure Tale	Mixed	5 males, 1 narrator	Failing; Obeying rules
First-Day Jitters	Humorous	1 female	New Christian; Obeying God
The Gardeners	Humorous	1 male, 1 female	New Age movement
Go Away God	Humorous	2 males, 1 female	Conscience; Guilt; Hearing God's voice
Horsefeathers and Nosefly	Humorous	2 male or female "helpers"	Christian living; Obedience
I Don't Want to Fight You Anymore	Serious	1 female	Relationship with God; Giving up control; Our value to God
Impressions, Inc.	Humorous	2 males, 1 female	Skin-deep Christianity

Title	Tone	Characters	Topics
Mere Technicality	Serious	1 male, 1 female	Living together; The cost of taking a stand for Christ
The Mystery of Robert Richardson	Mixed	3 males, 2 females, 1 narrator	Living the Christian life
The Right Thing	Serious	1 male	Costly obedience; Christian character; Persecution
10	Humorous	3 males, 2 females	First Commandment
_____	_____	_____	_____
_____	_____	_____	_____
_____	_____	_____	_____
_____	_____	_____	_____

 Songs

Title	Artist	Style	Tempo	Seeker-Sensitivity Rating
All I Ever Wanted	Margaret Becker	Pop/rock ballad	Slow/mid	4
Be the One	**Al Denson**	**Power ballad**	**Slow**	**7**
Casual Christian	**De Garmo & Key**	**Power ballad**	**Slow**	**6**
The Dilemma	Sandi Patti	Pop	Up	6
Ever Devoted	_Willow Creek Music_	_Ballad_	_Slow_	6
Fill Me, Lord	DeGarmo & Key	Ballad	Slow	2
For the Sake of the Call	Steven Curtis Chapman	Anthemic pop	Up	3
Heart's Cry	**Steven Curtis Chapman**	**Acoustic ballad**	**Mid/slow**	**7**
I Am Determined	Tim Shepherd	Inspirational ballad	Slow	2
I Choose to Follow	**Al Denson**	**Ballad**	**Slow**	**5**
I Want to Change	Russ Taff	MOR	Mid	7
If That's What It Takes	_Willow Creek Music_	_Pop/MOR_	_Mid/slow_	5
Lay It on Down	Bruce Carroll	Country	Mid/up	8
Look Me in the Eye	Margaret Becker	Pop ballad	Slow/mid	3
Love You With My Life	Steven Curtis Chapman	Pop	Up	5
Man of God	_Willow Creek Music_	_Pop/rock_	_Mid/up_	7
Mind, Body, Heart and Soul	**Bob Carlisle**	**Pop/rock**	**Up**	**9**
My Life Is in Your Hands	**Kathy Troccoli**	**Ballad**	**Slow**	**9**
My Soul Desire	Deniece Williams	R & B ballad	Slow	5
My Turn Now	Steven Curtis Chapman	Country bop	Up	6
The Narrow Way	Wayne Watson	Pop	Mid	6
Never Be an Angel	Margaret Becker	Pop	Mid	4

Title	Artist	Style	Tempo	Seeker-Sensitivity Rating
Show Yourselves to Be	Steven Curtis Chapman	Acoustic ballad	Slow/mid	4
Stranger to Holiness	Steve Camp	Ballad	Slow/mid	2
Surrender Medley	*Willow Creek Music*	*Ballad medley—duet*	*Slow*	6
There Is a Line	Susan Ashton	Folk pop	Mid	6
True Devotion	Margaret Becker	R & B/pop	Up	6
Walk in the Dark	Wayne Watson	Pop	Up	2
Whatever You Ask	**Steve Camp**	**Power ballad**	**Slow**	5
Who Makes the Rules	**Steven Curtis Chapman**	**Pop/folk rock**	**Up**	7
With All My Heart	Babbie Mason	Ballad	Slow	6
Would I Know You	**Wayne Watson**	**Ballad**	**Slow**	3
_____	_____	_____	_____	_____
_____	_____	_____	_____	_____
_____	_____	_____	_____	_____
_____	_____	_____	_____	_____

Movie Clips

Title: Chariots of Fire
Topic: Integrity; Standing up for what you believe in; TheSabbath
Description: Eric Liddell refuses to run on the Sabbath. The English Olympic Committee tries to make him compromise, but he stands firm.
Start Time: 1:28:15
Start Cue: "We decided to invite you in for a little chat"
End Time: 1:30:00
End Cue: "But I can't make that sacrifice"
Comments: _____
_____

Title: Indiana Jones and the Last Crusade
Topic: Faith; Trusting God when circumstances are confusing
Description: Indiana Jones faces a seemingly uncrossable chasm, but takes a "leap of faith" as he steps onto an invisible bridge. Illustrates faith, believing what can't be seen.
Start Time: 1:46:50
Start Cue: Indiana Jones walks through cave to the chasm
End Time: 1:48:45
End Cue: Indy throws sand on bridge to mark it—this can be cut earlier
Comments: _____
_____

Praise and Worship

This is a listing of songs (not worship choruses, but "specials") of worship.

 Songs

Title	Artist	Style	Tempo	Seeker-Sensitivity Rating
Almighty	**Wayne Watson**	**Praise & worship/pop**	**Up**	2
Always Before Me	**Steven Curtis Chapman**	**Worship ballad, in 3**	**Slow/mid**	1
Awesome God	**Rich Mullins**	**Pop anthem**	**Mid/up**	1
The Beauty of Holiness	**Steve Camp**	**Ballad**	**Slow**	1
Bless the Lord	**Steve Camp**	**Pop**	**Up**	1
Change in My Life	**John Pagano**	**Gospel**	**Mid/up**	9
Draw Me Near	**Al Denson**	**Ballad**	**Slow**	3
God Is Great	**Babbie Mason**	**R & B/pop**	**Up**	5
Here in the Quiet	*Willow Creek Music*	*Ballad*	*Slow*	4
He's Been Faithful	**Brooklyn Tabernacle Choir**	**Ballad with choir**	**Slow**	6
I Love You, Lord	The Archers	MOR	Mid	2
I'm Amazed	*Willow Creek Music*	*Ballad*	*Slow*	7
I Need to Stop	*Willow Creek Music*	*Pop*	*Up*	3
Listen to Our Hearts	**Geoff Moore & the Distance (with Steven Curtis Chapman)**	**Acoustic ballad—duet**	**Slow/mid**	2
Lord, I Want to Be Like Jesus	**Fernando Ortega**	**Ballad**	**Slow**	3
The Love of God	*Willow Creek Music*	*Acapella vocal group*	*Slow*	6
More Than Words	Steven Curtis Chapman	Acoustic guitar ballad	Mid/slow	4
My Redeemer Is Faithful and True	**Steven Curtis Chapman**	**Ballad**	**Slow**	9
Never Be Another	Paul Smith	Power ballad	Slow	8
Say the Name	Margaret Becker	Ballad	Slow/mid	4
We Believe in God	**Amy Grant**	**Acoustic ballad**	**Slow**	3
We've Got a Reason to Celebrate	**Billy and Sarah Gaines**	**R & B pop**	**Up**	3

Title	Artist	Style	Tempo	Seeker-Sensitivity Rating
Where Else Could I Go	*Willow Creek Music*	*Inspirational ballad*	*Slow*	8
Who Am I	**Margaret Becker**	**Power ballad**	**Slow**	7
Your Love	Alleluia Music	MOR—duet	Mid	4
Your Steadfast Love	Alleluia Music	MOR	Mid/slow	3
_____	_____	_____	_____	_____
_____	_____	_____	_____	_____
_____	_____	_____	_____	_____
_____	_____	_____	_____	_____
_____	_____	_____	_____	_____

Programming Tip

Spiritual authenticity

What we do for Christ is not nearly so important as who we are in him. As Christian artists, our highest priority must be to love Jesus above all else, to stay vitally connected to him, and as best we can, to live as he would live if he were in our place. "I am the vine, you are the branches. If a man remains in me, and I in him, he will bear much fruit; apart from me, you can do nothing" (John 15:5). Effective ministry can only flow out of a life and heart that are submitted to God.

Prayer

Might also include: *Quiet Time*

Message Titles

- ❏ Practicing the Presence of God
- ❏ Prayer Busters
- ❏ Two-Way Prayer
- ❏ *What Jesus Would Say to . . .* Bart Simpson
- ❏ **The Power of Prayer:** Amazing Answers to Prayer • God's Attitude Toward Prayer • How to Pray Authentically • Practicing the Presence of God • Prayer, Our Last Resort • Mountain-Moving Prayer • The Mystery of Unanswered Prayer
- ❏ **The Privilege of Prayer:** The Privilege of Prayer • Painfully Honest Prayers • Prayer Abuse • Dangerous Prayers

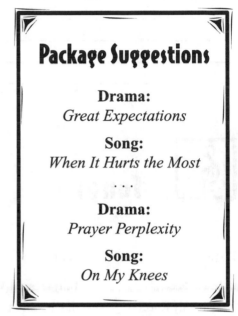

Package Suggestions

Drama:
Great Expectations

Song:
When It Hurts the Most

. . .

Drama:
Prayer Perplexity

Song:
On My Knees

_____

_____

_____

_____

Dramas

Title	Tone	Characters	Topics
Great Expectations	Serious	1 male, 2 females	Unanswered prayer
No Interruptions	Humorous	1 male	Quiet time; Prayer
Plane Talk	Humorous	2 males, 1 offstage voice (pilot)	Doubt; Skepticism; God's presence
Prayer Despair	Mixed	1 male, 2 females	Waiting for answers to prayer; Marriage; Process of change
Prayer Group Therapy	Humorous	2 males, 3 females	Prayer

Title	Tone	Characters	Topics
Prayer Perplexity	Humorous	2 males, 2 females	Prayer; The Lord's Prayer
Prayer Static	Serious	3 males, 1 female	Prayer; Misconceptions of God
Quiet Time?	Humorous	1 female	Prayer
Snow Job	Humorous	2 males, 1 female	Prayer abuse
Sweet Hour of Prayer	Humorous	2 males, 1 female	Prayer; Hypocrisy; Faith

 Songs

Title	Artist	Style	Tempo	Seeker-Sensitivity Rating
At Jesus' Feet	**Billy & Sarah Gaines**	**Ballad**	**Slow**	**6**
Down on My Knees	Susan Ashton	Folk rock	Mid/up	6
Draw Me Near	**Al Denson**	**Ballad**	**Slow**	**3**
Here in the Quiet	*Willow Creek Music*	*Ballad*	*Slow*	*4*
In His Presence	Sandi Patti	Traditional ballad	Slow	6
In His Sanctuary	**Morris Chapman & Friends**	**Ballad**	**Slow**	**6**
Midnight Oil	**Phillips, Craig and Dean**	**Acoustic ballad**	**Slow**	**7**
More Than Words	Steven Curtis Chapman	Acoustic guitar ballad	Mid/slow	4
On My Knees	**Willow Creek Music**	**Acoustic guitar ballad**	**Slow**	**5**
Prayer Medley	*Willow Creek Music*	*Ballad medley—trio*	*Slow*	*7*
Say It to Him	Teri Gibbs	Funky pop	Up	9
Still Listening	**Steven Curtis Chapman**	**Acoustic ballad**	**Slow/mid**	**7**
When God's People Pray	**Wayne Watson**	**Pop ballad**	**Mid/slow**	**3**

Movie Clips

Title: Shadowlands

Topic: Prayer

Description: A very short clip in which C. S. Lewis's friend tells him he knows God has answered his prayers for Joy's healing. Lewis's answer is a profound statement about prayer.

Start Time: 1:29:30

Start Cue: "Jack, what news?"

End Time: 1:30:00

End Cue: "It doesn't change God, it changes me"

Comments: May be too short except as a sermon illustration

_____

Title: Sister Act

Topic: Prayer

Description: Sister Mary Clarence is asked to pray at dinner, and the results are humorous.

Start Time: 0:23:15

Start Cue: Sister Mary Patrick raises her hand

End Time: 0:24:15

End Cue: Nuns echo "amen"

Comments: _____

_____

Title: Sister Act

Topic: Prayer abuse

Description: The nuns need a free helicopter ride to Reno to save Mary Clarence. When the pilot refuses, they start to pray very manipulative prayers.

Start Time: 1:21:15

Start Cue: "It's $1500 for the run to Reno"

End Time: 1:22:15

End Cue: Nuns in helicopter

Comments: _____

_____

Title: _____

Topic: _____

Description: _____

Start Time: _____

Start Cue: _____

End Time: _____

End Cue: _____

Comments: _____

_____

Relationship With God, General

Refers to the general idea of having a relationship with God, that God desires a relationship with us
See also: **Prayer**

Message Titles

- ❏ The Benefits of Knowing God
- ❏ Listening to God
- ❏ Ordering Your Spiritual World
- ❏ **Developing a Daring Faith:** Dialoging With God • Obeying God • Following God
- ❏ **Seven Wonders of the Spiritual World:** God Loves Me • God Can Be Trusted • God Forgives My Failures • God Transforms Me • God Guides Me • God Uses Me • God Satisfies Me

_____

_____

_____

_____

Dramas

Title	Tone	Characters	Topics
Another Day at the Bus Stop	Mixed	1 male, 1 female	Our relationship with God; Self-esteem
Any Time?	Mixed, mostly serious	1 male	Making time for God
The Big Question	Mixed, mostly humorous	1 male, 1 female, 1 child	The existence of God

Title	Tone	Characters	Topics
The Black Hole	Serious, but light	2 males, 1 female, 1 narrator	Filling the void; Contentment; God's love
I Don't Want to Fight You Anymore	Serious	1 female	Relationship with God; Giving up control; Our value to God
Idol Minds	Humorous	3 males, 2 females	False gods; Priorities
Impressions, Inc.	Humorous	2 males, 1 female	Skin-deep Christianity
Plane Talk	Humorous	2 males, 1 offstage voice (pilot)	Doubt; Skepticism; God's presence
Prayer Static	Serious	3 males, 1 female	Prayer; Misconceptions of God
Quiet Time?	Humorous	1 female	Prayer
Seeing Is Believing	Humorous	1 male, 1 female, 1 narrator	A Savior you can trust; Easy faith
Sitters, Strivers, Standers, and Saints	Mixed	4 either male or female, 1 narrator	God changing lives; God completing us
The Stickholders	Serious	3 males, 1 female, 1 narrator	Relationship with God; Freedom from rules
Street Chat	Humorous	4 males, 1 female	Search for meaning; Spirituality
Sweet Hour of Prayer	Humorous	2 males, 1 female	Prayer; Hypocrisy; Faith
Take Heart	Mixed; mime	2 males, 2 females	God heals the brokenhearted; Disappointment
Tom, Dick, and Mary	Serious	3 males, 1 female, 1 narrator	Hearing God's voice; Crowding God out of your life
You Cramp My Style	Serious	1 male, 1 female, 1 either male or female	Reasons why people don't believe; Society's view of God
_____	_____	_____	_____
_____	_____	_____	_____
_____	_____	_____	_____
_____	_____	_____	_____

Songs

Title	Artist	Style	Tempo	Seeker-Sensitivity Rating
At Jesus' Feet	Billy & Sarah Gaines	Ballad	Slow	6
Draw Me Near	Al Denson	Ballad	Slow	3
He Won't Let Me Down	Debbie McClendon	R & B/pop	Up	9

Title	Artist	Style	Tempo	Seeker-Sensitivity Rating
Heart's Cry	**Steven Curtis Chapman**	**Acoustic ballad**	**Mid/slow**	7
Heirlooms	Amy Grant	Ballad	Slow	8
Here in My Heart	Susan Ashton	Folk rock	Up	8
Here in the Quiet	*Willow Creek Music*	*Ballad*	*Slow*	4
Hunger and Thirst	Susan Ashton	Folk pop	Mid/up	6
I Am Determined	Tim Shepherd	Inspirational ballad	Slow	2
I Go to the Rock	**Dottie Rambo**	**Swing/big band**	**Mid**	7
I'm Amazed	*Willow Creek Music*	*Ballad*	*Slow*	7
In Christ Alone	**Michael English**	**Power ballad**	**Slow**	8
In His Presence	Sandi Patti	Traditional ballad	Slow	6
In His Sanctuary	Morris Chapman & Friends	Ballad	Slow	6
Jesus Loves Me	**Whitney Houston**	**R & B/pop**	**Slow/mid**	8
Man of God	*Willow Creek Music*	*Pop/rock*	*Mid/up*	7
Mind, Body, Heart and Soul	**Bob Carlisle**	**Pop/rock**	**Up**	9
More Than Words	Steven Curtis Chapman	Acoustic guitar ballad	Mid/slow	4
No One Knows My Heart	**Susan Ashton**	**Folk/pop ballad**	**Slow/mid**	9
On My Knees	*Willow Creek Music*	*Acoustic guitar ballad*	*Slow*	5
Prayer Medley	*Willow Creek Music*	*Ballad medley—trio*	*Slow*	7
Say It to Him	Teri Gibbs	Funky pop	Up	9
Say the Name	Margaret Becker	Ballad	Slow/mid	4
Still Listening	**Steven Curtis Chapman**	**Acoustic ballad**	**Slow/mid**	7
Want the World to Know	*Willow Creek Music*	*Pop*	*Up*	9
We Believe in God	**Amy Grant**	**Acoustic ballad**	**Slow**	3
What a Ride	*Willow Creek Music*	*Pop/rock*	*Up*	9
With All My Heart	Babbie Mason	Ballad	Slow	6
Would I Know You	**Wayne Watson**	**Ballad**	**Slow**	3
You're the One He Loves	Truth	Pop	Up	10

Movie Clips

Title: Chariots of Fire
Topic: Christian life; Endurance
Description: Eric Liddell gives a sermonette about running the race of faith.
Start Time: 0:25:35
Start Cue: "You came to see a race today"
End Time: 0:27:20
End Cue: "That is how you run a straight race"
Comments: _____
_____

Title: _____
Topic: _____
Description: _____
Start Time: _____
Start Cue: _____
End Time: _____
End Cue: _____
Comments: _____
_____

Programming Tip

Developing your gifts
In the parable of the talents, Jesus made it clear that he expects us to make the most of the gifts he has given. We are called to sharpen our skills and grow in our areas of expertise—to be the most useful tool in God's hands that we can be.

Sanctification/ Growing in Christ

Refers to the process of becoming like Christ
Might also include: *Growing in Christ, Spiritual Development*

Package Suggestion

Drama:
One Sunday in the Parking Lot

Song:
Changin'

Message Titles

- ❏ Building Bigger Hearts
- ❏ Do You Have What It Takes to Grow?
- ❏ **For Mature Audiences Only:** How to Stunt Your Spiritual Growth • Myths About Maturing • The Marks of a Mature Christian • What Motivates Mature Christians
- ❏ **The Seasons of a Spiritual Life:** The Season of Spiritual Seeking • The Season of Spiritual Infancy • The Season of Spiritual Adolescence • The Season of Spiritual Adulthood

_____
_____
_____
_____

Dramas

Title	Tone	Characters	Topics
It's a New Year . . . Again	Humorous	2 males, 1 female	New Year's; Growth/change is difficult
The Knowing Years	Mixed	3 females	Spiritual adolescence; Adolescence
Monday Night Meeting	Humorous	4 males	New Christian; Joy of Christian life; Discipleship

Title	Tone	Characters	Topics
One Sunday in the Parking Lot	Humorous	4 males or females	Pace of life; Making changes
Prayer Despair	Mixed	1 male, 2 females	Waiting for answers to prayer; Marriage; Process of change
Sitters, Strivers, Standers, and Saints	Mixed	4 either male or female, 1 narrator	God changing lives; God completing us
Welcome to the Family	Humorous	2 males, 1 female	New Christian; Growing in Christ
_____	_____	_____	_____
_____	_____	_____	_____
_____	_____	_____	_____
_____	_____	_____	_____
_____	_____	_____	_____

Songs

Title	Artist	Style	Tempo	Seeker-Sensitivity Rating
All I Ever Wanted	Margaret Becker	Pop/rock ballad	Slow/mid	4
Changin'	Acapella Vocal Band	Acapella vocal group	Up	8
Chippin' Away	*Willow Creek Music*	*Folk pop*	*Mid/up*	8
Heart's Cry	**Steven Curtis Chapman**	**Acoustic ballad**	**Mid/slow**	**7**
I Am Determined	Tim Shepherd	Inspirational ballad	Slow	2
I Stand, I Fall	*Willow Creek Music*	*Piano ballad*	*Slow*	7
I Want to Change	Russ Taff	MOR	Mid	7
If That's What It Takes	*Willow Creek Music*	*Pop/MOR*	*Mid/slow*	5
Look Me in the Eye	Margaret Becker	Pop ballad	Slow/mid	3
Lord, I Want to Be Like Jesus	**Fernando Ortega**	**Ballad**	**Slow**	**3**
Most of the Time	Glad	Piano ballad	Slow	4
Never Be an Angel	Margaret Becker	Pop	Mid	4
One Step at a Time	First Call	Pop vocal group	Up	8
Stranger to Holiness	Steve Camp	Ballad	Slow/mid	2
Take My Hand	**The Kry**	**Acoustic ballad**	**Mid/slow**	**9**
_____	_____	_____	_____	_____
_____	_____	_____	_____	_____
_____	_____	_____	_____	_____
_____	_____	_____	_____	_____

Movie Clips

Title: _____

Topic: _____

Description: _____

Start Time: _____

Start Cue: _____

End Time: _____

End Cue: _____

Comments: _____

_____

Programming Tip

Discover your own creative identity

Imitating other churches and creative programs has some value, but only as it enables you to forge your church's own style and way of doing things. What takes place at Willow Creek works there because it meets the need of the target audience and utilizes the specific gifts of the staff and volunteers. While some things that work elsewhere will succeed for you, your creative programs must reflect *your* audience and the gifts of *your* team. Allow the Holy Spirit to shape the unique way you will reach your congregation.

Sin

See also: **God's Forgiveness of Us, Grace, Guilt, Self-Control**

 Message Titles

- ☐ *Learning Through Life's Crises:* Learning Through Falling
- ☐ *Signs of the Times:* Dead End Road
- ☐ **Modern Day Madness:** The Agony of Escapism • The Pornography Problem • Hope for the Homosexual • Unwanted Pregnancies
- ☐ **The "S" Word:** Sin in a No-Fault Society • The High Cost of a Cheap Thrill • The Other "S" Word (Salvation)

_____

_____

_____

_____

Package Suggestion

Drama:
A Nice Guy

Song:
Face of Forgiveness

 Dramas

Title	Tone	Characters	Topics
All Gummed Up	Serious	1 male, 1 female, 1 offstage voice	Adultery; Dealing with past hurts; The pain of lies
Because I Love You	Serious	1 male, 1 female	Adultery; The consequences of sin
The Crowd, The Conscience, and Curt	Serious	2 males, 4 males or females	Broad vs. narrow way; Conscience; Peer pressure
A Failure Tale	Mixed	5 males, 1 narrator	Failing; Obeying rules
Forgive Again?	Serious	1 male, 1 female	Forgiving others
The Gardeners	Humorous	1 male, 1 female	New Age movement

Title	Tone	Characters	Topics
Go Away God	Humorous	2 males, 1 female	Conscience; Guilt; Hearing God's voice
It's Not My Fault	Humorous	4 females, 3 males	Sin; Taking responsibility for our sin; Excuses
Man of the Year	Serious	5 males, 1 female	Moralism; Our need for Christ
A Nice Guy	Serious	2 males	Regret; Admitting failures; Effects of sin; Confession
Straight-Jacketed	Serious	1 male	Bondage to past and to sin; Anger toward God
Taking Step Four	Humorous	1 female	Self-examination; Self-delusion; Confession of sin
"X" Marks the Spot	Serious; mime	1 female, 1 male, and 3 females or males	Sin; Redemption; Forgiveness; Guilt

Songs

Title	Artist	Style	Tempo	Seeker-Sensitivity Rating
Ball and Chain	**Susan Ashton**	**Folk/pop**	**Mid**	**9**
Behind Every Fantasy	*Willow Creek Music*	*Country pop*	*Up*	*10*
Call of the Wild	Susan Ashton	Country	Mid	10
Casual Christian	**De Garmo & Key**	**Power ballad**	**Slow**	**6**
Cross Medley	*Willow Creek Music*	*Ballad medley— hymns*	*Slow*	*7*
The Dilemma	Sandi Patti	Pop	Up	6
Down on My Knees	Susan Ashton	Folk rock	Mid/up	6
Face of Forgiveness	*Willow Creek Music*	*Ballad*	*Slow*	*10*
Forgive Me	Tim Miner	Ballad	Slow	4
The Great Divide	Point of Grace	Power ballad	Slow	9
I Stand, I Fall	*Willow Creek Music*	*Piano ballad*	*Slow*	*7*
Just Come In	Margaret Becker	Pop ballad	Slow	5
Mercy for the Memories	**Geoff Moore & the Distance**	**Folk/pop ballad**	**Slow**	**9**

Title	Artist	Style	Tempo	Seeker-Sensitivity Rating
Remember Your Chains	Steven Curtis Chapman	Acoustic MOR	Mid	2
Run Away	Steven Curtis Chapman	Pop	Up	7
Stranger to Holiness	Steve Camp	Ballad	Slow/mid	2
Who to Listen To	Amy Grant	Pop	Mid	8

Movie Clips

Title:	The Shawshank Redemption
Topic:	Regret; Consequences of sin
Description:	Red, a 40-year inmate, stands before the parole board and talks about his regret over his lost years.
Start Time:	2:05:30
Start Cue:	Bars slide open, door opens to parole board room
End Time:	2:07:32
End Cue:	Stop immediately after "I gotta live with that"
Comments:	

Title:	
Topic:	
Description:	
Start Time:	
Start Cue:	
End Time:	
End Cue:	
Comments:	

RELATIONSHIPS

Comforting Others

See also: **Hardship**

Message Titles

☐ *Love of Another Kind:* Comforting Love

_____

_____

_____

_____

Dramas

Title	Tone	Characters	Topics
Attack of the Well-Meaners	Mixed, mostly humorous	1 male, 2 females	Dealing with crisis; Friendship
The Breakfast Club	Mixed, mostly serious	4 males, 1 female	Friendship; Small groups; Friends in crisis
Mr. Hibbs' Day Off	Mixed; mime	3 males, 1 female, 1 child	Serving others; Self-denial; Being used by God
Shop Talk	Serious	2 males, 2 females	Failure; Adversity; Small groups
What Now?	Serious	2 males, 4 females	Coping with a crisis; Dealing with death
____	____	____	____
____	____	____	____
____	____	____	____
____	____	____	____

Songs

Title	Artist	Style	Tempo	Seeker-Sensitivity Rating
A Place to Call Home	*Willow Creek Music*	*Gospel ballad*	*Slow, in 3*	*10*
A Rose Is a Rose	Susan Ashton	Piano ballad	Slow	9
Be the One	**Al Denson**	**Power ballad**	**Slow**	**7**
The Extra Mile	Al Denson	Power Ballad	Slow	9
Helping Hand	Amy Grant	Pop	Mid/up	10
Holding Out Hope to You	Michael English	Power ballad	Slow	9
Let the Lord Love You	*Willow Creek Music*	*Acoustic guitar ballad*	*Slow*	*9*
Love Can Open the Door	Sandi Patti	Pop	Up	10
Not Too Far From Here	Kim Boyce	Ballad	Slow	7
Suffer in Silence	Susan Ashton	Folk/pop	Mid	10
_____	_____	_____	_____	_____
_____	_____	_____	_____	_____
_____	_____	_____	_____	_____
_____	_____	_____	_____	_____

Movie Clips

Title: _____

Topic: _____

Description: _____

Start Time: _____

Start Cue: _____

End Time: _____

End Cue: _____

Comments: _____

_____

Communication

See also: **Truth Telling**

Message Titles

- ❏ *The Age of Rage:* Expressing Anger Appropriately
- ❏ *The Age of Rage:* Responding to the Anger of Others
- ❏ *The Lost Art of Loving:* Please Speak My Language
- ❏ *Telling the Truth:* Expressing Positive Emotions
- ❏ *Telling the Truth:* Games People Play

_____

_____

_____

_____

Dramas

Title	Tone	Characters	Topics
The Luncheon	Serious	3 females	Mother/daughter conflict; Honesty in relationships
The Okra Windy Show	Humorous	3 males, 3 females	Honesty in relationships; Communication
A Problem of Perspective	Humorous	1 male, 1 female, 1 either male or female	Marriage; Marital conflict
Thanks for Listening	Humorous	1 male, 1 female, 1 male and 1 female teenager	Family; Listening

Songs

Title	Artist	Style	Tempo	Seeker-Sensitivity Rating
If I Had Only Known	Reba McEntire	Ballad	Slow	10
Only Here for a Little While	Billy Dean	Country	Mid/up	10
_____	_____	_____	_____	_____
_____	_____	_____	_____	_____
_____	_____	_____	_____	_____
_____	_____	_____	_____	_____

Movie Clips

Title: 8 Seconds

Topic: Regret; Communicating love

Description: A father, whose son has recently died, breaks down in remorse over not telling his son that he loved him.

Start Time: 1:27:10

Start Cue: Pallbearers carry casket out of church

End Time: 1:28:33

End Cue: "I loved him"

Comments: _____

_____

Title: _____

Topic: _____

Description: _____

Start Time: _____

Start Cue: _____

End Time: _____

End Cue: _____

Comments: _____

_____

Community

Different from **Small Groups** in that this topic speaks of the whole church, or groups of people within the church knowing, loving, and caring for each other—*being* the church to one another

See also: **The Church, Small Groups**

 ## Message Titles

- ❐ Discovering Community
- ❐ Making God's Dream (Community) Happen
- ❐ Only Community Is Forever
- ❐ The Reward for Relational Authenticity

_____

_____

_____

 ## Dramas

Title	Tone	Characters	Topics
The Breakfast Club	Mixed, mostly serious	4 males, 1 female	Friendship; Small groups; Friends in crisis
Don't Mention It	Mixed, mostly humorous	2 males, 2 females	Unemployment; Being open about problems
Just an Acquaintance	Mixed	2 males, 2 females	Relationships between men; Superficial relationships
Mr. X, Mr. Y, and Mr. Z	Humorous	4 males, 1 female, and a narrator	Friendship; Intimacy
Shop Talk	Serious	2 males, 2 females	Failure; Adversity; Small Groups
Something in Common	Mixed	3 females, 1 male	Starting relationships
_____	_____	_____	_____
_____	_____	_____	_____
_____	_____	_____	_____

Songs

Title	Artist	Style	Tempo	Seeker-Sensitivity Rating
Bridge Between Two Hearts	**Bob Carlisle**	**Pop**	**Up**	**9**
Gather at the River	Point of Grace	Pop	Up	8
I Believe in You	Steve Camp	Pop	Up	10
I Commit My Love to You	Twila Paris	Ballad	Slow	5
Isn't It Good	*Willow Creek Music*	*Ballad*	*Mid/slow*	*4*
Let's Build a Bridge	Michael English	Pop	Up	8
Let's Stand Together	**The Kry**	**Rock**	**Mid/up**	**1**
Love Can Build a Bridge	**The Judds**	**Ballad**	**Slow**	**10**
Somebody Make Me Laugh	**Patti Austin**	**Ballad**	**Slow**	**10**
Take My Hand	Russ Taff	Folk/rock	Mid	9
Undivided	**First Call**	**Ballad—trio**	**Slow**	**5**
We Are an Army	Trace Balin	Power ballad	Slow/mid	1
We Need Each Other	**Trace Balin**	**Power ballad**	**Slow/mid**	**7**
_____	_____	_____	_____	_____
_____	_____	_____	_____	_____
_____	_____	_____	_____	_____
_____	_____	_____	_____	_____

Movie Clips

Title: _____

Topic: _____

Description: _____

Start Time: _____

Start Cue: _____

End Time: _____

End Cue: _____

Comments: _____

_____

Control Issues

Message Titles

☐ *Love of Another Kind:* Love Busters

_____

_____

_____

_____

Package Suggestion

Drama:
Let Me Go

Song:
Let Me Go

Dramas

Title	Tone	Characters	Topics
Hungry Children	Very serious	1 male, 1 female, 1 boy, 1 teenage girl	Abusive parenting; Anger; Control issues
Let Me Go	Mixed	2 females	Parenting; Letting go of adult children
The Plate Spinner	Humorous	5 males, 4 females, 1 narrator	Pace of life; Being in control
Speak for Yourself	Humorous	3 males, 3 females	Being an enabler; Insecurity
Terminal Visit	Serious	3 females	Resurrecting relationships; Family conflict

Songs

Title	Artist	Style	Tempo	Seeker-Sensitivity Rating
In My Father's Hands	Susan Ashton	Folk/pop	Mid	9
Let Me Go	Susan Ashton	Folk ballad	Slow	10

Movie Clips

Title: Shadowlands

Topic: Control issues; Intimacy

Description: Joy confronts Jack on the fact that he has set up his world so that nobody can touch him—he has blocked intimacy by surrounding himself with people he can control.

Start Time: 1:05:55

Start Cue: "So what do you do here . . . think great thoughts?"

End Time: 1:07:37

End Cue: "You just don't like it. Nor do I"

Comments: _____

_____

Title: _____

Topic: _____

Description: _____

Start Time: _____

Start Cue: _____

End Time: _____

End Cue: _____

Comments: _____

_____

Draining Relationships

Message Titles

- ☐ *The Lost Art of Loving:* People Who Love Too Much
- ☐ *Love of Another Kind:* Loving Hard-to-Love People

_____

_____

_____

_____

_____

Dramas

Title	Tone	Characters	Topics
The Angry Woman	Serious	2 males, 3 females, 1 narrator	The roots of anger
Best Friends	Humorous	2 males, 2 females	Friendship; Insecurity; Needy people
Brother's Keeper	Serious	3 males	Unhealthy dependencies
No Thanks Giving	Serious	3 females	Truth telling; Family dynamics
Six Happy Hearts	Mixed	6 males or females	Laughter; A sour spirit affects others
Watching From the Window	Serious	1 female, 1 child	Stress of life; Challenge of motherhood; Draining relationships
What Are Friends for?	Serious	1 male, 2 females	Friendship; Truth telling

Songs

No songs specifically about Draining Relationships. *Look at* Our Value to God, Compassion, *and* Relational Conflict.

Title	Artist	Style	Tempo	Seeker-Sensitivity Rating
_____	_____	_____	_____	_____
_____	_____	_____	_____	_____
_____	_____	_____	_____	_____
_____	_____	_____	_____	_____

Movie Clips

Title: _____

Topic: _____

Description: _____

Start Time: _____

Start Cue: _____

End Time: _____

End Cue: _____

Comments: _____

_____

Programming Tip

Develop a "mission statement"

Everyone on the programming team—volunteers and staff members—should have a clear understanding of the mission, vision, and values of the team. Spend some time together developing a clear statement of purpose for your ministry. Then from time to time, take stock and evaluate how well you are accomplishing each part of the mission statement.

Family Relationships
~ Decay of the Family ~

Might also include: *Broken Families, Dysfunctional Families*
See also: **Divorce**

Package Suggestion

Drama:
Richard: 1992

Song:
Time to Return

Message Titles

- ☐ *Defining Family Values:* Endangered Values
- ☐ *Facing the Family Challenge:* Fragile—Handle With Care

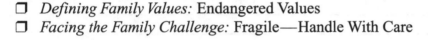

Dramas

Title	Tone	Characters	Topics
All Gummed Up	Serious	1 male, 1 female, 1 offstage voice	Adultery; Dealing with past hurts; The pain of lies
Hungry Children	Very serious	1 male, 1 female, 1 boy, 1 teenage girl	Abusive parenting; Anger; Control issues
I Know What You Want	Serious	2 males, 2 females	God's love; Dysfunctional families
The Intruder	Serious	1 male, 1 female	Self-image; Destructive parenting; God's love in spite of failure
No Thanks Giving	Serious	3 females	Truth telling; Family dynamics

Title	Tone	Characters	Topics
Straight-Jacketed	Serious	1 male	Bondage to past and to sin; Anger toward God
Richard: 1992	Serious	2 males, 1 female	Anger; Rebellion; Decay of the family
Tired of Trying	Serious	1 male, 2 females	Dealing with the anger of others; Confronting injustice

Songs

Many of these dramas leave the audience in a tender, vulnerable place. Responding with a song of Healing *or* God's Love, *such as* "Peace Be Still," *often works well.*

Title	Artist	Style	Tempo	Seeker-Sensitivity Rating
Cat's in the Cradle	Harry Chapin; Ugly Kid Joe	Folk	Mid	10
Time to Return	*Willow Creek Music*	*Ballad*	*Slow*	*8*

Movie Clips

Title: City Slickers
Topic: Dysfunctional families; Friendship
Description: Three friends share the best and worst days of their lives.
Start Time: 1:12:45
Start Cue: "All right, I got one"
End Time: 1:14:50
End Cue: "Same day"
Comments: Could start earlier, but Billy Crystal swears briefly during his worst-day description

Title: Dead Poet's Society

Topic: Destructive parenting

Description: Todd, a boarding school student, shares with a friend that his parents sent him the same birthday present that they gave him the previous year. Illustrates disconnected parenting.

Start Time: 1:05:40

Start Cue: "Todd?"

End Time: 1:07:30

End Cue: "You'll get another one next year"

Comments: _____

_____

Title: Forrest Gump

Topic: Child abuse; Bondage to the past

Description: Jenny and Forrest walk by the house where Jenny was abused as a child. She throws rocks at it.

Start Time: 1:45:30

Start Cue: After "Jenny, most of the times, was real quiet"

End Time: 1:46:50

End Cue: "Sometimes there just aren't enough rocks"

Comments: _____

_____

Title: Parenthood

Topic: Parental neglect; Dealing with past hurts

Description: Funny, bittersweet scene where young Gil (Steve Martin plays the adult Gil) is taken to a baseball game by his father and then left with an usher. We discover it's actually a combination of memories of his strained childhood.

Start Time: 0:00:05

Start Cue: Start at fade-up. This is the opening scene

End Time: 0:02:28

End Cue: "Strong, happy, confident kids"

Comments: Profanity immediately follows cutoff point

_____

Title: _____

Topic: _____

Description: _____

Start Time: _____

Start Cue: _____

End Time: _____

End Cue: _____

Comments: _____

_____

~ Destructive Parenting ~

Message Titles

- ❏ Fixing Broken Relationships
- ❏ *Facing the Family Challenge:* Fragile—Handle With Care
- ❏ *Parenthood:* Mistakes Parents Make

Package Suggestion

Drama:
Hungry Children

Song:
Peace Be Still

Dramas

Title	Tone	Characters	Topics
Expectations of the Expecting	Mixed	1 male, 1 female	Parenting; Affirming personality differences
Hungry Children	Very serious	1 male, 1 female, 1 boy, 1 teenage girl	Abusive parenting; Anger; Control issues
The Intruder	Serious	1 male, 1 female	Self-image; Destructive parenting; God's love in spite of failure
Reason Enough	Mixed, mostly serious	1 male, 1 female	Importance of faith grounded in reason
Richard: 1992	Serious	2 males, 1 female	Anger; Rebellion; Decay of the family
Tired of Trying	Serious	1 male, 2 females	Dealing with the anger of others; Confronting injustice
Wonderfully Made	Serious	2 females, 2 males, 1 narrator	Affirming a child's uniqueness

Songs

No specific songs on this topic. Look at God's Love, Healing, or Our Value to God as a contrast.

Title	Artist	Style	Tempo	Seeker-Sensitivity Rating
_____	_____	_____	_____	_____
_____	_____	_____	_____	_____
_____	_____	_____	_____	_____
_____	_____	_____	_____	_____

Movie Clips

Title: City Slickers
Topic: Dysfunctional families; Friendship
Description: Three friends share the best and worst days of their lives.
Start Time: 1:12:45
Start Cue: "All right, I got one"
End Time: 1:14:50
End Cue: "Same day"
Comments: Could start earlier, but Billy Crystal swears briefly during his worst-day description
_____

Title: Dead Poet's Society
Topic: Destructive parenting
Description: Todd, a boarding school student, shares with a friend that his parents sent him the same birthday present that they gave him the previous year. Illustrates disconnected parenting.
Start Time: 1:05:40
Start Cue: "Todd?"
End Time: 1:07:30
End Cue: "You'll get another one next year"
Comments: _____
_____

Title: Forrest Gump
Topic: Child abuse; Bondage to the past
Description: Jenny and Forrest walk by the house where Jenny was abused as a child. She throws rocks at it.
Start Time: 1:45:30
Start Cue: After "Jenny, most of the times, was real quiet"
End Time: 1:46:50

End Cue: "Sometimes there just aren't enough rocks"

Comments: _____

_____

Title: Indiana Jones and the Last Crusade
Topic: Father/son relationships
Description: Indiana Jones mildly confronts his father about the lack of a relationship between them.
Start Time: 1:13:45
Start Cue: "Remember the last time we had a quiet drink?"
End Time: 1:15:05
End Cue: "I can't think of anything"
Comments: Conversation is over a drink. May be offensive to some churches

_____

Title: Kramer vs. Kramer
Topic: The effect of divorce on children
Description: Dustin Hoffman reads a letter to his little boy from Meryl Streep, telling him why she left. The effects on the child are prominent.
Start Time: 0:21:50
Start Cue: Just before "Hey Billy!"
End Time: 23:45
End Cue: Scene ends with Billy staring at the TV
Comments: _____

_____

Title: Parenthood
Topic: Parental neglect; Dealing with past hurts
Description: Funny, bittersweet scene where young Gil (Steve Martin plays the adult Gil) is taken to a baseball game by his father and then left with an usher. We discover it's actually a combination of memories of his strained childhood.
Start Time: 0:00:05
Start Cue: Start at fade-up. This is the opening scene
End Time: 0:02:28
End Cue: "Strong, happy, confident kids"
Comments: Profanity immediately follows cutoff point

_____

Title: Parenthood
Topic: Unrealistic parental expectations
Description: Funny clip about parents' unrealistic expectations of their kids. Two parents lecture their daughter about not putting enough effort into her studies. At the end we realize she's 3 years old.
Start Time: 0:12:40
Start Cue: "Oh listen, Julie got 1291..."
End Time: 0:13:45
End Cue: "That's all I ask"
Comments: _____

_____

Title: Searching for Bobby Fischer

Topic: Fatherhood; Failure; Destructive parenting

Description: Eight-year-old Josh loses a chess match, and his dad angrily confronts him about losing. Illustrates a man who has invested too much in his son's success.

Start Time: 1:06:30

Start Cue: Shot of clock tower. "Seven moves" is first line

End Time: 1:08:20

End Cue: "Sorry"

Comments: _____

_____

Title: _____

Topic: _____

Description: _____

Start Time: _____

Start Cue: _____

End Time: _____

End Cue: _____

Comments: _____

_____

~ Family Conflict ~

See also: **Relational Conflict**

Message Titles

Package Suggestion
Drama: *Terminal Visit*
Song: *Beyond Justice to Mercy*

❏ Fixing Broken Relationships
❏ *Facing the Family Challenge:* Fragile—Handle With Care

_____
_____
_____
_____

Dramas

Title	Tone	Characters	Topics
Anything But Religion	Mixed, mostly serious	2 males, 2 females	Denominational differences; Families alienated because of religion
Brother's Keeper	Serious	3 males	Unhealthy dependencies
Finding Evidence	Serious	2 males, 1 female	Trust; Jumping to conclusions
Hungry Children	Very serious	1 male, 1 female, 1 boy, 1 teenage girl	Abusive parenting; Anger; Control issues
The Intruder	Serious	1 male, 1 female	Self-image; Destructive parenting; God's love in spite of failure
The Luncheon	Serious	3 females	Mother/daughter conflict; Honesty in relationships
Misjudged Love	Serious	2 males, 1 female	Homosexuality; AIDS; Father/son relationship
No Thanks Giving	Serious	3 females	Truth telling; Family dynamics
Remembrances	Serious	1 male, 1 female	Parent/child relationships; Forgiveness
Richard: 1992	Serious	2 males, 1 female	Anger; Rebellion; Decay of the family
Terminal Visit	Serious	3 females	Resurrecting relationships; Family conflict
Tired of Trying	Serious	1 male, 2 females	Dealing with the anger of others; Confronting injustice
Watching From the Window	Serious	1 female, 1 child	Stress of life; Challenge of motherhood; Draining relationships

 # Songs

Title	Artist	Style	Tempo	Seeker-Sensitivity Rating
Beyond Justice to Mercy	**Susan Ashton**	**Ballad**	**Slow**	**10**
Bridge Between Two Hearts	**Bob Carlisle**	**Pop**	**Up**	**9**
Common Ground	Sierra	Folk trio	Slow	9

Title	Artist	Style	Tempo	Seeker-Sensitivity Rating
The Last Song	**Elton John**	**Ballad**	**Slow**	**10**
The Living Years	Mike & the Mechanics	Pop	Mid/up	10
Love Conquers All	**Pam Thum**	**Pop**	**Up**	**10**
Meet in the Middle	**Diamond Rio**	**Country**	**Mid/up**	**10**
That's What Love Is For	Amy Grant	Power ballad	Slow	10

Movie Clips

Title: Hoosiers
Topic: Unconditional love; Forgiveness
Description: Dennis Hopper's character, a recovering alcoholic, is in the hospital drying out. His son visits him and tells him he loves him.
Start Time: 1:30:15
Start Cue: "No school this small"
End Time: 1:32:30
End Cue: "Anyway, no school this small has ever been in the state championship!"
Comments: Needs some setup for those who haven't seen the movie

Title: _____
Topic: _____
Description: _____
Start Time: _____
Start Cue: _____
End Time: _____
End Cue: _____
Comments: _____

~ Family Relationships, General ~

Message Titles

- ❏ **Defining Family Values:** Origin of Values • Transmitting Values • Endangered Values
- ❏ **Facing the Family Challenge:** Fragile—Handle With Care • Traits of a Healthy Family • Forming a Spiritual Foundation • The Future of the Family
- ❏ **Turning Houses Into Homes:** The Home as a Filling Station • The Home as a Training Center • The Home as a Trauma Center • The Home as a Seminary

_____

_____

_____

_____

Dramas

Title	Tone	Characters	Topics
Changes	Mixed, mostly serious	2 males, 2 females	Re-parenting parents; Family; Aging parents
Family Snapshots—Take I	Humorous	3 males, 2 females, 1 jr. high boy	Family communication
Family Snapshots—Take II	Humorous	2 males, 2 females, 1 jr. high boy	Families; Values; Priorities
Family Snapshots—Take III	Mixed; touching	1 male, 1 female	Parent/child relationships; Helping kids through hard times
Family Snapshots—Take IV	Serious	2 males, 3 females, 1 jr. high boy	Family; Self-sacrifice
First Things First	Humorous	1 male, 1 female, 1 female infant	New parents; Balancing children and marriage
Fishin'	Mixed; touching	2 males	Expressing positive emotions; Father/son relationships
For Better or Worse—Part VI	Mixed	3 males, 3 females	Family; Marriage

Title	Tone	Characters	Topics
Hungry Children	Very serious	1 male, 1 female, 1 boy, 1 teenage girl	Abusive parenting; Anger; Control issues
I Know What You Want	Serious	2 males, 2 females	God's love; Dysfunctional families
The Intruder	Serious	1 male, 1 female	Self-image; Destructive parenting; God's love in spite of failure
Masterpiece	Mixed; touching	1 male, 1 female, 2 teenage females	Self-esteem; Parenting
No Thanks Giving	Serious	3 females	Truth telling; Family dynamics
Reflections	Mixed	1 male, 2 females, 2 children	Motherhood
Remembrances	Serious	1 male, 1 female	Parent/child relationships; Forgiveness
The Speculators	Humorous	2 males, 1 female	Risk taking; Missed opportunities
Suit Yourself	Humorous	1 male, 2 females	Parenting; Letting kids make their own decisions
Thanks for Listening	Humorous	1 male, 1 female, 1 male and 1 female teenager	Family; Listening
Worth Keeping	Mixed; touching	1 male, 2 females	The nobility of motherhood; Single parenting

---

 # Songs

Title	Artist	Style	Tempo	Seeker-Sensitivity Rating
Cat's in the Cradle	Harry Chapin; Ugly Kid Joe	Folk	Mid	10
Hats	Amy Grant	Pop	Up	10
Heirlooms	**Amy Grant**	**Ballad**	**Slow**	**8**
How Could I Ask for More	Cindy Morgan	Piano ballad	Slow	9
I Want to Be Just Like You	**Phillips, Craig and Dean**	**MOR**	**Mid/slow**	**9**
If I Had Only Known	**Reba McEntire**	**Ballad**	**Slow**	**10**
Isn't It Good	*Willow Creek Music*	*Ballad*	*Mid/slow*	*4*
Let Me Go	**Susan Ashton**	**Folk ballad**	**Slow**	**10**

Title	Artist	Style	Tempo	Seeker-Sensitivity Rating
Midnight Oil	**Phillips, Craig and Dean**	**Acoustic ballad**	**Slow**	**7**
Only Here for a Little While	**Billy Dean**	**Country**	**Mid/up**	**10**
Thanks for So Much Love	Harry Newman	Ballad	Slow	10
_____	_____	_____	_____	_____
_____	_____	_____	_____	_____
_____	_____	_____	_____	_____

Movie Clips

Title: 8 Seconds
Topic: Regret; Communicating love
Description: A father, whose son has recently died, breaks down in remorse over not telling his son that he loved him.
Start Time: 1:27:10
Start Cue: Pallbearers carry casket from church
End Time: 1:28:33
End Cue: "I loved him"
Comments: _____
_____

Title: Dad
Topic: Father/son relationships
Description: Ted Danson and Jack Lemmon play a father and son. Lemmon is dying in a hospital bed, and they have a poignant exchange, ending with Danson crawling into bed with his dad.
Start Time: 1:46:20
Start Cue: "How you feeling?"
End Time: 1:50:35
End Cue: "I must have done something right." End after wide shot
Comments: _____
_____

Title: Father of the Bride
Topic: Parenthood; Father/daughter relationship
Description: Steve Martin plays basketball with his daughter as "My Girl" plays in background. Shows the warmth and fun of their relationship.
Start Time: 0:14:55
Start Cue: "Suppose you're not in the mood for a little one-on-one?"
End Time: 0:17:00
End Cue: Steve Martin and daughter walk off together
Comments: _____
_____

Title: Parenthood

Topic: Parental neglect; Dealing with past hurts

Description: Funny, bittersweet scene where young Gil (Steve Martin plays the adult Gil) is taken to a baseball game by his father and then left with an usher. We discover it's actually a combination of memories of his strained childhood.

Start Time: 0:00:05

Start Cue: Start at fade-up. This is the opening scene

End Time: 0:02:28

End Cue: "Strong, happy, confident kids"

Comments: Profanity immediately follows cutoff point

_____

Title: _____

Topic: _____

Description: _____

Start Time: _____

Start Cue: _____

End Time: _____

End Cue: _____

Comments: _____

_____

- Generation Gap -

See also: **Relational Conflict**

 # Message Titles

❑ Bridging the Generation Gap
❑ Intergenerational Community
❑ *Understanding the Times:* The '60s

_____
_____
_____
_____
_____

Dramas

Title	Tone	Characters	Topics
Finding Evidence	Serious	2 males, 1 female	Trust; Jumping to conclusions
Richard: 1968	Mixed	2 males, 2 females	Youthful idealism; Changing societal values; Generation gap; The '60s

Songs

Title	Artist	Style	Tempo	Seeker-Sensitivity Rating
The Living Years	Mike & the Mechanics	Pop	Mid/up	10
When We Fail Love	**Grover Levy**	**Piano ballad**	**Slow**	**10**

Movie Clips

Title: _____

Topic: _____

Description: _____

Start Time: _____

Start Cue: _____

End Time: _____

End Cue: _____

Comments: _____

_____

~ Parent-Child Relationships ~

Refers both to relationships between adult children and their parents and to parents with kids still in the home. This deals less with the challenges and "how-tos" of parenthood, and more with the relationships.

Message Titles

- ❏ The Launching Pad of Loving
- ❏ Leaving a Living Legacy
- ❏ Phantom Fathers
- ❏ Unforgettable Fathers
- ❏ *Facing the Family Challenge:* The Future of the Family
- ❏ *Fifth Commandment:* Honor Your Parents
- ❏ *Parenthood:* Re-parenting Parents

_____

_____

_____

_____

Dramas

Title	Tone	Characters	Topics
Changes	Mixed, mostly serious	2 males, 2 females	Re-parenting parents; Family; Aging parents
Definitely Safe	Serious— heartwarming	2 males, 1 female	Father's Day; Prodigal son; Unconditional love
Family Snapshots—Take I	Humorous	3 males, 2 females, 1 jr. high boy	Family communication
Family Snapshots—Take III	Mixed; touching	1 male, 1 female	Parent/child relationships; Helping kids through hard times
Finding Evidence	Serious	2 males, 1 female	Trust; Jumping to conclusions
Fishin'	Mixed; touching	2 males	Expressing positive emotions; Father/son relationships

Title	Tone	Characters	Topics
In the Dark	Serious	1 male, 1 female	Death of a child; Grief
The Intruder	Serious	1 male, 1 female	Self-image; Destructive parenting; God's love in spite of failure
Let Me Go	Mixed	2 females	Parenting; Letting go of adult children
Lucky Day at the Ballpark	Mixed	2 males, 1 boy	Father's Day; Proper priorities
The Luncheon	Serious	3 females	Mother/daughter conflict; Honesty in relationships
Masterpiece	Mixed; touching	1 male, 1 female, 2 teenage females	Self-esteem; Parenting
Misjudged Love	Serious	2 males, 1 female	Homosexuality; AIDS; Father/son relationship
A Mother's Day	Mixed	1 male, 2 females	Mother's Day
No Thanks Giving	Serious	3 females	Truth telling; Family dynamics
Quality Time	Serious	1 male, 1 female, 2 teenage girls	Fatherhood; Workaholism
Reflections	Mixed	1 male, 2 females, 2 children	Motherhood
Remembrances	Serious	1 male, 1 female	Parent/child relationships; Forgiveness
Richard: 1992	Serious	2 males, 1 female	Anger; Rebellion; Decay of the family
A Second Chance	Serious	3 males, 1 female	Decision making; Father/son relationships
Suit Yourself	Humorous	1 male, 2 females	Parenting; Letting kids make their own decisions
Worth Keeping	Mixed; touching	1 male, 2 females	The nobility of motherhood; Single parenting
_____	_____	_____	_____
_____	_____	_____	_____
_____	_____	_____	_____

Songs

Title	Artist	Style	Tempo	Seeker-Sensitivity Rating
Cat's in the Cradle	Harry Chapin; Ugly Kid Joe	Folk	Mid	10
I Want to Be Just Like You	**Phillips, Craig and Dean**	**MOR**	**Mid/slow**	9
The Last Song	**Elton John**	**Ballad**	**Slow**	10

Title	Artist	Style	Tempo	Seeker-Sensitivity Rating
The Living Years	Mike & the Mechanics	Pop	Mid/up	10
Let Me Go	**Susan Ashton**	**Folk ballad**	**Slow**	**10**
Midnight Oil	**Phillips, Craig and Dean**	**Acoustic ballad**	**Slow**	7
Thanks for So Much Love	Harry Newman	Ballad	Slow	10
You Don't Count the Cost	Billy Dean	Country ballad	Slow	10
___	___	___	___	___
___	___	___	___	___
___	___	___	___	___
___	___	___	___	___

 # Movie Clips

Title: 8 Seconds

Topic: Regret; Communicating love

Description: A father, whose son has recently died, breaks down in remorse over not telling his son that he loved him.

Start Time: 1:27:10

Start Cue: Pallbearers carry casket out of church

End Time: 1:28:33

End Cue: "I loved him"

Comments: _____
_____

Title: Dad

Topic: Father/son relationships

Description: Ted Danson and Jack Lemmon play a father and son. Lemmon is dying in a hospital bed, and they have a poignant exchange, ending with Danson crawling into bed with his dad.

Start Time: 1:46:20

Start Cue: "How you feeling?"

End Time: 1:50:35

End Cue: "I must have done something right." End after wide shot

Comments: _____
_____

Title: Dead Poet's Society

Topic: Destructive parenting

Description: Todd, a boarding school student, shares with a friend that his parents sent him the same birthday present that they gave him the previous year. Illustrates disconnected parenting.

Start Time: 1:05:40

Start Cue: "Todd?"

End Time: 1:07:30

End Cue: "You'll get another one next year"

Comments: _____

_____

Title: Father of the Bride

Topic: Parenthood; Letting go of adult children

Description: Steve Martin's daughter tells him she's getting married, and he sees her as a little girl telling him. Very short clip.

Start Time: 0:09:30

Start Cue: "I met somebody in Rome"

End Time: 0:10:45

End Cue: Little girl says, "We're getting married"

Comments: Might be used in conjunction with song "Watercolour Ponies" by Wayne Watson

_____

Title: Father of the Bride

Topic: Parenthood; Father/daughter relationship

Description: Steve Martin plays basketball with his daughter as "My Girl" plays in the background. Shows the warmth and fun of their relationship.

Start Time: 0:14:55

Start Cue: "Suppose you're not in the mood for a little one-on-one?"

End Time: 0:17:00

End Cue: Steve Martin and his daughter walk off together

Comments: _____

_____

Title: Indiana Jones and the Last Crusade

Topic: Father/son relationships

Description: Indiana Jones mildly confronts his father about the lack of a relationship between them.

Start Time: 1:13:45

Start Cue: "Remember the last time we had a quiet drink?"

End Time: 1:15:05

End Cue: "I can't think of anything"

Comments: Conversation is over a drink. May be offensive in some churches

_____

Title: Parenthood

Topic: Parental neglect; Dealing with past hurts

Description: Funny, bittersweet scene where young Gil (Steve Martin plays the adult Gil) is taken to a baseball game by his father and then left with an usher. We discover it's actually a combination of memories of his strained childhood.

Start Time: 0:00:05

Start Cue: Start at fade-up. This is the opening scene

End Time: 0:02:28

End Cue: "Strong, happy, confident kids"

Comments: Profanity immediately follows cutoff point

_____

~ Parenting ~

Refers primarily, though not exclusively, to parents with children still in the home

Message Titles

- ❏ Formula for a Successful Family (Ephesians 6:1–4)
- ❏ **Parenthood:** To Be or Not to Be • Raising Whole Children • Affirming Each Child's Uniqueness • Mistakes Parents Make • Re-parenting Parents
- ❏ **Turning Houses Into Homes:** The Home as a Filling Station • The Home as a Training Center • The Home as a Trauma Center • The Home as a Seminary

_____

_____

_____

_____

Dramas

Title	Tone	Characters	Topics
Expectations of the Expecting	Mixed	1 male, 1 female	Parenting; Affirming personality differences
Fat Chance	Mixed, mostly humorous	1 female	Parenting
Finding Evidence	Serious	2 males, 1 female	Trust; Jumping to conclusions
First Things First	Humorous	1 male, 1 female, 1 female infant	New parents; Balancing children and marriage
Guidance Counselors	Humorous	2 males, 1 female	The power of TV; Sources for values
Hungry Children	Very serious	1 male, 1 female, 1 boy, 1 teenage girl	Abusive parenting; Anger; Control issues
I Know What You Want	Serious	2 males, 2 females	God's love; Dysfunctional families
In the Dark	Serious	1 male, 1 female	Death of a child; Grief
The Intruder	Serious	1 male, 1 female	Self-image; Destructive parenting; God's love in spite of failure

Title	Tone	Characters	Topics
The Lamaze Class	Humorous	3 males, 4 females	Sources for values; Parenting
Let Me Go	Mixed	2 females	Parenting; Letting go of adult children
Little What's His Face	Mixed	3 males, 3 females	Christmas; Parenting
Lucky Day at the Ballpark	Mixed	2 males, 1 boy	Father's Day; Proper priorities
Masterpiece	Mixed; touching	1 male, 1 female, 2 teenage females	Self-esteem; Parenting
Misjudged Love	Serious	2 males, 1 female	Homosexuality; AIDS; Father/son relationship
No More Womb	Mixed	1 male, 1 female	State of the world; Fear of the unknown
On Track	Serious	2 males, 1 female	Forcing people into molds; Character building
One Day at the Zoo	Humorous	1 narrator, 3 males, 2 females, and some offstage voices	Fatherhood
Out of Control	Humorous	2 males, 1 female	Fatherhood; Parenting
Quality Time	Serious	1 male, 1 female, 2 teenage girls	Fatherhood; Workaholism
Reflections	Mixed	1 male, 2 females, 2 children	Motherhood
Remembrances	Serious	1 male, 1 female	Parent/child relationships; Forgiveness
Suit Yourself	Humorous	1 male, 2 females	Parenting; Letting kids make their own decisions
Wonderfully Made	Serious	2 females, 2 males, 1 narrator	Affirming a child's uniqueness
Worth Keeping	Mixed; touching	1 male, 2 females	The nobility of motherhood; Single parenting
_____	_____	_____	_____
_____	_____	_____	_____
_____	_____	_____	_____
_____	_____	_____	_____
_____	_____	_____	_____

Songs

Title	Artist	Style	Tempo	Seeker-Sensitivity Rating
Cat's in the Cradle	Harry Chapin; Ugly Kid Joe	Folk	Mid	10
I Want to Be Just Like You	**Phillips, Craig and Dean**	**MOR**	**Mid/slow**	**9**
Isn't It Good	*Willow Creek Music*	*Ballad*	*Mid/slow*	*4*
Let Me Go	**Susan Ashton**	**Folk ballad**	**Slow**	**10**
Midnight Oil	**Phillips, Craig and Dean**	**Acoustic ballad**	**Slow**	**7**
Only Here for a Little While	**Billy Dean**	**Country**	**Mid/up**	**10**
Somewhere in the World	Wayne Watson	Acoustic ballad	Slow	3
Thanks for So Much Love	Harry Newman	Ballad	Slow	10
_____	_____	_____	_____	_____
_____	_____	_____	_____	_____
_____	_____	_____	_____	_____
_____	_____	_____	_____	_____

Movie Clips

Title: Dad

Topic: Father/son relationships

Description: Ted Danson and Jack Lemmon play a father and son. Lemmon is dying in a hospital bed, and they have a poignant exchange, ending with Danson crawling into bed with his dad.

Start Time: 1:46:20

Start Cue: "How you feeling?"

End Time: 1:50:35

End Cue: "I must have done something right." End after wide shot

Comments: _____

_____

Title: Dead Poet's Society

Topic: Destructive parenting

Description: Todd, a boarding school student, shares with a friend that his parents sent him the same birthday present that they gave him the previous year. Illustrates disconnected parenting.

Start Time: 1:05:40

Start Cue: "Todd?"

End Time: 1:07:30

End Cue: "You'll get another one next year"

Comments: _____

_____

Title: Father of the Bride

Topic: Parenthood; Letting go of adult children

Description: Steve Martin's daughter tells him she's getting married, and he sees her as a little girl telling him. Very short clip.

Start Time: 0:09:30

Start Cue: "I met somebody in Rome"

End Time: 0:10:45

End Cue: Little girl says, "We're getting married"

Comments: Might be used in conjunction with song "Watercolour Ponies" by Wayne Watson

---

Title: Father of the Bride

Topic: Parenthood; Father/daughter relationship

Description: Steve Martin plays basketball with his daughter as "My Girl" plays in background. Shows the warmth and fun of their relationship.

Start Time: 0:14:55

Start Cue: "Suppose you're not in the mood for a little one-on-one?"

End Time: 0:17:00

End Cue: Steve Martin and daughter walk off together

Comments: _____

Title: Indiana Jones and the Last Crusade

Topic: Father/son relationships

Description: Indiana Jones mildly confronts his father about the lack of a relationship between them.

Start Time: 1:13:45

Start Cue: "Remember the last time we had a quiet drink?"

End Time: 1:15:05

End Cue: "I can't think of anything"

Comments: Conversation is over a drink. May be offensive in some churches

---

Title: Kramer vs. Kramer

Topic: Challenges of parenthood; Rebellion

Description: Dustin Hoffman's son refuses to eat his dinner and goes to eat ice cream instead. High identification for parents.

Start Time: 0:35:40

Start Cue: Begin at "It's Salisbury Steak"

End Time: 0:37:15

End Cue: Billy puts spoon in his mouth. Don't let it go past this

Comments: Can be used to show the challenges of parenthood or to illustrate rebellious human nature

---

Title: Kramer vs. Kramer

Topic: Effects of divorce on children

Description: Dustin Hoffman reads a letter to his little boy from Meryl Streep, telling him why she left. The effects on the child are prominent.

Start Time: 0:21:50

Start Cue: Just before "Hey Billy!"
End Time: 23:45
End Cue: Scene ends with Billy staring at the TV
Comments: _____
_____

Title: Kramer vs. Kramer
Topic: Divorce; Effects of divorce on children
Description: Billy tells his dad he thinks his mom left because he (Billy) was bad. Dustin Hoffman explains why he thinks she left. Very moving clip.
Start Time: 0:39:10
Start Cue: Billy turns on the light and says "Daddy, . . ."—mostly whispered
End Time: 0:41:40
End Cue: Dustin Hoffman closes the door
Comments: Video is dark, and audio is mostly whispered. Clip's effectiveness may vary, depending on the quality of church's equipment

Title: Parenthood
Topic: Parenthood
Description: Very short, funny clip shows the "joys" of parenthood—Steve Martin's daughter throws up on him.
Start Time: 0:06:45
Start Cue: "Hi, Daddy"
End Time: 0:07:12
End Cue: "Waiting for her head to spin around"
Comments: _____
_____

Title: Parenthood
Topic: Unrealistic parental expectations
Description: Funny clip about parents' unrealistic expectations of their kids. Two parents lecture their daughter about not putting enough effort into her studies. At the end we realize she's 3 years old.
Start Time: 0:12:40
Start Cue: "Oh listen, Julie got 1291"
End Time: 0:13:45
End Cue: "That's all I ask"
Comments: _____
_____

Title: Parenthood
Topic: Joys of parenthood
Description: Short but heartwarming clip where a boy tells his dad he wants to work where Dad does someday so they can still see each other every day.
Start Time: 1:03:25
Start Cue: Mom says, "Goodnight, sweetheart"
End Time: 1:04:10
End Cue: End before "Hubba Hubba"
Comments: _____
_____

Title:	Parenthood
Topic:	Frustrations of parenting
Description:	While looking for their son's retainer, parents talk about how difficult it is to know how to raise their son. Steve Martin says profound things about the reality of parenting.
Start Time:	1:13:30
Start Cue:	Steve Martin looking through garbage for retainer
End Time:	1:15:15
End Cue:	"Then they grow up to be like . . . me"
Comments:	_____
	_____

Title:	Parenthood
Topic:	Parenting
Description:	Funny scene. Steve Martin has his son play second base and has a daydream of his son graduating from college as valedictorian. When his son loses the game, he has a daydream of his son being a mad sniper shooting up the college, yelling "You made me play second base."
Start Time:	0:42:15
Start Cue:	"We're gonna need a new second baseman"
End Time:	0:46:50
End Cue:	"It's important to be supportive"
Comments:	_____
	_____

Title:	Parenthood
Topic:	Parenting; Ups and downs of parenting
Description:	Steve Martin and his wife argue about having another child. Grandma comes in and tells a story about a rollercoaster, which is a thinly veiled analogy to parenting.
Start Time:	1:48:40
Start Cue:	Steve Martin says, "I love you"
End Time:	1:51:15
End Cue:	"Well, I'll be seeing you in the car." Could also end at "If she's so brilliant, how come she's in the neighbor's car?"
Comments:	_____
	_____

Title:	Searching for Bobby Fischer
Topic:	Fatherhood; Failure; Destructive parenting
Description:	Eight-year-old Josh loses a chess match, and his dad angrily confronts him about losing. Illustrates a man who has invested too much in his son's success.
Start Time:	1:06:30
Start Cue:	Shot of clock tower. "Seven moves" is first line
End Time:	1:08:20
End Cue:	"Sorry"
Comments:	_____
	_____

Title: She's Having a Baby

Topic: Parenthood; Fear of parenthood

Description: Jake's wife tells him she stopped taking her birth-control pills. He screams and has a vision of being strapped to a speeding train car and crashing into a brick wall.

Start Time: 0:57:45/0:58:45

Start Cue: "Are you mad?"/"If I tell you something, will you promise"

End Time: 0:59:30

End Cue: Jake crashes into the wall

Comments: _____

_____

Title: _____

Topic: _____

Description: _____

Start Time: _____

Start Cue: _____

End Time: _____

End Cue: _____

Comments: _____

_____

Programming Tip

Great art

As a programmer, you will find it helpful to take in and experience great art in many forms. Visit art museums, listen to great music, attend live theater performances. Drink in the works of great poets, sculptors, architects, composers—artists who create works that are alive with brilliance and significance. As we understand why inspired art moves and changes us, we become more skilled in using the arts for God's purposes in the church.

Friendship

Message Titles

- ❏ Relationship Management
- ❏ The Rewards of Relationships
- ❏ Superficial or Significant?
- ❏ **Enriching Your Relationships:** Enriching Your Relationships
  • A Formula for Friendship • Relational Viruses • The Secret to
  Lasting Friendships
- ❏ **The Lost Art of Loving:** Why Aren't You Normal Like Me? • Please Speak My Language • Resurrecting Dying Loves • The Launching Pad of Love • People Who Love Too Much

_____
_____
_____
_____

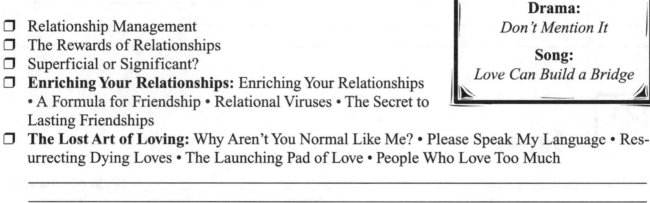

Package Suggestion

Drama:
Don't Mention It

Song:
Love Can Build a Bridge

Dramas

Title	Tone	Characters	Topics
Attack of the Well-Meaners	Mixed, mostly humorous	1 male, 2 females	Dealing with crisis; Friendship
Best Friends	Humorous	2 males, 2 females	Friendship; Insecurity; Needy people
The Breakfast Club	Mixed, mostly serious	4 males, 1 female	Friendship; Small groups; Friends in crisis
Can't Live Without 'Em	Mixed, mostly humorous	2 males, 2 females	Relationships; Unconditional love
Don't Mention It	Mixed, mostly humorous	2 males, 2 females	Unemployment; Being open about problems
For Better or Worse—Part VI	Mixed	3 males, 3 females	Family; Marriage
It's No Picnic	Humorous	3 males, 3 females	Work stress; Surface relationships

Title	Tone	Characters	Topics
Just an Acquaintance	Mixed	2 males, 2 females	Relationships between men; Superficial relationships
Mr. X, Mr. Y, and Mr. Z	Humorous	4 males, 1 female, and narrator	Friendship; Intimacy
Shop Talk	Serious	2 males, 2 females	Failure; Adversity; Small groups
Something in Common	Mixed	3 females, 1 male	Starting relationships
The Vacationers—Parts I and II	Humorous	2 males, 2 females	Personality differences; Friendships; Accepting others
What Are Friends for?	Serious	1 male, 2 females	Friendship; Truth telling
What Now?	Serious	2 males, 4 females	Coping with crisis; Dealing with death
_____	_____	_____	_____
_____	_____	_____	_____
_____	_____	_____	_____

 Songs

Title	Artist	Style	Tempo	Seeker-Sensitivity Rating
Bridge Between Two Hearts	**Bob Carlisle**	**Pop**	**Up**	**9**
The Extra Mile	Al Denson	Power Ballad	Slow	9
Holding Out Hope to You	Michael English	Power ballad	Slow	9
How Could I Ask for More	**Cindy Morgan**	**Piano ballad**	**Slow**	**9**
I Believe in You	Steve Camp	Pop	Up	10
Isn't It Good	*Willow Creek Music*	*Ballad*	*Mid/slow*	*4*
Let's Build a Bridge	Michael English	Pop	Up	8
Love Can Build a Bridge	**The Judds**	**Ballad**	**Slow**	**10**
Only Here for a Little While	**Billy Dean**	**Country**	**Mid/up**	**10**
Somebody Make Me Laugh	**Patti Austin**	**Ballad**	**Slow**	**10**
Suffer in Silence	Susan Ashton	Folk/pop	Mid	10
Take My Hand	Russ Taff	Folk/rock	Mid	9
That's What a Brother Is For	**Michael James**	**Ballad—male duet**	**Slow**	**5**
That's What Love Is For	Amy Grant	Power ballad	Slow	10
We Need Each Other	**Trace Balin**	**Power ballad**	**Slow/mid**	**7**
When We Fail Love	**Grover Levy**	**Piano ballad**	**Slow**	**9**
You Don't Count the Cost	Billy Dean	Country ballad	Slow	10
_____	_____	_____	_____	
_____	_____	_____	_____	
_____	_____	_____	_____	

Movie Clips

Title: Beaches
Topic: Friendship; Truth telling
Description: Two friends, estranged for years, come back together and confront each other.
Start Time: 1:09:20
Start Cue: "Well, look who's here"
End Time: 1:12:00
End Cue: "No, it was our fault"
Comments: Three objectionable words that might need to be bleeped

---

Title: City Slickers
Topic: Dysfunctional families; Friendship
Description: Three friends share the best and worst days of their lives.
Start Time: 1:12:45
Start Cue: "All right, I got one"
End Time: 1:14:50
End Cue: "Same day"
Comments: Could start earlier, but Billy Crystal swears briefly during his worst-day description

---

Title: Forrest Gump
Topic: Friendship; Laying your life down for a friend
Description: Forrest goes into the jungle of Vietnam to find his fallen friend, Bubba, and gets him out of the battle zone.
Start Time: 0:53:30
Start Cue: "I gotta find Bubba!"
End Time: 0:55:00
End Cue: Forrest runs out of frame, with jungle exploding behind him. Can also end at "That's all I have to say about that"
Comments: _____

Title: Forrest Gump
Topic: Love; Friendship
Description: Forrest, driving a shrimp boat, sees his friend Lt. Dan and jumps off the boat to greet him.
Start Time: 1:31:10
Start Cue: Shot of Forrest's hands steering the boat
End Time: 1:32:50
End Cue: "That's my boat." Can end earlier
Comments: _____

Title: Rudy

Topic: Friendship; Belief in each other

Description: Rudy's friend Pete gives him a Notre Dame jacket, symbolizing his belief in his friend's dream.

Start Time: 0:12:25

Start Cue: "What is today?"

End Time: 0:14:25

End Cue: Rudy blows out "candle," smiles at Pete

Comments: The Pete character lights a cigarette in the clip—some may be uncomfortable with this

_____

Title: Shadowlands

Topic: Control issues; Intimacy

Description: Joy confronts Jack on the fact that he has set up his world so that nobody can touch him—he has blocked intimacy by surrounding himself with people he can control.

Start Time: 1:05:55

Start Cue: "So what do you do here . . . think great thoughts?"

End Time: 1:07:37

End Cue: "You just don't like it. Nor do I"

Comments: _____
_____

Title: _____

Topic: _____

Description: _____

Start Time: _____

Start Cue: _____

End Time: _____

End Cue: _____

Comments: _____
_____

Programming Tip

Be an observer of your life
Be on the lookout for significance in the ordinary.
Often the things that happen to us during the day are
opportunities for the Holy Spirit to teach and touch us.
The insight and wisdom we gain at those times can
translate into powerful creative ideas. We need to be
careful not to let the hurry and pressure of ministry
deaden our ability to hear God's voice.

Love

See also: **God's Love**

Message Titles

- ❏ Building Bigger Hearts
- ❏ Loving Your Enemies
- ❏ **Giving and Receiving Love:** Gentleness • Trust • Sacrificial Love
- ❏ **The Lost Art of Loving:** Why Aren't You Normal Like Me? • Please Speak My Language • Resurrecting Dying Loves • The Launching Pad of Love • People Who Love Too Much
- ❏ **Love of Another Kind:** The Supremacy of Love • Bold Love • Loving Hard-to-Love People • Comforting Love • No Greater Love • When Love Breaks Down • The Sexual Side of Love • Love Busters • Love Never Fails
- ❏ **Loving Lessons:** Loving Lessons • Tender Love • Tough Love • Sacrificial Love • Steadfast Love • More About Tough Love • Radical Love

_____

_____

_____

_____

_____

Dramas

Title	Tone	Characters	Topics
Can't Live Without 'Em	Mixed, mostly humorous	2 males, 2 females	Relationships; Unconditional love
I Know What You Want	Serious	2 males, 2 females	God's love; Dysfunctional families
Married and Harried	Mixed	1 male, 1 female	Marriage; Going beyond feelings
Reflections	Mixed	1 male, 2 females, 2 children	Motherhood
The Story of Rachel	Serious	3 females	Care for the poor; Compassion

Title	Tone	Characters	Topics
Terminal Visit	Serious	3 females	Resurrecting relationships; Family conflict
_____	_____	_____	_____
_____	_____	_____	_____
_____	_____	_____	_____
_____	_____	_____	_____

Songs

Title	Artist	Style	Tempo	Seeker-Sensitivity Rating
Bridge Between Two Hearts	**Bob Carlisle**	**Pop**	**Up**	**9**
Desperado	Eagles	Ballad	Slow	10
Forever's as Far as I'll Go	Alabama	Country ballad	Slow	10
Helping Hand	Amy Grant	Pop	Mid/up	10
His Love Is Strong	**Clay Crosse**	**Pop**	**Up**	**10**
How Could I Ask for More	Cindy Morgan	Piano ballad	Slow	9
If I Had Only Known	**Reba McEntire**	**Ballad**	**Slow**	**10**
Love Can Build a Bridge	**The Judds**	**Ballad**	**Slow**	**10**
Love Can Open the Door	Sandi Patti	Pop	Up	10
Love Conquers All	**Pam Thum**	**Pop**	**Up**	**10**
Meet in the Middle	**Diamond Rio**	**Country**	**Mid/up**	**10**
There Is a Love	**Michael English**	**Pop**	**Up**	**9**
You Don't Count the Cost	Billy Dean	Country ballad	Slow	10
_____	_____	_____	_____	_____
_____	_____	_____	_____	_____
_____	_____	_____	_____	_____

Movie Clips

Title: 8 Seconds

Topic: Regret; Communicating love

Description: A father, whose son has recently died, breaks down in remorse over not telling his son that he loved him.

Start Time: 1:27:10

Start Cue: Pallbearers carry casket out of church

End Time: 1:28:33
End Cue: "I loved him"
Comments: _____

_____

Title: Forrest Gump
Topic: Friendship; Laying your life down for a friend
Description: Forrest goes into the jungle of Vietnam to find his fallen friend, Bubba, and runs him out of the battle zone.
Start Time: 0:53:30
Start Cue: "I gotta find Bubba!"
End Time: 0:55:00
End Cue: Forrest runs out of frame, with jungle exploding behind him. Can also end at "That's all I have to say about that"
Comments: _____

_____

Title: Forrest Gump
Topic: Love; Friendship
Description: Forrest, driving a shrimp boat, sees his friend Lt. Dan and jumps off the boat to greet him.
Start Time: 1:31:10
Start Cue: Shot of Forrest's hands steering the boat
End Time: 1:32:50
End Cue: "That's my boat." Can end earlier
Comments: _____

_____

Title: Hoosiers
Topic: Unconditional love; Forgiveness
Description: Dennis Hopper's character, a recovering alcoholic, is in the hospital drying out. His son visits him and tells him he loves him.
Start Time: 1:30:15
Start Cue: "No school this small"
End Time: 1:32:30
End Cue: "Anyway, no school this small has ever been in the state championship!"
Comments: Needs some setup for those who haven't seen the movie

_____

Title: _____
Topic: _____
Description: _____
Start Time: _____
Start Cue: _____
End Time: _____
End Cue: _____
Comments: _____

_____

Marriage and Dating
- Adultery -

See also: **Purity, Sex**

Package Suggestion

Drama:
Because I Love You

Song:
Can't We Try

Message Titles

- ❏ The High Cost of a Cheap Thrill
- ❏ Looking, Lusting or Loving?
- ❏ *Seventh Commandment:* Restrain Sexual Desires

_____
_____
_____
_____

Dramas

Title	Tone	Characters	Topics
All Gummed Up	Serious	1 male, 1 female, 1 offstage voice	Adultery; Dealing with past hurts; The pain of lies
Because I Love You	Serious	1 male, 1 female	Adultery; The consequences of sin
Richard: 1992	Serious	2 males, 1 female	Anger; Rebellion; Decay of the family

Songs

Title	Artist	Style	Tempo	Seeker-Sensitivity Rating
Behind Every Fantasy	*Willow Creek Music*	*Country pop*	*Up*	*10*
Call of the Wild	Susan Ashton	Country	Mid	10
Faithless Heart	Amy Grant	Ballad	Slow/mid	10
Run Away	Steven Curtis Chapman	Pop	Up	7
Walk on By	**Susan Ashton**	**Folk pop**	**Mid/up**	**8**
_____	_____	_____	_____	_____
_____	_____	_____	_____	_____
_____	_____	_____	_____	_____
_____	_____	_____	_____	_____

Movie Clips

Title:	City Slickers
Topic:	Adultery; Temptation
Description:	Billy Crystal's friend asks him if he would cheat on his wife if no one would ever know. His answer shows integrity.
Start Time:	0:44:38
Start Cue:	"What if you could have great sex"
End Time:	0:45:30
End Cue:	"I wouldn't like myself . . . that's all"
Comments:	May be too straightforward for some. Profanity precedes the clip

Title: _____

Topic: _____

Description: _____

Start Time: _____

Start Cue: _____

End Time: _____

End Cue: _____

Comments: _____

- Dating -

Message Titles

- ❏ How to Pick a Partner
- ❏ The Payoff for Sexual Purity
- ❏ *Fit to Be Tied:* Exposing the Marriage Myth
- ❏ *Fit to Be Tied:* The Keys to Compatibility
- ❏ *Fit to Be Tied:* Making Your Courtship Count

_____

_____

_____

Dramas

Title	Tone	Characters	Topics
For Better or Worse—Part I	Humorous	3 males, 3 females (offstage male and female voices)	Marriage
For Better or Worse—Part II	Humorous	2 males, 2 females	Marriage; Personality differences
For Better or Worse—Part III	Mixed	1 male, 1 female, 1 either male or female	Marriage; Dating
Hands Off	Humorous	1 male, 1 female	Dating; Sex; Temptation
Me, Myself, and Chris	Mixed	2 males, 1 female	Sex; Temptation; Dating
Mere Technicality	Serious	1 male, 1 female	Living together; The cost of taking a stand for Christ
A Real Man	Humorous	4 males, 1 female	The American male; Finding the right man
The Resolve Dissolve	Humorous	2 males, 1 female	Sexuality; Dating
Single?	Mixed	1 male, 1 female	Singleness; Loneliness; Fear of living alone
_____	_____	_____	_____
_____	_____	_____	_____

Songs

See also Love, Fulfillment, *and* Marriage and Dating

Title	Artist	Style	Tempo	Seeker-Sensitivity Rating
Somebody Love Me	Michael W. Smith	Power ballad	Slow	9
_____	_____	_____	_____	_____
_____	_____	_____	_____	_____
_____	_____	_____	_____	_____
_____	_____	_____	_____	_____

Movie Clips

Title:	She's Having a Baby
Topic:	Marriage; Reality of marriage
Description:	A young couple is at the altar. During the vows, the groom spaces out and hears the minister giving vows that are closer to reality. Very funny.
Start Time:	0:07:55
Start Cue:	"Kristen, wilt thou have"
End Time:	0:09:15
End Cue:	"I will"
Comments:	_____

Title: _____
Topic: _____
Description: _____
Start Time: _____
Start Cue: _____
End Time: _____
End Cue: _____
Comments: _____

- Divorce -

Message Titles

❐ Divorce and Remarriage
❐ *Fanning the Flames of Marriage:* The Keys to Conflict Resolution
❐ *Fit to Be Tied:* Now That I Married the Wrong Person

_____
_____
_____
_____

Package Suggestion

Drama:
Grand Canyon

Song:
Separate Lives

Dramas

Title	Tone	Characters	Topics
All Gummed Up	Serious	1 male, 1 female, 1 offstage voice	Adultery; Dealing with past hurts; The pain of lies
Grand Canyon	Serious	1 male, 1 female	Marital breakdown
Richard: 1992	Serious	2 males, 1 female	Anger; Rebellion; Decay of the family

Songs

Title	Artist	Style	Tempo	Seeker-Sensitivity Rating
Behind Every Fantasy	*Willow Creek Music*	*Country pop*	*Up*	*10*
Call of the Wild	Susan Ashton	Country	Mid	10
Can't We Try	**Dan Hill & Vonda Shepard**	**Pop ballad—duet**	**Slow**	**10**
Separate Lives	**Phil Collins & Marilyn Martin**	**Power ballad—duet**	**Slow**	**10**
_____	_____	_____	_____	_____
_____	_____	_____	_____	_____
_____	_____	_____	_____	_____
_____	_____	_____	_____	_____

Movie Clips

Title: Kramer vs. Kramer
Topic: Divorce
Description: Joanna tells Ted she is leaving him.
Start Time: 0:04:35
Start Cue: Door knock
End Time: 0:07:15
End Cue: Elevator door closes
Comments: Very real, painful clip showing the moment of separation. Might be very difficult for divorced people to watch

Title: Kramer vs. Kramer
Topic: Effects of divorce on children
Description: Father reads a letter to his little boy from the mother, telling him why she left. Effects on the child are powerfully shown.
Start Time: 0:21:50
Start Cue: Just before "Hey, Billy!"
End Time: 23:45
End Cue: Scene ends with Billy staring at the TV
Comments: _____

_____

Title: Kramer vs. Kramer
Topic: Divorce; Effects of divorce on children
Description: Billy tells his dad he thinks his mom left because he (Billy) was bad. Dad explains why he thinks she left. Very moving clip.

Start Time:	0:39:10
Start Cue:	Billy turns on light and says, "Daddy"
End Time:	0:41:40
End Cue:	Father closes door
Comments:	Video is dark, and audio is mostly whispered. Clip's effectiveness may vary according to the quality of the church's equipment

Title: _____

Topic: _____

Description: _____

Start Time: _____

Start Cue: _____

End Time: _____

End Cue: _____

Comments: _____

_____

- Intimacy -

Different from Romance—this involves the kind of knowing and being known that marriage was designed to produce.

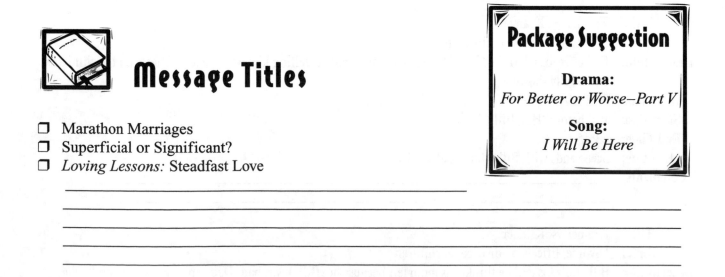

Message Titles

☐ Marathon Marriages
☐ Superficial or Significant?
☐ _Loving Lessons:_ Steadfast Love

_____

_____

_____

_____

Package Suggestion

Drama:
For Better or Worse–Part V

Song:
I Will Be Here

Dramas

Title	Tone	Characters	Topics
All Gummed Up	Serious	1 male, 1 female, 1 offstage voice	Adultery; Dealing with past hurts; The pain of lies
For Better or Worse–Part V	Mixed	1 male, 1 female	Marriage; Romance
Grand Canyon	Serious	1 male, 1 female	Marital breakdown
An Hour on Wednesday	Mixed— ends serious	1 male, 1 female	Marriage; Damaging effects of a fast-paced life
In Pursuit of Passion	Humorous	2 males, 2 females	Sex; Marriage
Just Say It!	Humorous	1 male, 1 female, 1 either male or female	Marriage communication; Importance of saying "I love you"
_____	_____	_____	_____
_____	_____	_____	_____
_____	_____	_____	_____
_____	_____	_____	_____
_____	_____	_____	_____

 # Songs

Title	Artist	Style	Tempo	Seeker-Sensitivity Rating
I Will Be Here	**Steven Curtis Chapman**	**Ballad**	**Slow**	**10**
Love and Learn	Steven Curtis Chapman	Pop/folk	Mid/slow	9
_____	_____	_____	_____	_____
_____	_____	_____	_____	_____
_____	_____	_____	_____	_____
_____	_____	_____	_____	_____
_____	_____	_____	_____	_____
_____	_____	_____	_____	_____
_____	_____	_____	_____	_____

Movie Clips

Title: Shadowlands

Topic: Control issues; Intimacy

Description: Joy confronts Jack [C. S. Lewis] on the fact that he has set up his world so that nobody can touch him—he has blocked intimacy by surrounding himself with people he can control.

Start Time: 1:05:55

Start Cue: "So what do you do here . . . think great thoughts?"

End Time: 1:07:37

End Cue: "You just don't like it. Nor do I"

Comments: _____

_____

Title: Shadowlands

Topic: Death; Sharing the dying process

Description: Jack and Joy talk about her imminent death. She makes a couple of profound statements about sharing the dying process.

Start Time: 1:45:30

Start Cue: "I don't want to be somewhere else anymore"

End Time: 1:47:55

End Cue: Jack and Joy kiss

Comments: _____

_____

Title: _____

Topic: _____

Description: _____

Start Time: _____

Start Cue: _____

End Time: _____

End Cue: _____

Comments: _____

_____

~ Male – Female Differences ~

See also: **Personality Differences**

Message Titles

- ❐ The Amazing American Female
- ❐ The Amazing American Male
- ❐ The Changing American Female
- ❐ The Changing American Male
- ❐ Loving a Man Without Losing Yourself
- ❐ When a Man Loves a Woman

_____
_____
_____
_____
_____

Dramas

Title	Tone	Characters	Topics
Feeling Opposition	Humorous	1 male, 1 female	Thinkers vs. feelers
For Better or Worse–Part V	Mixed	1 male, 1 female	Marriage; Romance
It's Only a Movie	Humorous	2 males, 2 females, 1 offstage voice	The power of media; The effects of what we see; Male/female differences
Just Looking	Mixed; light	1 male, 1 female	Eye causing you to stumble; Purity of thoughts

Songs

Title	Artist	Style	Tempo	Seeker-Sensitivity Rating
Meet in the Middle	Diamond Rio	Country	Mid/up	10

Movie Clips

Title: City Slickers
Topic: Differences between men and women
Description: Discussion about why men love baseball reveals some differences between men and women.
Start Time: 1:05:33
Start Cue: "Will you stop with Roberto Clemente?" or "So, do you hate baseball?"
End Time: 1:07:20
End Cue: "That was real"
Comments: _____
_____

Title: _____
Topic: _____
Description: _____
Start Time: _____
Start Cue: _____
End Time: _____
End Cue: _____
Comments: _____
_____

~ Marriage, General ~

Message Titles

- ☐ How to Pick a Partner
- ☐ **Fanning the Flames of Marriage:** Why Fires Burn Low • Help for Husbands • Wisdom for Wives • Keys to Conflict Resolution • Whatever Happened to Romance?
- ☐ **Fit to Be Tied:** Exposing the Marriage Myth • Keys to Compatibility • Making Your Courtship Count • Now That I Married the Wrong Person • Keeping Romance Alive • Strengthening Family Ties
- ☐ **Marriagewerks:** Demystifying Marriage • When a Man Loves a Woman • Loving a Man Without Losing Yourself • Marathon Marriages • Surviving a Spiritual Mismatch

_____

_____

_____

_____

Dramas

Title	Tone	Characters	Topics
All Gummed Up	Serious	1 male, 1 female, 1 offstage voice	Adultery; Dealing with past hurts; The pain of lies
Driven	Serious	1 male, 1 female	Workaholism; Marriage
First Things First	Humorous	1 male, 1 female, 1 female infant	New parents; Balancing children and marriage
For Better or Worse—Part I	Humorous	3 males, 3 females (offstage male and female voices)	Marriage
For Better or Worse—Part II	Humorous	2 males, 2 females	Marriage; Personality differences
For Better or Worse—Part III	Mixed	1 male, 1 female, 1 either male or female	Marriage; Dating

Title	Tone	Characters	Topics
For Better or Worse—Part IV	Mixed, mostly serious	1 male, 1 female	Marriage
For Better or Worse—Part V	Mixed	1 male, 1 female	Marriage; Romance
For Better or Worse—Part VI	Mixed	3 males, 3 females	Family; Marriage
Forgive Again?	Serious	1 male, 1 female	Forgiving others
Grand Canyon	Serious	1 male, 1 female	Marital breakdown
An Hour on Wednesday	Mixed— ends serious	1 male, 1 female	Marriage; Damaging effects of a fast-paced life
In Pursuit of Passion	Humorous	2 males, 2 females	Sex; Marriage
Just Say It!	Humorous	1 male, 1 female, 1 either male or female	Marriage communication; Importance of saying "I love you"
Married and Harried	Mixed	1 male, 1 female	Marriage; Going beyond feelings
Prayer Despair	Mixed	1 male, 2 females	Waiting for answers to prayer; Marriage; Process of change
A Problem of Perspective	Humorous	1 male, 1 female, 1 either male or female	Marriage; Marital conflict
Regarding Rodney	Humorous	4 males, 1 female	Workaholism; Marriage; Roles of men
Trying Time	Serious	1 male, 2 females	Marriage; Spiritual mismatch
_____	_____	_____	_____
_____	_____	_____	_____
_____	_____	_____	_____

Songs

Title	Artist	Style	Tempo	Seeker-Sensitivity Rating
Ball and Chain	Paul Overstreet	Country	Mid/up	10
Can't We Try	**Dan Hill & Vonda Shepard**	**Pop ballad—duet**	**Slow**	**10**
Faithless Heart	Amy Grant	Ballad	Slow/mid	10
Forever's as Far as I'll Go	Alabama	Country ballad	Slow	10
Go There With You	Steven Curtis Chapman	MOR	Mid	10
I Just Never Say It Enough	Wayne Watson	Ballad, in 3	Slow	8
I Will Be Here	**Steven Curtis Chapman**	**Ballad**	**Slow**	**10**
If You Could See What I See	Geoff Moore & the Distance	Folk ballad	Slow	10
Love and Learn	Steven Curtis Chapman	Pop/folk	Mid/slow	9
Love Conquers All	**Pam Thum**	**Pop**	**Up**	**10**

Title	Artist	Style	Tempo	Seeker-Sensitivity Rating
Meet in the Middle	**Diamond Rio**	**Country**	**Mid/up**	**10**
Separate Lives	**Phil Collins & Marilyn White**	**Power ballad—duet**	**Slow**	**10**
That's What Love Is All About	Michael Bolton	Ballad	Slow	10
That's What Love Is For	Amy Grant	Power ballad	Slow	10
You Don't Count the Cost	Billy Dean	Country ballad	Slow	10
_____	_____	_____	_____	_____
_____	_____	_____	_____	_____
_____	_____	_____	_____	_____

Movie Clips

Title:	8 Seconds
Topic:	Regret; Communicating love
Description:	A father, whose son has recently died, breaks down in remorse over not telling his son that he loved him.
Start Time:	1:27:10
Start Cue:	Pallbearers carry casket out of church
End Time:	1:28:33
End Cue:	"I loved him"
Comments:	_____

Title:	She's Having a Baby
Topic:	Marriage; Reality of marriage
Description:	A young couple are at the altar. During the vows, the groom spaces out and hears the minister giving vows that are closer to reality. Very funny.
Start Time:	0:07:55
Start Cue:	"Kristen, wilt thou have"
End Time:	0:09:15
End Cue:	"I will"
Comments:	_____

Title:	_____
Topic:	_____
Description:	_____
Start Time:	_____
Start Cue:	_____
End Time:	_____
End Cue:	_____
Comments:	_____

- Romance -

Message Titles

- ☐ Keeping Romance Alive
- ☐ Whatever Happened to Romance
- ☐ *The Lost Art of Loving:* Please Speak My Language

_____

_____

_____

_____

_____

Dramas

Title	Tone	Characters	Topics
For Better or Worse—Part II	Humorous	2 males, 2 females	Marriage; Personality differences
For Better or Worse—Part V	Mixed	1 male, 1 female	Marriage; Romance
In Pursuit of Passion	Humorous	2 males, 2 females	Sex; Marriage
Just Say It!	Humorous	1 male, 1 female, 1 either male or female	Marriage communication; Importance of saying "I love you"
Married and Harried	Mixed	1 male, 1 female	Marriage; Going beyond feelings

Songs

Title	Artist	Style	Tempo	Seeker-Sensitivity Rating
Forever's as Far as I'll Go	Alabama	Country ballad	Slow	10
I Just Never Say It Enough	Wayne Watson	Ballad, in 3	Slow	8
I Will Be Here	**Steven Curtis Chapman**	**Ballad**	**Slow**	**10**
That's What Love Is All About	Michael Bolton	Ballad	Slow	10

Movie Clips

Title: _____

Topic: _____

Description: _____

Start Time: _____

Start Cue: _____

End Time: _____

End Cue: _____

Comments: _____

_____

Programming Tip

Know your audience
Become a student of the cultural language of your
community. What kind of music do the people listen to
during the week? What kind of movies or television
shows are they watching? What books are they reading?
What issues concern them? To minister to someone,
you need to understand that person.

~ Sex ~

See also: **Purity, Romance, Self-Control**

Message Titles

- ☐ Christians in a Sex-crazed Culture
- ☐ The Difference Between Looking and Lusting
- ☐ Looking, Lusting or Loving?
- ☐ The Payoff for Sexual Purity
- ☐ *Money, Sex and Power:* Sex
- ☐ *Seventh Commandment:* Restrain Sexual Desires
- ☐ *Three Things God Loves (That Most People Don't Think He Does):* Lovemaking

_____
_____
_____
_____

Package Suggestion

Drama:
The Big Sell

Song:
Walk on By

Dramas

Title	Tone	Characters	Topics
All Gummed Up	Serious	1 male, 1 female, 1 offstage voice	Adultery; Dealing with past hurts; The pain of lies
Because I Love You	Serious	1 male, 1 female	Adultery; The consequences of sin
The Big Sell	Humorous	3 males, 2 females	Obsession with sex in society; Effect of the media
For Better or Worse—Part V	Mixed	1 male, 1 female	Marriage; Romance
Hands Off	Humorous	1 male, 1 female	Dating; Sex; Temptation
In Pursuit of Passion	Humorous	2 males, 2 females	Sex; Marriage
Just Looking	Mixed; light	1 male, 1 female	Eye causing you to stumble; Purity of thoughts

Title	Tone	Characters	Topics
Me, Myself, and Chris	Mixed	2 males, 1 female	Sex; Temptation; Dating
The Resolve Dissolve	Humorous	2 males, 1 female	Sexuality; Dating

Songs

Title	Artist	Style	Tempo	Seeker-Sensitivity Rating
Behind Every Fantasy	*Willow Creek Music*	*Country pop*	*Up*	*10*
Call of the Wild	Susan Ashton	Country	Mid	10
Run Away	Steven Curtis Chapman	Pop	Up	7
Strength in You	*Willow Creek Music*	*MOR pop*	*Slow/mid*	*10*
Walk on By	**Susan Ashton**	**Folk pop**	**Mid/up**	**8**

Movie Clips

Title: City Slickers

Topic: Adultery; Temptation

Description: Billy Crystal's friend asks him if he would cheat on his wife if no one would ever know. His answer shows integrity.

Start Time: 0:44:38

Start Cue: "What if you could have great sex"

End Time: 0:45:30

End Cue: "I wouldn't like myself . . . that's all"

Comments: May be too straightforward for some. Profanity precedes the clip

Personality Differences

Refers to the way God "wired us up"—"thinkers" vs. "feelers," etc.
See also: **Male–Female Differences**

Message Titles

- ❏ Affirming Your Uniqueness
- ❏ *The Lost Art of Loving:* Why Aren't You Normal Like Me?
- ❏ *Negotiating the Maze of Life:* Thinkers, Feelers and Procrastinators
- ❏ **Discovering the Way God Wired You Up:** Temperament • Emotions • Sexuality • Physically • Spiritually

_____
_____
_____
_____
_____

Dramas

Title	Tone	Characters	Topics
Expectations of the Expecting	Mixed	1 male, 1 female	Parenting; Affirming personality differences
Feeling Opposition	Humorous	1 male, 1 female	Thinkers vs. feelers
For Better or Worse–Part II	Humorous	2 males, 2 females	Marriage; Personality differences
Nothing in Common	Humorous	3 females, 1 male	Choosing platoon members; Affinity
Oh, What a Feeling!	Humorous	2 males, 1 female	Decision making; Self-control; Money management
On Track	Serious	2 males, 1 female	Forcing people into molds; Character building
A Problem of Perspective	Humorous	1 male, 1 female, 1 male or female	Marriage; Marital conflict

Title	Tone	Characters	Topics
The Vacationers–Parts I and II	Humorous	2 males, 2 females	Personality differences; Friendships; Accepting others
Wonderfully Made	Serious	2 females, 2 males, 1 narrator	Affirming a child's uniqueness
_____	_____	_____	_____
_____	_____	_____	_____
_____	_____	_____	_____
_____	_____	_____	_____

Songs

Title	Artist	Style	Tempo	Seeker-Sensitivity Rating
Bridge Between Two Hearts	Bob Carlisle	Pop	Up	9
Undivided	First Call	Ballad—trio	Slow	5
_____	_____	_____	_____	_____
_____	_____	_____	_____	_____
_____	_____	_____	_____	_____
_____	_____	_____	_____	_____
_____	_____	_____	_____	_____

Movie Clips

Title: _____

Topic: _____

Description: _____

Start Time: _____

Start Cue: _____

End Time: _____

End Cue: _____

Comments: _____

Relational Conflict

Forgiveness is a major theme here, though this listing deals with the entire process involved in resolving relational conflict.

See also: **God's Forgiveness of Us, Grace, Truth Telling**

 Message Titles

- ❒ The Keys to Resolving Conflict
- ❒ *Enriching Your Relationships:* Relational Viruses
- ❒ *The God of the Second Chance:* Giving Second Chances
- ❒ *The Lost Art of Loving:* Resurrecting Dying Loves
- ❒ *Relationships in the Kingdom:* Fixing Broken Relationships
- ❒ *Relationships in the Kingdom:* Loving Your Enemies
- ❒ *Telling the Truth:* Games People Play

_____

_____

_____

_____

 Dramas

Title	Tone	Characters	Topics
Famous Lost Words	Humorous	4 males, 1 female	Turning the other cheek; Boundaries
Finding Evidence	Serious	2 males, 1 female	Trust; Jumping to conclusions
Forgive Again?	Serious	1 male, 1 female	Forgiving others
In . . . We Trust	Serious	1 male	Trust; Difficulty trusting God
The Luncheon	Serious	3 females	Mother/daughter conflict; Honesty in relationships
No Thanks Giving	Serious	3 females	Truth telling; Family dynamics
The Okra Windy Show	Humorous	3 males, 3 females	Honesty in relationships; Communication

Title	Tone	Characters	Topics
Only Child	Serious	1 male, 2 females	Grace; Outrageous forgiveness; Doctrine of adoption
A Problem of Perspective	Humorous	1 male, 1 female, 1 male or female	Marriage; Marital conflict
Terminal Visit	Serious	3 females	Resurrecting relationships; Family conflict
What Are Friends for?	Serious	1 male, 2 females	Friendship; Truth telling
_____	_____	_____	_____
_____	_____	_____	_____
_____	_____	_____	_____
_____	_____	_____	_____

Songs

Title	Artist	Style	Tempo	Seeker-Sensitivity Rating
Beyond Justice to Mercy	**Susan Ashton**	**Ballad**	**Slow**	**10**
Bridge Between Two Hearts	**Bob Carlisle**	**Pop**	**Up**	**9**
Common Ground	Sierra	Folk trio	Slow	9
Forgive Me, Forgive You	Steve Camp	Gospel ballad	Slow/mid	7
Gather at the River	Point of Grace	Pop	Up	8
I Commit My Love to You	Twila Paris	Ballad	Slow	5
Let's Build a Bridge	Michael English	Pop	Up	8
Love Can Build a Bridge	**The Judds**	**Ballad**	**Slow**	**10**
Love Can Open the Door	Sandi Patti	Pop	Up	10
Love Conquers All	**Pam Thum**	**Pop**	**Up**	**10**
Meet in the Middle	**Diamond Rio**	**Country**	**Mid/up**	**10**
That's What Love Is For	Amy Grant	Power ballad	Slow	10
Undivided	**First Call**	**Ballad—trio**	**Slow**	**5**
When We Fail Love	**Grover Levy**	**Piano ballad**	**Slow**	**9**
Words	Kim Hill	Pop/rock	Up	10
_____	_____	_____	_____	_____
_____	_____	_____	_____	_____
_____	_____	_____	_____	_____
_____	_____	_____	_____	_____

Movie Clips

Title: Beaches
Topic: Friendship; Truth telling
Description: Two friends, estranged for years, come back together and confront each other.
Start Time: 1:09:20
Start Cue: "Well, look who's here"
End Time: 1:12:00
End Cue: "No, it was our fault"
Comments: Three objectionable words that might need to be bleeped

---

Title: Hoosiers
Topic: Unconditional love; Forgiveness
Description: Dennis Hopper's character, a recovering alcoholic, is in the hospital drying out. His son visits him and tells him he loves him.
Start Time: 1:30:15
Start Cue: "No school this small"
End Time: 1:32:30
End Cue: "Anyway, no school this small has ever been in the state championship!"
Comments: Needs some setup for those who haven't seen the movie

---

Title: _____
Topic: _____
Description: _____
Start Time: _____
Start Cue: _____
End Time: _____
End Cue: _____
Comments: _____

Small Groups

See also: **Friendship**

Message Titles

Package Suggestion

Drama:
The Breakfast Club

Song:
That's What a Brother Is For

❑ Jesus Forms a Small Group
❑ **Benefits of Brotherhood:** Overcoming Independence • Superficial or Significant • The Cost of Commitment • The Rewards of Relationships
❑ **Enlisting in Little Platoons:** The Purpose of Little Platoons • Picking Platoon Members • Problems in Little Platoons • The Rewards of Little Platoons • War Stories

_____

_____

_____

_____

Dramas

Title	Tone	Characters	Topics
The Breakfast Club	Mixed, mostly serious	4 males, 1 female	Friendship; Small groups; Friends in crisis
Just an Acquaintance	Mixed	2 males, 2 females	Relationships between men; Superficial relationships
Nothing in Common	Humorous	3 females, 1 male	Choosing platoon members; Affinity
Shop Talk	Serious	2 males, 2 females	Failure; Adversity; Small groups
Something in Common	Mixed	3 females, 1 male	Starting relationships

Songs

Title	Artist	Style	Tempo	Seeker-Sensitivity Rating
The Extra Mile	Al Denson	Power Ballad	Slow	9
I Believe in You	Steve Camp	Pop	Up	10
That's What a Brother Is For	**Michael James**	**Ballad—male duet**	**Slow**	5
We Need Each Other	Trace Balin	Power ballad	Slow/mid	7
_____	_____	_____	_____	_____
_____	_____	_____	_____	_____
_____	_____	_____	_____	_____
_____	_____	_____	_____	_____

Movie Clips

Title: Forrest Gump

Topic: Friendship; Laying your life down for a friend

Description: Forrest goes into the jungle of Vietnam to find his fallen friend, Bubba, and runs him out of the battle zone.

Start Time: 0:53:30

Start Cue: "I gotta find Bubba!"

End Time: 0:55:00

End Cue: Forrest runs out of frame, with jungle exploding behind him. Can also end at "That's all I have to say about that"

Comments: _____

_____

Title: _____

Topic: _____

Description: _____

Start Time: _____

Start Cue: _____

End Time: _____

End Cue: _____

Comments: _____

_____

Truth Telling

Refers to speaking the truth in love
See also: **Communication, Relational Conflict**

 ## Message Titles

❒ Simple Truth Telling
❒ *Loving Lessons:* Tough Love
❒ **Telling the Truth:** Secret Conversations • Five Deadly Lies • Truth or Consequences • Games People Play • Expressing Positive Emotions • Learning How to Hear the Truth

_____
_____
_____
_____
_____

 ## Dramas

Title	Tone	Characters	Topics
For Image Sake	Humorous	3 males, 1 female	Honesty; Pretense
The Luncheon	Serious	3 females	Mother/daughter conflict; Honesty in relationships
No Thanks Giving	Serious	3 females	Truth telling; Family dynamics
The Okra Windy Show	Humorous	3 males, 3 females	Honesty in relationships; Communication
What Are Friends For?	Serious	1 male, 2 females	Friendship; Truth telling

Songs

Title	Artist	Style	Tempo	Seeker-Sensitivity Rating
Only Here for a Little While	Billy Dean	Country	Mid/up	10

Movie Clips

Title:	Beaches
Topic:	Friendship; Truth telling
Description:	Two friends, estranged for years, come back together and confront each other.
Start Time:	1:09:20
Start Cue:	"Well, look who's here"
End Time:	1:12:00
End Cue:	"No, it was our fault"
Comments:	Three objectionable words that might need to be bleeped

Title: _____

Topic: _____

Description: _____

Start Time: _____

Start Cue: _____

End Time: _____

End Cue: _____

Comments: _____

SEEKER ISSUES

Apologetics

Refers to defending the faith

Might also include: *Atheism, Evolution vs. Creation, Evidence for Christianity, Reasons People Don't Believe*

 Message Titles

- ❐ Doubters Welcome
- ❐ Spiritual Sticking Points
- ❐ Where Does the Evidence Point?
- ❐ *What Jesus Would Say to* . . . Rob Sherman (a local atheist)
- ❐ **Believing the Unbelievable:** The Odds for Evolution • The Case for Creation • Myths or Miracles? • Are Science and Christianity Compatible?
- ❐ **The Case for Christ:** The Credibility of Christ's Claims • The Reality of the Resurrection • The Relevance of the Resurrection
- ❐ **Faith Has Its Reasons:** Reasons for Believing in God • Reasons for Believing in the Bible • Reasons for Believing in Jesus Christ • Reasons for Believing in the Resurrection • Reasons for Believing in Heaven and Hell

_____

_____

_____

_____

 Dramas

Title	Tone	Characters	Topics
Is "Nothing" Sacred?	Humorous	3 males, and at least 4 others in group	Evolution vs. Creation; Modern science
Mistaken Identity	Mixed	3 males, 2 females, 1 young girl	Christmas; Doubting
On the Outside	Serious	1 female or male	Being salt and light; Negative church experiences

Title	Tone	Characters	Topics
Reason Enough	Mixed, mostly serious	1 male, 1 female	Importance of faith grounded in reason
A Visitor	Serious	2 males, 1 female	Wolves in sheep's clothing; Discernment; Spiritual manipulation
Wait 'Til Halftime	Mixed	1 male, 1 female	Eternity; Heaven and hell; Evangelism
You Cramp My Style	Serious	1 male, 1 female, 1 either male or female	Reasons people don't believe; Society's view of God
_____	_____	_____	_____
_____	_____	_____	_____
_____	_____	_____	_____

Songs

For more song ideas, see Changed Life, Testimonial

Title	Artist	Style	Tempo	Seeker-Sensitivity Rating
No Better Place	Steven Curtis Chapman	Pop/folk rock	Up	7
Show Me the Way	Styx	Power ballad	Slow/mid	10
This Is the Life	Phillips, Craig and Dean	Pop/rock	Up	6
_____	_____	_____	_____	_____
_____	_____	_____	_____	_____
_____	_____	_____	_____	_____
_____	_____	_____	_____	_____

Movie Clips

Title: Sister Act

Topic: The church; Reasons why people don't go to church

Description: Humorous clip of a boring preacher and a horrible choir, illustrating a couple of reasons why people don't go to church.

Start Time: 0:30:25

Start Cue: "We are a small congregation this morning"

End Time: 32:25

End Cue: Whoopi Goldberg winces

Comments: _____

_____

Title: Shadowlands
Topic: Suffering; Pain; Why does God allow bad things to happen?
Description: C. S. Lewis delivers a speech about why God allows suffering.
Start Time: 0:10:00
Start Cue: "Yesterday I received a letter"
End Time: 0:11:40
End Cue: "Thank you very much"
Comments: The last line is a little hard to understand

_____

Title: _____
Topic: _____
Description: _____
Start Time: _____
Start Cue: _____
End Time: _____
End Cue: _____
Comments: _____
_____

Programming Tip

Drama: Keys to a good script
A good script—

- Grabs your attention and holds it
- Engages the congregation emotionally
- Relates closely to the theme of the message
- Is inventive
- Is concise
- Is believable—rooted in reality
- Creates strong audience identification

Basics of Christianity
~ Grace ~

A difficult concept for some seekers to understand, because it is foreign to human nature. This goes beyond the topic of **God's Forgiveness of Us** to understanding the heart of a God who would die in our place.

Message Titles

- ❑ Amazed by Grace
- ❑ The Difference Grace Makes
- ❑ The Grace of God
- ❑ Never Ending Grace
- ❑ Radical Love
- ❑ What's So Amazing About Grace?
- ❑ *Illustrating the Identity of God:* Our Gracious God
- ❑ *Yeah God:* For Being Gracious
- ❑ **Amazing Grace:** The God of Grace • The Gifts of Grace • Gracious Fathers
- ❑ **The God of the Second Chance:** Getting a Second Chance • Giving a Second Chance

_____

_____

_____

Package Suggestion

Drama:
Security Check

Song:
Only by Grace

Dramas

Title	Tone	Characters	Topics
Acting the Part	Serious	1 male, 2 females	Legalism; Living out our Christianity
The Book of Life	"Energetic mime"; mixed	3 males, 3 females	Baptism; Faith; Basic Christianity; Eternal life

Title	Tone	Characters	Topics
A Clean Slate	Serious	1 male, 2 or 3 males or females	Forgiveness; Redemption; Guilt
Keeping Tabs	Humorous	1 male, 1 female	Gifts of grace; Undeserved love
Measuring Up	Mixed; mime	2 males, 1 female, 1 other male or female	God's acceptance of us; Self-esteem
Only Child	Serious	1 male, 2 females	Grace; Outrageous forgiveness; Doctrine of adoption
The Prisoner	Serious	3 males, 1 female	Easter; Freedom from sin; New Christian
Security Check	Mixed	1 male, 1 female, 1 offstage voice	Salvation; Works vs. grace
"X" Marks the Spot	Serious; mime	1 female, 1 male, and 3 either female or male	Sin; Redemption; Forgiveness; Guilt
_____	_____	_____	_____
_____	_____	_____	_____
_____	_____	_____	_____

 # Songs

Title	Artist	Style	Tempo	Seeker-Sensitivity Rating
Cross Medley	*Willow Creek Music*	*Ballad medley— hymns*	*Slow*	7
Face of Forgiveness	*Willow Creek Music*	*Ballad*	*Slow*	10
The Great Divide	Point of Grace	Power ballad	Slow	9
His Grace Is Greater	Larnelle Harris	Inspirational ballad	Slow	8
I Don't Deserve Your Love	Trace Balin	Ballad	Slow	9
I Stand, I Fall	*Willow Creek Music*	*Piano ballad*	*Slow*	7
I'm Amazed	*Willow Creek Music*	*Ballad*	*Slow*	7
I've Been Released	*Willow Creek Music*	*Pop/rock— Chicago sound*	*Up*	9
Jesus Loves Me	**Whitney Houston**	**R & B/pop**	**Slow/mid**	8
Just Come In	Margaret Becker	Pop ballad	Slow	5
Love Is Always There	**Carolyn Arends**	**Folk/pop**	**Up**	9
The Love of God	*Willow Creek Music*	*Acapella vocal group*	*Slow*	6
Mercy for the Memories	**Geoff Moore & the Distance**	**Folk/pop ballad**	**Slow**	9

Title	Artist	Style	Tempo	Seeker-Sensitivity Rating
Miracle of Mercy	**Steven Curtis Chapman**	**Acoustic ballad**	**Slow**	**4**
Only by Grace	*Willow Creek Music*	*Pop/rock*	*Mid*	*10*
There Is a Love	**Michael English**	**Pop**	**Up**	**9**
Who Am I	Margaret Becker	Power ballad	Slow	7
Why Me	*Willow Creek Music*	*Ballad*	*Slow*	*9*
_____	_____	_____	_____	_____
_____	_____	_____	_____	_____
_____	_____	_____	_____	_____
_____	_____	_____	_____	_____

Movie Clips

Title: _____

Topic: _____

Description: _____

Start Time: _____

Start Cue: _____

End Time: _____

End Cue: _____

Comments: _____

~ Grace vs. Works/Legalism ~

Refers to the fact that eternal life cannot be earned, but is a gift through Christ alone. An issue that keeps many seekers from faith and keeps many believers from experiencing real freedom and joy.

Might also include: *Legalism*

Message Titles

- ☐ Averting Your Worst Nightmare
- ☐ The Difference Grace Makes
- ☐ Show Me the Way
- ☐ What's So Amazing About Grace?
- ☐ *Christianity's Toughest Competition:* Moralism

_____

_____

_____

Package Suggestion

Drama:
The Stickholders

Song:
If I Could Look Through Your Eyes

Dramas

Title	Tone	Characters	Topics
Acting the Part	Serious	1 male, 2 females	Legalism; Living out our Christianity
The Book of Life	"Energetic mime"; mixed	3 males, 3 females	Baptism; Faith; Basic Christianity; Eternal life
A Clean Slate	Serious	1 male, 2 or 3 males or females	Forgiveness; Redemption; Guilt
Keeping Tabs	Humorous	1 male, 1 female	Gifts of grace; Undeserved love
Security Check	Mixed	1 male, 1 female, 1 offstage voice	Salvation; Works vs. grace
The Stickholders	Serious	3 males, 1 female, 1 narrator	Relationship with God; Freedom from rules

Songs

Title	Artist	Style	Tempo	Seeker-Sensitivity Rating
The Great Divide	Point of Grace	Power ballad	Slow	9
He Won't Let You Go	**The Kry**	**Piano ballad**	**Slow**	**10**
If I Could Look Through Your Eyes	*Willow Creek Music*	*Piano ballad*	*Slow*	*10*
Only by Grace	*Willow Creek Music*	*Pop/rock*	*Mid*	*10*
What a Ride	*Willow Creek Music*	*Pop/rock*	*Up*	*9*
_____	_____	_____	_____	_____
_____	_____	_____	_____	_____
_____	_____	_____	_____	_____
_____	_____	_____	_____	_____

 Movie Clips

Title: _____

Topic: _____

Description: _____

Start Time: _____

Start Cue: _____

End Time: _____

End Cue: _____

Comments: _____

_____

~ Our Need for Christ ~

Refers to recognizing the need for a relationship with Christ
See also: **Guilt, Relationship With God—General**

Message Titles

- ☐ Averting Your Worst Nightmare
- ☐ Just What You're Looking for
- ☐ *Ordering Your Private World:* Ordering Your Spiritual World

_____

_____

_____

_____

Dramas

Title	Tone	Characters	Topics
Any Time?	Mixed, mostly serious	1 male	Making time for God
The Black Hole	Serious, but light	2 males, 1 female, 1 narrator	Filling the void; Contentment; God's love
Lizzy and Leroy	Humorous	1 male, 1 female, piano player (optional)	Life fulfillment; Material things don't satisfy
Man of the Year	Serious	5 males, 1 female	Moralism; Our need for Christ
Richard: 1992	Serious	2 males, 1 female	Anger; Rebellion; Decay of the family
The Safe	Mixed	1 male, 1 female, 3 either male or female	Inner strength; Needing God's strength
These Parts	Mixed	2 males, 1 female, 3 males or females, 1 child, 1 narrator	The Resurrection; Our need for Christ; Easter

Title	Tone	Characters	Topics
Wait 'Til Halftime	Mixed	1 male, 1 female	Eternity; Heaven and hell; Evangelism
What's the Ticket?	Mixed	2 females, 4 either male or female	Need for Christ; Contentment; Needs and wants
"X" Marks the Spot	Serious; mime	1 female, 1 male, 3 females or males	Sin; Redemption; Forgiveness; Guilt
You Cramp My Style	Serious	1 male, 1 female, 1 male or female	Reasons why people don't believe; Society's view of God
_____	_____	_____	_____
_____	_____	_____	_____
_____	_____	_____	_____
_____	_____	_____	_____

 # Songs

Title	Artist	Style	Tempo	Seeker-Sensitivity Rating
A Place to Call Home	*Willow Creek Music*	*Gospel ballad*	*Slow, in 3*	*10*
All That I Need	Steve Camp	Ballad	Slow	5
Ball and Chain	**Susan Ashton**	**Folk/pop**	**Mid**	**9**
Come Into My Life	Imperials	Power ballad	Slow	10
Desperado	Eagles	Ballad	Slow	10
The Difference	Paul Smith	Pop	Up	9
Heaven in the Real World	**Steven Curtis Chapman**	**Pop/rock**	**Up**	**7**
I Could Live Without You	Wayne Watson	Ballad	Slow	6
I'll Find You There	**The Kry**	**Folk/rock ballad**	**Slow**	**9**
Jesus Will Still Be There	**Point of Grace**	**Ballad**	**Slow**	**9**
Love That Will Not Let Me Go	**Steve Camp**	**Ballad**	**Slow**	**10**
Mercy for the Memories	**Geoff Moore & the Distance**	**Folk/pop ballad**	**Slow**	**9**
More to This Life	Steven Curtis Chapman	MOR pop	Mid/up	9
Only by Grace	*Willow Creek Music*	*Pop/rock*	*Mid*	*10*
People Need the Lord	Steve Green	Inspirational ballad	Slow	1
Show Me the Way	**Styx**	**Power ballad**	**Mid/slow**	**10**
Something to Hold On To	Truth	R & B/pop	Mid	10
Strength in You	*Willow Creek Music*	*MOR pop*	*Slow/mid*	*10*
Time to Return	*Willow Creek Music*	*Ballad*	*Slow*	*7*
We Believe in God	Amy Grant	Acoustic ballad	Slow	3

Title	Artist	Style	Tempo	Seeker-Sensitivity Rating
Where Else Could I Go	*Willow Creek Music*	*Inspirational ballad*	*Slow*	*8*
You're the One He Loves	**Truth**	**Pop**	**Up**	**10**
_____	_____	_____	_____	_____
_____	_____	_____	_____	_____
_____	_____	_____	_____	_____

Movie Clips

Title: _____

Topic: _____

Description: _____

Start Time: _____

Start Cue: _____

End Time: _____

End Cue: _____

Comments: _____

_____

~ Our Value to God ~

Refers to the essential truth that people matter to God
See also: **God's Love, Self-Esteem**

Message Titles

- ❏ Measuring How Much You Matter to God
- ❏ People Matter to God
- ❏ *Seven Wonders of the Spiritual World:* God Loves Me

_____

_____

_____

_____

Dramas

Title	Tone	Characters	Topics
Another Day at the Bus Stop	Mixed	1 male, 1 female	Our relationship with God; Self-esteem
The Intruder	Serious	1 male, 1 female	Self-image; Destructive parenting; God's love in spite of failure
The Lane of Life	Serious; mime	5 males or females, 1 offstage narrator	Salvation; Our value to God; Self-esteem
Measuring Up	Mixed; mime	2 males, 1 female, 1 male or female	God's acceptance of us; Self-esteem
Wonderfully Made	Serious	2 females, 2 males, 1 narrator	Affirming a child's uniqueness
_____	_____	_____	_____
_____	_____	_____	_____
_____	_____	_____	_____
_____	_____	_____	_____

 Songs

Title	Artist	Style	Tempo	Seeker-Sensitivity Rating
A Place to Call Home	*Willow Creek Music*	*Gospel ballad*	*Slow, in 3*	*10*
Almighty God	**Jim Murray**	**Traditional ballad**	**Slow**	**7**
His Eyes	**Steven Curtis Chapman**	**Acoustic guitar ballad**	**Mid/slow**	**9**
If I Could Look Through Your Eyes	*Willow Creek Music*	*Piano ballad*	*Slow*	*10*
In Heaven's Eyes	**Sandi Patty**	**Inspirational ballad**	**Slow**	**9**
Jesus Loves Me	**Whitney Houston**	**R & B/pop**	**Slow/mid**	**8**
Let the Lord Love You	*Willow Creek Music*	*Acoustic guitar ballad*	*Slow*	*9*
Love Is Always There	Carolyn Arends	Folk/pop	Up	9
The Love of God	*Willow Creek Music*	*Acapella vocal group*	*Slow*	*6*
The Prodigal (I'll Be Waiting)	Amy Grant	Ballad	Slow	7
There Is a Love	**Michael English**	**Pop**	**Up**	**9**
Treasure of You	Steven Curtis Chapman	Driving rock	Up	10
What I Wouldn't Give	*Willow Creek Music*	*Acoustic ballad*	*Slow*	*10*

Title	Artist	Style	Tempo	Seeker-Sensitivity Rating
Why Me	*Willow Creek Music*	*Ballad*	*Slow*	*9*
You're the One He Loves	Truth	Pop	Up	10

Movie Clips

Title: _____

Topic: _____

Description: _____

Start Time: _____

Start Cue: _____

End Time: _____

End Cue: _____

Comments: _____

_____

Programming Tip

Team building

Building strong, reliable volunteers is dependent on team members—

- Developing significant relationships with one another
- Being challenged and enjoying using their gifts
- Believing their service is significant
- Feeling respected

~ Salvation ~

Message Titles

- ☐ Averting Your Worst Nightmare
- ☐ Christianity 101
- ☐ The Doorway to Heaven
- ☐ How to Become a Christian
- ☐ Plain-English Christianity
- ☐ Show Me the Way
- ☐ *Private Conversations:* Jesus Talks to a Sinner
- ☐ *The "S" Word:* The Other "S" Word
- ☐ *A Taste of Christianity:* A Better Kind of Confidence
- ☐ **Your Ever-After:** Heaven • Hell • The Crimson Thread • One Eye on Eternity

_____
_____
_____
_____
_____

Package Suggestion

Drama:
"X" Marks the Spot

Song:
Cross Medley

Dramas

Title	Tone	Characters	Topics
The Black Hole	Serious, but light	2 males, 1 female, 1 narrator	Filling the void; Contentment; God's love
The Book of Life	"Energetic mime"; mixed	3 males, 3 females	Baptism; Faith; Basic Christianity; Eternal life
A Clean Slate	Serious	1 male, 2 or 3 males or females	Forgiveness; Redemption; Guilt
The Lane of Life	Serious; Mime	5 males or females, 1 offstage narrator	Salvation; Our value to God; Self-esteem
Measuring Up	Mixed; mime	2 males, 1 female, 1 male or female	God's acceptance of us; Self-esteem

Title	Tone	Characters	Topics
Only Child	Serious	1 male, 2 females	Grace; Outrageous forgiveness; Doctrine of adoption
The Prisoner	Serious	3 males, 1 female	Easter; Freedom from sin; New Christian
Security Check	Mixed	1 male, 1 female, 1 offstage voice	Salvation; Works vs. grace
These Parts	Mixed	2 males, 1 female, 3 males or females, 1 child, 1 narrator	The Resurrection; Our need for Christ; Easter
Wait 'Til Halftime	Mixed	1 male, 1 female	Eternity; Heaven and hell; Evangelism
"X" Marks the Spot	Serious; mime	1 female, 1 male, 3 females or males	Sin; Redemption; Forgiveness; Guilt
_____	_____	_____	_____
_____	_____	_____	_____
_____	_____	_____	_____
_____	_____	_____	_____
_____	_____	_____	_____

 Songs

Title	Artist	Style	Tempo	Seeker-Sensitivity Rating
A Place to Call Home	*Willow Creek Music*	*Gospel ballad*	*Slow, in 3*	10
All the Faith You Need	*Willow Creek Music*	*Pop/rock*	*Up*	10
Change in My Life	**John Pagano**	**Gospel**	**Mid/up**	**9**
Come Into My Life	Imperials	Power ballad	Slow	10
Cross Medley	*Willow Creek Music*	*Ballad medley— hymns*	*Slow*	7
The Great Divide	Point of Grace	Power ballad	Slow	9
He Won't Let You Go	**The Kry**	**Piano ballad**	**Slow**	**10**
I Found Myself in You	**Clay Crosse**	**Gospel ballad**	**Mid/slow**	**10**
I've Been Released	*Willow Creek Music*	*Pop/rock— Chicago sound*	*Up*	9
Love Is Always There	Carolyn Arends	Folk/pop	Up	9
The Love of God	*Willow Creek Music*	*Accapella vocal group*	*Slow*	6
Love That Will Not Let Me Go	**Steve Camp**	**Ballad**	**Slow**	**10**
Mercy for the Memories	**Geoff Moore & the Distance**	**Folk/pop ballad**	**Slow**	**9**
More Than Words	Steven Curtis Chapman	Acoustic guitar ballad	Mid/slow	4

Title	Artist	Style	Tempo	Seeker-Sensitivity Rating
Only by Grace	*Willow Creek Music*	*Pop/rock*	*Mid*	*10*
Show Me the Way	**Styx**	**Power ballad**	**Mid/slow**	**10**
There Is a Love	**Michael English**	**Pop**	**Up**	**9**
Want the World to Know	*Willow Creek Music*	*Pop*	*Up*	*9*
We Belong to Him	**Wayne Watson**	**MOR ballad**	**Slow/mid**	**2**
What I Wouldn't Give	*Willow Creek Music*	*Acoustic ballad*	*Slow*	*10*
Why Me	*Willow Creek Music*	*Ballad*	*Slow*	*9*
_____	_____	_____	_____	_____
_____	_____	_____	_____	_____
_____	_____	_____	_____	_____

Movie Clips

Title:	Indiana Jones and the Last Crusade
Topic:	Faith; Trusting God when circumstances are confusing.
Description:	Indiana Jones faces a seemingly uncrossable chasm, but takes a "leap of faith" as he steps onto an invisible bridge. Illustrates faith, believing what can't be seen.
Start Time:	1:46:50
Start Cue:	Indiana Jones walks through cave to the chasm
End Time:	1:48:45
End Cue:	Indy throws sand on bridge to mark it—can be cut earlier
Comments:	_____
	_____

Title:	_____
Topic:	_____
Description:	_____
Start Time:	_____
Start Cue:	_____
End Time:	_____
End Cue:	_____
Comments:	_____
	_____

fulfillment

Until we come to Christ, there is a void in our souls that we try desperately to fill. Nothing ultimately satisfies but a relationship with God.

 ## Message Titles

- ☐ Filling the Void
- ☐ *Seven Wonders of the Spiritual World:* God Satisfies Me
- ☐ *Surprised By God:* Surprised by God's Satisfaction
- ☐ **Money, Sex and Power:** Money • Sex • Power

_____

_____

_____

_____

 ## Dramas

Title	Tone	Characters	Topics
The Black Hole	Serious, but light	2 males, 1 female, 1 narrator	Filling the void; Contentment; God's love
Call Waiting	Mixed— ends serious	2 males	Marketplace pressures; Search for significance; Mid-life crisis
In Pursuit of Happiness	Mixed	1 male, 1 female	Contentment; Possessions
Lizzy and Leroy	Humorous	1 male, 1 female, piano player (optional)	Life fulfillment; Material things don't satisfy
The Lures of Life	Mixed mime; light	5 males, 1 female	Adventurism; Life fulfillment
Wasted	Mixed	2 males	Job satisfaction; Christians and work
What's the Ticket?	Mixed	2 females, 4 either male or female	Need for Christ; Contentment; Needs and wants
_____	_____	_____	_____
_____	_____	_____	_____
_____	_____	_____	_____

Songs

Title	Artist	Style	Tempo	Seeker-Sensitivity Rating
A Place to Call Home	*Willow Creek Music*	*Gospel ballad*	*Slow, in 3*	*10*
The Difference	Paul Smith	Pop	Up	9
Heaven in the Real World	**Steven Curtis Chapman**	**Pop/rock**	**Up**	**7**
I Could Live Without You	Wayne Watson	Ballad	Slow	6
I Found Myself in You	**Clay Crosse**	**Gospel ballad**	**Mid/slow**	**10**
Love That Will Not Let Me Go	**Steve Camp**	**Ballad**	**Slow**	**10**
More to This Life	Steven Curtis Chapman	MOR pop	Mid/up	9
Only You	*Willow Creek Music*	*Ballad*	*Slow*	*9*
Show Me the Way	**Styx**	**Power ballad**	**Mid/slow**	**10**
Somebody Make Me Laugh	**Patti Austin**	**Ballad**	**Slow**	**10**
Strength in You	*Willow Creek Music*	*MOR pop*	*Slow/mid*	*10*
Treasure	**Gary Chapman**	**Acoustic ballad**	**Slow**	**9**
What a Ride	*Willow Creek Music*	*Pop/rock*	*Up*	*9*
Where Else Could I Go	*Willow Creek Music*	*Inspirational ballad*	*Slow*	*8*

Movie Clips

Title:	City Slickers
Topic:	Disillusionment; Life fulfillment
Description:	Billy Crystal speaks at his son's school. Disillusioned with life in general, he gives a very funny, very depressing discourse on the stages of life.
Start Time:	0:44:38
Start Cue:	"As Danny said"
End Time:	0:45:30
End Cue:	"Any questions"
Comments:	

Title: Cool Runnings

Topic: Success; Ambition

Description: A bobsledder asks his coach why he cheated 20 years ago in the Olympics. The answer concerns the trap of success and its ultimate lack of fulfillment.

Start Time: 1:25:15

Start Cue: Coach enters hotel room

End Time: 1:27:15

End Cue: "When you cross that finish line, you'll know"

Comments: _____

_____

Title: She's Having a Baby

Topic: Life in suburbia; Emptiness of suburban life/American dream

Description: Funny parody of suburban life shows men in bad clothes dancing with lawnmowers, and their wives dancing around them with refreshments.

Start Time: 0:53:00

Start Cue: Start after the bicyclist leaves

End Time: 0:54:30

End Cue: End when music stops

Comments: _____

_____

Title: _____

Topic: _____

Description: _____

Start Time: _____

Start Cue: _____

End Time: _____

End Cue: _____

Comments: _____

_____

Life Foundation

Refers to the biblical rock vs. sand analogy; asks the question "What are you building your life on?"

See also: **God's Faithfulness**

 ## Message Titles

- ❏ A Better Kind of Confidence
- ❏ Defining Our Beliefs
- ❏ Staying Steady in the Storm
- ❏ Unmasking Your Master
- ❏ *What Jesus Would Say to . . .* Bill Gates

_____

_____

_____

_____

 ## Dramas

Title	Tone	Characters	Topics
Chameleon	Mixed	3 males	Controlling our emotions; God's presence in our lives
The Game of Life	Humorous	1 male, 1 female, 1 narrator	Decision making; Search for meaning
Is "Nothing" Sacred?	Humorous	3 males, and at least 4 others in group	Evolution vs. Creation; Modern science
Lifetime Deal	Serious	2 males	Workaholism
Lizzy and Leroy	Humorous	1 male, 1 female, piano player (optional)	Life fulfillment; Material things don't satisfy
The Lures of Life	Mixed mime; light	5 males, 1 female	Adventurism; Life fulfillment

Title	Tone	Characters	Topics
One Step Up, One Step Down	Serious	4 males (1 can be female)	Ambition; Priorities
Richard: 1985	Serious	2 males	Workaholism; Materialism vs. idealism
The Safe	Mixed	1 male, 1 female, 3 males or females	Inner strength; Needing God's strength
Security Check	Mixed	1 male, 1 female, 1 offstage voice	Salvation; Works vs. grace
_____	_____	_____	_____
_____	_____	_____	_____
_____	_____	_____	_____
_____	_____	_____	_____

Songs

Title	Artist	Style	Tempo	Seeker-Sensitivity Rating
A Place to Call Home	*Willow Creek Music*	*Gospel ballad*	*Slow, in 3*	10
Build My World Around You	**Sandi Patty**	**Pop**	**Up**	**9**
Ever Devoted	*Willow Creek Music*	*Ballad*	*Slow*	6
Foundations	Geoff Moore & the Distance	Folk/pop ballad	Slow/mid	8
From Here on Out	*Willow Creek Music*	*MOR pop*	*Mid*	8
The Future	First Call	Pop vocal group	Up	8
He Won't Let Me Down	**Debbie McClendon**	**R & B/pop**	**Up**	**9**
Heaven in the Real World	**Steven Curtis Chapman**	**Pop/rock**	**Up**	**7**
His Love Is Strong	**Clay Crosse**	**Pop**	**Up**	**10**
I Found Myself in You	**Clay Crosse**	**Gospel ballad**	**Mid/slow**	**10**
I Go to the Rock	**Dottie Rambo**	**Swing/big band**	**Mid**	**7**
In My Father's Hands	**Susan Ashton**	**Folk/pop**	**Mid**	**9**
The Love of God	Phillip Bailey	Ballad	Slow	8
Love That Will Not Let Me Go	**Steve Camp**	**Ballad**	**Slow**	**10**
No Better Place	**Steven Curtis Chapman**	**Pop/folk rock**	**Up**	**7**
Place in This World	Michael W. Smith	Power ballad	Slow	9
Rock Steady	Wayne Watson	Pop/rock	Up	7
Solid as the Rock	**Michael English**	**Pop**	**Up**	**8**
Something to Hold on To	Truth	R & B/pop	Mid	10
Strength in You	**Willow Creek Music**	**MOR pop**	**Slow/mid**	**10**

Title	Artist	Style	Tempo	Seeker-Sensitivity Rating
Thy Word	Amy Grant	Ballad	Slow	4
Treasure	**Gary Chapman**	**Acoustic ballad**	**Slow**	**9**
What a Ride	*Willow Creek Music*	*Pop/rock*	*Up*	9
___	___	___	___	___
___	___	___	___	___
___	___	___	___	___
___	___	___	___	___

 # Movie Clips

Title: _____

Topic: _____

Description: _____

Start Time: _____

Start Cue: _____

End Time: _____

End Cue: _____

Comments: _____

_____

Programming Tip

Drama: Being real

Look for sketches that focus on real people dealing with real issues. Often the best dramas are written as a person goes back into the emotional "tunnel" and recalls a real experience. Why? Because it is real. When reviewing a script, ask yourself these questions: Is the dialogue consistent with the way people talk? Do the characters behave as people do? Is there honesty and integrity in the way the issues are dealt with?

Misconceptions of Christianity

Many people don't believe because of a distorted view of God or of the Christian life.
See also: **Grace vs. Works, God's Character—General, Joy of the Christian Life**

 ## Message Titles

- ❏ Five Deadly Lies
- ❏ Fully Informed Followers
- ❏ *A Taste of Christianity:* A Better Kind of Freedom
- ❏ *What Jesus Would Say to . . .* Oprah Winfrey
- ❏ **Three Things God Loves (That Most People Think He Doesn't):** Leisure • Laughter • Love-making

_____

_____

_____

_____

 ## Dramas

Title	Tone	Characters	Topics
Acting the Part	Serious	1 male, 2 females	Legalism; Living out our Christianity
D-Day	Humorous	2 males, 1 female	Misconceptions about Christianity
Fully Devoted Sailors	Humorous	1 male, 1 female, 7 males or females	Joy of Christian life; Misconceptions of Christianity

Title	Tone	Characters	Topics
"It"	Humorous	2 males, 1 female	Becoming a Christian doesn't mean having no problems; Vulnerability of new believers
The Lures of Life	Mixed mime; light	5 males, 1 female	Adventurism; Life fulfillment
Monday Night Meeting	Humorous	4 males	New Christian; Joy of Christian life; Discipleship
No Fun	Humorous	3 males, 1 female	Christian lifestyle; Misconceptions about Christianity
A Problem of Perception	Humorous	3 males, 1 female	Misconceptions about Christianity; Christian life
Pulpit Talk	Humorous	3 males, 2 females	Stereotypical church experiences; Sermons; Intro to Sermon on the Mount
Will the Real God Please Stand Up?	Humorous	3 males, 1 female	God's character; What is God like? Second Commandment
_____	_____	_____	_____
_____	_____	_____	_____
_____	_____	_____	_____
_____	_____	_____	_____
_____	_____	_____	_____

Songs

Title	Artist	Style	Tempo	Seeker-Sensitivity Rating
The Great Adventure	Steven Curtis Chapman	Pop/rock	Up	5
No Better Place	**Steven Curtis Chapman**	**Pop/folk rock**	**Up**	**7**
Only by Grace	*Willow Creek Music*	*Pop/rock*	*Mid*	*10*
This Is the Life	**Phillips, Craig and Dean**	**Pop/rock**	**Up**	**6**
What a Ride	*Willow Creek Music*	*Pop/rock*	*Up*	*9*
_____	_____	_____	_____	_____
_____	_____	_____	_____	_____
_____	_____	_____	_____	_____
_____	_____	_____	_____	_____
_____	_____	_____	_____	_____

Movie Clips

Title: Sister Act
Topic: The church; Reasons people don't go to church
Description: Humorous clip of a boring preacher and a horrible choir, illustrating a couple of reasons why people don't go to church.
Start Time: 0:30:25
Start Cue: "We are a small congregation this morning"
End Time: 32:25
End Cue: Whoopi Goldberg winces
Comments: _____
_____

Title: _____
Topic: _____
Description: _____
Start Time: _____
Start Cue: _____
End Time: _____
End Cue: _____
Comments: _____
_____

Programming Tip

Prayer is the programmer's greatest tool
It may seem like stating the obvious, but prayer is essential to the creative process. We do the work of planning and preparing, but it is only God who can take our efforts and gifts and produce life change. When we ask him to inspire us and to have his way in the creative process, we will marvel at powerful programming "moments" that can only be explained by the work of the Holy Spirit.

New Christians

Refers to the specific issues that face brand-new or young believers
See also: **Baptism**

 ## Message Titles

❏ *The Seasons of a Spiritual Life:* The Season of Spiritual Infancy

_____

_____

_____

 ## Dramas

Title	Tone	Characters	Topics
Call of the Wild	Mixed	1 male, 1 female	Serving God; Serving in a place consistent with your gifts and temperament
A Day in the Life	Humorous	5 males	Christians in the marketplace; New Christian
First-Day Jitters	Humorous	1 female	New Christian; Obeying God
"It"	Humorous	2 males, 1 female	Becoming a Christian doesn't mean having no problems; Vulnerability of new believers
Monday Night Meeting	Humorous	4 males	New Christian; Joy of Christian life; Discipleship
The Prisoner	Serious	3 males, 1 female	Easter; Freedom from sin; New Christian
Welcome to the Family	Humorous	2 males, 1 female	New Christian; Growing in Christ
_____	_____	_____	_____
_____	_____	_____	_____
_____	_____	_____	_____

Songs

Title	Artist	Style	Tempo	Seeker-Sensitivity Rating
All the Faith You Need	*Willow Creek Music*	*Pop/rock*	*Up*	*10*
Come Into My Life	Imperials	Power ballad	Slow	10
From This Moment On	**Newsong**	**Ballad**	**Slow**	**8**
He Won't Let You Go	**The Kry**	**Piano ballad**	**Slow**	**10**
I Found Myself in You	**Clay Crosse**	**Gospel ballad**	**Mid/slow**	**10**
I've Been Released	*Willow Creek Music*	*Pop/rock— Chicago sound*	*Up*	*9*
I'm Amazed	*Willow Creek Music*	*Ballad*	*Slow*	*7*
Take My Hand	**The Kry**	**Acoustic ballad**	**Mid/slow**	**9**
Want the World to Know	*Willow Creek Music*	*Pop*	*Up*	*9*

Movie Clips

Title: _____

Topic: _____

Description: _____

Start Time: _____

Start Cue: _____

End Time: _____

End Cue: _____

Comments: _____

Other Religions

We have also included Roman Catholicism here because of some of the methodological and sometimes theological differences between Catholics and Protestants.

 ## Message Titles

- ☐ What Protestants Can Learn From Catholics
- ☐ What Catholics Can Learn From Protestants
- ☐ **Alternatives to Christianity:** The New Age Movement • Contemporary Cults • Major World Religions
- ☐ **The Rise of Satanism:** The Secret World of Satan Worship • A Biography of Satan • Overcoming Satanic Opposition

_____
_____
_____
_____
_____

 ## Dramas

Title	Tone	Characters	Topics
Anything But Religion	Mixed, mostly serious	2 males, 2 females	Denominational differences; Families alienated because of religion
The Conversion	Serious	2 males, 1 female	Hinduism
Differences	Humorous	2 males, 1 female	Catholicism vs. Protestantism
Faith in Jeapordy	Mixed	2 females, 2 males	Mormonism
Family Values	Serious	2 females, 2 males	Cults; Broken families
The Gardeners	Humorous	1 male, 1 female	New Age movement
Is "Nothing" Sacred?	Humorous	3 males, and at least 4 others in group	Evolution vs. Creation; Modern science

Title	Tone	Characters	Topics
Nothing to It	Mixed	2 males, 2 females	Satanism; Spiritual warfare
Winning Strategy	Mixed	2 males, 4 males or females	Good vs. evil; Busyness

Songs

It is difficult to pin down specific songs for this topic, but with theological issues it often works well to use songs that affirm who God is. See God's Character–General, Lordship of Christ.

Title	Artist	Style	Tempo	Seeker-Sensitivity Rating

Movie Clips

Title: _____

Topic: _____

Description: _____

Start Time: _____

Start Cue: _____

End Time: _____

End Cue: _____

Comments: _____

_____

Spiritual Seeking

Affirming and encouraging the seeking process

Package Suggestion

Drama:
Reason Enough

Song:
A Place to Call Home

Message Topics

- ❐ The Benefits of Being a Seeker
- ❐ Doubters Welcome
- ❐ The Rewards of Spiritual Risk Taking
- ❐ Show Me the Way
- ❐ *The Seasons of a Spiritual Life:* The Season of Spiritual Seeking
- ❐ *What Jesus Would Say to . . .* Peter Jennings

_____

_____

_____

Dramas

Title	Tone	Characters	Topics
The Big Question	Mixed, mostly humorous	1 male, 1 female, 1 child	The existence of God
The Game of Life	Humorous	1 male, 1 female, 1 narrator	Decision making; Search for meaning
Is "Nothing" Sacred?	Humorous	3 males, and at least 4 others in group	Evolution vs. Creation; Modern science
The Lures of Life	Mixed mime; light	5 males, 1 female	Adventurism; Life fulfillment
Reason Enough	Mixed, mostly serious	1 male, 1 female	Importance of faith grounded in reason
Street Chat	Humorous	4 males, 1 female	Search for meaning; Spirituality

Title	Tone	Characters	Topics
Wait 'Til Halftime	Mixed	1 male, 1 female	Eternity; Heaven and hell; Evangelism

_____ _____ _____ _____

_____ _____ _____ _____

_____ _____ _____ _____

Songs

Title	Artist	Style	Tempo	Seeker-Sensitivity Rating
A Place to Call Home	_Willow Creek Music_	_Gospel ballad_	_Slow, in 3_	_10_
All the Faith You Need	_Willow Creek Music_	_Pop/rock_	_Up_	_10_
Come Into My Life	Imperials	Power ballad	Slow	10
Heaven in the Real World	**Steven Curtis Chapman**	**Pop/rock**	**Up**	**7**
I Found Myself in You	**Clay Crosse**	**Gospel ballad**	**Mid/slow**	**10**
More to This Life	Steven Curtis Chapman	MOR pop	Mid/up	9
Place in This World	Michael W. Smith	Power ballad	Slow	9
Show Me the Way	**Styx**	**Power ballad**	**Mid/slow**	**10**
Treasure	**Gary Chapman**	**Acoustic ballad**	**Slow**	**9**
You're the One He Loves	**Truth**	**Pop**	**Up**	**10**

_____ _____ _____ _____ _____

_____ _____ _____ _____ _____

_____ _____ _____ _____ _____

_____ _____ _____ _____ _____

Movie Clips

Title: _____

Topic: _____

Description: _____

Start Time: _____

Start Cue: _____

End Time: _____

End Cue: _____

Comments: _____

_____

SOCIAL ISSUES

Abortion

Message Titles

- ☐ *Modern-day Madness:* Unwanted Pregnancies
- ☐ *Our Modern Moral Trifecta:* Abortion

_____
_____
_____
_____
_____

Dramas

Title	Tone	Characters	Topics
Catch 22	Serious	2 females	Abortion
The Painful Process	Serious	1 female	Abortion

Songs

Songs of tenderness and compassion work well with these dramas. See God as a Refuge, God's Love, God's Tenderness, Our Value to God.

Title	Artist	Style	Tempo	Seeker-Sensitivity Rating
In Heaven's Eyes	Sandi Patti	Inspirational ballad	Slow	9
Peace Be Still	Al Denson	Ballad	Slow	10

Movie Clips

Title: _____

Topic: _____

Description: _____

Start Time: _____

Start Cue: _____

End Time: _____

End Cue: _____

Comments: _____

_____

Caring for the Poor

See also: **Compassion**

 Message Titles

❏ *Becoming a Contagious Christian:* Compassion
❏ *What Jesus Would Say to . . .* Mother Teresa

_____
_____
_____
_____
_____

 Dramas

Title	Tone	Characters	Topics
Am I Missing Something?	Serious	3 males, 2 females	Attitudes in serving; Giving; Self-deception; Rationalizing
Fourth of July	Mixed	1 male, 2 females, 1 child	Fourth of July; The homeless
The Story of Rachel	Serious	3 females	Care for the poor; Compassion
Suit and Volly	Humorous	2 males, 2 females	Motives in serving others

 **Songs**

Title	Artist	Style	Tempo	Seeker-Sensitivity Rating
Heaven in the Real World	**Steven Curtis Chapman**	**Pop/rock**	**Up**	7
Helping Hand	Amy Grant	Pop	Mid/up	10
Love Can Open the Door	Sandi Patti	Pop	Up	10
Not Too Far From Here	Kim Boyce	Ballad	Slow	7
We Are the People	Bob Carlisle	Power ballad	Slow	5

 Movie Clips

Title:	_____
Topic:	_____
Description:	_____
Start Time:	_____
Start Cue:	_____
End Time:	_____
End Cue:	_____
Comments:	_____
	_____

Homosexuality

Might also include: *AIDS*

Message Titles

- ☐ Hope for the Homosexual
- ☐ The Truth About Homosexuality
- ☐ *Our Modern Moral Trifecta:* Homosexuality

_____

_____

_____

_____

_____

Dramas

Title	Tone	Characters	Topics
Just As I Am	Serious	1 male	Homosexuality
Misjudged Love	Serious	2 males, 1 female	Homosexuality; AIDS; Father/son relationship

364

Songs

Title	Artist	Style	Tempo	Seeker-Sensitivity Rating
The Last Song	Elton John	Ballad	Slow	10
_____	_____	_____	_____	_____
_____	_____	_____	_____	_____
_____	_____	_____	_____	_____
_____	_____	_____	_____	_____
_____	_____	_____	_____	_____

 # Movie Clips

Title: _____

Topic: _____

Description: _____

Start Time: _____

Start Cue: _____

End Time: _____

End Cue: _____

Comments: _____

_____

The Power of the Media

Message Titles

- ☐ Sources for Values
- ☐ Spiritual Eyesight
- ☐ *What Jesus Would Say to . . .* Murphy Brown
- ☐ *What Jesus Would Say to . . .* Oprah Winfrey
- ☐ *What Jesus Would Say to . . .* Rush Limbaugh

Dramas

Title	Tone	Characters	Topics
The Big Sell	Humorous	3 males, 2 females	Obsession with sex in society; Effect of the media
Confessions of an Ad-aholic	Humorous	1 male, 1 female	Materialism; Power of the media; The American dream
Guidance Counselors	Humorous	2 males, 1 female	The power of TV; Sources for values
It's Only a Movie	Humorous	2 males, 2 females, 1 offstage voice	The power of media; The effects of what we see; Male/female differences

Songs

Title	Artist	Style	Tempo	Seeker-Sensitivity Rating
Couch Potato	Billy Crockett	Acoustic pop	Up	10
Who to Listen To	Amy Grant	Pop	Mid	8
Words	**Kim Hill**	**Pop/rock**	**Up**	**10**
_____	_____	_____	____	____
_____	_____	_____	____	____
_____	_____	_____	____	____
_____	_____	_____	____	____

Movie Clips

Title: _____

Topic: _____

Description: _____

Start Time: _____

Start Cue: _____

End Time: _____

End Cue: _____

Comments: _____
_____

Racism

Message Titles

☐ *Our Modern Moral Trifecta:* Racism

_____
_____
_____

Dramas

Title	Tone	Characters	Topics
Half-Baked	Humorous	1 male, 2 females	Racism; Prejudice

Songs

Title	Artist	Style	Tempo	Seeker-Sensitivity Rating
In Heaven's Eyes	**Sandi Patty**	**Inspirational ballad**	**Slow**	**9**
Someday	Grover Levy	Pop	Mid/up	9
Undivided	First Call	Trio ballad	Slow	4

Movie Clips

Title: The Man Without a Face
Topic: Prejudice; Racism
Description: Mel Gibson plays a disfigured teacher who recites a portion of Shakespeare's *Merchant of Venice* about prejudice against Jews. The clip is all the more poignant because of his disfigured face.
Start Time: 0:49:30
Start Cue: "I hold the world but as the world"
End Time: 0:50:40
End Cue: "Shall we not revenge"
Comments: Last line is quite harsh, though honest

Title: _____
Topic: _____
Description: _____
Start Time: _____
Start Cue: _____
End Time: _____
End Cue: _____
Comments: _____

Programming Tip

Choose a creative environment

Where you hold your creative meetings is very important. Creative people typically need an environment that feels comfortable and eases tension. Avoid fluorescent lights and cramped spaces. Meet in a place that will enhance, not inhibit, the creative process.

The State of the World

Refers to the decay of American society

Package Suggestion

Drama:
No More Womb

Song:
Time to Return

Message Titles

☐ *Understanding the Times:* The Nineties
☐ **Changing Times:** The Changing American Male • The Changing American Female • The Changing American Child • Changing American Sexuality • The Changing American Dream • The Changing American Church

_____
_____
_____
_____

Dramas

Title	Tone	Characters	Topics
No More Womb	Mixed	1 male, 1 female	State of the world; Fear of the unknown

Songs

Title	Artist	Style	Tempo	Seeker-Sensitivity Rating
Heaven in the Real World	**Steven Curtis Chapman**	**Pop/rock**	**Up**	7
The Only Hope	Babbie Mason	Ballad	Slow	5
Time to Return	*Willow Creek Music*	*Ballad*	*Slow*	7
___	___	___	___	___
___	___	___	___	___
___	___	___	___	___
___	___	___	___	___

 # Movie Clips

Title: _____

Topic: _____

Description: _____

Start Time: _____

Start Cue: _____

End Time: _____

End Cue: _____

Comments: _____

_____

Song Index

A Beautiful Place
  Artist: Wayne Watson
  Album/Label: A Beautiful Place, Dayspring
  Style: MOR ballad
  Tempo: Mid/slow
  Seeker-Sensitivity Rating: 9
  Themes: Romans 8:28; The benefits of trials

A Place Called Hope
  Artist: Michael English
  Album/Label: Hope, Warner Alliance
  Style: Pop gospel
  Tempo: Mid/up
  Seeker-Sensitivity Rating: 8
  Themes: Hope for the broken-hearted
  Comments: Never used at Willow Creek

A Place to Call Home
  Artist: Willow Creek Music
  Album/Label: A Place to Call Home, Word/Maranatha!
  Style: Gospel ballad
  Tempo: Slow, in 3
  Seeker-Sensitivity Rating: 10
  Themes: Filling the void, Salvation, Healing
  Comments: Works well out of several dramas, especially those ending with a character who feels lost

A Rose Is a Rose
  Artist: Susan Ashton
  Album/Label: Susan Ashton, Sparrow
  Style: Piano ballad
  Tempo: Slow
  Seeker-Sensitivity Rating: 9
  Themes: Encouragement—stay true to who you are
  Comments: May need contextual setup to work. Never used at Willow Creek

All I Ever Wanted
  Artist: Margaret Becker
  Album/Label: Simple House, Sparrow
  Style: Pop/rock ballad
  Tempo: Slow/mid
  Seeker-Sensitivity Rating: 4
  Themes: Statement of devotion to Christ

All That I Need
  Artist: Steve Camp
  Album/Label: Consider the Cost, Sparrow
  Style: Ballad
  Tempo: Slow
  Seeker-Sensitivity Rating: 5
  Themes: Need for Christ; Hardship of Christian life

All the Faith You Need
  Artist: Willow Creek Music

Album/Label: None
  Style: Pop/rock
  Tempo: Up
  Seeker-Sensitivity Rating: 10
  Themes: Faith; Affirmation of seeking process
  Comments: Strong opener, especially for evangelistic services

Almighty
  Artist: Wayne Watson
  Album/Label: Home Free, Dayspring
  Style: Praise & worship/pop
  Tempo: Up
  Seeker-Sensitivity Rating: 2
  Themes: Praise & Worship; God's power

Almighty God
  Artist: Jim Murray
  Album/Label: Christians Arise, Word
  Style: Traditional ballad
  Tempo: Slow
  Seeker-Sensitivity Rating: 7
  Themes: God's protection, tender grace
  Comments: Also works well as female solo

Altar of Ego
  Artist: Carolyn Arends
  Album/Label: I Can Hear You, Reunion
  Style: Folk/pop
  Tempo: Mid/up
  Seeker-Sensitivity Rating: 6
  Themes: Pride, ego, thinking more highly of ourselves than we ought to
  Comments: Clever writing—may be a bit hard to catch and track the words. Great hook phrase—could be used in a sermon. Never used at Willow Creek

Always Before Me
  Artist: Steven Curtis Chapman
  Album/Label: Coram Deo 2, Sparrow
  Style: Worship ballad, in 3
  Tempo: Slow/mid
  Seeker-Sensitivity Rating: 1
  Themes: Worship; Holding God above all else

Another Time, Another Place
  Artist: Sandi Patti (with Wayne Watson)
  Album/Label: Another Time, Another Place, Word
  Style: Power ballad
  Tempo: Slow
  Seeker-Sensitivity Rating: 8
  Themes: Heaven; Longing for Heaven

Ask Me
  Artist: Amy Grant
  Album/Label: Heart in Motion, Myrrh

Style: Pop
  Tempo: Mid
  Seeker-Sensitivity Rating: 9
  Themes: Child Abuse
  Comments: Very volatile subject, and some of the images in this song may be overwhelming—handle with extreme care

At Jesus' Feet
  Artist: Billy & Sarah Gaines
  Album/Label: Love's the Key, Benson
  Style: Ballad
  Tempo: Slow
  Seeker-Sensitivity Rating: 6
  Themes: Relationship with God; Being in God's presence
  Comments: Has worked in Willow Creek seeker services as a picture of a relationship with God

Audience of One
  Artist: Willow Creek Music
  Album/Label: A Place to Call Home, Word/Maranatha!
  Style: Power ballad
  Tempo: Slow
  Seeker-Sensitivity Rating: 8
  Themes: Pleasing God, not men; Ministry motives
  Comments: Strong statement of ministry/personal motives

Away in a Manger
  Artist: Steven Curtis Chapman
  Album/Label: Sparrow Christmas, Sparrow
  Style: Folk pop
  Tempo: Mid
  Seeker-Sensitivity Rating: 10
  Themes: Christmas

Awesome God
  Artist: Rich Mullins
  Album/Label: Winds of Heaven . . . Stuff of Earth, Reunion
  Style: Pop anthem
  Tempo: Mid/up
  Seeker-Sensitivity Rating: 1
  Themes: God's power; Praise & Worship

Ball and Chain
  Artist: Susan Ashton
  Album/Label: Wakened by the Wind, Sparrow
  Style: Folk/pop
  Tempo: Mid
  Seeker-Sensitivity Rating: 9
  Themes: Freedom from sin; Salvation
  Comments: Poetic lyrics-might be tough to track lyrically in some settings. Strong images

Ball and Chain
    Artist: Paul Overstreet
    Album/Label: Heroes, Word
    Style: Country
    Tempo: Mid/up
    Seeker-Sensitivity Rating: 10
    Themes: Marriage; Joy of marriage

The Beauty of Holiness
    Artist: Steve Camp
    Album/Label: Mercy in the Wilderness, Warner Alliance
    Style: Ballad
    Tempo: Slow
    Seeker-Sensitivity Rating: 1
    Themes: Worship; God's holiness

Be the One
    Artist: Al Denson
    Album/Label: Be the One, Benson
    Style: Power ballad
    Tempo: Slow
    Seeker-Sensitivity Rating: 7
    Themes: Call to commitment, to make a difference in others' lives
    Comments: Mostly aimed at Christians, but works for Seekers as well as a call to be a difference-maker

Behind Every Fantasy
    Artist: Willow Creek Music
    Album/Label: A Place to Call Home, Word/Maranatha!
    Style: Country pop
    Tempo: Up
    Seeker-Sensitivity Rating: 10
    Themes: Temptation, consequences of sin
    Comments: "Behind every fantasy is a harsh reality," is the "hook" and basic message of the song

Beyond Justice to Mercy
    Artist: Susan Ashton
    Album/Label: Wakened by the Wind, Sparrow
    Style: Ballad
    Tempo: Slow
    Seeker-Sensitivity Rating: 10
    Themes: Relational breakdown, forgiveness
    Comments: Powerful song—follows several dramas well

Bless the Lord
    Artist: Steve Camp
    Album/Label: Mercy in the Wilderness, Warner Alliance
    Style: Pop
    Tempo: Up
    Seeker-Sensitivity Rating: 1
    Themes: Praise; Psalm 103

Bound to Come Some Trouble
    Artist: Rich Mullins
    Album/Label: Never Picture Perfect, Reunion
    Style: Ballad
    Tempo: Slow
    Seeker-Sensitivity Rating: 10
    Themes: Hardship—Jesus understands, He will be there
    Comments: Can also work as a female solo

Bridge Between Two Hearts
    Artist: Bob Carlisle

Album/Label: Bob Carlisle, Sparrow
    Style: Pop
    Tempo: Up
    Seeker-Sensitivity Rating: 9
    Themes: Relationships; God's love joining peoples' hearts
    Comments: Key might need to be lowered

Build My World Around You
    Artist: Sandi Patty
    Album/Label: Find it on the Wings, Word
    Style: Pop
    Tempo: Up
    Seeker-Sensitivity Rating: 9
    Themes: Life foundation
    Comments: Good opener

Busy Man
    Artist: Steven Curtis Chapman
    Album/Label: For the Sake of the Call, Sparrow
    Style: Pop
    Tempo: Mid/up
    Seeker-Sensitivity Rating: 10
    Themes: Pace of life; Materialism

Call of the Wild
    Artist: Susan Ashton
    Album/Label: Susan Ashton, Sparrow
    Style: Country
    Tempo: Mid
    Seeker-Sensitivity Rating: 10
    Themes: Faithfulness in marriage, consequences of sin
    Comments: Story song—needs to be communicated well to avoid loss of focus. Could be enhanced by drama or video. Never used at Willow Creek

Can't We Try
    Artist: Dan Hill & Vonda Shepard
    Album/Label: Dan Hill; Dan Hill's Greatest Hits, Columbia
    Style: Pop ballad—duet
    Tempo: Slow
    Seeker-Sensitivity Rating: 10
    Themes: Marital breakdown; Marital healing.
    Comments: Good song to follow a drama showing marital conflict

Casual Christian
    Artist: De Garmo & Key
    Album/Label: Commander Sozo . . ., Frontline/Benson
    Style: Power ballad
    Tempo: Slow
    Seeker-Sensitivity Rating: 6
    Themes: Authenticity; Commitment to Christ

Cat's in the Cradle
    Artist: Harry Chapin
    Album/Label: Harry Chapin Anthology, Elektra
    Style: Folk
    Tempo: Mid
    Seeker-Sensitivity Rating: 10
    Themes: Parenting; Having time for your kids; Regret
    Comments: Just the opening guitar riff provokes an emotional response. A very strong song

Change in My Life
    Artist: John Pagano
    Album/Label: Leap of Faith Soundtrack, MCA
    Style: Gospel
    Tempo: Mid/up
    Seeker-Sensitivity Rating: 9
    Themes: Changed life; Testimonial
    Comments: Works best with a medium-large vocal group, but can be done with smaller group. Great testimonial song

Changin'
    Artist: Acapella Vocal Band
    Album/Label: What's Your Tag Say, Word
    Style: Acapella vocal group
    Tempo: Up
    Seeker-Sensitivity Rating: 8
    Themes: Sanctification, making changes
    Comments: Relatively difficult, but fun if you can pull it off. Works well coming out of the drama "One Sunday in the Parking Lot"

Charm Is Deceitful
    Artist: Kim Hill
    Album/Label: Talk About Life, Reunion
    Style: Ballad
    Tempo: Slow
    Seeker-Sensitivity Rating: 5
    Themes: Proverbs 13 woman
    Comments: Language is a little Christian for an unchurched audience, but can still work

Chippin' Away
    Artist: Willow Creek Music
    Album/Label: None
    Style: Folk pop
    Tempo: Mid/up
    Seeker-Sensitivity Rating: 8
    Themes: Sanctification; God gently changing me

Come Into My Life
    Artist: Imperials
    Album/Label: Love's Still Changin' Hearts, Star Song
    Style: Power ballad
    Tempo: Slow
    Seeker-Sensitivity Rating: 10
    Themes: Decision for Christ— "crossing the line"; Salvation

Common Ground
    Artist: Sierra
    Album/Label: Sierra, Star Song
    Style: Folk trio
    Tempo: Slow
    Seeker-Sensitivity Rating: 9
    Themes: Relational breakdown; Finding a point of understanding

Couch Potato
    Artist: Billy Crockett
    Album/Label: The Basic Stuff, Urgent
    Style: Acoustic pop
    Tempo: Up
    Seeker-Sensitivity Rating: 10
    Themes: TV; Sloth
    Comments: Funny song about the negative effects of TV would be especially fun with a vocalist who can play the guitar as well. Never done at Willow Creek

Crisis Mode
 Artist: Willow Creek Music
 Album/Label: None
 Style: Piano ballad
 Tempo: Slow
 Seeker-Sensitivity Rating: 9
 Themes: Pace of life

Cross Medley
 Artist: Willow Creek Music
 Album/Label: None, Willow Creek
 Style: Ballad medley—hymns
 Tempo: Slow
 Seeker-Sensitivity Rating: 7
 Themes: The cross; Atonement; Grace
 Comments: Combines "How Great Thou Art," "It Is Well," "Nothing But the Blood," and "Jesus Paid It All"

Desperado
 Artist: Eagles
 Album/Label: Eagles Live; Greatest Hits, 1971-1976; Desperado, Asylum
 Style: Ballad
 Tempo: Slow
 Seeker-Sensitivity Rating: 10
 Themes: Decision song—get off the fence

The Difference
 Artist: Paul Smith
 Album/Label: Human Touch, Star Song
 Style: Pop
 Tempo: Up
 Seeker-Sensitivity Rating: 9
 Themes: Fulfillment in Christ

The Dilemma
 Artist: Sandi Patti
 Album/Label: Le Voyage,
 Style: Pop
 Tempo: Up
 Seeker-Sensitivity Rating: 6
 Themes: John 7—I do the things I don't want to do
 Comments: Some strong lyrics that may be missed in a one-time hearing. Never done at Willow Creek

Do I Trust You
 Artist: Twila Paris
 Album/Label: The Warrior is a Child, Benson
 Style: MOR
 Tempo: Mid
 Seeker-Sensitivity Rating: 5
 Themes: Trust in God

The Door
 Artist: Al Denson
 Album/Label: Reasons, Benson
 Style: Power ballad
 Tempo: Slow
 Seeker-Sensitivity Rating: 1
 Themes: Evangelism

Down on My Knees
 Artist: Susan Ashton
 Album/Label: Wakened by the Wind, Sparrow
 Style: Folk rock
 Tempo: Mid/up
 Seeker-Sensitivity Rating: 6
 Themes: Need for Christ; Repentance
 Comments: This song may go over some

peoples' heads in a one-time hearing. May work better in a "Baby-buster"-targeted service. Never used at Willow Creek

Down the Road
 Artist: Triloje
 Album/Label: Triloje,
 Style: Acapella vocal group
 Tempo: Slow
 Seeker-Sensitivity Rating: 6
 Themes: Heaven; Understanding hardship
 Comments: May be out of print

Draw Me Near
 Artist: Al Denson
 Album/Label: Reasons, Benson
 Style: Ballad
 Tempo: Slow
 Seeker-Sensitivity Rating: 3
 Themes: Worship; Relationship with God
 Comments: Good call to worship song

Eleanor Rigby
 Artist: Beatles
 Album/Label: Revolver, Capitol
 Style: Acoustic ballad
 Tempo: Slow/mid
 Seeker-Sensitivity Rating: 10
 Themes: Loneliness
 Comments: We did this with an acoustic guitar accompaniment and a slower tempo—very effective

Ever Devoted
 Artist: Willow Creek Music
 Album/Label: Ever Devoted, Willow Creek
 Style: Ballad
 Tempo: Slow
 Seeker-Sensitivity Rating: 6
 Themes: Devotion to God; Emptiness without God

Every Step I Take
 Artist: Bob Carlisle
 Album/Label: Bob Carlisle, Sparrow
 Style: Bluesy pop
 Tempo: Mid
 Seeker-Sensitivity Rating: 9
 Themes: Faith; Taking a step
 Comments: States that God will provide power along the way, as we take steps of faith

The Extra Mile
 Artist: Al Denson
 Album/Label: The Extra Mile, Benson
 Style: Power Ballad
 Tempo: Slow
 Seeker-Sensitivity Rating: 9
 Themes: Friendship; Standing by one another

Face of Forgiveness
 Artist: Willow Creek Music
 Album/Label: None
 Style: Ballad
 Tempo: Slow
 Seeker-Sensitivity Rating: 10
 Themes: Grace, forgiveness

Facts Are Facts
 Artist: Steven Curtis Chapman
 Album/Label: Heaven in the Real World,

Sparrow
 Style: Rock/pop
 Tempo: Up
 Seeker-Sensitivity Rating: 4
 Themes: God fulfills His promises; Call to commitment

Faith, Hope and Love
 Artist: Point of Grace
 Album/Label: Point of Grace, Word
 Style: Pop vocal group
 Tempo: Up
 Seeker-Sensitivity Rating: 9
 Themes: Hardship; Faith
 Comments: The vocal intro is difficult—leave plenty of time to rehearse

Faithless Heart
 Artist: Amy Grant
 Album/Label: Lead Me On, Myrrh
 Style: Ballad
 Tempo: Slow/mid
 Seeker-Sensitivity Rating: 10
 Themes: Marriage; Staying faithful
 Comments: Might work well with an appropriate drama

Fill Me Lord
 Artist: De Garmo & Key
 Album/Label: Mission of Mercy, Forefront
 Style: Ballad
 Tempo: Slow
 Seeker-Sensitivity Rating: 2
 Themes: Obedience, yieldedness
 Comments: From an older album that may be hard to locate

For the Sake of the Call
 Artist: Steven Curtis Chapman
 Album/Label: For the Sake of the Call, Sparrow
 Style: Anthemic pop
 Tempo: Up
 Seeker-Sensitivity Rating: 3
 Themes: Commitment to the cause of Christ; Answering the call
 Comments: Would be great with a strong choir

For Who He Really Is
 Artist: Steven Curtis Chapman
 Album/Label: Real Life Conversations, Sparrow
 Style: Folk/pop ballad
 Tempo: Mid/slow
 Seeker-Sensitivity Rating: 1
 Themes: Spiritual authenticity; Lifestyle evangelism

Forever's as Far as I'll Go
 Artist: Alabama
 Album/Label: Pass It On Down; Greatest Hits, vol. III, RCA
 Style: Country ballad
 Tempo: Slow
 Seeker-Sensitivity Rating: 10
 Themes: Marriage; Love; Marital commitment

Forgive Me
 Artist: Tim Miner
 Album/Label: A True Story, Frontline

Style: Ballad
Tempo: Slow
Seeker-Sensitivity Rating: 4
Themes: Confession; Brokenness
Comments: Key might need to be lowered

Forgive Me, Forgive You
Artist: Steve Camp
Album/Label: Doing My Best, vol. 1, Sparrow
Style: Gospel ballad
Tempo: Slow/mid
Seeker-Sensitivity Rating: 7
Themes: Forgiveness, healing broken relationships
Comments: Needs the right situation to work—lyrics might be a bit confusing otherwise

Foundations
Artist: Geoff Moore & the Distance
Album/Label: Foundations, Sparrow
Style: Folk/pop ballad
Tempo: Slow/mid
Seeker-Sensitivity Rating: 8
Themes: Christ as the foundation of life; Rock vs. sand

Friend of a Wounded Heart
Artist: Wayne Watson
Album/Label: Watercolour Ponies, Dayspring
Style: Power ballad
Tempo: Slow
Seeker-Sensitivity Rating: 8
Themes: Hardship, pain; God's love for the broken-hearted

From Here On Out
Artist: Willow Creek Music
Album/Label: None
Style: MOR pop
Tempo: Mid
Seeker-Sensitivity Rating: 8
Themes: Trusting God

From This Moment On
Artist: Newsong
Album/Label: All Around the World, Benson
Style: Ballad
Tempo: Slow
Seeker-Sensitivity Rating: 8
Themes: Encouraging a new Christian
Comments: Great song for baptism

The Future
Artist: First Call
Album/Label: Undivided, Dayspring
Style: Pop vocal group
Tempo: Up
Seeker-Sensitivity Rating: 8
Themes: Trusting God for the future

Gather at the River
Artist: Point of Grace
Album/Label: The Whole Truth, Word
Style: Pop
Tempo: Up
Seeker-Sensitivity Rating: 8
Themes: Forgiveness

Gentle Hands
Artist: Truth

Album/Label: Second to None, Benson
Style: Traditional ballad
Tempo: Slow
Seeker-Sensitivity Rating: 8
Themes: God's tenderness; Protection

Go There With You
Artist: Steven Curtis Chapman
Album/Label: The Great Adventure, Sparrow
Style: MOR
Tempo: Mid
Seeker-Sensitivity Rating: 10
Themes: Marriage, commitment in marriage

God Is Great
Artist: Babbie Mason
Album/Label: With All My Heart, Word
Style: R & B/pop
Tempo: Up
Seeker-Sensitivity Rating: 5
Themes: Praise

God Is in Control
Artist: Twila Paris
Album/Label: Beyond a Dream, Star Song
Style: Pop/rock
Tempo: Up
Seeker-Sensitivity Rating: 1
Themes: God's sovereignty
Comments: Encouraging Praise anthem

The Great Adventure
Artist: Steven Curtis Chapman
Album/Label: The Great Adventure, Sparrow
Style: Pop/rock
Tempo: Up
Seeker-Sensitivity Rating: 5
Themes: The adventure of the Christian life.
Comments: Works well coming out of video—i.e., the "yee-hah" scene in *City Slickers*

The Great Divide
Artist: Point of Grace
Album/Label: The Whole Truth, Word
Style: Power ballad
Tempo: Slow
Seeker-Sensitivity Rating: 9
Themes: Salvation; The cross
Comments: Never used at Willow Creek

Hard Times
Artist: Wayne Watson
Album/Label: A Beautiful Place, Dayspring
Style: Ballad
Tempo: Slow
Seeker-Sensitivity Rating: 4
Themes: Hardship; Holding on to Christ in the midst of hardship
Comments: Never used at Willow Creek

Hats
Artist: Amy Grant
Album/Label: Heart in Motion, Myrrh
Style: Pop
Tempo: Up
Seeker-Sensitivity Rating: 10
Themes: Challenges of motherhood; Multiplicity of the roles of a mother
Comments: Fun song that could be augmented by drama during the song, illustrating the challenge of modern motherhood

He Covers Me
Artist: Steve Camp
Album/Label: One on One, Doing My Best, vol. 1, Sparrow
Style: Power ballad
Tempo: Slow/mid
Seeker-Sensitivity Rating: 4
Themes: Longing for Heaven, release from sin; God's sustenance

He Won't Let Me Down
Artist: Debbie McClendon
Album/Label: Count it All Joy, Sparrow
Style: R & B/pop
Tempo: Up
Seeker-Sensitivity Rating: 9
Themes: God's faithfulness
Comments: Good opener, but a bit dated. Works well to update with a hip-hop feel. We do it as a female group song, sharing the lead

He Won't Let You Go
Artist: The Kry
Album/Label: You, Freedom/Malaco
Style: Piano ballad
Tempo: Slow
Seeker-Sensitivity Rating: 10
Themes: God's faithful love; Assurance—God will never leave or forsake you
Comments: Poignant song, great "moment" potential

He'll Find a Way
Artist: Billy and Sarah Gaines
Album/Label: He'll Find a Way, Benson
Style: MOR ballad—duet
Tempo: Slow/mid
Seeker-Sensitivity Rating: 8
Themes: God's ability to handle our problems

He's All You Need
Artist: Steve Camp
Album/Label: One on One, Doing My Best, vol. 1, Sparrow
Style: Ballad
Tempo: Slow
Seeker-Sensitivity Rating: 8
Themes: Sufficiency of Christ; Grace
Comments: Second verse is a little closer to a believer's experience than that of a seeker, but can still relate

He's Been Faithful
Artist: Brooklyn Tabernacle Choir
Album/Label: Live . . . Again, Word
Style: Ballad with choir
Tempo: Slow
Seeker-Sensitivity Rating: 6
Themes: God's faithfulness
Comments: Great testimony song

Healing River
Artist: Willow Creek Music
Album/Label: A Place to Call Home, Word/Maranatha!
Style: Ballad
Tempo: Slow/mid
Seeker-Sensitivity Rating: 9
Themes: Healing; Heaven

Heart's Cry
Artist: Steven Curtis Chapman

Album/Label: The Great Adventure, Sparrow
Style: Acoustic ballad
Tempo: Mid/slow
Seeker-Sensitivity Rating: 7
Themes: Desire to be like Christ
Comments: Works in seeker services as a testimonial, and opportunity to eavesdrop on a committed Christian

Heaven in the Real World
Artist: Steven Curtis Chapman
Album/Label: Heaven in the Real World, Sparrow
Style: Pop/rock
Tempo: Up
Seeker-Sensitivity Rating: 7
Themes: Need for Christ; Need for hope

Heirlooms
Artist: Amy Grant
Album/Label: Christmas album, Myrhh
Style: Ballad
Tempo: Slow
Seeker-Sensitivity Rating: 8
Themes: Christmas; Family; Relationship with Christ

Helping Hand
Artist: Amy Grant
Album/Label: House of Love, Myrhh
Style: Pop
Tempo: Mid/up
Seeker-Sensitivity Rating: 10
Themes: Helping others; Servanthood
Comments: We've used this to a mixed response

Here in My Heart
Artist: Susan Ashton
Album/Label: Angels of Mercy, Sparrow
Style: Folk rock
Tempo: Up
Seeker-Sensitivity Rating: 8
Themes: God's faithful love
Comments: Great groove, though the message may be hard to catch in a one-time hearing. Solid opener for a "Baby Buster"-oriented service

Here in the Quiet
Artist: Willow Creek Music
Album/Label: None
Style: Ballad
Tempo: Slow
Seeker-Sensitivity Rating: 4
Themes: Worship; Desire for intimacy with God

Heroes
Artist: Paul Overstreet
Album/Label: Heroes, Word
Style: Country
Tempo: Mid/slow
Seeker-Sensitivity Rating: 8
Themes: Heroes; Courage

Hiding Place
Artist: Steven Curtis Chapman
Album/Label: First Hand, Sparrow
Style: Pop ballad
Tempo: Mid/slow

Seeker-Sensitivity Rating: 9
Themes: God as a refuge

Higher Ways
Artist: Steven Curtis Chapman
Album/Label: For the Sake of the Call, Sparrow
Style: Acoustic guitar ballad
Tempo: Slow/mid
Seeker-Sensitivity Rating: 8
Themes: Trusting God in hardship, confusing circumstances
Comments: Some of the images may be hard to track in a one-time hearing

His Eyes
Artist: Steven Curtis Chapman
Album/Label: Real Life Conversations, Sparrow
Style: Acoustic guitar ballad
Tempo: Mid/slow
Seeker-Sensitivity Rating: 9
Themes: God's omnipresence; His watchful care over us; Diversity in the character of Christ

His Grace Is Greater
Artist: Larnelle Harris
Album/Label: I've Just Seen Jesus, Impact/Benson
Style: Inspirational ballad
Tempo: Slow
Seeker-Sensitivity Rating: 8
Themes: God's grace

His Love Is Strong
Artist: Clay Crosse
Album/Label: Time to Believe, Reunion
Style: Pop
Tempo: Up
Seeker-Sensitivity Rating: 10
Themes: God's love
Comments: Great opener. Can also be sung by a female

His Strength Is Perfect
Artist: Steven Curtis Chapman
Album/Label: Real Life Conversations, Sparrow
Style: Ballad
Tempo: Slow
Seeker-Sensitivity Rating: 9
Themes: God's strength in our weakness
Comments: Works well as a female solo also, with key change

Holding Out Hope to You
Artist: Michael English
Album/Label: Hope, Warner Alliance
Style: Power ballad
Tempo: Slow
Seeker-Sensitivity Rating: 9
Themes: Friendship; Enduring hardship together
Comments: Never used at Willow Creek

Home Free
Artist: Wayne Watson
Album/Label: Home Free, Dayspring
Style: Ballad
Tempo: Slow/mid
Seeker-Sensitivity Rating: 6

Themes: Death; Heaven;
Comments: Lyrics are pretty specific, so it might be hard to find the right place for this song. Never done at Willow Creek

Honesty
Artist: Margaret Becker
Album/Label: Immigrant's Daughter, Sparrow
Style: Power ballad
Tempo: Slow
Seeker-Sensitivity Rating: 9
Themes: Honesty with God; Anger

How Could I Ask for More
Artist: Cindy Morgan
Album/Label: Real Life, Word
Style: Piano ballad
Tempo: Slow
Seeker-Sensitivity Rating: 9
Themes: Thanksgiving for the simple pleasures of life
Comments: We've used the original recording with a media, showing slides of families

Hunger and Thirst
Artist: Susan Ashton
Album/Label: Angels of Mercy, Sparrow
Style: Folk pop
Tempo: Mid/up
Seeker-Sensitivity Rating: 6
Themes: Hunger for God
Comments: Never done at Willow Creek

I Am Determined
Artist: Tim Shepherd
Album/Label: Tim Shepherd, Diamante
Style: Inspirational ballad
Tempo: Slow
Seeker-Sensitivity Rating: 2
Themes: Commitment to Christ
Comments: Language is quite "churchy," but a strong statement for believers. When we do it, we change the word "invincible" to "obedient"

I Believe in You
Artist: Steve Camp
Album/Label: Justice, Sparrow
Style: Pop
Tempo: Up
Seeker-Sensitivity Rating: 10
Themes: Friendship; encouragement
Comments: May need to be lowered slightly

I Choose to Follow
Artist: Al Denson
Album/Label: The Extra Mile, Benson
Style: Ballad
Tempo: Slow
Seeker-Sensitivity Rating: 5
Themes: Commitment; Discipleship

I Commit My Love to You
Artist: Twila Paris
Album/Label:
Style: Ballad
Tempo: Slow
Seeker-Sensitivity Rating: 5
Themes: Relational conflict
Comments: Speaks more to conflict within

the body of Christ, but can also relate to seeker

I Could Live Without You
Artist: Wayne Watson
Album/Label: The Fine Line, Dayspring
Style: Ballad
Tempo: Slow
Seeker-Sensitivity Rating: 6
Themes: Need for Christ, Fullness of life in Christ
Comments: The phrase "not a chance of escaping hell" may be a bit harsh for unconditioned seekers, but a strong song

I Don't Deserve Your Love
Artist: Trace Balin
Album/Label: Champions, Dayspring
Style: Ballad
Tempo: Slow
Seeker-Sensitivity Rating: 9
Themes: God's gracious, undeserved love
Comments: Never done at Willow. Piano part may need to be simplified

I Found Myself in You
Artist: Clay Crosse
Album/Label: Time to Believe, Reunion
Style: Gospel ballad
Tempo: Mid/slow
Seeker-Sensitivity Rating: 10
Themes: Salvation; Search for meaning
Comments: The title line may need setup for clarity, and the key may need to be lowered. Strong song

I Go to the Rock
Artist: Dottie Rambo
Album/Label: Songs for Sunday, Benson
Style: Swing/big band
Tempo: Mid
Seeker-Sensitivity Rating: 7
Themes: Life foundation; Stability of Christ
Comments: This song has worked well for us with a big band treatment

I Just Never Say It Enough
Artist: Wayne Watson
Album/Label: Home Free,
Style: Ballad, in 3
Tempo: Slow
Seeker-Sensitivity Rating: 8
Themes: Marriage; Speaking love to spouse
Comments: A touching song from husband to wife. Never done at Willow Creek

I Love You Lord
Artist: The Archers
Album/Label: Colors of Your Love, Star Song
Style: MOR
Tempo: Mid
Seeker-Sensitivity Rating: 2
Themes: Love for God; Worship
Comments: Works best as a trio—1 female, 2 male

I Miss the Way
Artist: Michael W. Smith
Album/Label: i 2 (EYE), Reunion
Style: Ballad
Tempo: Slow

Seeker-Sensitivity Rating: 1
Themes: Backsliding
Comments: Song from one friend to another, pleading with him/her to come back to Christ. Could be a little finger-pointing if not handled tenderly. Never used at Willow Creek

I Need to Stop
Artist: Willow Creek Music
Album/Label: None
Style: Pop
Tempo: Up
Seeker-Sensitivity Rating: 3
Themes: Praise and Worship; Pace of life; "Assembling of the Saints"

I Stand, I Fall
Artist: Willow Creek Music
Album/Label: None
Style: Piano ballad
Tempo: Slow
Seeker-Sensitivity Rating: 7
Themes: Sanctification; Failure; Grace
Comments: Very transparent song, allows people to see the reality of the Christian growth process

I Want to Be Just Like You
Artist: Phillips, Craig and Dean
Album/Label: Lifeline, Star Song
Style: MOR
Tempo: Mid/slow
Seeker-Sensitivity Rating: 9
Themes: Parenthood
Comments: Great song on fatherhood—we have used slides of families in conjunction with a live performance

I Want to Change
Artist: Russ Taff
Album/Label: Walls of Glass, Myrrh
Style: MOR
Tempo: Mid
Seeker-Sensitivity Rating: 7
Themes: Becoming like Jesus; Desire to change

I Will Be Free
Artist: Cindy Morgan
Album/Label: Reason to Live, Word
Style: Ballad
Tempo: Slow
Seeker-Sensitivity Rating: 7
Themes: Heaven; Healing; Freedom

I Will Be Here
Artist: Steven Curtis Chapman
Album/Label: More to This Life, Sparrow
Style: Ballad
Tempo: Slow
Seeker-Sensitivity Rating: 10
Themes: Marriage; Commitment to Spouse
Comments: Beautiful statement of marital commitment; Has been covered by country artist Billy Dean

I'll Be Believing
Artist: Point of Grace
Album/Label: Point of Grace, Word

Style: Pop vocal group
Tempo: Up
Seeker-Sensitivity Rating: 9
Themes: Faith

I'll Find You There
Artist: The Kry
Album/Label: I'll Find You There, Freedom/Malaco
Style: Folk rock ballad
Tempo: Slow
Seeker-Sensitivity Rating: 9
Themes: God's faithfulness; God meets our needs
Comments: Has an alternative, anthemic feel. Especially good for "buster"-oriented services

I'm Amazed
Artist: Willow Creek Music
Album/Label: Ever Devoted, Willow Creek
Style: Ballad
Tempo: Slow
Seeker-Sensitivity Rating: 7
Themes: God's goodness; Grace
Comments: Can be used in a number of contexts—a real "moment" song

I'm Depending On You
Artist: Harv & Edythe
Album/Label: Streets of Gold, Randolph Productions/Campus Crusade
Style: MOR
Tempo: Mid
Seeker-Sensitivity Rating: 7
Themes: Dependence on Christ in hard times

I'm in a Hurry (and Don't Know Why)
Artist: Alabama
Album/Label: American Pride, RCA
Style: Country pop
Tempo: Up
Seeker-Sensitivity Rating: 10
Themes: Pace of life
Comments: Works well out of "Plate Spinners" drama, or as a fun opener

I've Been Released
Artist: Willow Creek Music
Album/Label: A Place to Call Home, Word/Maranatha!
Style: Pop/rock—Chicago sound
Tempo: Up
Seeker-Sensitivity Rating: 9
Themes: Freedom from sin

If I Could Look Through Your Eyes
Artist: Willow Creek Music
Album/Label: Ever Devoted, Willow Creek
Style: Piano ballad
Tempo: Slow
Seeker-Sensitivity Rating: 10
Themes: Self-esteem; Our value to God; God's view of us
Comments: Great song on our value to God

If I Had Only Known
Artist: Reba McEntire
Album/Label: 8 Seconds Soundtrack, MCA
Style: Ballad
Tempo: Slow
Seeker-Sensitivity Rating: 10
Themes: Regret for unspoken love

Comments: We have used the recorded version in conjunction with the movie clip from *8 Seconds*—very motivating

If That's What It Takes
  Artist: Willow Creek Music
  Album/Label: Ever Devoted, Willow Creek
  Style: Pop/MOR
  Tempo: Mid/slow
  Seeker-Sensitivity Rating: 5
  Themes: Willingness to be broken; Desire to be like Christ

If You Could See Me Now
  Artist: Truth
  Album/Label: Something to Hold On To, Integrity
  Style: Ballad
  Tempo: Slow
  Seeker-Sensitivity Rating: 5
  Themes: Heaven; Death of a loved one
  Comments: Lyrics are very specific-from the voice of a Christian who was in great physical pain, and is now in Heaven—must be used carefully

If You Could See What I See
  Artist: Geoff Moore & the Distance
  Album/Label: Evolution, Forefront
  Style: Folk ballad
  Tempo: Slow
  Seeker-Sensitivity Rating: 10
  Themes: Marriage; Self-esteem
  Comments: Song from a husband to his wife, stating the beauty he sees in her, in spite of what she sees in herself. Never used at Willow Creek

In Christ Alone
  Artist: Michael English
  Album/Label: Michael English, Warner Alliance
  Style: Power ballad
  Tempo: Slow
  Seeker-Sensitivity Rating: 8
  Themes: Sufficiency of Christ; Giving God the glory

In Heaven's Eyes
  Artist: Sandi Patti
  Album/Label: Make His Praise Glorious, Word
  Style: Inspirational ballad
  Tempo: Slow
  Seeker-Sensitivity Rating: 9
  Themes: You matter to God; Self-esteem
  Comments: Beautiful statement of our value to God

In His Presence
  Artist: Sandi Patti
  Album/Label: Make His Praise Glorious, Word
  Style: Traditional ballad
  Tempo: Slow
  Seeker-Sensitivity Rating: 6
  Themes: God's presence; Prayer

In His Sanctuary
  Artist: Morris Chapman & Friends
  Album/Label: Voice of Praise, Maranatha!
  Style: Ballad

Tempo: Slow
Seeker-Sensitivity Rating: 6
Themes: Prayer; Relationship with God
Comments: This song can be used to give seekers a glimpse inside the prayer life of a Christian

In My Father's Hands
  Artist: Susan Ashton
  Album/Label: Wakened by the Wind, Sparrow
  Style: Folk/pop
  Tempo: Mid
  Seeker-Sensitivity Rating: 9
  Themes: God is able; Trusting God, letting Him have control

Isn't it Good
  Artist: Willow Creek Music
  Album/Label: None
  Style: Ballad
  Tempo: Mid/slow
  Seeker-Sensitivity Rating: 4
  Themes: The Church; Community
  Comments: We've used this in seeker services effectively, even though it has a church/community focus

Jesus Loves Me
  Artist: Whitney Houston
  Album/Label: Bodyguard Soundtrack, Arista
  Style: R & B/pop
  Tempo: Slow/mid
  Seeker-Sensitivity Rating: 8
  Themes: God's love

Jesus Will Still Be There
  Artist: Point of Grace
  Album/Label: Point of Grace, Word
  Style: Ballad
  Tempo: Slow
  Seeker-Sensitivity Rating: 9
  Themes: God's love for the broken-hearted

Just Come In
  Artist: Margaret Becker
  Album/Label: Immigrant's Daughter, Sparrow
  Style: Pop ballad
  Tempo: Slow
  Seeker-Sensitivity Rating: 5
  Themes: God's forgiveness; Leaving behind past failure
  Comments: Ethereal treatment on original recording may not transfer well to some live settings—may need to be re-arranged

Keep the Flame Burning
  Artist: Debby Boone
  Album/Label: Surrender, Lamb & Lion
  Style: MOR
  Tempo: Mid
  Seeker-Sensitivity Rating: 5
  Themes: Following Christ with passion; Endurance

King of the Jungle
  Artist: Steven Curtis Chapman
  Album/Label: Heaven in the Real World, Sparrow
  Style: Pop shuffle with African touches
  Tempo: Mid/up
  Seeker-Sensitivity Rating: 9

Themes: Pace of life; God's sovereignty
Comments: Fun song—may be too light musically for some churches. Never used at Willow Creek

The Last Song
  Artist: Elton John
  Album/Label: The One, MCA
  Style: Ballad
  Tempo: Slow
  Seeker-Sensitivity Rating: 10
  Themes: AIDS; Father/son relationship

Lay It On Down
  Artist: Bruce Carroll
  Album/Label: The Great Exchange, Word
  Style: Country
  Tempo: Mid/up
  Seeker-Sensitivity Rating: 8
  Themes: Materialism; Worldliness

Let Me Go
  Artist: Susan Ashton
  Album/Label: Angels of Mercy, Sparrow
  Style: Folk ballad
  Tempo: Slow
  Seeker-Sensitivity Rating: 10
  Themes: Letting go of adult children; Parenting
  Comments: The drama "Let Me Go" was written to precede this song

Let the Lord Love You
  Artist: Willow Creek Music
  Album/Label: A Place to Call Home, Word/Maranatha!
  Style: Acoustic guitar ballad
  Tempo: Slow
  Seeker-Sensitivity Rating: 9
  Themes: Self-esteem; God's love
  Comments: Works well out of self-esteem oriented dramas

Let's Build a Bridge
  Artist: Michael English
  Album/Label: Michael English, Warner Alliance
  Style: Pop
  Tempo: Up
  Seeker-Sensitivity Rating: 8
  Themes: Relationships; Unity
  Comments: Lyrics are a bit confusing, but musically very strong

Let's Stand Together
  Artist: The Kry
  Album/Label: I'll Find You There, Freedom/Malaco
  Style: Rock
  Tempo: Mid/up
  Seeker-Sensitivity Rating: 1
  Themes: Commitment; Unity
  Comments: Strong anthemic call to commitment. Might be a little "edgy" for some churches

Lion and the Lamb
  Artist: Maranatha! Singers
  Album/Label: Praise 14, Maranatha!
  Style: Ballad—trio
  Tempo: Slow

Seeker-Sensitivity Rating: 4
Themes: Character, person of Christ

Listen to Our Hearts
  Artist: Geoff Moore & the Distance (with Steven Curtis Chapman)
  Album/Label: A Friend Like U, Forefront
  Style: Acoustic ballad—duet
  Tempo: Slow/mid
  Seeker-Sensitivity Rating: 2
  Themes: Praise & worship; Love for God

The Living Years
  Artist: Mike & the Mechanics
  Album/Label: The Living Years, Atlantic
  Style: Pop
  Tempo: Mid/up
  Seeker-Sensitivity Rating: 10
  Themes: Regret over unspoken words to a father.
  Comments: Works best with a large vocal group, especially a mixture of children and adults

Look Me in the Eye
  Artist: Margaret Becker
  Album/Label: Simple House, Sparrow
  Style: Pop ballad
  Tempo: Slow/mid
  Seeker-Sensitivity Rating: 3
  Themes: Desire to be like Christ

Lord, I Want to Be Like Jesus
  Artist: Fernando Ortega
  Album/Label: In a Welcome Field, Urgent
  Style: Ballad
  Tempo: Slow
  Seeker-Sensitivity Rating: 3
  Themes: Worship; Sanctification

Lord of All
  Artist: First Call
  Album/Label: Something Takes Over, Dayspring
  Style: Ballad—trio
  Tempo: Slow
  Seeker-Sensitivity Rating: 6
  Themes: Praise & worship; God's sovereignty, majesty

Love and Learn
  Artist: Steven Curtis Chapman
  Album/Label: Heaven in the Real World, Sparrow
  Style: Pop/folk
  Tempo: Mid/slow
  Seeker-Sensitivity Rating: 9
  Themes: Working through marital difficulty
  Comments: Might work will coming right out of a drama

Love Can Build a Bridge
  Artist: The Judds
  Album/Label: Love Can Build a Bridge, Curb/RCA
  Style: Ballad
  Tempo: Slow
  Seeker-Sensitivity Rating: 10
  Themes: Relationships, love
  Comments: Works especially well with a choir, though not necessary

Love Can Open the Door
  Artist: Sandi Patti
  Album/Label: Le Voyage, Word
  Style: Pop
  Tempo: Up
  Seeker-Sensitivity Rating: 10
  Themes: Power of love to break down relational walls
  Comments: Good opener for relationships, reaching out to others

Love Conquers All
  Artist: Pam Thum
  Album/Label: Faithful, Benson
  Style: Pop
  Tempo: Up
  Seeker-Sensitivity Rating: 10
  Themes: Power of love to break down walls; God's love
  Comments: Great opener

Love Has Come
  Artist: Amy Grant
  Album/Label: Christmas Album, Myrhh
  Style: MOR
  Tempo: Mid
  Seeker-Sensitivity Rating: 8
  Themes: Christmas; God's gift of love

Love Is Always There
  Artist: Carolyn Arends
  Album/Label: I Can Hear You, Reunion
  Style: Folk/pop
  Tempo: Up
  Seeker-Sensitivity Rating: 9
  Themes: Nobody is beyond salvation
  Comments: Try it with an "unplugged" feel and look. Never used at Willow Creek

The Love of God
  Artist: Phillip Bailey
  Album/Label: Triumph, Myrrh LA
  Style: Ballad
  Tempo: Slow
  Seeker-Sensitivity Rating: 8
  Themes: God's love

The Love of God
  Artist: Willow Creek Music
  Album/Label: None
  Style: Acapella vocal group
  Tempo: Slow
  Seeker-Sensitivity Rating: 6
  Themes: God's love
  Comments: Acapella treatment of this hymn has been one of our strongest moments at a seeker service

Love That Will Not Let Me Go
  Artist: Steve Camp
  Album/Label: Justice, Doing My Best, vol. 1, Sparrow
  Style: Ballad
  Tempo: Slow
  Seeker-Sensitivity Rating: 10
  Themes: God's steadfast love
  Comments: A great song. Title is a great phrase to work into the message

Love You With My Life
  Artist: Steven Curtis Chapman
  Album/Label: More to This Life, Sparrow

Style: Pop
Tempo: Up
Seeker-Sensitivity Rating: 5
Themes: "If you love Me, you will obey My commandments".
Comments: Intro is hard to recreate effectively live

Man of God
  Artist: Willow Creek Music
  Album/Label: A Place to Call Home, Word/Maranatha!
  Style: Pop/rock
  Tempo: Mid/up
  Seeker-Sensitivity Rating: 7
  Themes: A man's commitment to integrity

Meet in the Middle
  Artist: Diamond Rio
  Album/Label: Diamond Rio, Arista
  Style: Country
  Tempo: Mid/up
  Seeker-Sensitivity Rating: 10
  Themes: Marriage; Relational conflict

Mercy for the Memories
  Artist: Geoff Moore & the Distance
  Album/Label: Foundations, Sparrow
  Style: Folk/pop ballad
  Tempo: Slow
  Seeker-Sensitivity Rating: 9
  Themes: Forgiveness; Healing of the past

Midnight Oil
  Artist: Phillips, Craig and Dean
  Album/Label: Phillips, Craig and Dean, Star Song
  Style: Acoustic ballad
  Tempo: Slow
  Seeker-Sensitivity Rating: 7
  Themes: Mothers; Prayer

Mighty Lord
  Artist: Kathy Troccoli
  Album/Label: Portfolio, Reunion
  Style: Funky pop
  Tempo: Up
  Seeker-Sensitivity Rating: 8
  Themes: God's power; God's character

Mind, Body, Heart and Soul
  Artist: Bob Carlisle
  Album/Label: Bob Carlisle, Sparrow
  Style: Pop/rock
  Tempo: Up
  Seeker-Sensitivity Rating: 9
  Themes: Testimony—changed life; Commitment to Christ

Miracle of Mercy
  Artist: Steven Curtis Chapman
  Album/Label: Heaven in the Real World, Sparrow
  Style: Acoustic ballad
  Tempo: Slow
  Seeker-Sensitivity Rating: 4
  Themes: God's grace; Our weakness—flesh vs. spirit

Money Is a Powerful Thing
  Artist: Willow Creek Music
  Album/Label: None

Style: Motown/pop
Tempo: Up
Seeker-Sensitivity Rating: 10
Themes: Power of money

More Than Words
    Artist: Steven Curtis Chapman
    Album/Label: More to This Life, Sparrow
    Style: Acoustic guitar ballad
    Tempo: Mid/slow
    Seeker-Sensitivity Rating: 4
    Themes: Progression from prayer to God's Word to the fact that who God is goes beyond our words to the fact that Christ's sacrifice backed up His words with action
    Comments: Wonderfully complex song—may be hard to nail down to a specific topic

More to This Life
    Artist: Steven Curtis Chapman
    Album/Label: More to This Life, Sparrow
    Style: MOR Pop
    Tempo: Mid/up
    Seeker-Sensitivity Rating: 9
    Themes: Emptiness of life without Christ; Christ gives life purpose, meaning
    Comments: Strong song, but hasn't completely clicked at Willow yet—we're not sure why

Most of the Time
    Artist: Glad
    Album/Label: No Less Than All, Benson/Greentree
    Style: Piano ballad
    Tempo: Slow
    Seeker-Sensitivity Rating: 4
    Themes: How unlike Christ I am; Sanctification
    Comments: A bit dated, and the vocal range is difficult, but some strong, transparent lyrics

The Music of Christmas
    Artist: Steven Curtis Chapman
    Album/Label: The Music of Christmas, Sparrow
    Style: Folk pop
    Tempo: Mid
    Seeker-Sensitivity Rating: 10
    Themes: Christmas

My Life Is in Your Hands
    Artist: Kathy Troccoli
    Album/Label: Kathy Troccoli, Reunion
    Style: Ballad
    Tempo: Slow
    Seeker-Sensitivity Rating: 9
    Themes: Trust in God

My Redeemer Is Faithful and True
    Artist: Steven Curtis Chapman
    Album/Label: First Hand, Sparrow
    Style: Ballad
    Tempo: Slow
    Seeker-Sensitivity Rating: 9
    Themes: God's faithfulness
    Comments: Strong song; Term "Redeemer" may need to be explained to a seeker audience

My Soul Desire
    Artist: Deniece Williams
    Album/Label: So Good to Know, Sparrow

Style: R & B ballad
Tempo: Slow
Seeker-Sensitivity Rating: 5
Themes: Commitment; Serving God

My Turn Now
    Artist: Steven Curtis Chapman
    Album/Label: Real Life Conversations, Sparrow
    Style: Country bop
    Tempo: Up
    Seeker-Sensitivity Rating: 6
    Themes: Responding to God's love in obedience and service.
    Comments: Works well with vocal group. May be too light musically for some churches

The Narrow Way
    Artist: Wayne Watson
    Album/Label: Giants in the Land, Dayspring
    Style: Pop
    Tempo: Mid
    Seeker-Sensitivity Rating: 6
    Themes: Discipleship; Morality

Never Be An Angel
    Artist: Margaret Becker
    Album/Label: Simple House, Sparrow
    Style: Pop
    Tempo: Mid
    Seeker-Sensitivity Rating: 4
    Themes: Desire to change, to be like Christ
    Comments: Probably works best with a 35-under audience. Never used at Willow Creek

Never Be Another
    Artist: Paul Smith
    Album/Label: Live and Learn, Dayspring
    Style: Power ballad
    Tempo: Slow
    Seeker-Sensitivity Rating: 8
    Themes: God's character, uniqueness

No Better Place
    Artist: Steven Curtis Chapman
    Album/Label: For the Sake of the Call, Sparrow
    Style: Pop/folk rock
    Tempo: Up
    Seeker-Sensitivity Rating: 7
    Themes: Fulfillment, joy of the Christian life
    Comments: Great for youth ministries, also works for adults

No More Night
    Artist: Morris Chapman
    Album/Label: Lately, Word
    Style: Inspirational
    Tempo: Slow
    Seeker-Sensitivity Rating: 6
    Themes: Heaven

No One Knows My Heart
    Artist: Susan Ashton
    Album/Label: Wakened by the Wind, Sparrow
    Style: Folk/pop ballad
    Tempo: Slow/mid
    Seeker-Sensitivity Rating: 9
    Themes: God knows me, loves me; Yieldedness

Not Too Far From Here
    Artist: Kim Boyce

Album/Label: By Faith, Warner Alliance
Style: Ballad
Tempo: Slow
Seeker-Sensitivity Rating: 7
Themes: Compassion for the hurting and poor

On My Knees
    Artist: Willow Creek Music
    Album/Label: A Place to Call Home, Word/Maranatha!
    Style: Acoustic guitar ballad
    Tempo: Slow
    Seeker-Sensitivity Rating: 5
    Themes: Prayer, intimacy with God
    Comments: Can work in a seeker context as a demonstration of the inner life of a believer

One of Us
    Artist: Geoff Moore & the Distance
    Album/Label: A Place to Stand, Sparrow
    Style: Ballad
    Tempo: Slow
    Seeker-Sensitivity Rating: 8
    Themes: Christ's humanity, understanding of us

One Step at a Time
    Artist: First Call
    Album/Label: Undivided, Dayspring
    Style: Pop vocal group
    Tempo: Up
    Seeker-Sensitivity Rating: 8
    Themes: Faith; God will give us power along the way as we step out
    Comments: May be a bit dated

Only by Grace
    Artist: Willow Creek Music
    Album/Label: A Place to Call Home, Word/Maranatha
    Style: Pop/rock
    Tempo: Mid
    Seeker-Sensitivity Rating: 10
    Themes: Grace vs. works
    Comments: Works well for "target weekends," to explain that you can't earn your way to heaven, but that God offers the grace gift of salvation

Only Here for a Little While
    Artist: Billy Dean
    Album/Label: Young Man, Capitol/SBK
    Style: Country
    Tempo: Mid/up
    Seeker-Sensitivity Rating: 10
    Themes: Make the most of your time on earth

The Only Hope
    Artist: Babbie Mason
    Album/Label: A World of Difference, Word
    Style: Ballad
    Tempo: Slow
    Seeker-Sensitivity Rating: 5
    Themes: Need for Christ in a decaying world

Only You
    Artist: Willow Creek
    Album/Label: None
    Style: Ballad
    Tempo: Slow

Seeker-Sensitivity Rating: 9
Themes: Fulfillment in Christ

Only Your Love
Artist: Margaret Becker
Album/Label: Grace, Sparrow
Style: Pop/MOR
Tempo: Mid
Seeker-Sensitivity Rating: 6
Themes: Gods love; Joy of Christian life
Comments: Never used at Willow Creek

Original Love
Artist: Imperials
Album/Label: Love's Still Changing Hearts, Star Song
Style: Pop
Tempo: Up
Seeker-Sensitivity Rating: 9
Themes: Testimony; God's love
Comments: Bridge could come off preachy—needs to be delivered compassionately

Our God Is With Us
Artist: Steven Curtis Chapman
Album/Label: The Music of Christmas, Sparrow
Style: Folk pop
Tempo: Mid
Seeker-Sensitivity Rating: 9
Themes: Christmas; The birth of Christ bringing hope

Peace Be Still
Artist: Al Denson
Album/Label: Al Denson, Benson
Style: Ballad
Tempo: Slow
Seeker-Sensitivity Rating: 10
Themes: God's peace, comfort for the hurting
Comments: Great song to come out of a drama that ends with a hurting character

People Need the Lord
Artist: Steve Green
Album/Label: Steve Green, Sparrow
Style: Inspirational ballad
Tempo: Slow
Seeker-Sensitivity Rating: 1
Themes: Evangelism

Place in This World
Artist: Michael W. Smith
Album/Label: Go West Young Man, Reunion
Style: Power ballad
Tempo: Slow
Seeker-Sensitivity Rating: 9
Themes: Identity; Direction for life
Comments: Geared toward a younger audience, but has potential as a cry for direction

Power of God
Artist: Imperials
Album/Label: This Year's Model, Myrrh
Style: Pop/rock
Tempo: Up
Seeker-Sensitivity Rating: 5
Themes: God's power in me; I can do all things through Christ

Prayer Medley
Artist: Willow Creek Music
Album/Label: None

Style: Ballad medley-trio
Tempo: Slow
Seeker-Sensitivity Rating: 7
Themes: Prayer; Relationship with God
Comments: Includes "On My Knees," "In His Sanctuary," and "Here in the Quiet"

The Prodigal (I'll Be Waiting)
Artist: Amy Grant
Album/Label: Unguarded, Myrrh
Style: Ballad
Tempo: Slow
Seeker-Sensitivity Rating: 7
Themes: Prodigal son theme; Unconditional love
Comments: Needs to be set up with a drama or Scripture reading/comments slot

Reaching
Artist: Carolyn Arends
Album/Label: I Can Hear You, Reunion
Style: Ballad
Tempo: Slow
Seeker-Sensitivity Rating: 6
Themes: Longing for heaven
Comments: Very poignant song. Be careful not to use it out of context

Remember Your Chains
Artist: Steven Curtis Chapman
Album/Label: Heaven in the Real World, Sparrow
Style: Acoustic MOR
Tempo: Mid
Seeker-Sensitivity Rating: 2
Themes: Remembering life before Christ; Freedom from sin

Rock Steady
Artist: Wayne Watson
Album/Label: Field of Souls, Warner Alliance
Style: Pop/rock
Tempo: Up
Seeker-Sensitivity Rating: 7
Themes: God's faithfulness in spite of my shortcomings

Run Away
Artist: Steven Curtis Chapman
Album/Label: First Hand, Sparrow
Style: Pop
Tempo: Up
Seeker-Sensitivity Rating: 7
Themes: Fleeing temptation

Run to the Battle
Artist: Steve Camp
Album/Label: Doing My Best, vol. 1, Sparrow
Style: Pop/rock
Tempo: Up/mid
Seeker-Sensitivity Rating: 1
Themes: Exhortation-call to spiritual battle
Comments: Good motivational song

Safe
Artist: Steve Archer
Album/Label: Action, Home Sweet Home
Style: Ballad—duet
Tempo: Slow/mid
Seeker-Sensitivity Rating: 8

Themes: God as a refuge
Comments: We haven't used this in some time

Say It to Him
Artist: Teri Gibbs
Album/Label: Turn Around, Canaan/Word
Style: Funky pop
Tempo: Up
Seeker-Sensitivity Rating: 9
Themes: Prayer; Friendship with God

Say the Name
Artist: Margaret Becker
Album/Label: Soul, Sparrow
Style: Ballad
Tempo: Slow/mid
Seeker-Sensitivity Rating: 4
Themes: Relationship with Christ; Name of Jesus
Comments: Never used at Willow Creek

Seize the Day
Artist: Carolyn Arends
Album/Label: I Can Hear You, Reunion
Style: Folk pop, in 3
Tempo: Mid
Seeker-Sensitivity Rating: 8
Themes: Risk taking; Following your dreams
Comments: Strong song—might work with a scene from *Dead Poets' Society*. Never used at Willow Creek

Separate Lives
Artist: Phil Collins & Marilyn White
Album/Label: White Nights Soundtrack, Atco
Style: Power ballad—duet
Tempo: Slow
Seeker-Sensitivity Rating: 10
Themes: Marital breakdown; Divorce
Comments: Can be a powerful song following a drama like "Grand Canyon"

Shepherd of My Heart
Artist: Sandi Patti
Album/Label: Morning Like This, Word
Style: Ballad
Tempo: Slow
Seeker-Sensitivity Rating: 4
Themes: Trust in God

Show Me the Way
Artist: Styx
Album/Label: Edge of the Century; Greatest Hits, A & M
Style: Power ballad
Tempo: Slow/mid
Seeker-Sensitivity Rating: 10
Themes: Seeker's cry for an answer

Show Yourselves to Be
Artist: Steven Curtis Chapman
Album/Label: For the Sake of the Call, Sparrow
Style: Acoustic ballad
Tempo: Slow/mid
Seeker-Sensitivity Rating: 4
Themes: John 15; Bearing fruit; Being connected to Christ

Solid as the Rock
Artist: Michael English
Album/Label: Michael English, Warner

Alliance
Style: Pop
Tempo: Up
Seeker-Sensitivity Rating: 8
Themes: Foundation of Christ

Somebody Love Me
Artist: Michael W. Smith
Album/Label: Change Your World, Reunion
Style: Power ballad
Tempo: Slow
Seeker-Sensitivity Rating: 9
Themes: Self esteem; Need for love; Singleness
Comments: Geared toward more of a high school-aged audience, but might work for adults in the right context

Somebody Make Me Laugh
Artist: Patti Austin
Album/Label: That Secret Place, MCA/GRP
Style: Ballad
Tempo: Slow
Seeker-Sensitivity Rating: 10
Themes: Fulfillment; Longing for more
Comments: First part of first verse seems a little out of place in church, but a powerful song. We've used the original recording in conjunction with drama

Something to Hold On To
Artist: Truth
Album/Label: Something To Hold On To, Integrity
Style: R & B/pop
Tempo: Mid
Seeker-Sensitivity Rating: 10
Themes: Life Foundation
Comments: Musically difficult

Somewhere in the World
Artist: Wayne Watson
Album/Label: Giants in the Land, Dayspring
Style: Acoustic ballad
Tempo: Slow
Seeker-Sensitivity Rating: 3
Themes: Parenthood—prayer for son's future wife

Still Listening
Artist: Steven Curtis Chapman
Album/Label: Heaven in the Real World, Sparrow
Style: Acoustic ballad
Tempo: Slow/mid
Seeker-Sensitivity Rating: 7
Themes: Prayer

Stranger to Holiness
Artist: Steve Camp
Album/Label: Shake Me to Wake Me, Sparrow
Style: Ballad
Tempo: Slow/mid
Seeker-Sensitivity Rating: 2
Themes: Our sinfulness; How unlike God we are
Comments: Key may need to be lowered; may be a bit dated, but some strong lyrics

Strength in You
Artist: Willow Creek Music

Album/Label: A Place to Call Home, Word/Maranatha!
Style: MOR pop
Tempo: Slow/mid
Seeker-Sensitivity Rating: 10
Themes: Foundation of life

Suffer in Silence
Artist: Susan Ashton
Album/Label: Wakened by the Wind, Sparrow
Style: Folk/pop
Tempo: Mid
Seeker-Sensitivity Rating: 10
Themes: Offering to share pain of a friend, letting people in to the healing process
Comments: Some beautiful lyrics, may be a bit esoteric for some settings

Surrender Medley
Artist: Willow Creek Music
Album/Label: Ever Devoted, Willow Creek
Style: Ballad medley—duet
Tempo: Slow
Seeker-Sensitivity Rating: 6
Themes: Submission to Christ
Comments: Includes "My Life Is in Your Hands," "Holy Spirit, Take Control," "Living Sacrifice," "Take My Life"

Take My Hand
Artist: The Kry
Album/Label: You, Freedom/Malaco
Style: Acoustic ballad
Tempo: Slow/mid
Seeker-Sensitivity Rating: 9
Themes: Trusting God in faith—taking a step
Comments: Compelling song—It helps if you have 2 strong male vocalists, but not critical

Take My Hand
Artist: Russ Taff
Album/Label: The Way Home,
Style: Folk/rock
Tempo: Mid
Seeker-Sensitivity Rating: 9
Themes: Friendship; Desire for community
Comments: Can be a strong song, especially for a younger audience, but the speak/singing feel of the verses may not work in some settings

Thankful
Artist: Willow Creek Music
Album/Label: Ever Devoted, Willow Creek
Style: Pop
Tempo: Up
Seeker-Sensitivity Rating: 7
Themes: Thanksgiving; God's faithfulness, goodness

Thanks for So Much Love
Artist: Harry Newman
Album/Label: Journey,
Style: Ballad
Tempo: Slow
Seeker-Sensitivity Rating: 10
Themes: Song of thanks for a Mother's love and sacrifice.
Comments: Song written by a Willow Creek

vocalist for his mother—you can get a copy by calling (847)765-6222

That's What a Brother Is For
Artist: Michael James
Album/Label: Shoulder to the Wind, Reunion
Style: Ballad—male duet
Tempo: Slow
Seeker-Sensitivity Rating: 5
Themes: Men's friendship, small groups
Comments: Can also work as a solo. If you do it as a duet, make sure the men authentically have a relationship—it will enhance the moment

That's What Love Is All About
Artist: Michael Bolton
Album/Label: The Hunger, Columbia
Style: Ballad
Tempo: Slow
Seeker-Sensitivity Rating: 10
Themes: Building a lasting marriage
Comments: Key may need to be lowered

That's What Love Is For
Artist: Amy Grant
Album/Label: Heart in Motion, Myrrh
Style: Power ballad
Tempo: Slow
Seeker-Sensitivity Rating: 10
Themes: Love overcoming relational or marital conflict
Comments: Never used at Willow Creek

There Is a Line
Artist: Susan Ashton
Album/Label: Susan Ashton, Sparrow
Style: Folk pop
Tempo: Mid
Seeker-Sensitivity Rating: 6
Themes: No compromise, statement of commitment to integrity
Comments: May be a bit hard to track lyrically

There Is a Love
Artist: Michael English
Album/Label: Hope, Warner Alliance
Style: Pop
Tempo: Up
Seeker-Sensitivity Rating: 9
Themes: God's love for the broken-hearted; God's love

They Could Not
Artist: Sandi Patti
Album/Label: Lift Up the Lord, Impact/Benson
Style: Inspirational ballad
Tempo: Slow
Seeker-Sensitivity Rating: 5
Themes: Easter; The Resurrection

This Baby
Artist: Steven Curtis Chapman
Album/Label: The Music of Christmas, Sparrow
Style: Pop
Tempo: Up
Seeker-Sensitivity Rating: 9
Themes: Christmas

This Is the Life
  Artist: Phillips, Craig and Dean
  Album/Label: Phillips, Craig and Dean, Star Song
  Style: Pop/rock
  Tempo: Up
  Seeker-Sensitivity Rating: 6
  Themes: Joy of the Christian life
  Comments: Second half of the second verse is very finger-pointing at seekers. Be careful

Thy Word
  Artist: Amy Grant
  Album/Label: Straight Ahead, Myrrh
  Style: Ballad
  Tempo: Slow
  Seeker-Sensitivity Rating: 4
  Themes: God's Word; Guidance

Time Out
  Artist: Clark Sisters
  Album/Label: Heart and Soul, Rejoice
  Style: R & B
  Tempo: Up
  Seeker-Sensitivity Rating: 9
  Themes: Pace of life, hurry

Time to Return
  Artist: Willow Creek Music
  Album/Label: None
  Style: Ballad
  Tempo: Slow
  Seeker-Sensitivity Rating: 7
  Themes: Decaying world; Need for Christ

Treasure
  Artist: Gary Chapman
  Album/Label: The Light Inside, Reunion
  Style: Acoustic ballad
  Tempo: Slow
  Seeker-Sensitivity Rating: 9
  Themes: Fulfillment in Christ
  Comments: Already great song was recently improved with slightly updated treatment

Treasure of You
  Artist: Steven Curtis Chapman
  Album/Label: Heaven in the Real World, Sparrow
  Style: Driving rock
  Tempo: Up
  Seeker-Sensitivity Rating: 10
  Themes: Our value to God
  Comments: Great statement to seekers. May be too edgy musically for some churches. Never used at Willow Creek

True Devotion
  Artist: Margaret Becker
  Album/Label: Grace, Sparrow
  Style: R & B/Pop
  Tempo: Up
  Seeker-Sensitivity Rating: 6
  Themes: Devotion to Christ
  Comments: Never used at Willow Creek

Undivided
  Artist: First Call
  Album/Label: Undivided, Dayspring
  Style: Ballad—trio
  Tempo: Slow
  Seeker-Sensitivity Rating: 5
  Themes: Unity in the body of Christ

Comments: More church-oriented, dealing with denominational differences, but can work in a seeker context when talking about unity

Up From the Dead
  Artist: Dana Key
  Album/Label: The Journey, Forefront
  Style: Pop
  Tempo: Mid
  Seeker-Sensitivity Rating: 8
  Themes: Easter; Resurrection

Via Dolorosa
  Artist: Sandi Patti
  Album/Label: Songs From the Heart, Impact/Benson
  Style: Inspirational Ballad
  Tempo: Slow
  Seeker-Sensitivity Rating: 7
  Themes: Easter; Suffering of Christ

Walk in the Dark
  Artist: Wayne Watson
  Album/Label: A Beautiful Place, Dayspring
  Style: Pop
  Tempo: Up
  Seeker-Sensitivity Rating: 2
  Themes: Faith; Trusting God in confusing circumstances
  Comments: The image of "walking in the dark" with Jesus may be confusing to some, though it makes sense in context

Walk On By
  Artist: Susan Ashton
  Album/Label: Angels of Mercy, Sparrow
  Style: Folk pop
  Tempo: Mid/up
  Seeker-Sensitivity Rating: 8
  Themes: Temptation

Want the World to Know
  Artist: Willow Creek Music
  Album/Label: None
  Style: Pop
  Tempo: Up
  Seeker-Sensitivity Rating: 9
  Themes: Testimony

We Are an Army
  Artist: Trace Balin
  Album/Label: Champions, Dayspring
  Style: Power ballad
  Tempo: Slow/mid
  Seeker-Sensitivity Rating: 1
  Themes: Spiritual warfare; The church; Unity
  Comments: Strong anthemic song

We Are the People
  Artist: Bob Carlisle
  Album/Label: Bob Carlisle, Sparrow
  Style: Power ballad
  Tempo: Slow
  Seeker-Sensitivity Rating: 5
  Themes: Call to compassion
  Comments: Song is aimed at Christians, but can also be used to challenge anyone to make a difference in someone else's life. Verses are a bit confusing

We Believe in God
  Artist: Amy Grant

Album/Label: Songs From the Loft, Reunion
  Style: Acoustic ballad
  Tempo: Slow
  Seeker-Sensitivity Rating: 3
  Themes: Creed; Need for Christ

We Belong to Him
  Artist: Wayne Watson
  Album/Label: The Fine Line, Dayspring
  Style: MOR ballad
  Tempo: Slow/mid
  Seeker-Sensitivity Rating: 2
  Themes: Christ died for us—we are His

We Need Each Other
  Artist: Trace Balin
  Album/Label: Champions, Dayspring
  Style: Power ballad
  Tempo: Slow/mid
  Seeker-Sensitivity Rating: 7
  Themes: Relationships community
  Comments: Best done with a group of singers who have strong relationships with each other

We've Got a Reason to Celebrate
  Artist: Billy and Sarah Gaines
  Album/Label: He'll Find a Way, Benson
  Style: R & B pop
  Tempo: Up
  Seeker-Sensitivity Rating: 3
  Themes: Praise & worship; God's greatness

What a Ride
  Artist: Willow Creek Music
  Album/Label: A Place to Call Home, Word/Maranatha!
  Style: Pop/rock
  Tempo: Up
  Seeker-Sensitivity Rating: 9
  Themes: Joy, thrill of the Christian life
  Comments: Very fun song live

What I Wouldn't Give
  Artist: Willow Creek Music
  Album/Label: None
  Style: Acoustic ballad
  Tempo: Slow
  Seeker-Sensitivity Rating: 10
  Themes: Our value to God
  Comments: From Christ's perspective, so it probably needs some kind of a set-up

Whatever You Ask
  Artist: Steve Camp
  Album/Label: After God's Own Heart, Doing My Best, vol. 1, Sparrow
  Style: Power ballad
  Tempo: Slow
  Seeker-Sensitivity Rating: 5
  Themes: Obedience; Commitment
  Comments: Strong song of desired obedience—there is also an updated version on Generation Y's debut album, with a female lead

When God's People Pray
  Artist: Wayne Watson
  Album/Label: Home Free, Dayspring
  Style: Pop ballad
  Tempo: Mid/slow
  Seeker-Sensitivity Rating: 3
  Themes: Prayer; The power of prayer

When It Hurts the Most
Artist: Brent Lamb
Album/Label: Outside These Walls, Diadem
Style: Ballad
Tempo: Slow
Seeker-Sensitivity Rating: 9
Themes: God's strength in our hardship; Growth through pain
Comments: Could come across as an "easy answer," if not used properly

When We Fail Love
Artist: Grover Levy
Album/Label: Grover Levy, Myrrh
Style: Piano ballad
Tempo: Slow
Seeker-Sensitivity Rating: 9
Themes: Failure in relationships; Forgiveness
Comments: Poignant song. Chorus might be a little wordy—hard to follow in a one-time hearing, but worth a listen

When You Are a Soldier
Artist: Steven Curtis Chapman
Album/Label: For the Sake of the Call, Sparrow
Style: Keyboard ballad
Tempo: Slow/mid
Seeker-Sensitivity Rating: 4
Themes: The Christian life is hard—God will be there

Where Else Could I Go
Artist: Willow Creek Music
Album/Label: None
Style: Inspirational ballad
Tempo: Slow
Seeker-Sensitivity Rating: 8
Themes: Need for Christ; Fulfillment in Christ

Where Would I Be Now
Artist: Willow Creek Music
Album/Label: None
Style: Ballad-Broadway feel
Tempo: Slow
Seeker-Sensitivity Rating: 6
Themes: Good Friday; Atonement
Comments: Powerful song for a Good Friday service

Who Am I
Artist: Margaret Becker
Album/Label: The Reckoning; Steps of Faith, Sparrow
Style: Power ballad
Tempo: Slow
Seeker-Sensitivity Rating: 7
Themes: Grace; God's unconditional love

Who Makes the Rules
Artist: Steven Curtis Chapman
Album/Label: More to This Life, Sparrow

Style: Pop/folk rock
Tempo: Up
Seeker-Sensitivity Rating: 7
Themes: Authenticity; Life foundation; Worldliness
Comments: Lyrically geared to Christians, but has worked in seeker services—title can be used in message

Who to Listen To
Artist: Amy Grant
Album/Label: Unguarded, Myrrh
Style: Pop
Tempo: Mid
Seeker-Sensitivity Rating: 8
Themes: Decision-making; Sources for values
Comments: A large part of the interlude can be omitted for live performance

Why Me
Artist: Willow Creek Music
Album/Label: A Place to Call Home, Word/Maranatha!
Style: Ballad
Tempo: Slow
Seeker-Sensitivity Rating: 9
Themes: God's undeserved, sacrificial love
Comments: Works well for Good Friday

Wings of Love
Artist: Imperials
Album/Label: This Year's Model,
Style: Pop
Tempo: Up
Seeker-Sensitivity Rating: 8
Themes: God's protection; God as a refuge

With All My Heart
Artist: Babbie Mason
Album/Label: With All My Heart, Word
Style: Ballad
Tempo: Slow
Seeker-Sensitivity Rating: 6
Themes: Commitment; Discipleship

Words
Artist: Kim Hill
Album/Label: Brave Heart, Reunion
Style: Pop/rock
Tempo: Up
Seeker-Sensitivity Rating: 10
Themes: The tongue; Slander
Comments: When we did this at Willow Creek, we did in conjunction with the drama "The Killing Spree," which we transitioned to during the Beatle-esque interlude. We finished the song after the drama

Would I Know You
Artist: Wayne Watson
Album/Label: Watercolour Ponies, Dayspring
Style: Ballad

Tempo: Slow
Seeker-Sensitivity Rating: 3
Themes: Spiritual Authenticity
Comments: Strong message of self-examination—very convicting

You Don't Count the Cost
Artist: Billy Dean
Album/Label: Billy Dean, Capitol/SBK
Style: Country ballad
Tempo: Slow
Seeker-Sensitivity Rating: 10
Themes: Love; The sacrifice of love, what it compels us to do

You're the One He Loves
Artist: Truth
Album/Label: Something to Hold On To, Integrity
Style: Pop
Tempo: Up
Seeker-Sensitivity Rating: 10
Themes: Our value to God
Comments: Great opener

You've Got to Stand for Something
Artist: Aaron Tippin
Album/Label: You've Got to Stand for Something, RCA/BMG
Style: Country
Tempo: Up
Seeker-Sensitivity Rating: 10
Themes: Integrity

Your Love
Artist: Alleluia Music
Album/Label: Your Love, Integrity
Style: MOR—duet
Tempo: Mid
Seeker-Sensitivity Rating: 4
Themes: God's love; Praise & worship

Your Love Stays With Me
Artist: Gary Chapman
Album/Label: Everyday Man, Reunion
Style: Piano ballad
Tempo: Slow
Seeker-Sensitivity Rating: 10
Themes: God's unfailing, faithful love
Comments: Album may be out of print; Russ Taff did a very different version on a recent album. I prefer Chapman's simpler version, if you can find it

Your Steadfast Love
Artist: Alleluia Music
Album/Label: Come and Worship, Alleluia Music/Integrity
Style: MOR
Tempo: Mid/slow
Seeker-Sensitivity Rating: 3
Themes: God's faithful love; Praise & worship

Drama Index

ACTING THE PART by Sharon Sherbondy

Carol is having a difficult time putting her faith into action. Specifically, she's driving her husband crazy with her list of "don'ts." Like many sincere but misinformed believers, she has an exaggerated view of how God calls us to live.

Suggested Topics: Legalism, Living out our Christianity

Characters: 1 male, 2 females

WCCC Series Title: How Christianity Complicates Your Life

ADULTEROUS WOMAN/SOLDIER AT THE CROSS by Judson Poling

(These are two monologues, either of which could stand alone.)
The first story is told by the woman caught in adultery (John 8), though it is some time after the fact. She has just witnessed Jesus' crucifixion, especially ironic because there was nothing she could do to help Him even though His encounter with her spared her life. She recounts the shame of that day, the travesty of justice, and the tenderness of Jesus who not only treated her with dignity and saved her life, but also forgave her sin. She knows even though He's now dead, she'll see Him again, and until that day will always hold in her heart the freedom and new start He gave her.

Suggested Topics: Good Friday, Grace, God's tenderness, The woman caught in adultery

Characters: 1 female

WCCC Series Title: Good Friday

The second monologue recounts the experience of one of the soldiers at the cross. He has mixed feelings about the whole ordeal, wondering why Rome has taken to killing off such apparently harmless victims. When he wrestles with what he's done, especially in light of Jesus' readiness to forgive all who hurt him, he blurts out to the heavens that he had to do it—he had orders. Maybe this guy was the Messiah, maybe not. But God should have made it more obvious. He should have sent someone who at least looked more impressive so everybody would know.

Suggested Topics: Good Friday, Skeptical reactions to Jesus

Characters: 1 male

WCCC Series Title: Good Friday

ALL GUMMED UP by Judson Poling

It's fifteen minutes before Jennifer's wedding and she's sitting outside at the bus stop talking to an old man. She's attempting to sort out her feelings of mistrust toward her father. When she was 12 she discovered her father was having an affair and she still hasn't recovered. Now she wonders if she can trust her fiance. The old man encourages her to see her fiance for who he is, not for who her father was.

Suggested Topics: Adultery, Dealing with past hurts, The pain of lies

Characters: 1 male, 1 female, 1 offstage male voice

WCCC Series Title: Seventh Commandment; Restrain Sexual Desires

ALL I WANT FOR CHRISTMAS by Judson Poling

This sketch examines the difficulty people have in restraining their material desires. The setting is a shopping mall at Christmas time. Parents are trying to convince their daughter that adding a 7th Barbie doll to her collection isn't necessary. Through a brief series of events, she ends up talking to two other adults and ironically, she's able to poignantly explain how she's trying to be less greedy.

Suggested Topics: Greed, Desire to acquire possessions

Characters: 3 males, 2 females, 1 female child

WCCC Series Title: Tenth Commandment; Restrain Material Desires

AM I MISSING SOMETHING? by Donna Lagerquist

When amiable businessman and city council candidate Robert Dibbons is honored as the "Giver of the Week" by a local newspaper, everyone is thrilled! However, one employee soon begins to question her boss's sincerity. She recounts a painful memory of her father giving her leftover presents from work; items that cost him nothing monetarily or emotionally. In a frustrating conclusion, Mr. Dibbons fails to see the harm in something being "mutually beneficial." We know, however, that he volunteers to promote himself and gives only out of his excess.

Suggested Topics: Attitudes in serving, Giving, Self-deception, Rationalizing

Characters: 3 males, 2 females

WCCC Series Title: Building Bigger Hearts; The Story Of Three Hearts

THE ANGRY WOMAN by Judson Poling

As we look back over Jean's life, several episodes of disappointment and humiliation show us why she's an angry woman: nagging from her mother, embarrassment from a teacher, being dumped by a boyfriend, and disparagement from her alcoholic husband. She "never said what she needed to say" which has kept her from expressing her true feelings—she's bottled them up so that now they leak out in the wrong places, leaving her angry and lonely. "Because she didn't say what she needed to say, she's said what she didn't want to say—and now doesn't know what to say."

Suggested Topics: The roots of anger

Characters: 2 males, 3 females, 1 narrator

WCCC Series Title: The Age Of Rage; The Roots Of Rage

ANOTHER DAY AT THE BUS STOP by Judson Poling

A modern retelling of the story of the woman at the well from John 4. A "woman of the evening" meets a stranger at a bus stop, who not only shows her kindness, but even asks for a sip of her Coke. She is unaccustomed to being treated as a person, but the stranger amazes her even more by claiming to be Jesus. Though she is skeptical, His ability to sympathetically describe so many details about her life convinces her He's real—and as He leaves, she haltingly expresses her desire to talk with Him again.

Suggested Topics: Our relationship to God, Self-esteem

Characters: 1 male, 1 female

WCCC Series Title: Private Conversations—Jesus Talks to a Sinner

ANY TIME? by Sharon Sherbondy

In this sketch we see how an "everyman" character responds to God's desire to be a part of his life. In his college years he is too busy with studies and asks God to come back when he is more settled. In his early adulthood he has too many responsibilities but this time asks God to come back when he is retired. In his retirement he is glad to see God but isn't prepared for the challenge of meeting with Him regularly.

Suggested Topics: Making time for God

Characters: 1 male

WCCC Series Title: Fourth Commandment; Remember the Sabbath Day

ANYTHING BUT RELIGION by Sharon Sherbondy

Ruth and Hank are on their way to visit their daughter, Cheryl, and her husband, Brian. All are hoping to have a "nice" evening, but it's unlikely because no matter how hard they try, they end up fighting over religion. The reason: Ruth and Hank are Catholic, and Cheryl has left the Church and has become a Protestant like her husband. The sketch honestly presents the misunderstandings and hurt feelings that often result from this very common family tension.

Suggested Topics: Denominational differences, Families alienated because of religion

Characters: 2 males, 2 females

WCCC Series Title: What Catholics Can Learn From Protestants

ATTACK OF THE WELL-MEANERS by Various Authors

When Gwen's father takes ill, two of her friends fly in to console her. The comedy occurs as they attempt to help Gwen deal with this tragedy and fail completely to offer what Gwen really needs.

Suggested Topics: Dealing with crisis, Friends

Characters: 1 male, 2 females

WCCC Series Title: Strength for the Storms of Life; Strength Storms Produce

BE LIKE MIKE by Brian Svenkeson

In this lighthearted drama, an average man, Bob, falls asleep and dreams he is Michael Jordan. At first he enjoys the fame and recognition—but various "takers" make him wish he could be left alone. When the scene climaxes with a scientist cornering him to get his DNA for Jurassic Park, he utters the words of the commercial: "Can you imagine if I were just a basketball player?" They all respond at once "No!" and Bob is left with the nightmare that people will always want a piece of those who are in the limelight.

Suggested Topics: Fame, Pressures of success

Characters: 4 males, 2 females (actors play multiple roles)

WCCC Series Title: What Jesus Would Say To … Michael Jordan

BECAUSE I LOVE YOU by Sharon Sherbondy

Michelle has planned a romantic dinner for Eric only to have it spoiled by a piece of junk mail. Michelle had an affair four years earlier with a man who worked at the company that sent the letter. Suddenly the romantic evening turns into a major argument, as Eric reveals his deep hurt and continual lack of trust, even after four years. The sketch ends with the couple alienated and hurting.

Suggested Topics: Adultery, The consequences of sin

Characters: 1 male, 1 female

WCCC Series Title: The "S" Word; The High Cost of a Cheap Thrill

BEST FRIENDS by Sharon Sherbondy

The kids are off camping and a husband and wife are looking forward to a romantic weekend alone. They are interrupted by the neighbors who come loaded down with games, munchies, and sleeping bags determined to keep the couple company. The neighbors are actually a very needy couple whose complaints and insensitivity lead to a delightfully comic resolution.

Suggested Topics: Friendship, Insecurity

Characters: 2 males, 2 females

WCCC Series Title: Ordering Your Private World; Your Relational World

THE BIG QUESTION by Sharon Sherbondy

Brian and Lisa are in a panic as they decide how to explain the "facts of life" to their young daughter Amy. Much to their surprise, Amy doesn't have questions about sex, but about the existence of God. She wants to know where God lives and if He's good. As a result of the conversation, Brian and Lisa begin questioning if they believe in God and what they know about Him.

Suggested Topics: The existence of God

Characters: 1 male, 1 female, 1 child

WCCC Series Title: Faith Has Its Reasons; Reasons for Believing in God

THE BIG SELL by Sharon Sherbondy and Steve Pederson

An ad agency is contracted to devise an ad campaign for a new soft-drink product, "Rejuven-ade." The product manager comes in just as the team is thinking up ways to make the beverage sell. True to Madison Avenue, the ideas quickly turn toward sexual themes, and instead of extolling the family values the product manager wanted, the campaign's slogan becomes, "Don't drink it 'cause you're thirsty, drink it 'cause you're hot." On a roll, though oblivious to the fact the product manager left because he didn't like it, they move to their next account, "Catalina Gourmet Cat Food." Within seconds, the ideas have turned to—you guessed it—"erotic."

Suggested Topics: Obsession with sex in society, Effect of the media

Characters: 3 males, 2 females

WCCC Series Title: The Payoff of Sexual Purity

THE BLACK HOLE by Various Authors

Joe, an average guy, and Jane, an average girl, were created by God, and He loved them very much. Like all of us, they have a definite need for Him, but typically they try to fill the "black hole" with relationships, status, and possessions. Until they ask God's forgiveness and are filled by Him, they live empty lives.

Suggested Topics: Contentment, God's love, Filling the void

Characters: 2 males, 1 female, 1 narrator

WCCC Series Title: Easter Celebration; God's Wake Up Calls; Surprised By God's Truth

THE BOOK OF LIFE by Donna Lagerquist

An energetic mime that shows how and how not to have one's name written in the Book of Life and thus obtain entrance into heaven. In this parable, a bicyclist ponders his/her flat tire and becomes a witness to several people (of varied occupations/ backgrounds) getting "called" by a Maitre D' (God) to enter through a door (heaven). Whenever the door is open, there's the sound of a great party. When the Maitre D' finds a person's name in the Book of Life they are allowed to enter through the door. The bicyclist tries to enter, but his/her name is not in the Book. The Maitre D' tries to explain that in order to have one's name in the Book, they must give Him their heart. Not satisfied with that, the bicyclist tries money, good deeds, and even sneaking into heaven before finally trusting his/her heart to God.

Suggested Topics: Baptism, Faith, Basic Christianity, Eternal life

Characters: 3 females, 3 males

WCCC Series Title: Baptism Service

THE BOY WHO NEVER GOT DIRTY by Various Authors

A lighthearted tale of a boy named LeRoy Boskowitz. He never got dirty, took risks, or helped others because he was afraid of getting hurt. He remained this way into adulthood until his wife Stella got fed up and devised a plan which led LeRoy to experience the joy of serving others.

Suggested Topics: Service, Risk taking

Characters: 1 male, 1 female, 1 narrator

WCCC Series Title: Seven Wonders of the Spiritual World; God Uses Me

THE BREAKFAST CLUB by Sharon Sherbondy

The cost of building relationships can be high but the rewards can be just as great. A group of four men meet together once a week to hold each other accountable, encourage one another, and share in each other's lives. In a busy world one meeting a week can be an inconvenience but when a crisis occurs that investment can really pay off.

Suggested Topics: Friendship, Friends in crisis

Characters: 4 males, 1 female

WCCC Series Title: Enlisting in Platoons; The Rewards of Little Platoons

THE BROTHERHOOD by Various Authors

We have an exaggerated view of a serious problem when the local chapter of the International Order of the Brotherhood of Fellow Workaholics meets. Their motto is "Work hard, die young, and leave a haggard-looking corpse." One of the members shares his "testimony" of how he came dangerously close to becoming a well-balanced person.

Suggested Topics: Workaholism, Balancing your life

Characters: 2 males, 4 either male or female

WCCC Series Title: Taking Care Of Business; What Drives The Workaholic?

BROTHER'S KEEPER by Various Authors

How would you handle someone wanting to be included in every part of your life? This sketch shows us how Larry deals with his needy brother

Jack. Larry's frustrations finally bring him to a confrontation with Jack. At first we think Jack understands the point, but he simply has refocused his attention elsewhere.
Suggested Topics: Unhealthy dependencies
Characters: 3 males
WCCC Series Title: The Lost Art of Loving; People Who Love Too Much

THE BROW BEATER by Various Authors

Norman just can't seem to forget his past failures and just in case he might he carries with him a "Brow Beater's Book." This comprehensive guide to all of his failures reminds him that he's a second class citizen and keeps him in his place. His date for the evening tries to explain the freeing power of forgiveness and how that can change his outlook on life.
Suggested Topics: Self-esteem, Failures, Forgiveness
Characters: 1 male, 1 female
WCCC Series Title: Resolving Regrets

CALL OF THE WILD by Sharon Sherbondy

Charlie's in for a shock when Marla comes home from church. She heard a message on taking a step of faith and letting God have complete charge of the direction of our lives. The night before she saw a special on needy people in Africa and now she's convinced God has called her there. Marla ignores that her personality and skills are completely out of sync with a ministry in Africa and that her own community is a more suitable mission field.
Suggested Topics: Serving God
Characters: 1 male, 1 female
WCCC Series Title: Seven Wonders of the Spiritual World; God Guides Me; The Greatest Adventure on Earth

CALL WAITING by Judson Poling

Two men in an office anticipate a reprimand for their failure to get the loan the company needs for expansion. Though they tease each other good-naturedly about what they will have to endure, Allan is having deeper questions about his significance to the company—and in reality, his significance as a person. His income has not matched his hopes, and he's had to watch others rise higher and faster in the corporate structure. He's having, in the words of Chris, a poorly timed "mid-life crisis." Chris decides to go and hide out from the dreaded call. Now left alone, Allan sits in his office contemplating the conversation and whether he should quit or stay. The phone rings. He stares at it as the lights fade.
Suggested Topics: Mid-life crisis, Marketplace pressures, Search for significance
Characters: 2 males
WCCC Series Title: Four Advantages Christians Have at Work

CAN'T LIVE WITHOUT 'EM by Donna Lagerquist

A sweeping look at the various relationships that affect us throughout life. An on-stage narrator and actors recreate scenes from childhood, high school, college, and marriage that illustrate in a comic way the many frustrations of living with imperfect people. Clothes, brains, beauty, neatness, even store-bought rather than home-made cakes—all affect whether we're accepted or rejected. The difficulty of loving others unconditionally is contrasted with words from the Sermon on the Mount (and other passages) that show Christianity's striking—and challenging—counter-cultural stance.
Suggested Topics: Relationships, Unconditional love
Characters: 2 males, 2 females
WCCC Series Title: The Greatest Sermon in History

CATALOG-ITIS by Judson Poling

This is an exaggerated look at one family's struggle with compulsive shopping. Arn and Peggy are unable to control their desire for more possessions and confuse wants with needs. Their attempt to buy a legitimate household necessity turns into a mad frenzy for more, more, more!
Suggested Topics: Self-control, Contentment
Characters: 1 male, 1 female, 2 jr. high age girls
WCCC Series Title: Rare and Remarkable Virtues; Self-Control

CATCH 22 by Sharon Sherbondy

A woman contemplating an abortion confides in a friend. The ensuing dialogue explores the difficulty, agony, and emotions associated with this issue. In a surprise twist, the friend admits that she had had an abortion herself—and still suffers from the guilt. There are no pat answers here, but no one will miss the power of this real-life drama.
Suggested Topics: Abortion
Characters: 2 females
WCCC Series Title: Modern-day Madness; Unwanted Pregnancies

CHAMELEON by Sharon Sherbondy

Jeff is taken by surprise when his father's behavior is determined by the happenings around him. One minute Jeff's father is affectionate and singing his praises, but as soon as Dad receives bad news he verbally attacks Jeff and questions his motives. Jeff is exhausted when this happens twice in a short period of time.
Suggested Topics: God's presence in our lives, Controlling our emotions
Characters: 3 males
WCCC Series Title: Stability in a Changing World

CHANGES by Sharon Sherbondy

Karen and Russ are having dinner with Karen's parents. For some reason, during this visit she is struck with the aging of her parents. A combination of their helplessness and Karen's memories of past times together make her sad, yet at the same time she is filled with a love for these two special people in her life.
Suggested Topics: Re-parenting parents, Family
Characters: 2 males, 2 females
WCCC Series Title: Parenthood—Part 5: Re-parenting Parents

CHECK MATES by Sharon Sherbondy

The subject of finances brings fear to the heart of Rob and excitement to Judy. In the midst of trying to balance their checkbook, Judy and Rob discover that their significant debt is a shared problem. To correct the situation, they decide to get rid of all their credit cards. When they actually try to do it, however, they rationalize and end up keeping most of the cards and destroying only two.
Suggested Topics: Personal finances, Debt
Characters: 1 male, 1 female
WCCC Series Title: The Day WCCC Told the Truth-Part 2

A CLEAN SLATE by Various Authors

An "everyman" character delivers three brief monologues. After each one, 2 or 3 guilt figures with small black slates mark down his "sins" while saying, "God is gonna get you for that!" Guilt ridden "everyman" has finally had enough and he cries out to God only to discover that instead of "getting him," God forgives him. The guilt figures disappear and "everyman" discovers in their place a large clean slate.
Suggested Topics: Forgiveness, Redemption, Guilt
Characters: 1 male, 2 or 3 males or females
WCCC Series Title: Celebration of Baptism

THE COMFORT ZONE by Judson Poling

Ken and Karla spend another "comfortable" night at home. Their lives are always very comfortable, a fact to which they repeatedly refer. Any disturbance either by way of TV, career opportunity from a friend, intruding neighbors—even a life-threatening piece of popcorn stuck in Karla's throat—is met with their same commitment to remain … comfortable. This comic sketch shows that in the end, the desire to avoid risks can actually mean death, not life.
Suggested Topics: Risk taking
Characters: 1 male, 2 females (1 TV announcer on tape)
WCCC Series Title: Games We Play—Risk

CONFESSIONS OF AN AD-AHOLIC by Judson Poling

Al and Alice are "ad-aholics," individuals addicted to advertisements. They explain how the addiction started, progressed, and eventually ruined their lives. This satire shows how chasing the American dream of having more can be a nightmare.

Suggested Topics: American dream, Possessions, Contentment, Self-control
Characters: 1 male, 1 female
WCCC Series Title: Changing Times—The Changing American Dream; A New Way of Thinking

CONVERSATIONS by Judson Poling

Phil is waiting to talk to his boss, accompanied by another man. We quickly find out this other person is a personified critical voice, heard and seen only by him but always there. As the conversation with Barb, his boss, gets going, the critical voice constantly interrupts making Phil say things he really doesn't want to. He eventually must excuse himself, knowing the voice has won again, and has convinced him he's a failure. As Phil exits, Barb comments to herself on Phil's erratic behavior—only to be shamed by her own critical voice!
Suggested Topics: Self-esteem, Self-criticism, Failure
Characters: 2 males, 1 female, 1 offstage female voice
WCCC Series Title: When I'm Mad at Myself

CONVERSATIONS IN A FIELD by Judson Poling

Two lilies and two ravens become discontent with their lot. After worrying themselves into a worried frenzy, they realize that God created them to enjoy being lilies and ravens, and that He will care for their needs.
Suggested Topics: Anxiety, Worry
Characters: 2 males, 2 females
WCCC Series Title: Illustrating the Identity of God; Our Providing God; The Pleasure of Playing God

THE CONVERSION by Judson Poling

Todd, an appealing college student, discusses with his parents his recent conversion to Hinduism. Todd's dad doesn't understand how he could "turn his back on his country and his family's faith." Todd feels they don't know enough about Hinduism to make a judgment.
Suggested Topics: Hinduism
Characters: 2 males, 1 female
WCCC Series Title: Alternatives to Christianity; Major World Religions

COUNTING THE COST by Debra Poling

These are three separate monologues representing true accounts of the price people paid to follow Christ. The first is a man who turned down a promotion because it would take him and his family away from a church where they were growing. The second is a woman who gave up marriage because the man was not a fully devoted follower of Christ. The third is a Jewish couple who risked alienation when they claimed Jesus as their Messiah.
Suggested Topics: Commitment to Christ, Sacrifice, Spiritual maturity
Characters: 2 males, 2 females
WCCC Series Title: Seasons of a Spiritual Life; Spiritual Adulthood

CREDIT DUE by Donna Lagerquist

Miss Patsy is the host of a local kids television show, but definitely has some problems liking her job—and kids. Norah, a make-up person on the set offers some helpful ideas for the show. Though Miss Patsy appears to disdain Norah, she uses her idea anyway, without giving her credit. It isn't the first time either, and in the end, Norah knows she's being used, but doesn't know what to do.
Suggested Topics: When others use you
Characters: 2 males, 2 females, two children's voices offstage
WCCC Series Title: The Greatest Sermon in History

THE CROWD, THE CONSCIENCE, AND CURT by Judson Poling

As a young boy at the playground, Curt meets "The Crowd," that collection of voices that tells him to travel the broad way with everyone else. They hold up their happy face masks, assuring him their way leads to fulfillment. In junior high they tell him to cheat. At that point, he hears from "The Conscience," who warns him to protect his character. Later in life, the Crowd entices him with an adulterous affair, while the Conscience urges him to keep his promises. Divorce follows. Finally, Curt faces a spiritual crossroads. Once again the Crowd beckons him on the

broad path. Conscience tries in vain to keep him from going with the voices he's become accustomed to heeding. In the end, they show their true colors with haunting masks in torment.
Suggested Topics: Broad versus narrow way, Conscience, Peer pressure at all ages
Characters: 2 males, 4 males or females for the Crowd
WCCC Series Title: The Greatest Sermon in History

A DAY IN THE LIFE by Judson Poling

This unique drama is really a series of short, interconnected vignettes which illustrate in a humorous way a new Christian going about his first day at work after his conversion. To perform this sketch, the pastor must actually interact with the actor playing the new Christian, interspersing his message throughout the vignettes, As the new believer faces a hectic morning commute, an obnoxious co-worker, and the temptation to lie to keep a sale, the scenes cover three broad topics of interest for new Christians. They are: making time for God in the midst of a busy schedule, forgiving those who wrong you, and steering through ethical dilemmas in the workplace.
Suggested Topics: New Christian, Basic Christian lifestyle, Christians in the marketplace
Characters: 5 males (or adapted for females)
WCCC Series Title: Capturing the Heart of Christianity

D-DAY by Sharon Sherbondy

Humorous sketch about a businessman, Rob, whose wife and co-worker find his calendar at work filled with thrill-seeking activities, up until a day marked "D-Day"—then there's nothing scheduled after it. They first think he's going through a mid-life crisis, then fear he is going to die. When Rob comes into his office, he informs them that "D-Day" refers to the "decision" to become a Christian. He has filled his calendar with fun things, because once "D-Day" arrives, "it's all over!"
Suggested Topics: Misconceptions about Christianity
Characters: 2 males, 1 female
WCCC Series Title: Yeah God

DEFINITELY SAFE by Donna Lagerquist

It's Father's Day and a college age son and father talk on their back porch. The son, Mark, has been sensing his mother's anger toward him and finally gets the explanation: both parents are disappointed in Mark because he's lied to them about dropping out of school. Mark confesses readily, and verbally beats himself up for being such a failure, especially compared to his successful older sister. The father, though angry, wants Mark to come home so they can work things out. Mark marvels at his dad's patience. As they play a quick baseball skirmish, the father calls his son "safe—definitely safe." The obvious double entendre of his words touch us with the never-ending love of a committed father.
Suggested Topics: Father's Day; Prodigal son
Characters: 2 males, 1 female
WCCC Series Title: Father's Day; Leaving a Living Legacy

DIFFERENCES by Donna Lagerquist

A bag lady innocently and humorously opens up the otherwise "sensitive" topic of Catholicism versus Protestantism when she happens upon two ministers—one of each denomination—on a street corner and wrongly assumes they are friends. With childlike wonder she questions them on topics such as confession, communion, and why they wear what they do. Despite her light-heartedness and attempts at bringing them together, friction between the two men remains obvious and unresolved.
Suggested Topics: Catholicism vs. Protestantism; Friction among believers
Characters: 2 males, 1 female
WCCC Series Title: What Protestants Can Learn From Catholics

DON'T MENTION IT by Donna Lagerquist

An evening together for two couples is strained because one of the men is unemployed. While the host wife is (comically) going overboard trying to be sensitive to the unemployed couple's embarrassment, the unemployed man just wishes he could stay at home so he wouldn't have to deal with other people and their reaction to his condition. Finally the two husbands speak openly about the situation, with the host husband confessing he too was unemployed for a while and went through all the feelings associated with that time of hardship. The sketch ends on a light note with the two men realizing it's better to "mention it"—instead of hiding the need to talk about what is really going on.

Suggested Topics: Unemployment, Honesty about negative feelings, Community

Characters: 2 males, 2 females

WCCC Series Title: Do You Have What It Takes to Grow; Carry the Message

DONUTS AND DEADBEATS by Sharon Sherbondy

Joyce is on a diet again but Dick is paying the price. As he describes it, after 10 minutes on the diet she becomes "cranky and neurotic and even suicidal." So they make a deal: he will be her support and encouragement as long as his food intake remains the same. Can Joyce handle temptation? Will Dick cheer her on? The ending is very true to the "real world" we all live in.

Suggested Topics: Discipline, Physical health

Characters: 1 male, 1 female

WCCC Series Title: Fit for Life

DRIVEN by Donna Lagerquist

In the car on the way to an awards banquet for his being salesman of the year, Doug and Nancy get in a fight. She is becoming more and more frightened of the man he's becoming as he claws his way to success. He can't see the way both he and his family are paying a price for his drivenness. He also can't see how part of his problem is his trying to please his deceased father's wishes for him. In the end, Nancy gets out of the car and leaves Doug to his success act. As the lights fade, Doug lays on the horn, frustrated and alone.

Suggested Topics: Workaholism, Marriage

Characters: 1 male, 1 female

WCCC Series Title: A Hunger for Healing

EARLY ONE MORNING JUST AFTER THE DAWN OF HISTORY AS WE KNOW IT by Judson Poling

Two cavemen stumble upon each other, and immediately establish their respective territories. They quickly discover this is not enough to satisfy their need to feel superior, so they begin a one-upmanship game that starts with a stone rock for a chair and ends with a Laz-y-Boy recliner! Just when you think things couldn't be weirder, another caveman shows up … with a cellular phone! He outdoes the other two hands down! This entire sketch is done without any dialog—just actions, props, and "grunts."

Suggested Topics: Materialism; Keeping up with the Joneses

Characters: 3 males

WCCC Series Title: The Profit of Financial Integrity

THE EGGSHELL FAMILY by Judson Poling

A comic sketch in which a couple agonize over every decision, from whether or not to watch TV to answering the door. The son is a rather normal fellow who cannot tolerate his parents' indecisiveness. The uncle enters and is a mirror image of the father. After great difficulty deciding which car to drive, the family leaves for a restaurant. We can only wonder what happens when they are confronted with a menu!

Suggested Topics: Decision making

Characters: 2 males, 1 female, 1 either male or female

WCCC Series Title: The Art of Decision Making; Decisions, Decisions, Decisions

THE EGGSHELLS BREAK OUT by Judson Poling

The Eggshell family is back again, and this time they're ready to take on the world—or are they? This overly cautious family looks at the high price of breaking out their shells and taking risks.

Suggested Topics: Risk taking, Facing challenges

Characters: 3 males, 1 female

WCCC Series Title: Facing Up to Fear; The Fear of Failure

EVERYTHING'S RELATIVE by Judson Poling

Sid's pleas for a break don't move the policeman giving him a ticket—instead a lecture ensues on the importance of upholding the law. Once at home, Sid falls asleep and dreams of being burglarized. In the dream, the policeman and thief merely echo Sid's earlier lines to the policeman concerning how to show "mercy." When Sid wakes up, he has a new appreciation for a standard of right and wrong.

Suggested Topics: God's holiness, Benefits of God's laws

Characters: 3 males, 1 female

WCCC Series Title: Surprised by God; Surprised by God's Holiness

EXPECTATIONS OF THE EXPECTING by Judson Poling

Dirk and Claire are expecting their first child—but they're finding out just how much they're expecting of that child. Dirk, the perfectionist, has a life of education and achievement all laid out; Claire is mostly laid back about it. The soon-to-be-parents are copies of their own parents' expectations, and they're only now realizing how different those expectations are. The sketch ends on a positive note as both affirm the differences in each other that together will help bring about balance in their child's life.

Suggested Topics: Parenting, Affirming personality differences

Characters: 1 male, 1 female

WCCC Series Title: Parenthood—Part 4; Mistakes Parents Make

A FAILURE TALE by Donna Lagerquist

Once upon a time there was a kingdom that was ruled by a very kind and loving king. We see what happens when the king confronts three of the subjects who have violated the rule of making firearms. How will they react to deliberately disobeying rules that create serious consequences for not only themselves but those around them? You can expect denial, admission, and forgiveness at the conclusion of the tale.

Suggested Topics: Failing, Obeying rules

Characters: 5 males, 1 narrator

WCCC Series Title: Learning Through Life's Crises; Learning Through Failing

FAITH IN JEOPARDY by Cathy Peters

Two couples get together for an evening and through a game of Jeopardy discover where their faith lies. Bruce and Annette, a semi-churched couple, find out Jim and Carol have recently made a commitment to the Mormon Church. At first there doesn't seem to be any major difference in what they believe, but as the game goes on it reveals some alarming aspects of Mormon theology.

Suggested Topics: Mormonism

Characters: 2 females, 2 males

WCCC Series Title: Alternatives to Christianity; Contemporary Cults

FAMILY SNAPSHOTS—TAKE I by Sharon Sherbondy

The first of five sketches involving a typical family. Linda, the mother, is visiting with an old friend when the kids come home. Chaos breaks out as the children (Chris, a typical 8th-grade boy; Jenny, a high school student; and Ned, who is home visiting from college) get Linda more and more embarrassed at the impression they are making on her friend. When the father arrives a decision is made that things have to change.

Suggested Topics: Family, Communication

Characters: 3 males, 2 females, 1 junior high boy

WCCC Series Title: Turning Houses Into Homes; The Home as a Filling Station

FAMILY SNAPSHOTS—TAKE II by Sharon Sherbondy

In an effort to get closer, our family has decided to spend the evening playing Scruples (a board game asking the players how they would react to specific situations). The game reveals that the time parents invest in teaching children values and priorities is well worth it.

Suggested Topics: Values, Priorities

Characters: 2 males, 2 females, 1 junior high boy
WCCC Series Title: Turning Houses Into Homes; The Home as a Training Center

FAMILY SNAPSHOTS—TAKE III by Sharon Sherbondy

This touching sketch looks at the special relationship between parent and child, particularly father and daughter. Mike is distracted with work and surprised when Jenny says she feels neglected. After talking about a sensitive issue Jenny is dealing with, Mike recommits himself to being available to her.
Suggested Topics: Parent/child relationships
Characters: 1 male, 1 female
WCCC Series Title: Turning Houses Into Homes; The Home as a Trauma Center

FAMILY SNAPSHOTS—TAKE IV by Sharon Sherbondy

The family has decided to take in a teenage friend of Jenny's whose family asked her to leave when they discovered she was pregnant. The characters learn that "integrity and concern for your fellow man" takes sacrifice.
Suggested Topics: Family, Self-sacrifice
Characters: 2 males, 3 females, 1 junior high boy
WCCC Series Title: Turning Houses Into Homes; The Home as a Seminary

FAMILY SNAPSHOTS—TAKE V: CHRISTMAS EVE

It's Christmas Eve and the family is getting ready for church when they receive a phone call saying the service has been cancelled because of the heavy snow. Mom comes up with the idea that the family do their own version of the Christmas story. Despite the older children's moanings and humorous interpretations, the scene ends with a touching moment when Dad reads the story of Christ's birth.
Suggested Topics: Christmas
Characters: 2 males, 2 females, 1 junior high boy
WCCC Series Title: Christmas Eve—1987

FAMILY VALUES by Judson Poling

Paula and her mom meet after what appears to have been a long separation. Her mother wants her to come home with her, but Paula indicates she wants to stay. We finally discover that Paula has joined some kind of cult. As Mom describes the life she wants Paula to come home to, we realize that a party-hearty brother and mom's on-again, off-again romance makes for a less than appealing home life. Still the control of the cult group makes us see that Paula has been brainwashed. A member of the group enters to escort Paula back. Paula decides to go with him and Mom is left calling for her daughter in an empty room.
Suggested Topics: Cults, Broken families
Characters: 2 females, 2 males
WCCC Series Title: Religion Run Amok; How Good Groups Go Bad

FAMOUS LOST WORDS by Judson Poling

Turn the other cheek? Give to whoever asks? Are these commands meant to be taken literally? In this "drama within a drama" the actors break from reading Jesus' words when one of them confesses he's skeptical. The words sound noble enough, but nobody he knows really lives them. Two brief scenes recounted from the actors' lives show in a lighthearted way the extremes of, on the one hand allowing yourself to be walked on and, on the other hand setting up inflexible boundaries. Can either of these be right? What did Jesus really mean? The sketch ends without resolution, the actors—and the audience—left with the unanswered question.
Suggested Topics: Turning the other cheek, Healthy boundaries/unhealthy submission
Characters: 4 males, 1 female
WCCC Series Title: The Greatest Sermon in History

FAT CHANCE by Sharon Sherbondy

Sharon is trying to get a few minutes alone to talk to God about her struggles as a parent. However, the kids (only heard by her) are constantly interrupting outside the bedroom door. We witness the typical parental tension between wanting to do the right things, and fearing doing the wrong things. The sketch takes a light-hearted, but also poignant look at every parent's struggle.
Suggested Topics: Parenting
Characters: 1 female
WCCC Series Title: Parenthood—Part 2: Raising Whole Children; Parenthood—Part 1: To Be or Not to Be

FEELING OPPOSITION by Donna Lagerquist

Phil and Kate visit their lawyer friend to draw up a will. Kate becomes very emotional as she envisions the will being needed (i.e., herself or Phil dying). Phil, being "practical," tries to convince Kate she's over-reacting (as usual). As they comically reach the point of actually signing the will, Phil gets a little surprise that releases an "over-reaction" on his part ... much to Kate's delight.
Suggested Topics: Thinkers vs. feelers
Characters: 1 male, 1 female
WCCC Series Title: Discovering the Way God Wired You Up—Emotions

FINAL JUDGMENT by Judson Poling

A historical trial is taking place to determine God's guilt for allowing undue and unjust suffering in the world. The prosecuting attorney calls three witnesses: a nerd who says God has no compassion on His creation, Ms. Lonely Heart who struggles with her lack of companionship, and Rev. Pat Answers who gives easy but empty answers to people's pain and suffering. The defendant's only witness is a small child.
Suggested Topics: Suffering
Characters: 4 males, 2 females, 1 child
WCCC Series Title: Strength Through the Storms of Life; Why Storms Strike

FINDING EVIDENCE by Sharon Sherbondy

Vicki and Russ come across a bag of cocaine in their son's room. They confront him with assumptions and accusations before he has had a chance to explain. He is angry that they've jumped to conclusions and informs them that he took the bag away from a friend who is trying to kick the habit. Russ's response is one of disbelief. The audience is left to decide for themselves who to believe.
Suggested Topics: Recognizing the truth, Jumping to conclusions, Trust
Characters: 2 males, 1 female
WCCC Series Title: Faith and the Front Page

FIRST-DAY JITTERS by Sharon Sherbondy

Over the weekend, Claire has made a decision to accept Christ as her Savior. It's Monday morning and she's having a conversation with God about how she expects her day to go. Claire has gone to some unnecessary extremes, like an oversized Bible and saying "Praise the Lord" often, to demonstrate her changed life. God impresses upon her the need to die to her old nature.
Suggested Topics: New Christians, Obeying God, Witnessing
Characters: 1 female
WCCC Series Title: Life in the Comfort Zone

FIRST THINGS FIRST by Sharon Sherbondy

This sketch takes a humorous look at the home that allows children to become the central focus. Kathy and Greg have been parents for 10 months and their lives have changed drastically! Kathy is especially finding it difficult to adapt to the new demands of a baby and still maintain a marriage.
Suggested Topics: New parents, Priorities, Balancing children and marriage
Characters: 1 male, 1 female, 1 female infant
WCCC Series Title: Dangers in the Modern Home

FISHIN' by Steve Pederson

It's not easy for some of us to say "I love you and appreciate what you do for me." That's the case with this father and son. They accomplish little fishing but they do manage to break the ice and share how they really feel about each other.

Suggested Topics: Expressing positive emotions, Father and son relationships

Characters: 2 males

WCCC Series Title: Telling the Truth to Each Other; Learning How to Hear Truth; Father's Day—1989

FOR BETTER OR WORSE—PART I by Sharon Sherbondy

Paula and Marsha have dragged their husbands to ballroom dance lessons in hopes of doing something fun and exciting for their marriages. Joining them are Paula's sister, Lisa, and her fiance, Dan. Lisa and Dan's gushy demonstrations of their love totally turn off Steve and Kurt. Paula and Marsha on the other hand remind them that they used to be just like that—"but then they had to go and get married."

Suggested Topics: Marriage

Characters: 3 males, 3 females (offstage male and female voices)

WCCC Series Title: Fit to Be Tied; Exposing the Marriage Myth

FOR BETTER OR WORSE—PART II by Sharon Sherbondy

Dan and Lisa are coming to Steve and Paula's house for the evening. Steve's not very excited about the idea until Paula mentions that Dan and Lisa have never had a fight. Suddenly Steve is bringing out the cards and together they begin setting up the young lovers' doom. Except things don't exactly turn out as planned—or do they?

Suggested Topics: Marriage, Temperament

Characters: 2 males, 2 females

WCCC Series Title: Fit to Be Tied; Keys to Compatibility

FOR BETTER OR WORSE—PART III by Donna Lagerquist

The sketch opens with Marsha and Kurt in their first marriage counseling session. The sketch is a mix of humor and soberness as the two reveal the story of their courtship. The conclusion leaves the audience with the idea that a healthy marriage begins before the wedding day.

Suggested Topics: Courtship, Marriage

Characters: 1 male, 1 female, 1 either male or female

WCCC Series Title: Fit to Be Tied; Making Your Courtship Count

FOR BETTER OR WORSE—PART IV by Sharon Sherbondy

Dan and Lisa have been married for a while and love is still in the air—or so Lisa tells Paula over the phone. Lisa also talks of her anger and frustration with her dad's controlling and authoritative personality. When Dan comes home, Lisa's happy marriage slowly begins to unravel as she sees clearly for the first time that she's married a man just like her father.

Suggested Topics: Marriage

Characters: 1 male, 1 female

WCCC Series Title: Fit to Be Tied; Now That I Married the Wrong Person

FOR BETTER OR WORSE—PART V by Sharon Sherbondy

It's 11:15 p.m. Steve's asleep on the couch. Paula heads for bed when suddenly Steve wakes up and wants to "you know." Paula becomes furious. What ensues is an honest look at the pain Paula has in feeling like "the last thought of the day."

Suggested Topics: Marriage

Characters: 1 male, 1 female

WCCC Series Title: Fit to Be Tied; Keeping Romance Alive

FOR BETTER OR WORSE—PART VI by Donna Lagerquist

The three couples introduced to the audience in Part I are reunited at a Christmas Party. The scene opens with the group watching home movies. A few of the characters share childhood memories, impressing us with the importance of family relationships. The sketch closes with Marsha and Kurt sharing the news of their pregnancy. We see how each of the couples has worked and is continuing to work on their marriage and the blessings they receive.

Suggested Topics: Family, Family of God, The importance of friends

Characters: 3 males, 3 females

WCCC Series Title: Fit to Be Tied; Strengthening Family Ties

FOR IMAGE SAKE by Cathy Peters

Bob will do anything to get ahead and now he's paying the price. He has lied to everyone at work about his family and possessions. Bob comically scrambles to make things appear true when his boss invites himself to dinner in order to meet his family.

Suggested Topics: Honesty

Characters: 3 males, 1 female

WCCC Series Title: Telling the Truth to Each Other; Truth or Consequences

FOR THE LOVE OF MONEY by Cathy Peters

This six-character "rap" takes a look at people's unhealthy obsessions with money. Credit Card Carla, Loan Shark Larry, Status Sam, Gullible Gloria, Miser Mike, and Tina Teenager are the characters that rap their views.

Suggested Topics: Money

Characters: 3 males, 3 females

WCCC Series Title: Money, Sex, and Power; Money

FORGIVE AGAIN? by Sharon Sherbondy

Susan is furious. She's just spent another evening humiliated by her husband Jerry's stories. It seems that every time they're with friends she becomes the brunt of Jerry's jokes. And this time she's had it. She's not going to be so quick to forgive as she has in the past.

Suggested Topics: Forgiving others

Characters: 1 male, 1 female

WCCC Series Title: The God of the Second Chance; Giving Second Chances

FOURTH OF JULY by Donna Lagerquist

A family watching fireworks is joined by the likable bag lady Vivian. The son, Elliott, takes a real liking to her, but his parents are naturally standoffish. Elliott can't understand why she doesn't have the benefits associated with living in America the land of opportunity, especially when Vivian is truly patriotic (in her eccentric sort of way). The sketch ends as the parents awkwardly decide to move to a different spot to get away from her in spite of Elliott's protest.

Suggested Topics: Fourth of July, The homeless

Characters: 1 male, two females, one child

WCCC Series Title: After the Fireworks

FULL-SERVICE STATIONS AND OTHER MYTHS by Donna Lagerquist

Jane has to deliver a company presentation on the importance and benefits of service. Instead, she reviews her frustrating experiences with a gas station attendant, an answering service operator, a night watchman, and the police department. She is left pondering, "Whatever happened to the idea of one person serving another?"

Suggested Topics: Serving

Characters: 1 male, 1 female

WCCC Series Title: Rediscovering the Kingdom of God

FULLY DEVOTED SAILORS by Donna Lagerquist

Demonstrates the misunderstanding many have regarding life as a fully devoted follower of Christ by comparing life as a sailor to life as a Christian. Too often people assume Christianity promises them a miserable existence, void of any pleasure. But commitment to Christ produces joy, not drudgery.

Suggested Topics: Joy, Misconceptions of following Christ

Characters: 1 male, 1 female, 7 either male or female

WCCC Series Title: The Benefits of Knowing God

FUNNY GIRL by Donna Lagerquist

Margo, the "funny girl," tells her story of being overweight from her youth. As a child, she is teased by her brother, in high school she learns how to generate laughter from embarrassment, and by college has discovered making people laugh is the only way to get them to notice her and like her. She even tries a stint as a stand-up comic—though in the end, as she huddles in a closet with a Twinkie, she still feels lost in the crowd.

Suggested Topics: Being an outsider, Need for acceptance

Characters: 1 male, 2 females (multiple roles for 1 man and 1 woman)

WCCC Series Title: What Jesus Would Say to … Madonna

THE GAME OF LIFE by Steve Pederson and Judson Poling

This sketch is a parody on the board game "The Game Of Life." An "everyman" character spins the wheel and begins the game. He's confronted along the way with choices that will determine the game's outcome. He loses, but when the narrator gets ready to put the game away the man's wife stops him. She thinks if the right choices are made she'll do better.

Suggested Topics: Search for meaning, Spiritual seeking

Characters: 1 male, 1 female, 1 narrator

WCCC Series Title: The Seasons of a Spiritual Life; Spiritual Seeking; Negotiating the Maze of Life; God's Role in Decision Making

THE GARDENERS by Judson Poling

To explain the New Age Movement this sketch goes back to the Garden of Eden. Similar to those following the New Age philosophy, Adam and Eve want to be gods and control their own destiny. Through humor, aspects of the New Age are exposed.

Suggested Topics: New Age movement

Characters: 1 male, 1 female

WCCC Series Title: Alternatives to Christianity; The New Age Movement

GETTING THE NOD by Judson Poling

Doug and Mark have two different ways of viewing and handling failure. Mark plays the corporate game but finds out Doug's honesty earns him the respect of his boss. It also earns him the opportunity at a second chance.

Suggested Topics: Honesty, Integrity, Handling failures, Business ethics

Characters: 2 males, 1 either male or female

WCCC Series Title: Guess Who's Coming to Dinner

GO AWAY GOD by Various Authors

This is a commercial for "Go Away God," a new product guaranteeing to ease one's conscience and drown out God's "still small voice." A salesman, with the help of two customers, shows us the effectiveness of these pills which allow people to do what they want without the consequences of guilt. In the end, we witness the futility of such an approach.

Suggested Topics: Listening to God, Leadings from God

Characters: 2 males, 1 female

WCCC Series Title: Leadings From God; The Importance of Leadings

GOING PUBLIC by Donna Lagerquist

This sketch is a modern-day allegory about "going public" with your faith. Henry Parker Brown goes to his neighborhood barber shop. In his world, however, everyone wears trench coats, sunglasses, gloves—in short, everyone is a secret agent afraid of being seen or recognized. As Henry announces his plans to go public, the others in the shop are aghast. As he peels off the layers, he encourages them to go public too, but no one else will follow. Henry exits elated, and they wonder if maybe they ought to consider it too.

Suggested Topics: Baptism (public confession of Christ), Living openly for Christ

Characters: 2 males, 2 females, 1 offstage narrator

WCCC Series Title: Baptism

GOOD FRIDAY 1990 by Steve Pederson and Judson Poling

Included are two short sketches, the first one features Mary Magdalene and Judas, the second one Mary Magdalene and Joseph of Arimathea. Mary encounters Judas as he is leaving the upper room to betray Christ. Not realizing his intentions, Mary tells Judas she has been sent by Joseph (a member of the Sanhedrin, but a follower of Christ) to warn Jesus of impending danger. Eventually Mary realizes what Judas is about to do. The second sketch takes place outside the High Priest's

chamber where Jesus is being interrogated by the Sanhedrin. Joseph has left because he can no longer tolerate what is going on. He meets Mary, who awaits news; together they reflect on what Jesus means to them, fully realizing what will likely happen to their Master.

Suggested Topics: Good Friday

Characters: 2 males, 1 female

WCCC Series Title: Good Friday Service 1990

GOOD FRIDAY 1991, SCENE I by Steve Pederson and Judson Poling

This sketch and the following one both portray Jesus and the disciples in a very human, touching, and even at times humorous light. The emphasis is on trying to make the gospel accounts contemporary without dating them, and on wanting the audience to see the characters and identify with them. Jesus is the Son of God, but His role as Servant is stressed in these sketches. The sketch focuses on the foot-washing episode. Peter, John, and Mary prepare the Upper Room, discussing the imminent danger Jesus faces. The supper begins but Jesus immediately explains His mission among them through the act of washing their feet. The scene ends with Jesus admonishing them to "serve others, even as I have served you." (*Note:* This sketch can be used with or without Scene II.)

Suggested Topics: Good Friday, Serving others

Characters: Jesus character, 12 disciples, 2 females

WCCC Series Title: Good Friday Service 1991

GOOD FRIDAY 1991, SCENE II by Judson Poling

This second sketch picks up later in the "Last Supper" scene. Thomas expresses concern that Jesus didn't exploit the opportunities the masses' enthusiasm offered Him. Mary agrees, adding the warning that word on the street is He's soon to be betrayed. Jesus, of course, knows all this, but takes it one step further—one of them will be the betrayer. After all deny this (Peter most vehemently), Jesus explains their need to abide in Him to bear fruit. Tension breaks out between Peter and Thomas over the "number two spot," but Jesus adds to his prediction of His betrayal the warning to Peter that he will deny Him. Once again, Jesus returns to the "servant" theme and ends with the establishment of the Eucharist as Judas slips out to seal both their fates. (*Note:* This sketch can be used with or without Scene I.)

Suggested Topics: Good Friday

Characters: Jesus character, 12 disciples, 2 females

WCCC Series Title: Good Friday Service 1991

GRAND CANYON by Daniel S. Johnson

In a doleful poetic style, a husband and wife tell the story of disillusionment and deterioration within their relatively short marriage. Expectations haven't been met, and both aren't sure they can go on. Options of a divorce and an affair look enticing. In a surprise twist, the story ends with the wife receiving a doctor's report: "I have good news for you."

Suggested Topics: Marriage

Characters: 1 male, 1 female

WCCC Series Title: The Greatest Sermon in History

GREAT EXPECTATIONS by Sharon Sherbondy

It seems as if Kathy and Greg's long awaited prayer has finally been answered. In a few hours they will be parents. Unexpectedly, the birth mother changes her mind about the adoption. Kathy and Greg are again left childless and broken wondering why God hasn't answered their prayers.

Suggested Topics: Unanswered prayer

Characters: 1 male, 2 females

WCCC Series Title: The Power of Prayer; The Mystery of Unanswered Prayer

GUIDANCE COUNSELORS by Judson Poling

Two parents meet with a school counselor to discuss the problems their third-grade son is having in school. The counselor is concerned that their son's view of reality is distorted because of too much TV. The parents, who seem to sincerely want to help their son, point out that a similar problem occurred with friends of theirs whose daughter got involved with the wrong crowd and for that reason had trouble in school. Their friends, however, are Dan and Rosanne from the TV show *Rosanne.* In the discussion that follows, the parents talk about some of their other friends: Laura and Rob Petrie, the Bradys, the Waltons, the Huxtables, Barney and Betty Rubble—all as if they were real people in their lives. It's now clear to the counselor where the boy's problems come from—and he wants to refer them to a therapist. Not wanting a complete stranger, they come up with an idea: how about Bob Newhart! When the counselor points out he's been canceled, the couple screams in disbelief.

Suggested Topics: Sources for values, The power of TV, Parenting
Characters: 2 males, 1 female
WCCC Series Title: God Talk; What Jesus Would Say to … Murphy Brown

HALF-BAKED by Donna Lagerquist

In this light comedy, a woman becomes frustrated at her bakery because they can't find her cheesecake order, and the clerk behind the counter doesn't speak English well. She expresses her frustration to her friend who is with her, and the friend is surprised at the borderline racist comments she makes. As she finally slams her receipt on the counter and demands her money back, the clerk points out that she'll have to go to another bakery—because that's where she ordered her cheesecake!

Suggested Topics: Racism, Prejudice
Characters: 1 male, 2 females
WCCC Series Title: One Modern Moral Trifecta; Racism

HANDS OFF by Sharon Sherbondy

The sketch opens with dating couple Randy and Lana enjoying a romantic dinner for two. The rest of the evening takes a comical twist as we watch this couple keep true to their "decision to not … you know. …" They are hit from all sides of our culture—radio, magazines, tv, movies, and peers. The audience will be laughing as they watch this couple avoid these snares, but will be left with a real picture of the struggles singles face.

Suggested Topics: Sex, Dating, Temptation
Characters: 1 male, 1 female
WCCC Series Title: Changing Times; Changing American Sexuality

HANK'S HANDLES by Judson Poling

Hank, our main character, demonstrates to the audience how he manages the many demands in his life. He keeps everyone on strings and controls their interactions. Of course, life isn't easily manipulated—and Hank becomes tied up in knots.

Suggested Topics: Time management
Characters: 5 males, 3 females
WCCC Series Title: Signs of the Times; Reduce Speed

HAPPY EASTER by Donna Lagerquist

Through short vignettes, we see the confusion about the meaning of Easter. A 10-year-old struggles to accept her silly looking polka-dot Easter dress made by grandma, which matches her mom's. When Dad enters, he's wearing a polka-dot tie and lapel hankie made from the same cloth! In the next scene, two moms cheer on their kids at an Easter-egg hunt. A dad enters dressed up as the "Easter Barney" (the costume store was out of bunny costumes, only Barney the Dinosaur). Other than candy, eggs, and prizes no one has a clue as to what Easter is all about. Finally a grad student daughter and mother argue about going to a family gathering at Aunt Fran's. The daughter wants to head for Florida to avoid the hassles of having to explain her broken engagement to the rest of the family and painfully reminds her mother of the shame of her recent divorce. She laments the scorn she'll receive because of how she "can't keep a man around, just like my mother." The on-stage narrator sums up at the end that despite the obvious lack of personal happiness for many, it is the empty tomb that gives us hope.

Suggested Topics: Easter
Characters: 3 males, 5 females, 1 ten-year-old girl (by double casting, all adult parts can be played by 2 women and 2 men)
WCCC Series Title: Easter Celebration 1994

HONESTLY SPEAKING by Debra Poling

We all struggle with allowing God to recreate and redefine us despite our insecurities and past failures. It's hard to stop telling ourselves things we've become so accustomed to hearing in our own head: "I'm dumb!" "No one really likes me" or "I'm worthless." A dinner party with a few friends becomes a very awkward situation when Penny's negative self-talk overwhelms her.

Suggested Topics: Positive self-talk, Self-esteem
Characters: 3 males, 3 females
WCCC Series Title: Telling the Truth to Yourself; Secret Conversations

HORSEFEATHERS AND NOSEFLY by Judson Poling

Dr. Horsefeathers and his assistant Clarence Nosefly offer help to people trying to live the Christian life. They offer outlandish products such as the "straight jacket of morality," which protects people from doing things wrong. Their approach clearly illustrates the ridiculousness of easy answers to problems we face in the Christian life.

Suggested Topics: Christian living, Obedience
Characters: 2 male or female "helpers"
WCCC Series Title: Christianity 101; The Miracle of the Christian Life

AN HOUR ON WEDNESDAY by Sharon Sherbondy

Chris and Laura are a couple living in the fast track. Their highly scheduled existence leaves them little time for each other. When Laura reveals she is pregnant, Chris's machine-like response is "February is a bad month." Laura ends up hurt by his insensitivity. While much of the sketch is comic, it moves toward a very poignant ending.

Suggested Topics: Marriage, Damaging effects of a fast-paced life
Characters: 1 male, 1 female
WCCC Series Title: Honest to God

HUNGRY CHILDREN by Donna Lagerquist

A sobering look at the destructive effects of careless family communication. As a family eats their supper, Dad's sour, hostile attitude takes its toll on Mom and the kids. He's critical and complaining and no one escapes his attacks. When he picks on his teenage daughter for how she's starving herself, she runs out of the room exasperated. Her little brother want to go "give her something," but Dad insists no one should cater to her. But the brother doesn't want to give her food—he wants to give her a hug.

Suggested Topics: Parenting, Poor family communication, Anger, Control issues
Characters: 1 male, 1 female, 1 boy, 1 teenage girl
WCCC Series Title: Facing the Family Challenge; Fragile: Handle With Care

I DON'T WANT TO FIGHT YOU ANYMORE by Debra Poling

This monologue eavesdrops on a conversation between a woman and God. She describes her frustration at obeying God in an effort to be the new creation He desires. He demands a lot. She reminds God that she lacked a loving father role model in her earthly father. She felt controlled by her father, and now isn't sure she's willing to let God control her life. But she's tired of fighting, and needs to make a decision.

Suggested Topics: Relationship with God, Giving up control, Our value to God
Characters: 1 female
WCCC Series Title: Developing a Daring Faith; Obeying God; God's Outrageous Claims; Unmasking Our Future

I KNOW WHAT YOU WANT by Judson Poling

Using a combination of two dramatic styles—choral speaking and short monologue—four characters representing the child roles of a dysfunctional family (i.e., super achiever, clown, scapegoat, and lost child) reflect on learning the rules of life's most important game: "I know what you want." They each relate the formative experiences from their childhood that taught them how to relate to other's expectations. As adults, they now believe they've got it all figured out, but then God shows up with totally foreign expectations. Having never experienced this kind of unconditional love, they are now left with the question, "I wonder what He wants?"

Suggested Topics: Evangelism, God's love, Dysfunctional families
Characters: 2 males, 2 females
WCCC Series Title: Building Bigger Hearts—Part III

IDOL MINDS by Cathy Peters

An angel is sent to Chicago to find one person faithful to God. He finds this isn't an easy task. He talks with four people, Sam the Gam, a man whose main interest is women, Gwendolyn Gucci, who's sold out to keeping up with the latest fashions, Barry Bear Fan, whose devotion belongs to the Chicago Bears, and Nellie New Age, who believes there is a "god" in each of us.

Suggested Topics: Priorities, No other gods before Him
Characters: 3 males, 2 females
WCCC Series Title: God Has Feelings Too; What Makes God Jealous

IMPRESSIONS, INC. by Judson Poling

With spiritual makeovers as his specialty, Dr. P. W. Donnenuff "assists" a new customer at his Impressions, Inc. consulting firm. From knee-expanders that give the impression of having spent hours in prayer to onion ring "glasses" that keep the wearer's eyes in a perpetual state of tears of repentance, Dr. Donnenuff remakes his clients so they can "look" like spiritual giants ("without any thyroid complications"). This is a humorous spoof of applying Christianity from the outside in—with minimal cost at a fraction of the effort.

Suggested Topics: Skin-deep Christianity, Christian in appearance only
Characters: 2 males, 1 female
WCCC Series Title: It's My Turn Now; Cosmetic Christianity

IN PURSUIT OF HAPPINESS by Sharon Sherbondy

Janice seems to have everything she needs but she can't keep up with everything she wants. Her husband thinks she expects too much out of life. That scares and saddens Janice because nothing seems to fill the emptiness she's feeling.

Suggested Topics: Contentment, Possessions
Characters: 1 male, 1 female
WCCC Series Title: What Can Fill an Empty Frame?

IN PURSUIT OF PASSION by Judson Poling

Jerry has planned a romantic evening for two, but much to his surprise Dawn isn't interested. Earlier that day they had an argument which is yet to be resolved. Dawn wants to talk about it, but Jerry wants to resolve it in the bedroom. Two modern day "experts" (Dr. Ruth and the Church Lady from *Saturday Night Live*) enter the scene to offer their advice on sexual satisfaction in marriage.

Suggested Topics: Sex, Marriage
Characters: 2 males, 2 females
WCCC Series Title: Money, Sex, and Power; Sex

IN THE DARK by Donna Lagerquist

As a couple prepares to go out with friends, the wife tries to re-record the answering machine message. In doing so, she hears a previously unheard message from her husband and young daughter. She is visibly moved—painfully, we realize her daughter is dead. The husband re-enters, and the two come once again to an apparently oft repeated place of grief and anger. In the end, she can't go out with the friends as planned, and the lights fade as she hugs her daughter's picture.

Suggested Topics: Death of a child; Grief
Characters: 1 male, 1 female
WCCC Series Title: The Greatest Sermon in History

THE INTRUDER by Sharon Sherbondy

A woman is studying for a nursing exam when the voice of her father comes back to haunt her. His criticisms, sneers, and lack of support verbalized over the years are now virtually resident in her even though he's been dead for two years. He steps out onto the stage and the two continue talking though he is only a phantom. He calls attention to her failed marriage and supposed neglect of her kids, all intended to make her feel inadequate. Even her newfound relationship with God is fodder for his belittling comments. The sketch ends with his final jeer: "Who knows you better than your father?"

Suggested Topics: Self-image, Destructive parenting, God's love in spite of failure
Characters: 1 male, 1 female
WCCC Series Title: The Greatest Sermon in History; God's Inclination

IN ... WE TRUST by Judson Poling

In this monologue, a man struggles with trust in the everyday relationships of life. His son has had a recent accident, so he is reluctant to trust his driving. His wife has embarrassed him in front of some coworkers, as well as upset his placid marriage with demands he be more sensitive and meet her needs. Every relationship in his life, he confesses, boils down to somebody "using" somebody else, a point with which he bluntly stabs the audience. Then there's trust in God, a whole different subject. Or is it?

Suggested Topics: Trust, Difficulty trusting God, Father/husband role
Characters: 1 male
WCCC Series Title: Giving and Receiving Love; Trust

IS "NOTHING" SACRED? by Judson Poling

Sam is invited by his friend Mark to a meeting of a new religious group that combines faith with science. As the meeting begins, Sam realizes this is a bizarre group. The "Nihilo Master" leads the members in the ritual, and he unveils the meaning behind all of life and the source of everything that is—a big zero. Everything has come from nothing, everything is going toward nothing, therefore everyone and everything is nothing. This is the message of modern scientific "religion" and this humorous satire leaves the audience laughingly aware of the logical outcome of this prevailing worldview.

Suggested Topics: Evolution, Creation, Modern science
Characters: 3 males, and at least 4 others in group
WCCC Series Title: Believing the Unbelievable; The Case for Creation

"IT" by Judson Poling

This parody shows how people become deceived into believing that a relationship with Christ will keep away much of the suffering and pain of life. "Real Life" catches up with a happy couple and dumps a "load" of problems on them. They try to make Real Life go away by threatening to have "It" get after him. They come to find that they have only made themselves easier targets by ignoring Real Life.

Suggested Topics: Dealing with problems, Vulnerability of new believers
Characters: 2 males, 1 female
WCCC Series Title: Dealing With Discouragement

IT'S A NEW YEAR ... AGAIN by Judson Poling

It's a new year and Fred is already feeling rather defeated as he reviews his New Year's resolutions. Annie, of broadway musical fame, enters optimistically singing of tomorrow's possibilities. She almost has Fred believing he will succeed in bringing about significant change in his life, when Church Lady, of *Saturday Night Live*, enters rebuking Fred for being a "worthless slug of a human being." In the end, Fred is defeated, opting to watch a football game instead of working on areas of his life that need changing.

Suggested Topics: New Year's, Significant growth/change is difficult
Characters: 2 males, 1 female
WCCC Series Title: Navigating the Nineties

IT'S NO PICNIC by Donna Lagerquist

When Al brings a cooler to his company picnic containing his lap top computer and files, his wife, Cindy, tries to explain to him how ridiculous he is acting. Al is confident that his boss will only talk "work," and wants to be prepared. However, Cindy shows Al the invitation to the picnic which contains a stipulation: no "work talk" is allowed. Instead of relaxing with that information, Al's paranoia increases as he wonders what he'll talk about to people he barely recognizes away from the office! Once they find a group of "picnickers" and join them, Al's fears become humorously valid. The group has a very difficult time talking about anything other than work issues. It's sad commentary on the types of relationships Al has at work. Sadder still (yet quite funny), in the end we find out that Al and Cindy are in the wrong place and thus have joined the wrong company picnic.

Suggested Topics: Work stress, Surface relationships, Our sin
Characters: 3 males, 3 females
WCCC Series Title: Keeping Your Head Up When Your Job Gets You Down

IT'S NOT MY FAULT by Donna Lagerquist

In the setting of a high school principal's office, we see a humorous portrayal of people "passing the buck" for their wrong-doing. When her daughter is caught smoking in the school bathroom, Mrs. Randall sets out to prove that it was not her daughter's fault. In defense-attorney-style, she calls various people "forward" (to the principal's desk) and accuses them of their part in the "crime." Each character pleads innocence by pointing at another, who in turn, does the same. In the end, we find a room full of flustered people, none of whom are willing to take responsibility for their offense.

Suggested Topics: Sin, Taking responsibility for our sin
Characters: 4 females, 3 males
WCCC Series Title: The "S" Word—Sin

IT'S ONLY A MOVIE by Judson Poling

Gina and Bruce are getting ready for a night out with friends. When Lori and Eric arrive, all are concerned it's too cold to go out, so they decide to rent a movie. The problem is they can't agree on what kind to get—and their interests divide strictly along gender lines! The women want romance and adventure—a "chick flick"—while the men want fast cars and guns. They decide to all go together to find something at the video store they can agree on. In the second part of the drama, the women are watching the last few minutes of *Dr. Zhivago,* Kleenex in hand as the men come upstairs from watching their movie, Die Hard 1 and 2. Earlier the women chided the men on the affect movies have on their testosterone levels, but the men now point out how the women have been taken in. The men are smug about their ability to stay in control of their feelings, despite what they watch. After Eric and Lori leave however, we hear Eric yelling offstage at someone who cuts him off as he drives away. Gina gives him a cold stare, and he sheepishly realizes he too has been affected by what he sees.

Suggested Topics: The effects of what we see, Male/female differences, Power of media
Characters: 2 males, 2 females, 1 offstage male voice
WCCC Series Title: The Greatest Sermon in History; Spiritual Eyesight

JUST AN ACQUAINTANCE by Donna Lagerquist

Julie surprises her fiancé, Gary, by dropping by the restaurant where he is waiting to meet his out of town friend Andy. As the subject of the best man is broached, Gary seems defensive. He has no best friend … "its a girl thing." Julie points out that Andy would qualify, though Gary thinks his brother should do it because he "owes him." Just then Andy comes by, and Julie has to leave. As Gary and Andy get reacquainted, it is obvious their lives are going in separate directions. Gary is embarrassed when Andy finds out that he's a waiter at the restaurant they're at. Instead of drawing closer, the two talk of sports and other superficialities, and in the end, when Andy's off making a call, Gary tells his waitress Andy is merely "a guy I went to college with … just an acquaintance."

Suggested Topics: Relationships among men, Community
Characters: 2 males, 2 females
WCCC Series Title: The Reward for Relational Authenticity

JUST AS I AM by Various Authors

In this monologue (based on the true experience of a homosexual) a man openly and honestly addresses a church congregation. He recounts his struggle, including the lack of understanding by his friends and his father. The rejection caused him to seek solace in bars and alcohol, but the experience left him empty. He is thinking of turning his struggles over to Christ, but wonders if the church is ready for the likes of him.

Suggested Topics: Homosexuality
Characters: 1 male
WCCC Series Title: Modern-day Madness; Hope for the Homosexual

JUST IN CASE by Various Authors

Margaret is accosted by a high pressure salesman promising her assurance if God should fail her. This "Just in Case Kit" (parodies Ephesians 6) includes items like the "knee pads of pessimism," the "shield of fallacy" the "helmet of humanism" and the "almighty machete." This ridiculous sketch confronts us with our own level of trust in God.

Suggested Topics: Trusting God, Almighty God
Characters: 1 male, 1 female
WCCC Series Title: Seven Wonders of the Spiritual World; God Can Be Trusted; Can I Trust a Silent God

JUST LOOKING by Sharon Sherbondy

A wife confronts her husband with shocking news: she has "found something" in their teenage son's room. When she pulls out the swimsuit issue of a sports magazine, the husband shrugs it off as nothing to be concerned about. Her anxiety about their son's sexual purity takes a surprising turn as she reveals the hurt she has felt all these years about how her husband notices other women. She is embarrassed—and scared. She's not getting any younger and she wants to know her husband won't be lured by another woman's beauty. For the first time he sees what his careless gazes cost his wife. At the conclusion, he vows, "There's only one woman for me—" but he is good-naturedly chased off when he teases, "and she's right here on page 23, did you see her?"

Suggested Topics: Eye causing you to stumble, Purity of thoughts
Characters: 1 male, 1 female
WCCC Series Title: The Greatest Sermon in History

JUST SAY IT! by Donna Lagerquist

In an attempt to get her husband to say he loves her, Terri installs a subliminal message system. This machine gets Ed to say all those things she's been longing to hear. However, Terri discovers they don't satisfy her because Ed isn't saying them on his own.

Suggested Topics: Marriage communication, Importance of saying I love you
Characters: 1 male, 1 female, 1 either male or female
WCCC Series Title: The Lost Art of Loving; Please Speak My Language

KEEPING TABS by Sharon Sherbondy

Nancy is so compulsive in her need not be obligated to anyone that she keeps tabs on everything she and her husband receive. She believes that nothing is given without something being expected in return. Anonymously, flowers arrive and Nancy threatens to call the florist to find out who she "owes." When her husband confesses that he sent them "just because he loves her" she thinks it is because he wants something.

Suggested Topics: Gifts of grace
Characters: 1 male, 1 female
WCCC Series Title: Amazing Grace; The Gifts of Grace; Surprised by God; Surprised by God's Love

THE KILLING SPREE by Sharon Sherbondy

Most of us believe we have nothing to worry about when it comes to the sixth Commandment. But this sketch helps us take a comical look at the murder we commit with our mouth. During a conversation, Jane enters the "Twilight Zone" where consequences of her caustic tongue are deadly. It's too late when Jane realizes the lesson, she's already "killed" her best friend, her dog, her daughter, and a solicitor.

Suggested Topics: Sixth Commandment, Gossip
Characters: 1 male, 3 females
WCCC Series Title: Sixth Commandment; Respect Human Life

THE KNOWING YEARS by Donna Lagerquist

This sketch looks at the season of omniscience, adolescence. Ruthie, Kate, and Mandy are three high school cheerleaders who think they know more about life and what matters than the adults around them.

Suggested Topics: Spiritual adolescence, adolescence

Characters: 3 females
WCCC Series Title: Seasons of a Spiritual Life; Spiritual Adolescence

THE LAMAZE CLASS by Judson Poling

Paul and Lynn Eggshell return, this time as part of a Lamaze class preparing for their baby's arrival. As usual, they are petrified by the slightest unusual sound, circumstance, or challenge. When the conversation in the class gets around to what values parents should give to their children, Paul and Lynn panic at their absence of clear, firmly held values. What store would you go to get values? True Value (hardware store)? Given their lack in this area, Lynn decides to wait to have the baby, but Paul points out it's too late now!

Suggested Topics: Sources for values, Parenting
Characters: 3 males, 4 females
WCCC Series Title: Defining Family Values; Origin of Values

THE LANE OF LIFE by Deb Poling

A mime with narration. A person walking down life's lane hears and believes what others are saying: "You're ugly!" "You're stupid!" "You're worthless." But a kindly stranger offers a new perspective: "You matter to God!" At first unconvinced, the person gradually comes to believe this wonderful news … and reaches out to share it with others.

Suggested Topics: Salvation, Evangelism, Self-esteem
Characters: 5 either male or female, 1 offstage narrator
WCCC Series Title: Easter Celebration; People Matter to God; Celebration of Baptism
Note: This sketch is very similar to a later version of this sketch titled You Matter To God

LET ME GO by Judson Poling

A mom is visiting her "twentysomething" daughter who has just moved into her first apartment on her own. Mom has been organizing the house all day when Deb comes home from work. She is put off by all the changes her mother has made to her living space, though Mom shrugs it off, thinking she's been doing Deb a favor. Alphabetizing her soup cans is one thing, but when Deb discovers her mom has also interfered with a romantic relationship, she explodes. After some harsh words, Mom weakens, hurt that her role as mother is no longer needed (she's also just recently been widowed). Deb tries to apologize, and explains she wants a mother, not a caretaker. But Mom is uncertain how she can be one without the other.

Suggested Topics: Parenting, Letting go of adult children
Characters: 2 females
WCCC Series Title: Facing the Family Challenge; The Future of the Family

LIFE CYCLE by Sharon Sherbondy

Two women find themselves next to each other on exercise bikes at the health club. They begin conversing and discover they are both worn-out moms who use the health club as an escape—anything "to get out of the house." Almost by accident, Linda tells Ann that she is also in a Bible study group. When she realizes Ann is non-churched, Linda gets nervous, pedals faster, and somewhat self-consciously talks about a few practical dimensions of her faith. By the time Ann leaves, it's clear that the women enjoy an affinity which will likely result in future deeper conversations.

Suggested Topics: Witnessing, Making a difference, Starting new relationships
Characters: 2 females
WCCC Series Title: For Mature Audiences Only—What Motivates Mature Christians

LIFESTYLES OF THE OBSCURED AND INDEBTED by Cathy Peters

This sketch takes an exaggerated look at how people mismanage money in order to "keep up with the Joneses." It begins when Stanley and Henrietta Havemore notice a new car in Charlie Contendo's driveway. We see a chain reaction of spending spread throughout the neighborhood. When Charlie finally enters the scene at the end, everyone is in for a surprise.

Suggested Topics: Money, coveting, possessions

Characters: 4 males, 3 females
WCCC Series Title: Your Money Matters; Determining a Standard of Living

LIFETIME DEAL by Brian Svenkeson/Steve Pederson/Mark Demel

Jack and David have negotiated to sell the company they've worked ten years to build. Jack is elated at the $9 million offer an investment group has proposed, but David can only find fault. As they try to decide on what they're going to do, Jack challenges David on his over-commitment to his business. When David defensively answers that he's invested his life here, Jack agrees: "You've invested your life; I've invested my time." Jack leaves, pleading with David to consider the offer. After Jack is gone, David calls his wife and unexpectedly tells her that the deal fell through, and that he's planning to buy Jack out.

Suggested Topics: Work, Workaholism
Characters: 2 males
WCCC Series Title: Your Work Matters to God

LITTLE WHAT'S HIS FACE by Sharon Sherbondy

A young couple still in the hospital try to name their infant son born just before Christmas. Extended family members get involved in the debate and finally a decision is made. The second half of this drama focuses on the father who performs a monologue telling his infant son what he promises to give him for Christmas. The father confesses that someday he'll fail his son, but the Savior never will.

Suggested Topics: Christmas, Parenting
Characters: 3 males, 3 females
WCCC Series Title: Christmas Eve 1986

LIZZIE AND LEROY by Sharon Sherbondy

This is a familiar tale of how "things" don't provide ultimate fulfillment. The melodramatic Southern belle, Lizzie, tells the tragic story of how her husband's promotion in a chicken ranch ultimately provided them with everything they wanted, except happiness. LeRoy eventually leaves Lizzie in search of "it." Lizzie ends up alone, hoping LeRoy will return with news of what he's discovered.

Suggested Topics: Only God satisfies, Material goods don't provide ultimate happiness
Characters: 1 male, 1 female, piano player (optional)
WCCC Series Title: Surprised by God; Surprised by God's Satisfaction

LONELY AT THE TOP by Judson Poling

An obviously overworked politician talks on the phone with his assistant about delegates from a Political Action Committee who dropped by unexpectedly. He manages to stall them for a few minutes, during which he laments the incessant demands on him to please and appease. He also vilifies those around him who constantly want to use him. In fact, just recently he was forced to get rid of a group's political enemy when he himself found the man rather harmless, if not a bit interesting. As he musters up the energy to meet the delegation in his waiting room, he can't understand what crisis could be so urgent—he got rid of their enemy on Friday, so why do they have to bother him on Sunday morning? As he walks out, we realize Pilate—dressed in a modern suit—is about to find out about the resurrection of Jesus.

Suggested Topics: The perils of power, A leader's need for divine help, Easter
Characters: 1 male
WCCC Series Title: The Greatest Sermon in History

LUCKY DAY AT THE BALLPARK by Sharon Sherbondy

Josh (about 13) and his grandfather are at a Cubs ball game. Josh has been anxiously waiting for his dad to arrive, but he doesn't appear until the game is almost finished. The grandfather is upset with his son's seeming insensitivity to Josh's needs. In spite of marriage problems which plague the father, the grandfather tells him that he is the most important person in Josh's life and that he needs to "be there" for him. It's obvious the grandfather's challenge has been heard, because the father changes some future plans to accommodate his son. The sketch ends with Josh catching a fly ball, which he then gives to his dad.

Suggested Topics: Father's Day, Proper priorities
Characters: 2 males, 1 boy
WCCC Series Title: Father's Day

THE LUNCHEON by Sharon Sherbondy

This sketch painfully portrays a deteriorating mother-daughter relationship. From the moment they are seated in the restaurant, Susan begins defensively fielding her mom's disapproving comments. When Susan can take it no more, she lets her mother know how she really feels. To Susan's surprise, her mom has some dissatisfied and hurt feelings, too. The scene ends with the two ready to try some changes.

Suggested Topics: Motherhood, Family relationships, Honesty
Characters: 3 females
WCCC Series Title: Telling Truth to Each Other; Expressing Positive Emotions

THE LURES OF LIFE by Debra Poling

This mime features Charlie Chaplin and the Keystone Cops. Charlie illegally gets money and experiences the pleasure money can buy: a girlfriend, a cruise, world travels. But not before having to outwit the Keystone Cops. With the cops off his trail, he and his girlfriend are free to pursue pleasure. Chaplin eventually realizes, however, the emptiness of this lifestyle and walks away from it all.

Suggested Topics: Adventurism, The pleasures of the world don't satisfy
Characters: 5 males, 1 female
WCCC Series Title: Christianity's Greatest Competition; Adventurism

MAN OF THE YEAR by Judson Poling

Richard Hanson is honored as "Man of the Year," yet as he begins to give his speech, memories of his past come back to haunt him. Though his outward appearance seems noble enough, the realities of the other side of his life show him up for the sinner he is—even the Man of the Year needs a Savior from moral imperfections.

Suggested Topics: Moralism, Our need for grace
Characters: 5 males, 1 female
WCCC Series Title: Christianity's Greatest Competition; Moralism

MARRIED AND HARRIED by Judson Poling

When Mary and Harry first meet they fall deeply in love and try very hard to please one another. Not being able to deny their feelings, they get married. Reality soon sets in and they learn that love doesn't "just happen." It's something that they have to work at.

Suggested Topics: Marriage
Characters: 1 male, 1 female
WCCC Series Title: Fanning the Flames of Marriage; Why Fires Burn Low

MASTERPIECE by Sharon Sherbondy

A family getting ready to leave for the grandparents' house experience the usual hassle trying to get out the door. What's different this time is that Mom and teenage daughter stay behind to talk about her struggles with her self-esteem. Mom is able to reaffirm her beauty and uniqueness—she is a "masterpiece."

Suggested Topics: Self-esteem, Parenting
Characters: 1 male, 1 female, 2 teenage females
WCCC Series Title: When Temptation Lurks

ME, MYSELF, AND CHRIS by Sharon Sherbondy

Bill and his alter ego battle over the temptation of premarital sex. Bill's alter ego tries every possible tactic and argument but to no avail, Bill sticks to his principles.

Suggested Topics: Sex, Temptation, Dating
Characters: 2 males, 1 female
WCCC Series Title: When Temptation Lurks

MEASURING UP by Judson Poling

In this mime, a boy discovers early in life what others think of him. His friends don't let him play with them—he doesn't "measure up." They show this graphically by pulling out measuring tapes and laughing as they shake their heads and leave their tapes around his neck. When he goes home as a teenager, his family has their measuring tapes too, and intimidate him with them. He enters adulthood with his failed attempts at measuring up still around his neck. Even in business, he can't seem to keep up with peers who make it clear that he doesn't measure up. Finally he is ready to hang himself with the tapes he's collected over the years, but God breaks through. God tells him that someone else has already measured up for him—Jesus died so he wouldn't have to keep trying to make the grade. At God's command, the man shreds the tape measures that have choked him his whole life, and gratefully begins the relationship God has initiated.

Suggested Topics: God's acceptance of us, Self-esteem
Characters: 2 males, 1 female, 1 other male or female
WCCC Series Title: The Greatest Sermon in History

MERE TECHNICALITY by Sharon Sherbondy

Mark comes home and announces to Karen that they're going on a trip together to Cancun, compliments of his business. Karen is not exactly overjoyed, and Mark thinks it's because of the fight they had that morning. It turns out she's uncomfortable with the fact they're living together but aren't married. She's been going back to church, and although she loves him, she wants the relationship to be right. Mark is angry Karen is taking her religion so seriously, and goes upstairs in a huff. Karen is left alone, and curls up with a blanket to sleep on the couch.

Suggested Topics: Living together vs. marriage, The cost of taking a stand for Christ
Characters: 1 male, 1 female
WCCC Series Title: The Greatest Sermon in History; Unmasking Your Master

MERRY CHRISTMAS WITH LOVE by Judson Poling

It's Christmas Eve and Mildred, a widow, is alone because of a heavy snowfall. She looks back at a happier Christmas and asks God to comfort her loneliness. He surprises her with a visit from some carolers.

Suggested Topics: Christmas
Characters: 1 female, 3 male or female carolers
WCCC Series Title: Christmas Eve 1985

THE MIRROR THOUGHT OF IT by Donna Lagerquist

Norm Anderson is being shown a home in the prestigious neighborhood of Beachwood Hills Estates. His eccentric realtor, Mrs. Foley, extols the value of the home and the neighborhood. When she leaves the room for a few minutes, he begins to measure to see if his bed will fit—and hears a voice. It's the mirror talking to him. Norm thinks it's a friend playing a practical joke, but the mirror's detailed knowledge of his life quickly convinces him the voice is in fact the mirror image of his life. The mirror questions Norm's motives for wanting to move, and makes him think about his restlessness and compulsion to want more. When Mrs. Foley returns, he leaves, convinced he doesn't need the "tropic-simulated greenhouse." She's bewildered—but then hears the mirror call her name.

Suggested Topics: Materialism, Workaholism, Striving for more
Characters: 1 male, 1 female, 1 offstage voice
WCCC Series Title: Summer Reflections; Come Unto Me

MISJUDGED LOVE by Brian Svenkeson and Steve Pederson

As an older man enters a hospital room, we learn from his conversation with the nurse that he's here to visit his adult son. When Eddie his son comes in, he is obviously quite sick. As the conversation continues, the awful truth comes out ... he has AIDS. The dad has had trouble accepting both the illness and the lifestyle that produced it. But when all is said and done, Eddie is his son, the son he loves, the son he will stand with till the end.

Suggested Topics: Father's Day, Homosexuality, AIDS
Characters: 2 males, 1 female
WCCC Series Title: Father's Day: Dads ... Whatever You Do

MISTAKEN IDENTITY by Donna Lagerquist

A park district production of the Christmas story causes one woman to question what she believed when she was a girl. She remembers celebrating Christ's birth and then three months later being confused when celebrating his death and resurrection. How did he grow up so fast? Did events happen the way the Bible says? This sketch provides an opportunity to recognize the questions of those who are not regular attenders.

Suggested Topics: Christmas
Characters: 3 males, 2 females, 1 young girl
WCCC Series Title: Christmas Eve 1988

MONDAY NIGHT MEETING by Judson Poling

Wally, a new Christian, struggles with how to act out his faith. In an effort to be godly he overspiritualizes everything and eliminates leisure from his life. Three of the guys from his small group (Bible study) try to explain and demonstrate that a serious commitment to God doesn't negate fun and enjoyment from life.

Suggested Topics: New Christians, Realistic expectations, Discipleship
Characters: 4 males
WCCC Series Title: Telling the Truth to Yourself; Five Deadly Lies

A MOTHER'S DAY by Donna Lagerquist

It's Mother's Day and Julie is disappointed and a little angry that her mother, (an actress in California) isn't able to stay with her and her new-born son while her husband is out of town. Julie reluctantly agrees to her husband's idea of hiring a nanny to come and help while he's gone. When the foreign nanny, Sophie, arrives, Julie is pleasantly surprised by her homey touches, despite a heavy accent and comical mannerisms. However, as time passes, Sophie's homey touches seem all too familiar to what Julie experienced as a child. Finally, to Julie's great surprise, Sophie removes her disguise and reveals her true identity … Julie's mom.

Suggested Topics: Mother's Day
Characters: 1 male, 2 females
WCCC Series Title: Surprised by God; Surprised by God's Power

MR. HIBBS' DAY OFF by Various Authors

This simple but effective mime tells the story of a man whose day off goes differently than he planned. While on his way to the zoo, Mr. Hibbs is confronted by many needy people: a young girl upset over her lost balloon, a woman who has just been robbed, and a hungry, homeless man. Mr. Hibbs stops and helps each person, buying a balloon for the girl, giving his coat to the woman, and lunch to the man. When Mr. Hibbs finally gets to the zoo, it is closed. He is upset, even angry. On his way home, however, he is reminded how meaningful his day has been when the kindness he had earlier demonstrated is returned to him.

Suggested Topics: Serving others, Self-denial, Being used by God
Characters: 3 males, 1 female, 1 child
WCCC Series Title: Becoming a Contagious Christian; Sacrifice

MR. PEEPERS GOES TO SLEEP by Donna Lagerquist

Lisa wants to know why Mr. Peepers, her pet bird, won't move anymore. When her dad says the bird is dead, Lisa demands that he make it "undead." Lisa's mom feels that Lisa isn't old enough to understand death. Lisa's grandmother believes that most people don't understand or accept death. A young child's first experience with death forces the adults in her life to examine their own fears and beliefs.

Suggested Topics: Death, Facing the truth
Characters: 1 male, 2 females, 1 child
WCCC Series Title: Facing Up to Fear; The Fear of Death

MR. P. NOCCHIO by Judson Poling

A man with a very large nose enters a therapist's office. He complains of problems going back to his childhood which have become worse in recent months. At first the therapist thinks he must be talking about self-esteem issues from his big nose. But the client explains his nose is a symptom, that the real problem is he keeps stretching the truth. He is, in fact, Pinocchio—now grown up. The therapist tries to be sympathetic, but alternates between believing Mr. Nocchio's story and wondering if this guy's just plain nuts. The therapist concludes the time with the promise of a quick cure—a lie which causes his nose to suddenly grow as well!

Suggested Topics: Honesty

Characters: 2 males, or 1 female and 1 male
WCCC Series Title: Do You Have What It Takes to Grow? Asking God to Remove Shortcomings

MR. X, MR. Y, AND MR. Z by Judson Poling

Three superficially related neighbors maintain their space and protect themselves from intimacy. Mr. Z, however, is changed by a newcomer, Mr. Smith ("the one with the funny name") who helps him see the joys of stepping out of his comfort zone. Though experiencing some embarrassment and then returning to his protective environment, it is a new beginning—a true friendship has been born, and Mr. Z will never be the same.

Suggested Topics: Friendship, Intimacy
Characters: 4 males, 1 female, 1 narrator
WCCC Series Title: Benefits of Brotherhood; Superficial or Significant

THE MYSTERY OF ROBERT RICHARDSON by Judson Poling

This sketch is comprised of five different monologues which all comment on the character of Robert Richardson, through various stages of his life. The stories told make us realize that Robert was a person who lived a Christ glorifying life.

Suggested Topics: Living the Christian life
Characters: 3 males, 2 females, 1 narrator
WCCC Series Title: How to Be Strong When It Counts

THE NATURE OF LIFE by Sharon Sherbondy

This two-part drama shows a family of four going camping. In the first part, the family is setting up camp, but the kids with their headphones and blow-dryers aren't exactly in the camping mood, and Dad wonders why they even bothered to come. The second part opens later that night with Dad looking through his telescope. At first, no one else is interested, but then the son sees a shooting star. Whithin a few minutes, father and son end up in a shared moment, marveling God's creation.

Suggested Topics: Family, Wonder of creation
Characters: 2 males, 2 females
WCCC Series Title: Family Night

A NICE GUY by Donna Lagerquist

Glen was recently hired to teach 5th grade and brought along a friend, Bill, to help set up the room. Coincidently, this was Bill's alma mater, and Bill shares some funny stories from those years. The mood abruptly changes, however, when Bill discovers the room's radiator still has a bend in it from when he was there. In that spot, a boy in his class, Bobby Heaver was tied to the radiator and had his pants pulled down in front of class. Bill feels the guilt of his participation that day—and also knowing Bobby later committed suicide. Bill knows everyone thinks he's a nice guy on the outside, but his capacity to hurt another human being haunts him. When left alone for a few minutes, Bill tries to apologize to Bobby.

Suggested Topics: Step 5 (12 steps), Admitting failures, Effects of sin
Characters: 2 males
WCCC Series Title: Do You Have What It Takes to Grow? Tell Somebody

NICE TO HAVE AROUND by Donna Lagerquist

This mime demonstrates how the Bible is sometimes viewed as just a nice "item" to have in a household. The narrative shows a woman encountering her Bible at various stages of her life: infancy, childhood, adolescence, marriage, midlife, and eventually at her death. Though the encounters and uses for her Bible are numerous, never once, do they involve opening it and reading it.

Suggested Topics: Attitudes toward the Bible
Characters: 2 males, 1 female
WCCC Series Title: Faith Has Its Reasons; Reasons for Believing in the Bible

NO FUN by Judson Poling

Ginny and Steve, out on a "date," discuss the difficulty they face because of Steve's aunt being in for a visit. Ginny tries to suggest ways they could all have fun, but Steve knows better—his aunt just doesn't ever have fun. The waiter shows Steve's aunt back to the table—and it's the Church Lady (from *Saturday Night Live*). After a brief discussion with Steve and Ginny about the evils of "worldly amusement," she launches into a "rap" and brings home her perspective: "No fun—that's the spiritual life!"

Suggested Topics: Christian lifestyle, Misconceptions about Christianity
Characters: 3 males, 1 female (Church Lady is played by a male)
WCCC Series Title: A Taste of Christianity; A Better Kind of Freedom

NO INTERRUPTIONS by Sharon Sherbondy

This monologue describes one man's struggle with a quiet time. Our character has evaluated his life and assessed a lack of balance and a need for replenishing. So he's instructed his wife and children that he's not to be interrupted for any reason while he's praying. As the sketch progresses, we see he's more than willing to be interrupted.

Suggested Topics: Quiet time, Prayer
Characters: 1 male
WCCC Series Title: Bringing Out the Best in People; Bringing Out the Best in Yourself

NO MORE WOMB by Donna Lagerquist

This sketch takes both a comic and serious look at the issues facing children today. The scene begins inside the womb, where our two characters—a set of fraternal twins—discuss the things they are most looking forward to. As the discussion progresses, they talk about that which they are most afraid of: not being accepted by their peers … not doing well academically … being abducted or abused.

Suggested Topics: The world children face today, Fear of the unknown
Characters: 1 male, 1 female
WCCC Series Title: Changing Times; The Changing American Child

NO THANKS GIVING by Donna Lagerquist

The scene opens with Terri busily placing name cards around her dining room table set for 10. A friend stops by to encourage her not to get too caught up in pleasing others. Then Terri sits and "pre-enacts" what she thinks will happen during the meal. Via a tape, we hear the voices of various family members complaining or needing something, and especially Terri's mother, finding fault in just about everything Terri does. Overwhelmed, she cries out about how tired she is of taking care of everyone else and of pretending that everything is "nice" … and she decides things will be different this year. Terri's caught off guard when her mother enters the dining room and immediately begins "altering" the seating assignments and centerpiece. The confidence Terri had gained moments earlier falls to the wayside in her mother's presence.

Suggested Topics: Truth telling, Needy people
Characters: 3 females
WCCC Series Title: Enriching Your Relationships; Rational Viruses

NOTHING IN COMMON by Steve Pederson

How much in common is necessary to create a platoon? Three prominent women—Katherine Hepburn, Abby Van Buren, and Roseanne Barr—are brought together by a television producer because they represent a cross-section of celebrity women of the '80s. Their goal is to speak on issues that affect today's women. The few things they have in common, being famous and female, mislead the producer to believe they could work together.

Suggested Topics: Choosing platoon members
Characters: 3 females, 1 male
WCCC Series Title: Enlisting in Platoons; Picking Platoon Members

NOTHING TO IT by Donna Lagerquist

After a Halloween party, two couples wind down chatting about what they believe to be "harmless demonic" activities. Three of them wear ghoulish costumes, one is dressed as Bo Peep. "Bo" is uncomfortable with the topic of conversation, yet the others coax her on saying she's making a big deal out of nothing. They continue by reminiscing about Ouija boards, rabbit's feet, childhood voodoo spells, and decide to reen-

act one of their slumber party levitations. Bo resists this too, yet in predictable repetition, the others remind her once again, "There's nothing to it!"

Suggested Topics: Satanism, Spiritual warfare
Characters: 2 males, 2 females
WCCC Series Title: The Rise of Satanism; The Secret World of Satan Worship

THE OFFERING by Judson Poling

It's time for the offering and four people express their reasons for giving. The first chooses not to give because he believes his tithe could be used more wisely by himself. The second gives because of the recognition he might receive. The third hates giving because she feels God is never satisfied with what she offers. The fourth enjoys giving because it is his opportunity to say thanks to God.

Suggested Topics: Tithing
Characters: 3 males, 1 female
WCCC Series Title: Your Money Matters; Discovering The Rewards Of Giving

OH, WHAT A FEELING! by Debra Poling

A husband and wife are out to buy a car—a stripped-down, bottom-of-the-line model. He cautions her to not get carried away with the emotional appeal of the salesman, but to let him be in charge of making the deal. He winds up getting "lost in the feeling" and buying a loaded, top-of-line model.

Suggested Topics: Decision making
Characters: 2 males, 1 female
WCCC Series Title: Negotiating the Maze of Life; Thinkers, Feelers, and Procrastinators

THE OKRA WINDY SHOW by Cathy Peters

This parody of a popular talk show examines the games people play in relationships. Okra Windy, the talk show personality, has three guests who explain their strategy to get what ever they want. Each of her guests, Mary Manipulato, Harry Hintman, and Dr. Buscalliano, have exaggerated approaches to achieve their goals.

Suggested Topics: Honesty in relationships, Communication
Characters: 3 males, 3 females
WCCC Series Title: Telling the Truth to Each Other; Games People Play

THE OLD MAN AND THE LAUNDROMAT by Donna Lagerquist

John, in his sixties, was recently widowed and is now having to do his laundry at the laundromat. Through the course of a conversation with a woman there, he shares his grief, anger, and struggles to do anything—even the laundry—since his wife's death. While helping John "sort," the woman uncovers an inflatable Christmas ornament, a memento of his wife which he keeps because "she blew it up." When the woman's daughter innocently unplugs the ornament, John yells out, and replugs it. Once left alone, he realizes he must let go and slowly lets the air out gently against his cheek.

Suggested Topics: Letting go, Grieving, Dealing with death
Characters: 1 male, 1 female, 1 child
WCCC Series Title: Disappointment With God; When God Seems Silent

ON THE OUTSIDE by Donna Lagerquist

In this monologue, a woman sitting on a park bench across from a church recounts her experience growing up when every week, she sat in church "third row, left of center." Her happy Christian family illusion was shattered one day when her mother announced she and her father were getting a divorce. Now, the "divorcee and her kids" sat in the back of the church, outcasts and unwelcome. She angrily recounts her disappointment at how little those who were supposed to be the "light of the world, salt of the earth" did for her during those difficult years. When she grew up, the woman left the church—and hasn't been back. The closest she gets is "the second park bench, left of the sidewalk."

Suggested Topics: Being salt and light; How churches can sometimes drive people away from God

Characters: 1 female
WCCC Series Title: The Greatest Sermon in History

ON TRACK by Judson Poling

Don and Ruth are having a tough time understanding their son Kevin's attraction to computers. They want him to be involved with sports because of the friends he'll make and the experience it will bring. Computers "can't build character." What they fail to see is Kevin's uniqueness and how best to encourage him.

Suggested Topics: Character building, Forcing people into a mold
Characters: 2 males, 1 female
WCCC Series Title: Bringing Out the Best in People; The How-to's

ON VACATION by Judson Poling

Peter and Nancy are on a plane to a much needed vacation in Colorado. However, he has a hard time relaxing. A combination of guilt, (he'll miss his small group Bible Study), burnout, and another passenger's attempts to witness to him, eventually push him over the edge.

Suggested Topics: Guilt, Leisure time, Inability to slow down
Characters: 2 males, 1 female, 1 either male or female
WCCC Series Title: Ordering Your Private World; Your Recreational World

ONE DAY AT THE ZOO by Judson Poling

This sketch takes a humorous look at a futuristic view of a zoo that houses some endangered species and one of the last examples of a paternal normalus (father) now residing in a zoo. The father interacts with automated facsimiles of his predators: office dictatorus (boss), secretaria hot-to-trotus (seductress), neighborous influencius (friend), and nagus ad infinitum (wife).

Suggested Topics: Father's Day
Characters: 1 narrator, 3 males, 2 females and some offstage voices
WCCC Series Title: Amazing Grace; Gracious Fathers

ONE STEP UP, ONE STEP DOWN by Judson Poling

In this narrated mime, an everyman character faces ambition and the high price it solicits. To be at the top costs him family, friendships, and integrity, but he was left with wealth, a big office, and acceptance. Everyman has difficulty feeling that satisfaction he thought success would bring.

Suggested Topics: Ambition, Priorities
Characters: 4 males (1 can be female)
WCCC Series Title: Taking Care of Business; The Character Crisis

ONE SUNDAY IN THE PARKING LOT by Judson Poling

If cars in a church parking lot could talk, what would they say? This light-hearted sketch answers that question as four cars—an Escort, a BMW, a Celebrity, and a Honda—come to life. One car in particular laments being "driven" all the time and wonders if it's worth it to go on. The key to longevity? Making changes, especially before things get so bad. In regard to the need for preventative maintenance the cars' needs are no different than ours. The sketch ends on a humorous note as the cars play their favorite game, "Parking Lot Shuffle," and move to another spot to confuse their owners.

Suggested Topics: Pace of life
Characters: 4 males or females
WCCC Series Title: For Mature Audiences Only; Marks of a Mature Christian

ONLY CHILD by Donna Lagerquist

Elise is at her college friend Andy's home while Andy's mom is preparing supper. While they make small talk, Mom looks at a package which has arrived in the mail—and is shocked. It's addressed to her deceased son, Jason, who was killed by a drunk driver four years earlier. Andy finally enters, and Mom leaves upset. Andy must finish telling the story about how a crazy kid in a stolen car killed Jason, and didn't even have to go to prison. Instead, the family adopted him. Elise suddenly understands— Andy is the one who hit and killed Jason four years ago, and who was brought into the family and raised as their own.

Suggested Topics: Grace, Outrageous forgiveness, The doctrine of adoption
Characters: 1 male, 2 females
WCCC Series Title: The Greatest Sermon in History

OUT OF CONTROL by Sharon Sherbondy

Steve has the afternoon to prove that he is not a P.O.P. (Push Over Parent). The outcome is that Nick, his son, easily manipulates and controls his father.

Suggested Topics: Father's Day, Parenting
Characters: 2 males and 1 female
WCCC Series Title: Father's Day; Rediscovering Discipline

THE PAINFUL PROCESS by Donna Lagerquist

In this monologue, a woman recounts her struggle to overcome the pain of her abortion. As she remembers the events of that day, she compares the descriptions others gave her to dry cleaning—to having a spot removed. But although that's what she was told it was like, she feels lied to. Yes, there was some physical pain, but that passed fairly quickly. What followed—and haunts her—is the emotional pain. "They told me lots of women have abortions and never think about it again. I'm not one of them." She bluntly tells the audience, "I didn't just remove a spot."

Suggested Topics: Abortion
Characters: 1 female
WCCC Series Title: Our Modern Moral Trifecta

PARLOR TALK by Donna Lagerquist

Bill and Ray meet at a funeral parlor—where both of them are the ones who've died. Ray's wake is heavily attended, mostly by business associates. Bill recently moved from out of town so only his wife, Elaine, is there. As she sits alone and Bill tries in vain to talk to her, Bill's doctor comes in. She tells Elaine about the profound impact Bill's life had, especially on another cancer patient, a little boy named Joey. Despite the small showing at his funeral, Bill's life was a testimony to caring for others, while Ray, although popular even in death, laments he poured his life into his business and "never even got a gold watch!"

Suggested Topics: Death, Living for others, Workaholism
Characters: 3 males, 2 females
WCCC Series Title: The Greatest Sermon in History; The Truth About Heavenly Treasures

PASTOR GENERAL Donna Lagerquist

A couple, new to the area, come to visit Reverend Howitzer at the Army of God Church to ask him a few questions about the church. Reverend Howitzer's dictatorial leadership style comes out in full force as this humorous sketch unfolds.

Suggested Topics: Abusive leadership, The church, Authoritarianism
Characters: 2 males, 2 females

PERMANENT SOLUTION by Sharon Sherbondy

Mary Ann's got a tough career decision to make so she heads to her hair dresser's for some respected advice. Before she can get that, she's bombarded with "advice" from two other women who base their wisdom on talk shows, gossip magazines, and fortune tellers.

Suggested Topics: Decision-making, Whom to listen to
Characters: 4 females
WCCC Series Title: Negotiating the Maze of Life; Developing a Personal Board of Directors

PLANE TALK by Judson Poling

Dan, a nervous, talkative passenger engages Bill, a seasoned business traveler on a plane trip. The conversation turns to spiritual matters when Bill casually observes he saw Dan pray before his meal. Bill expresses his skepticism about God's involvement in the everyday affairs of life—at the very moment the captain announces an engine failure! Bill suddenly becomes panic-stricken, and all his poised confidence gives way to desperate (and comical) pleas for God to help. When the captain announces the crisis has passed and they will be landing soon, Bill goes back to his "got-it-all-together" facade, as if nothing has happened. The

saying "There are no atheists in foxholes" finds an amusing, contemporary counterpart in this sketch.
Suggested Topics: God's presence, Faith, God's feelings
Characters: 2 males, 1 offstage voice (pilot)
WCCC Series Title: The Power of Prayer; Practicing the Presence of God

THE PLATE SPINNER by Donna Lagerquist

In this narrated story (the narrator is the only speaking part), Hank Spinner finds his life is becoming overwhelming. At first, everything is "Hunkey Dorey." He keeps his boss, Mr. Hunkey, and his wife, Dorey, quite happy (represented by him spinning imaginary plates on wooden poles each character holds). He is further challenged when Peachy, his daughter, and Keen, a new account require his attention. Add to those obligations Oakey, a health club membership, Dokey, a counselor, and his aging parents, Nitty and Gritty, and Hank now has a Hunkey Dorey Peechy Keen Oakey Dokey Nitty Gritty life. Keeping all those plates spinning has him on the edge of a breakdown!
Suggested Topics: Pace of life, Being in control
Characters: 5 males, 4 females, 1 narrator
WCCC Series Title: Do You Have What It Takes To Grow? Admitting Our Powerlessness Over Sin (Step 1)

PRAYER DESPAIR by Judson Poling

When JoAnn complains about her husband's lack of interest in her, Valerie questions whether she has asked God to change Glenn. JoAnn replies she has, "but nothing happens, he's still the same." In the end, we discover it is JoAnn who is insensitive to the change taking place in Glenn.
Suggested Topics: Waiting for answers to prayer, Marriage
Characters: 1 male, 2 females
WCCC Series Title: The Power of Prayer; Prayer … Our Last Resort

PRAYER GROUP THERAPY by Donna Lagerquist

Four would be pray-ers meet for group therapy. In this case, each member has some sort of common prayer dysfunction. Doug is into "holy language" and his prayers are full of outbursts and alleluias that disrupt the others. Margaret uses prayer as a vehicle for gossip. Amy is timid and uses only memorized or formula prayers. Jay doesn't really pray at all because he has concluded God knows everything so He certainly doesn't need any prayers to inform Him of a request. Karen, the facilitator, tries to get everyone to participate in a simple time of prayer, but as each person's warped perspective on prayer kicks in, the results are disastrous—in an outlandishly comical way!
Suggested Topics: Prayer
Characters: 2 males, 3 females
WCCC Series Title: Capturing the Heart of Christianity

PRAYER PERPLEXITY by Judson Poling

Several brief scenes illustrate comically the confusion in our culture about prayer. In the first scene, a group of people pray fervently—to rip off the heads of the opposing team! Then a child's nighttime prayer becomes a confusing theology lesson from mom who doesn't really understand why we pray. Next, a man prays for the meal, and puts on a holy sounding prayer voice complete with religious vocabulary. A teenager prays for justice on her ex-friend who stole her boyfriend. A shipwrecked man promises God anything, but backs out of it all when rescued. A memorized mealtime prayer doesn't quite fit—at a funeral! Finally, a committee trying to update prayer go to ridiculous lengths. In the end, the actors paraphrase the Lord's prayer, and we see the wonderful simplicity of Jesus' model.
Suggested Topics: The Lord's Prayer, Prayer
Characters: 2 males, 2 females
WCCC Series Title: The Greatest Sermon in History

PRAYER STATIC by Judson Poling

Jim, a typical man, explains to the audience how static has interfered with his prayer life. Every time he prays Jim hears, "Boy, is God ticked at you!" or "He doesn't like it when you get too personal!" or "There's no

one to rely on but yourself!" We view three scenes from Jim's life illustrating how this static originated.
Suggested Topics: Prayer
Characters: 3 males, 1 female
WCCC Series Title: The Power of Prayer; God's Attitude Toward Prayer

THE PRISONER by Donna Lagerquist

A three-part drama. In the first scene we meet Joey, a prisoner. He receives an unexpected visit from the warden, who tells him the governor has granted him clemency. The scene ends with him dazed in joyous disbelief. In the next scene, a janitor drops by. He can't understand why Joey is still in his cell playing cards. Joey is actually more comfortable staying there—it's what he's used to. In the third scene, Joey's sister has arrived to take him home. Although it doesn't make sense, Joey's not sure he can leave. The scene ends as his sister takes his hand and literally walks him into the freedom of his new life.
Suggested Topics: Easter, Basic Christianity, New Christian
Characters: 3 males, 1 female
WCCC Series Title: Easter Celebration 1993

A PROBLEM OF PERCEPTION by Sharon Sherbondy

Did you know that Christians always wear black? And they never mow the lawn on Wednesdays? This sketch takes a comical look at three people's misconceptions of what the Christian life is like.
Suggested Topics: The Christian life, Misconceptions about Christianity
Characters: 3 males, 1 female
WCCC Series Title: The Adventure of Christianity

A PROBLEM OF PERSPECTIVE by Judson Poling

A tired husband returns home at the end of a work day to his equally tired wife. In the few moments as they talk, their exhaustion and unmet needs create a tense (but comical) exchange. The scene freezes and a counselor appears and explains that he'd like to hear what happened from each of their perspectives. The scene is replayed twice, once from each point of view and it's hard to believe they're describing the same situation!
Suggested Topics: Marriage, Truth telling
Characters: 1 male, 1 female, 1 either male or female
WCCC Series Title: Fanning the Flames of Marriage; Keys to Resolving Conflict; The Age of Rage; Expressing Anger Appropriately

PULPIT TALK by Donna Lagerquist and Steve Pederson

In this broadly comic sketch, a narrator introduces us to a pulpit, wondering what our reaction to it is. With the help of other characters, we experience a variety of sermons that could be found in an average church on a typical Sunday: the Sominex, the Terminex, and the Feel-Good. But none of these compare to the greatest sermon of all known as the Sermon on the Mount, and this drama ends with the opening lines of that sermon. If a more broad emphasis is desired an alternate ending of Scripture verses in provided which focuses on the power of God's Word.
Suggested Topics: Introduction to the Sermon on the Mount; Stereotypical church experiences, How does God speak?
Characters: 3 males, 2 females
WCCC Series Title: The Greatest Sermon in History

THE QUAGMIRE by Various Authors

An "everyman" character explains to the audience his reasons for heading to the Quagmire. It isn't a pleasant place; in fact, most people there are miserable, but it's attractive because it's an escape. Halfway through this sketch, God reminds the character He loves him and will guide him through to higher ground.
Suggested Topics: Failure, Self-esteem, Trusting God
Characters: 1 male or female
WCCC Series Title: From Stuck to Starting Over

QUALITY TIME by Judson Poling

This sketch takes a look at the philosophy of "quality time" between parents and children. We see a father who has a difficult time controlling his pre-occupation with business and keeping up with his daughters' lives. The daughters contemplate a friend's situation whose parents are divorced and wonder if her one afternoon a week with her dad isn't better than the "quality time" they have each day.

Suggested Topics: Fathers
Characters: 1 male, 1 female, 2 teenage girls
WCCC Series Title: Understanding Dad's Dilemma

QUIET TIME? by Sharon Sherbondy

This sketch focuses on the difficulty so many have in giving God their complete attention during their devotional time. This new mom unsuccessfully tries to combat the distractions and situational demands surrounding her. This comical sketch has application to many.

Suggested Topics: Prayer
Characters: 1 female
WCCC Series Title: The Power of Prayer; Amazing Answers to Prayer; Faith's First Steps

THE QUITTER by Judson Poling

Warren's been unemployed for seven months and it's been a tough struggle. To get everyone "off his back" he decided to tell them he had a new job and for a week has been hanging out at the shopping mall from 9 to −5. When the truth comes out, Warren and everyone else have a hard time with the fact he quit trying.

Suggested Topics: Quitting, Failure
Characters: 2 males, 1 female
WCCC Series Title: Anyone Can Quit

A REAL HERO by Judson Poling

Mark knows his life is going nowhere but can't figure out who could "mentor" him to a better future. He falls asleep in his TV chair, and Johnny Carson shows up in his living room, complete with a line-up of guests. First Superman, then Rambo, and finally President Bush all try to give Mark advice on life. He finally realizes he is dreaming.

Suggested Topics: Manhood, Heroes, Christian men
Characters: 6 males
WCCC Series Title: Everyday Heroes: Hallmarks of a Hero

A REAL MAN by Judson Poling

One evening Cheryl decides to list the qualities she's looking for in a "real man." Much to her surprise her dreams come true and she's faced with three men; a rugged individualist, a twentieth-century entrepreneur, and a poetic type. After seeing their strengths and weaknesses she rejects them all and concludes she needs a man who can make her laugh.

Suggested Topics: The American male, Finding the right man
Characters: 4 males, 1 female
WCCC Series Title: Changing Times; Changing American Male

REASON ENOUGH by Sharon Sherbondy

During her weekly counseling session Susan discusses everything from what's on television to whether she believes in God. Susan doesn't believe in God but not because she doesn't want to. Growing up she wasn't given any reasons for believing and now as an adult she doesn't know where to go for answers.

Suggested Topics: Importance of faith grounded in reason
Characters: 1 male, 1 female
WCCC Series Title: Fully Informed Followers

REFLECTIONS by Sharon Sherbondy

It's Mother's Day again, and Lois takes a look back at her years as a mother. Her reflecting reveals the pain, humor, and joy that she experienced. She concludes that motherhood is a privilege and has added to her life.

Suggested Topics: Mother's Day, Mother-child relationships
Characters: 1 male, 2 females, 2 children either male or female
WCCC Series Title: The Lost Art of Loving; The Launching Pad of Loving

REGARDING RODNEY by Donna Lagerquist

In this broadly comic sketch, the scene opens on a police line-up. Mrs. Devero tries to pick out her husband Rodney with the assistance of a police officer. The problem is that he is a totally different person at work, and because the day before he had come home early still in his "work mode," she mistook him for a burglar! She finally picks him out of the line-up, but he still hasn't changed to "home Rodney." By the end of their conversation, Rodney leaves frustrated at her inability to grasp he can't be two people at once. She in turn asks the officer to call the other men back into the line-up to see if one of them might be better than her husband!

Suggested Topics: Workaholism, Roles of men, Marriage
Characters: 4 males, 1 female
WCCC Series Title: Marriage Werks; When a Man Loves a Woman

REMEMBRANCES by Judson Poling

While helping their mother move, Jerry and Sue talk about their father, who has recently died. Jerry is angry because although he had access to his father's property (boat, car, money) he felt his father was never there for him. Later, he is alone and stumbles across some letters he wrote to his father. While reading one, he painfully becomes aware that at one time there was a significant relationship between them.

Suggested Topics: Parent/child relationships, Forgiveness, Fifth Commandment
Characters: 1 male, 1 female
WCCC Series Title: Fifth Commandment; Honor Your Parents

THE RESOLVE DISSOLVE by Judson Poling

Steve and Jean separately vow to never get involved in a romantic relationship again. Just as they're convinced a vow of celibacy or a convent is their only hope, they meet. Promises melt in the warmth of sexual attraction. But never fear, Church Lady (of *Saturday Night Live*) comes to the rescue and pours her "little bit superior" cold water over the budding romance.

Suggested Topics: Sexuality, Romance, Singleness, Dating, Moral issues
Characters: 2 males, 1 female
WCCC Series Title: Discovering the Way God Wired You Up Sexually

RICHARD: 1968 by Donna Lagerquist

(The first sketch in a four-part series.) Richard, a hippie-type college student is invited home to meet Mr. and Mrs. Matson, the parents of his girlfriend, "M.A." It is the classic but comical encounter of radical values versus mainstream, conservative America. As the father grills Richard about his eating—and "weed" consumption—habits, Richard counters with concerns about the war in Vietnam. With both parents in the kitchen, he and M.A. talk about how trapped the older generation seems. Richard leaves on an angry note, challenging M.A. to choose which side she'll be on, quoting "The Times They Are a-Changin'."

Suggested Topics: Youth idealism, Changing societal values, Generation gap
Characters: 2 males, 2 females
WCCC Series Title: Understanding the Times; The '60s

RICHARD: 1974 by Sharon Sherbondy

(The second sketch in a four-part series.) Richard is sitting in a bar on the night of President Nixon's resignation. He and others around him lament the jobs they don't have. M.A., his wife, comes in looking for him. His pride is wounded, both because of his unemployment and because he's a Vietnam veteran with no respect or appreciation from society. It's doubly ironic, because he opposed the war but was drafted and was forced to go. In the end, a friendly bartender—a vet himself—counsels Richard, and the two fellow soldiers share some moments of identification. The bartender encourages Richard to go back to his wife, and consider the job offer from his much-hated father-in-law. Richard reluctantly takes the advice, and the two part with a nostalgic military salute.

Suggested Topics: Dillusionment with life, Crumbling dreams, Pushing away loved ones

Characters: 5 males, 1 female
WCCC Series Title: Understanding the Times; The '70s

RICHARD: 1985 by Judson Poling

After coming home late at night, Richard finds himself looking down the barrel of his father-in-law's rifle, who thinks he's a prowler. Once they settle down, their conversation turns to the changes in Richard's life: his growing interest in making money, his extensive time commitments at work, and the loss of his youthful idealism. The father-in-law knows all too well how short life is, especially now that he has lost his own wife. He finally decides to go to bed, 'warning' Richard he may kidnap his 10-year-old and play hookey with him the next day. Richard calls out after him not to 'corrupt' his boy, but as he considers why he's so concerned, he realizes he's not sure the path of college and career will truly make his son happy.

Suggested Topics: Workaholism, Materialism vs. idealism, Fathers
Characters: 2 males
WCCC Series Title: Understanding the Times; The '80s

RICHARD: 1992 by Donna Lagerquist

(The last sketch in a four part series.) Richard's college age son, Zach, enters the living room just as Richard settles in with a late night snack. Tension fills the air: Zach got thrown out of his mother's house. Richard is now divorced, and Zach has grown up to be a rebellious, troubled young man. Richard chastises his son for having a girlfriend in his room—as his own live-in girlfriend enters. Awkward greetings are exchanged and she exits. The conversation now crescendos as father and son express their lifetime of rage. After all is said and done, Zach angrily sums up: "We sure don't have much, do we, Dad?"

Suggested Topics: Anger, Rebellion, Decay of the family
Characters: 2 males, 1 female
WCCC Series Title: Understanding the Times; The '90s

THE RIGHT NICHE by Cathy Peters

In an effort to find the right job, Bob Bounce-around goes to the Max-A-Million Professional Career Counseling Agency. During the interview the job counselor discovers his real desire is to be a fireman and Bob discovers he has a knack for job counseling.

Suggested Topics: Job satisfaction, Finding the right niche
Characters: 2 males, 1 female
WCCC Series Title: Taking Care of Business; Keys to Job Satisfaction

THE RIGHT THING by Various Authors

A reflective monologue set in front of the home of a man who was just fired from his job as a reporter because he chose to help someone in need and missed his story. We hear him struggle with how to tell his wife and children and to understand why doing the right thing in God's eyes can sometimes be very difficult. (Suggestion: Follow with verses pertaining to the Christian struggle or God's seeing what is done in secret.)

Suggested Topics: Christian character, Costly obedience, Persecution
Characters: 1 male
WCCC Series Title: Difference Makers

THE SAFE by Judson Poling

An "everyman" character demonstrates to the audience how a safe which contains all of his inborn and personal resources can solve anything that comes his way. We see how he effectively handles the IRS, employees, and health problems, but to his surprise the resources in his safe won't subdue a spiritual "crisis" as easily.

Suggested Topics: Inner strength, Depend on God's strength, Storms of life
Characters: 1 male, 1 female, 3 either male or female
WCCC Series Title: Connecting With the Source of Strength

A SECOND CHANCE by Sharon Sherbondy

Al and Marge have made a difficult and seemingly illogical decision to let Al's father, Earl, move in with them. Both feel strongly that God has led them to this decision and even when challenged by another believer and Earl's difficult personality, they plan to trust in God's leading.

Suggested Topics: Decision making, Hard choices, Father/son relationships
Characters: 3 males, 1 female
WCCC Series Title: The Art of Decision Making; Father Knows Best

SECURITY CHECK by Sharon Sherbondy

Roy is nervously pacing at what appears to be an airport terminal. Sue joins him and in the course of their conversation we discover they have died and are now on the outskirts of heaven waiting for their name to be called. Roy is counting on his duffel bag "trophies," his life's accomplishments, as his ticket to get in. Sue's counting on the fact that the price has been paid "already." In the end, Sue's name is called, and Roy is left clutching his trophies.

Suggested Topics: Salvation, Works vs. grace
Characters: 1 male, 1 female, voice on tape
WCCC Series Title: A Taste of Christianity; A Better Kind of Confidence

SEEING IS BELIEVING by Various Authors

A commercial for the "Bonco-God-O-Matic" causes two typical people, Bob and Jane, to replace Christ with a tangible, "comfortable" god. Thus, they avoid church, prayer, worship, and serving. This god is easy, but will he provide help for the problems of life?

Suggested Topics: A Savior you can trust, The emptiness of an easy faith
Characters: 1 male, 1 female, 1 narrator
WCCC Series Title: Where Is God in the Star Trek Cast?

A SERF'S TALE by Judson Poling

In this zany sketch, a medieval serf and his wife recount their botched attempt at grabbing for the "good life." In their longing to break out of their mere peasant's existence, they hatch a plan for the husband to be indentured to two lords—strictly forbidden by the law of the land which says, "one lord only." For a while the plan works, but in his exhaustion, the serf's duplicity is discovered and the lords both banish them. In the end they share the simple but stinging moral of their saga: "You cannot serf two masters."

Suggested Topics: Serving two masters, Materialism
Characters: 1 male, 1 female
WCCC Series Title: You Can't Serve Two Masters

SHOP TALK by Donna Lagerquist

Vic has lost the family business. When friends come by to comfort him, he finds it hard to receive their help. He can't get it out of his mind that he destroyed the business started by his grandfather 73 years earlier. His pain and anger with himself keep him from benefiting from the help they are trying to offer. They continue to stand with him, and in the end affirm one more time, "We're here for you ... all of us."

Suggested Topics: Unemployment, Adversity, Small groups
Characters: 2 males, 2 females
WCCC Series Title: Capturing the Heart of Christianity; Discovering Community

SINGLE? by Donna Lagerquist

Two old acquaintants meet on a chairlift at a ski slope. They engage in small talk, by use of one word questions and answers. The conversation reveals a lot more than either intend, specifically their feelings about being single.

Suggested Topics: Being single, Loneliness, Fear of living alone
Characters: 1 male, 1 female
WCCC Series Title: Facing Up to Fear; The Fear of Living Alone

SITTERS, STRIVERS, STANDERS, AND SAINTS by Judson Poling

An underachiever ("Sitter"), an overachiever ("Striver"), and an opinionated analyzer ("Stander") receive a visit from God. Each person discovers he or she is living in some excess, and finds he or she needs some quality another person possesses. When each makes a move according to God's gentle nudge, he or she becomes a more balanced, fulfilled person.

Suggested Topics: God uses me, God can change me

Characters: 4 either male or female, 1 narrator
WCCC Series Title: Celebration of Baptism

SIX HAPPY HEARTS by Donna Lagerquist

A mime based on Proverbs 17:22: "A cheerful heart is good medicine, but a downcast spirit dries up the bones." Six friends drive their cars (chairs) to a place they all choose to rendezvous for laughter and fun. However, one of the friends is obviously unhappy. One by one, his downcast spirit affects each of his friends. The chairs are used to create the different places these friends go; a movie theater, roller coaster, restaurant, and living room. In the end, the six friends return to their homes—all negatively affected by the one, downcast spirit.

Suggested Topics: Laughter, A sour spirit affects others
Characters: 6 males or females
WCCC Series Title: Three Things That God Loves … Laughter

SNOW JOB by Donna Lagerquist

Mr. and Mrs. Kneely use—rather, abuse—prayer in order to get things done that they'd rather not do themselves. They send their daughter off to the store just minutes before her new boyfriend arrives at their house. The boyfriend then becomes prey to the Kneelys' dramatic prayers for God to send someone into their life to shovel the snow, take out the garbage, etc. Organ music, threats, and bribery are all a part of their outlandish prayers. The exaggerated situation presents a humorous look at the sad reality of people who abuse prayer.

Suggested Topics: Prayer abuse
Characters: 2 males, 1 female
WCCC Series Title: Privilege of Prayer; Prayer Abuse

SOMEBODY'S GOT TO DO IT by Sharon Sherbondy

Somehow the word has been spread that in order to serve God and the church, you've got to suffer doing it or it doesn't count. That's why Paul is avoiding Reverend Roper's phone call. But to the surprise of Paul, and Shirley, his wife, he discovers a new word in serving: joy!

Suggested Topics: Spiritual gifts, Serving
Characters: 1 male, 1 female
WCCC Series Title: Discovering the Way God Wired You Up—Spiritually

SOMETHING IN COMMON by Donna Lagerquist and Steve Pederson

How does a friendship start? What does it take to build significant relationships? In this sketch we see four complete strangers develop a "platoon." Over the weeks while watching their girls in gymnastics we see that common interests, risk-taking, and time, are a few of the keys to developing close friendships.

Suggested Topics: Starting relationships
Characters: 3 females, 1 male
WCCC Series Title: Enlisting in Platoons; The Purpose Of Little Platoons

SPEAK FOR YOURSELF by Donna Lagerquist

Vicki has always been quiet but things have gotten ridiculous. Joe, her husband, does all the talking for her. Some mutual friends confront Joe about his enabling Vicki to stay in her comfort zone. They agree that the rest of the evening Joe will only speak for himself and allow his wife to talk. Everyone is pleasantly surprised at Vicki's reaction.

Suggested Topics: Insecurity, Being an enabler
Characters: 3 males, 3 females
WCCC Series Title: From Stuck to Making a Difference

THE SPECULATORS by Various Authors

Alfred, Cora, and their daughter, Tammy, have made thinking about living an end in itself. Humorously they verbalize the possibilities of their day, without actually doing anything. Tammy encourages her parents to consider having a weekly family time. However, when Alfred and Cora realize this will necessitate taking action to make some changes in their lives, they decide they'd rather not think about it.

Suggested Topics: Risk taking, Missed opportunities
Characters: 2 males, 1 female,
WCCC Series Title: Opportunity Knocks; The Determining Factor

THE STICKHOLDERS by Debra Poling

This mime takes a creative look at how we tend to view God as all "rules and regulations," rather than as someone who wants a relationship with us. The "everyman" character soon learns that if he obeys life's rules he'll get along just fine. But when he disobeys, the consequences are answering to the Stickholders. But God's stick, a shepherd staff, is different. The man learns he can lean on the staff and rest from his rules.

Suggested Topics: Relationship with God, Resting from rules
Characters: 3 males, 1 female, 1 narrator
WCCC Series Title: Developing a Daring Faith; Dialoguing With God; Easter Celebration 1989

STOLEN JESUS by Donna Lagerquist

This setting for this Christmas-season drama is a vandalized nativity scene in the middle of a large city. All that remains of the nativity is the stable, hay, and manger. A woman, Barbara, is frustrated with the holidays and in particular a home in turmoil. While carrying just-bought gifts home, she breaks the heel on her shoe, sits on a park bench, and encounters Vivian, a bag lady. Vivian has taken up residency in the "stable." Through the course of their conversation, Barbara moves from fear and disgust to actually confiding in, and having true compassion for Vivian. Vivian's homespun wisdom and quiet simple view of Jesus deeply touch Barbara—and the audience.

Suggested Topics: Christmas
Characters: 2 females
WCCC Series Title: Christmas Eve 1989

THE STORY OF RACHEL by Donna Lagerquist

Three women tell the same story from their own perspective. One day, while feeding ducks in the park, Mary Pat has her bag of bread crumbs stolen by Rachel, a street girl. The scene is witnessed by Jean. Their descriptions of what happened are interwoven throughout, showing how the three women view Rachel's poverty—and theft—in totally different ways. Rachel sees it as her only way to survive; Mary Pat, though Rachel's target, sees past her offense and tries to reach out to help her—first, practically, and then in personal ways; and Jean watches all this, and thinks it foolishness for anyone to reach out to a street urchin.

Suggested Topics: Care for the poor, Forgiving others
Characters: 3 females
WCCC Series Title: What Jesus Would Say to … Mother Teresa

STRAIGHT-JACKETED by Various Authors

A man in a straight jacket talks to the audience about his painful past. He's chosen his life of bondage because it keeps him from having to get vulnerable. His constriction keeps him safe. His father was an alcoholic and beat his mom, his wife left him, and now he stays in his cocoon. Even if he did want to be free, he observes without emotion, "I don't know how to get out."

Suggested Topics: Bondage to sin and our past, Anger toward God
Characters: 1 male
WCCC Series Title: Do You Have What It Takes to Grow? Conscious Contact With God (Step11)

STREET CHAT by Judson Poling

This drama takes a humorous look at the question "what helps you keep your spiritual life going?" The interviewer meets four characters, a Carl Sagan–type, a Rod Sterling clone from *The Twilight Zone*, a Shirley MacLaine devotee, and the Church Lady from *Saturday Night Live*.

Suggested Topics: Search for meaning, Spirituality
Characters: 4 males, 1 female
WCCC Series Title: Ordering Your Private World; Your Spiritual World

SUIT AND VOLLY by Donna Lagerquist

Vivian, the bag lady, explains to her fellow homeless friend, Earl, that two people she names "Suit and Volly" are the soup servers today at the soup kitchen and that they make her angry. Suit always wears his suit and makes sure he lets everyone know he is a prominent lawyer who takes time to do community service. Volly prides herself on her dedication to volunteer anywhere and everywhere. Eventually Earl convinces Vivian to join him, and once at the kitchen, Suit and Volly live up to their nicknames. Suit soon leaves to get back to the office, Volly goes off to volunteer somewhere else. Finally Earl serves Vivian her meal, for the right reasons with the right heart.

Suggested Topics: Genuine commitment, Service
Characters: 2 males, 2 females
WCCC Series Title: Everyday Heroes—Heroes of the Heart

SUIT YOURSELF by Donna Lagerquist

Dan has just returned home from shopping for a bathing suit with his daughter Tracey. Marlene stayed home, dreading the annual argument over what is modest enough for parents but stylish enough for a teenager. While Tracey visits outside with the neighbor kids, Dan and Marlene discuss the shopping trip. Tracey bought a suit, but Dan hasn't seen it, deciding instead to trust his daughter's judgment after expressing his concerns. Marlene considers his deference to Tracey a cop-out and worries about what others will think of them as parents if Tracey shows up at church camp in a string bikini. Just then, a neighbor brings in the shopping bag Tracey left outside. What kind of suit did Tracey buy? The drama ends as both parents lunge for the bag to find out!

Suggested Topics: Parenting, Letting kids make their own decisions
Characters: 1 male, 2 females
WCCC Series Title: Facing the Family Challenge; Forming a Spiritual Foundation

THE SURPRISE PARTY by Donna Lagerquist

It's Dennis's birthday and he is sure that his wife has organized a surprise party for him. While with a friend, Larry, he repeatedly tries to get him to break down and admit that a surprise party is in the works. Larry is unsuccessful in convincing Dennis that he knows nothing about a party. Once home, both Dennis and Larry are surprised! There is a party—but it's for Larry! In the end, when his wife finds him off by himself, Dennis reluctantly shares his embarrassment and disappointment.

Suggested Topics: Disappointments are a part of life
Characters: 2 males, 1 female
WCCC Series Title: Disappointment With God; What Causes Disappointment?

SWEET HOUR OF PRAYER by Sharon Sherbondy

In this lighthearted satire, an elderly woman who is outwardly pious is suddenly broken in on by a would-be robber. Her trust in God is shaken as her prayers are unanswered and the robber's threats go unchallenged. He leaves her tied up, penniless, and very angry at God. Suddenly a policeman comes in: the thief has been caught and she is freed. Outwardly she rejoices, but she realizes her prayer life is less than dynamic.

Suggested Topics: Prayer, Hypocrisy, Faith
Characters: 2 males, 1 female
WCCC Series Title: The Fight for Spiritual Vitality

TAKE HEART by Debra Poling

This solo mime shows a woman in three different stages of life; as a child, a teenager, and a woman in the workplace. In each stage the narrative demonstrates how the woman essentially suffers a broken heart. In the end it is God who not only mends her heart, but returns it to her full and strong.

Suggested Topics: God heals the brokenhearted, Disappointment
Characters: 2 males, 2 females
WCCC Series Title: Sandy: A Heart for God

TAKING STEP FOUR by Sharon Sherbondy

In this lighthearted monologue, a women reads from the book *Hunger for Healing* about taking Step 4 (from 12 Step programs). She has prepared herself to "take a searching and fearless moral inventory" with paper, pen, Kleenex … and food. As she begins, she humorously retreats to blaming others and missing the whole point of the step. The need for

honesty in self-examination comes through powerfully—yet in a disarmingly funny way.

Suggested Topics: Self-delusion, Confession of sin
Characters: 1 female
WCCC Series Title: Do You Have What It Takes to Grow?; Making a Moral Inventory (Step 4)

10 by Judson Poling

To introduce a series on the Ten Commandments and to present the First Commandment—"Honor God as God"—the audience meets the character "10." In this sketch, "10" is an on-the-street reporter quizzing people on their knowledge of the Ten Commandments. He also speaks directly to the audience concerning impressions that the Ten Commandments are dated and nitpicky. (*Note:* "10" also appears in other dramas.)

Suggested Topics: First Commandment
Characters: 3 males, 2 females
WCCC Series Title: First Commandment; Honor God as God

TERMINAL VISIT by Debra Poling

Two grown sisters meet in an airport. Their relationship has become superficial, and now their inability to communicate about hidden hurts has built a wall. Instead of feeling close and supported, they experience disappointment in each other.

Suggested Topics: Resurrecting relationships, Confronting family hurts
Characters: 3 females
WCCC Series Title: The Lost Art of Loving; Resurrecting Dying Loves

THANKS FOR LISTENING by Sharon Sherbondy

A family decides to picnic outside although it's quite cold. As they engage in typical "busy family" dinner conversation, Mark, the teenage son, tries to talk about his baseball game. He is interrupted throughout his story. Several times he is asked to begin again, only to be repeatedly ignored. In the end, everyone complains it's too cold, so they head back in. Mark is left at the table alone. He decides to finish his story, talking enthusiastically as if everyone was still there. He thanks them all for listening, though he sits with no one left to hear.

Suggested Topics: Family, Listening
Characters: 1 male, 1 female, 1 male and 1 female teenager
WCCC Series Title: Facing the Family Challenge; Traits of a Healthy Family

THESE PARTS by Judson Poling

In the land of "These Parts," where everyone has only part sight, part hearing, and one arm, a Stranger appears who tells a family they can be whole. After consulting the experts, the Stranger is rejected and killed. But he returns to life and again offers to give them sight, hearing, and use of both arms. When the family consults the experts they say it's impossible. Only the child remains, and only the child receives … "a hug with both arms."

Suggested Topics: The Resurrection, Our need for Christ, Easter
Characters: 2 males, 1 female, 3 either male or female, 1 child, 1 narrator
WCCC Series Title: Faith Has Its Reasons; Reasons for Believing in the Resurrection; Surprised by God; Surprised by God's Church

A THIEF'S CAROL by Sharon Sherbondy

In the spirit of Dickens's *Christmas Carol,* our character "10" (see the script "10") pays a visit to Rouge (a Scrooge-like character). During the night, "10" escorts three people from Rouge's past, whom he's stolen from, deceived, and defrauded. By the end of the evening, Rouge is ready to change his life and make restitution for his wrongdoings.

Suggested Topics: Eighth Commandment, Stealing
Characters: 3 males, 2 female
WCCC Series Title: Eighth Commandment; Respect the Property of Others

TIRED OF TRYING by Donna Lagerquist

Kate tries to make the best of the dilemma she faces when her son invites his grandfather (her father) to his birthday party. He is a "miserable man." At first Kate stifles her anger towards him as she has all her life. However, when forced to protect her son from emotional abuse from his grandfather, she ends up honestly and powerfully confronting her father.

Suggested Topics: Dealing with the anger of others
Characters: 1 male, 2 females
WCCC Series Title: The Age of Rage; Responding to the Anger of Others

TIRED WHEN NEEDED by Sharon Sherbondy

Mr. Watson has locked himself up in a motel room to get away from people and their demands on his time. However, Mrs. Willoughby has tracked him down to request his involvement in just one more worthy cause. He tries reason, but even a direct no doesn't work with Mrs. Willoughby—until he cracks!

Suggested Topics: Burnout, Saying "no"
Characters: 1 male, 1 female
WCCC Series Title: Redefining Commitment

TOM, DICK, AND MARY by Judson Poling

Sometimes the noise in people's lives prevents them from hearing God's message of love. Tom couldn't hear God because he was always on his soap box. Dick's ears were filled with the sound of his money machine. And Mary filled her world with the television, the radio, and the walkman. When their lives are quieted, all three discover they are miserable and very much alone.

Suggested Topics: Closing God out
Characters: 3 males, 1 female, 1 narrator
WCCC Series Title: Leadings From God; How to Receive God's Leadings

TRYING TIME by Donna Lagerquist

Paula is a believer and Marty is not. While shopping, they meet a friend Connie, who enthusiastically tells Paula her son just became a Christian. When she leaves, Paula and Marty have a hard conversation because Marty can't share Paula's enthusiasm for spiritual things. He knows she's not happy with him the way he is, and she knows he's angry that she has changed since they got married. Both are frustrated that, though they love each other, a major area of life is a constant sore spot.

Suggested Topics: Marriage, Beloved unbeliever, Evangelism
Characters: 1 male, 2 females
WCCC Series Title: Marriage Werks; Surviving Spiritual Mismatch

UNAVERAGE JOE by Sharon Sherbondy

This sketch is a lighthearted retelling of the angel's visit to Joseph before he attempted to divorce Mary. In a contemporary setting (complete with stereotypic Jewish accents), a good Jewish boy, Joseph, awakens his good Jewish parents in the middle of the night to tell them that he's had an encounter with an angel. His wife to be, Mary, is pregnant and will have a child, God's Son—or so says the angel. Mom and Dad can't believe it. They argue, with each other, with Joseph—and in the end admit they will try to stay open but that it will be hard to accept the loss of honor to their family name. Joseph replies this willingness to sacrifice reputation is not merely for the love of a woman, it is for the love of his God. He can do no other.

Suggested Topics: Christmas, God's call
Characters: 2 males, 1 female
WCCC Series Title: Giving and Receiving Love

UP ON THE ROOF by Donna Lagerquist

When stressed-out Wally is sent up to the roof of his office building to check on his boss' TV reception, he discovers a real problem. A bag lady is using the antenna for a clothesline while she retreats to the roof to "get away from it all." However, through the course of lighthearted conversation with the lady and her homespun wisdom, Wally discovers a problem more serious than the antenna debris. His personal life has become overwhelming and he is exhausted. Just as Wally begins to absorb the peaceful rooftop environment, his boss interrupts by calling on Wally's cordless phone. Wally hurries to return back to work but has obviously been touched by the woman's concern for him and her words

of wisdom to visit the roof as often as he needs in order to handle life one little battle at a time.

Suggested Topics: Emotional refueling, Building compassion
Characters: 1 male, 1 female
WCCC Series Title: Building Bigger Hearts—Part I

THE VACATIONERS—PARTS I AND II by Judson Poling

This is a two-part sketch that takes a comedic look at how two couples survive the planning of a mutual vacation. The couples come to the realization that they have some very different ideas on how to plan and enjoy their time together. While on the vacation, the reality of the couples' differences seems like a nightmare. As they calm down, they realize that there is no right or wrong way to do things, just different preferences.

Suggested Topics: Personality differences, Friendships, Accepting others
Characters: 2 males, 2 females
WCCC Series Title: The Lost Art of Loving; Why Aren't You Normal Like Me?

VINCE BUELLER'S DAY OFF by Sharon Sherbondy

This is Vince's first day off in two weeks. He vowed to spend the day relaxing, but ends up driving his wife crazy by "fixing" everything he sets his eyes on.

Suggested Topics: Workaholism, Importance of rest/leisure
Characters: 1 male, 1 female, 1 boy
WCCC Series Title: Three Things That God Loves (That Most People Think He Doesn't); Leisure

A VISITOR by Sharon Sherbondy

Howard, a recent widower, is visited in his home by Mr. Kendall from Tree of Life ministries. When Howard's adult daughter Penny drops by to bring supper, she begins to question Mr. Kendall about his "ministry" and finds him evasive. As she continues to press him, it becomes clear her father is being duped into giving a large contribution, manipulated by his own emotional vulnerability and Mr. Kendall's connivery. Penny finally insists Mr. Kendall leave, and as he goes, bids him, "Happy hunting!"

Suggested Topics: Being wise as serpents, Spiritual manipulation, Wolves in sheep's clothing
Characters: 2 males, 1 female
WCCC Series Title: The Greatest Sermon in History

WAIT 'TIL HALFTIME by Sharon Sherbondy

Larry is into the Bulls basketball game when Beth comes in suggesting they do something more social for the evening. When she suggests inviting over another couple, Craig and Robin, he becomes especially disinterested. He doesn't like their Christianity, while she finds them interesting, caring people. The exchange is mostly lighthearted until the end when she expresses concern for his eternal well-being. He quips about burial in "asbestos underwear" to try to fend her off. In his mind, eternity can wait until half-time.

Suggested Topics: Evangelism, Heaven and hell
Characters: 1 male, 1 female
WCCC Series Title: Case for Christ; Relevance of the Resurrection

THE WALL by Donna Lagerquist

The setting is the Vietnam War Memorial. At one end of the Wall, two army buddies reminisce about a friend they lost in the war, and how he had personally affected their lives. Further down the wall a woman talks to and remembers her brother, whose name is also on the Wall. A warm, reflective mood is broken when a "vacationing" family invades the area, taking pictures and making insensitive comments. The family soon learns the difference between touring monuments and visiting/remembering loved ones.

Suggested Topics: Significance of remembering, i.e., Communion
Characters: 3 males, 2 females, 1 child
WCCC Series Title: It's My Turn Now; The Significance of the Sacraments

WASTED by Judson Poling

Cliff, a janitor, is showing Brett, a new employee, the ropes. Brett is a student intent on moving ahead, and dreams of someday working in an office like the one they're cleaning. The scene changes and now Brett does work there, and Cliff stops by on his way out to a fishing trip. Brett's harried and envies Cliff's freedoms. The scene changes again to a night at the office: Brett has moved up the ladder and is working late again. He is confronted by Cliff, and explains that Cliff doesn't understand the pressure of a man in Brett's position. Cliff confesses that he envies what Brett has done with his life. Both realize neither career has been perfect, and neither knows what to do. We're left knowing both white collar and blue collar jobs have difficulties—but how to cope is left unspecified.

Suggested Topics: Christians and work
Characters: 2 males
WCCC Series Title: The Day Wccc Told the Truth—Part 4

WATCHING FROM THE WINDOW by Sharon Sherbondy

Carol is standing in front of her house with a suitcase in her hand. She is contemplating walking out on her family. At first, she seems somewhat cold and hard, but gradually our empathy is aroused because we realize that she has been beaten down by the people in her life who take from her but give nothing back.

Suggested Topics: Draining relationships, Challenge of motherhood
Characters: 1 female, 1 child
WCCC Series Title: Building Bigger Hearts: Part II

WELCOME TO THE FAMILY by Sharon Sherbondy

Judy and Fred are overwhelmed by a pushy salesman offering them a "Lifestyle for God package." They are new Christians, both confused and vulnerable, and while wanting to grow in their faith, they are unsure how to respond to the salesman's offer.

Suggested Topics: Growing in Christ, Spiritual infancy and/or gullibility
Characters: 2 males, 1 female
WCCC Series Title: Seasons of a Spiritual Life; Spiritual Infancy

WHAT ARE FRIENDS FOR? by Sharon Sherbondy

Wayne has just arrived home from work and greets Joan who doesn't really seem to hear him. She's preoccupied with thoughts of her recent conversation with her friend Sue. Sue is coming over to "talk" because she needs it. Wayne is tired of Sue and her problems and finds an excuse to leave. Sue has marital and family problems that require professional counseling, but she won't go. Joan doesn't know how to tell Sue the truth because she's afraid Sue will feel hurt. In the meantime these "talks" have caused a strain in Joan's marriage. Finally, Joan has a difficult but truthful conversation with Sue, once again suggesting she see a counselor. Sue feels betrayed. The telephone rings and Sue hands the phone to Joan as she exits. "Relax, it's not me!"

Suggested Topics: Friendship, Truth telling
Characters: 1 male, 2 females
WCCC Series Title: Enriching Your Relationships; Secret to Lasting Friendships

WHAT IF … by Donna Lagerquist

In this lighthearted sketch, a man nervously tries to get to sleep, anxious about a variety of concerns. He goes in and out of dreams where his boss, a doctor, his wife, and even two movers show up to torment him. All the characters come back at the end and talk directly to the audience, quoting the familiar words from the Sermon on the Mount about being anxious for nothing, and seeking first the kingdom. Easier said than done!

Suggested Topics: Worry
Characters: 3 males, 1 female
WCCC Series Title: The Greatest Sermon in History; Why Worry

WHAT NOW? by Sharon Sherbondy

This sketch opens with a group of friends reminiscing about the good times they've shared. Slowly the audience discovers that the reason they gathered is to support their friend after the sudden death of her husband. She has caring friends and family to support her but that isn't enough. She doesn't know how she'll face the challenges of being a widow and single parent.

Suggested Topics: Coping with a crisis, Dealing with death
Characters: 2 males, 4 females
WCCC Series Title: Learning Through Life's Crises; Learning Through Losing

WHAT'S THE TICKET? by Sharon Sherbondy

Joyce is frustrated with her lack of contentment. She lives her life with determination when it comes to getting what she wants and thinks she needs. Each year she searches out her Christmas present from her husband, unwraps it and takes it back to get what she really wants. She's also dedicated to trying to win the lottery so she can get the things she needs (new wardrobe, new furniture) to go along with her color scheme.

Suggested Topics: Need for Christ, Contentment, Needs and wants
Characters: 2 females, 4 either male or female
WCCC Series Title: Seven Wonders of the Spiritual World; God Satisfies Me

WHEEL OF POWER by Cathy Peters

This sketch exemplifies the "wheel of power" or pecking order people experience today. We watch how people misuse the power they've been given or have taken.

Suggested Topics: Power
Characters: 4 males, 1 female, 1 child
WCCC Series Title: Money, Sex, and Power; Power

WILL THE REAL GOD PLEASE STAND UP by Sharon Sherbondy

On her 35th birthday Ginger is plagued by a series of nagging questions and at the top of the list is "What happens when I die?" Three characters appear representing different views of God she has been taught at various stages in her life. The sheriff who keeps track of everything, the mechanic who fixes things, and the grandfather who just wants her to feel good. None of them represent the true complete view of God.

Suggested Topics: Second Commandment, What is God like?
Characters: 3 males, 1 female
WCCC Series Title: Second Commandment; Refuse to Reduce God; It's a Good Thing I'm Not God

WINNING STRATEGY by Various Authors

At what appears to be a high level corporate board meeting, officers discuss plans for expansion. It gradually becomes apparent these people are really devils planning to enslave humanity. A unique idea is suggested by a relatively low-ranking participant: make people self-reliant, busy … in a word, "successful." Tragedies make people recognize their need, but preoccupation with gain keeps them away from God. The new idea is received warmly—and all get to work.

Suggested Topics: Good vs. evil
Characters: 2 males, 4 males or females
WCCC Series Title: Rise of Satanism; Biography of Satan

WONDERFULLY MADE by Donna Lagerquist

A creative interpretation of the statement in Psalm 139 of how God knits us together in our mother's womb and has a plan for our life. We see a child, Elizabeth, assigned qualities by God while in her mother's womb. She is to be a dancer, a left-handed painter, an introvert, and strong-willed. She knows she is loved and made just right. However, once she is born, these feelings change because her parents' aspirations for her are quite different than what she was "told" in the womb. Her father replaces ballet shoes with soccer shoes. Her mother makes her keep her left hand behind her back so that her penmanship doesn't look funny. Their "redirection" through the years physically and emotionally stifles who Elizabeth was meant to be, and she grows up a very sad and confused child.

Suggested Topics: Affirming a child's uniqueness

Characters: 2 females, 2 males, 1 narrator
WCCC Series Title: Parenthood—Part 3; Affirming Each Child's Uniqueness

WORTH KEEPING by Donna Lagerquist

Moving into a new home sets the scene for a touching encounter between Dan, a newly hired Major League baseball player, and his mother, who raised him alone. When Dan leaves to move the truck, his mother shares her box of memories with Dan's wife. Among the Little League snapshots and trophies, there is also an afghan that she knitted during his high school games. Dan had spoken of it, but didn't know his mother had kept it until the box is unpacked. As Dan and his mother continue to sort through the box, Dan realizes the major role his mother played in his achievement of becoming a Major League player.

Suggested Topics: Mother's Day, Single parenting
Characters: 1 male, 2 females
WCCC Series Title: The Nobility of Motherhood

"X" MARKS THE SPOT by Judson Poling and Steve Pederson

This mime take a look at people's efforts to get rid of their sin: "X." Our characters meet three people who claim to have the answer to their problem. The first tries to make it go away, the second tries to hide it, and the last offers the only hope, the cross. The score that accompanied this mime is not available, however we have provided comments so you can create your own.

Suggested Topics: Sin, Redemption, Forgiveness, Guilt
Characters: 1 female, 1 male, and 3 either female or male
WCCC Series Title: Baptism Celebration; The "S" Word; The Other "S" Word

YOU CRAMP MY STYLE by Donna Lagerquist

Three people, who are very much individuals, give three monologues which are inter-cut with each other. The first is a too-busy businessman in his car on his car phone. The second is a woman in an airport phone booth on her way to a new life in a new location. The third is an energetic DJ processing music requests in his studio. One by one we see each of them receive a phone call from God. And, one by one we see each of them explain why they have no need for Him.

Suggested Topics: Reasons people don't believe, How society views God
Characters: 1 male, 1 female, 1 either male or female
WCCC Series Title: Christianity's Greatest Competition; Individualism

This resource was created to serve you.

It is just one of many ministry tools that are part of the Willow Creek Resources® line, published by the Willow Creek Association together with Zondervan Publishing House. The Willow Creek Association was created in 1992 to serve a rapidly growing number of churches from all across the denominational spectrum that are committed to helping unchurched people become devoted followers of Christ.

The vision of the Willow Creek Association is to help churches better relate God's solutions to the needs of seekers and believers. Here are some of the ways it does that:

- **Church Leadership Conferences**—3½-day events, generally held at Willow Creek Community Church in South Barrington, IL, that are being used by God to help church leaders find new and innovative ways to fulfill and expand their ministries.
- **The Leadership Summit**—a once-a-year event designed to increase the leadership effectiveness of pastors, ministry staff, and volunteer church leaders.
- **Willow Creek Resources®**—to provide churches with a trusted channel of ministry resources in areas of leadership, evangelism, spiritual gifts, small groups, drama, contemporary music, and more. For more information, call Willow Creek Resources® at 800/876-7335. Outside the U.S. call 610/532-1249.
- **WCA Monthly Newsletter**—to inform you of the latest trends, events, news, and resources.
- **The Exchange**—to assist churches in recruiting key staff for ministry positions.
- **The Church Associates Directory**—to keep you in touch with over 1000 other WCA member churches.

For conference and membership information please write or call:

Willow Creek Association
P.O. Box 3188
Barrington, IL 60011-3188
(847) 765-0070